Against Itself

THE FEDERAL THEATER AND WRITERS' PROJECTS IN THE MIDWEST

Paul Sporn

Wayne State University Press

Detroit

Copyright © 1995 by Wayne State University Press,
Detroit, Michigan 48201. All rights are reserved.
No part of this book may be reproduced without formal permission.
Manufactured in the United States of America.
99 98 97 96 95   5 4 3 2 1

Library of Congress Cataloging-in-Publication Data

Sporn, Paul, 1921–

   Against itself : the Federal Theater and Writers' Projects in the Midwest
/ Paul Sporn.

      p. cm.

   Includes bibliographical references and index.

   ISBN 0–8143–2590–4 (pbk. : alk. paper)

   1. Federal Theatre Project (U.S.)—History. 2. Federal Writers Project—
History. 3. Theater—Middle West—History—20th century. 4. American
literature—Middle West—History and criticism. I. Title

PN2270.F43S66   1995

792'.0973—dc20   94–43427

DESIGNER
Mary Krzewinski

Cover illustrations courtesy of the Library of Congress Federal Theatre
Project Collection, George Mason University.

For
Jo

CONTENTS

4 The Making and Unmaking of Populist Esthetics: The Midwest Achievement of the FWP and FTP

PREFACE

Collectivity is an issue that comes up again and again in this study. The collective lives of the least favored members of communities that were themselves dis-esteemed are at the heart of the literature, theater, and federal patronage explored therein. But all works are entangled in collectivity. So it is with this busy and ranging book, which has taken twelve years to make, although its sensibility is a product also of experiences and encounters that go much farther back in time.

It could not be what it has become without the many contributions of my colleagues and students in the English Department of Wayne State University. In the period of its making, the English Department itself became transformed from old tradition to new theoretical custom. Wherever the book has taken theoretical flight, it owes much to the informed excitement this change exposed me to. I read several sections of the book at the department's Faculty Forum, where my colleagues and students responded with insightful criticism. Theory is a heady enchantment, and the extent to which I've been able to keep its feet on the ground, to nurture it with the flesh and blood of the real world, I owe to other collectives. One of them is made up of the tool grinders and assembly-line workers in the Chevy engine plant in Tonawanda, New York, where I worked for several years before coming back to the academic world. They taught me lessons about friendship and working worlds that differ from those of privileged culture. These have sustained me in teaching at Wayne and writing this book. So have my friends and comrades of left-wing days. They had visions of making a new kind of life for the dispossessed of the world, even when their conviction and eagerness in reaction to a hostile dominant culture drove many of them into inflexible thought and practice.

Families are also collectives. I want to acknowledge the contributions made by my father Harry Sporn and my mother Ida Tepper, both now dead. They lived through the depression years which this work covers, on several occasions taking me to see the park productions of the Federal Theater Project's caravan theater. My father had the silent courage of so many who labored in this country's factories. He would take off for work at a Brooklyn garment plant in the dark hours before I was awake and trudge home late in the day, never complaining but always a loyal union man. My mother was a magician who transformed the pennies and hardships of those days into a home filled with comforting warmth and delectable food of her own skillful making. Their spirit is an informing element in my attempt to bring the immigrant cultures of those days alive in this study.

The belief that sounds throughout the work that diverse publics and cultures, and in particular African Americans and European Americans, have the stuff to be true to themselves and still embrace each other in respect and love has been strengthened by my son Peter Sporn and his wife Barbara Ransby and by my daughter Pam Sporn and her husband Pablo Foster. Their children Jason and Asha Ransby Sporn and Lelanie Sporn Foster combine in their own flesh the dream the book points to in examining the successes and failures of Great Depression patronage.

This book would not have been possible without our present-day form of patronage. The bulk of the research for it was enabled by a generous grant for the academic year 1980–81 from the National Endowment for the Humanities. The Michigan Council for the Humanities also provided funds in 1979 and 1980. Wayne State University, through its Office of Research and Sponsored Programs and the encouragement of the late Albert Barucha-Ried, the dean of Graduate Studies at the time, kept the project moving ahead with a grant-in-aid in 1979 and a research development award in 1982. In 1992 the vice-president for Graduate Studies at Wayne, Garrett T. Heberlein, approved a subvention for editorial assistance toward which the English Department, at the prompting of its chair, Professor Lesley Brill, added matching funds. In all these grant matters, Daniel J. Graf, the director of Research and Sponsored Programs at Wayne, proved to be an exceptionally skillful mediator.

Libraries and archives have been of enormous assistance. The most important among these are the Library of Congress; the National Archives; the Federal Theater Collection at George Mason University in Fairfax, Virginia; the Franklin Delano Roosevelt Library at Hyde Park, New York; and the Lincoln Center Library of Performing Arts in New York City. The Michigan resources that were indispensable were the Bentley Historical Library in Ann Arbor; the Rare Book Room at the Harlan Hatcher Graduate Library of the University of Michigan; the Burton Historical Collection, the E. Azalia Hackley Collection, and the Department of Music and Performing Arts, all at the Detroit Public Library; the Michigan State University Library; and the Michigan State Archives. Elsewhere in the Midwest, I had the cooperation of the Illinois Historical Library in Springfield, the Chicago

Historical Museum, and the University of Chicago's Regenstein Library. The two major resources at Wayne State University were the Archives of Urban and Labor Affairs at the Walter Reuther Library and the Folklore Archives at Purdy Library.

Several librarians and archivists were particularly fine examples of cooperation and service. Dr. Ronald S. Wilkinson, Specialist in American Cultural History at the Manuscript Division of the Library of Congress, deserves special mention for the clue he gave to the vast Federal Writers' unsorted holdings at the Library's Landover warehouse. Paul T. Heffron, former acting chief of the division, opened warehouse doors. The division's Richard Bickell and Joseph Sullivan were well-informed archivists who were also skilled crowbar manipulators. Both their professional and manual skills facilitated my first view of long buried Midwest manuscripts. Professors Lorraine Brown and John O'Connor, and Research Assistant Jeanne Burch of the George Mason Federal Theater Collection were very helpful in the early years of the project. The courtesy and genuine interest in my research of all the staff at Wayne's Archives of Urban and Labor Affairs and particularly Carrolyn Davis always made working there productive and pleasurable. Margaret Ward and Benedict Markowski of the Burton Historical Collection led me to information about the Midwest African-American community and the Polish-American community of the first third of the twentieth century that improved and deepened my account of those two cultures.

My research assistant Violet Kristoff is due a multitude of thanks. She transcribed my research scrawls and taped interviews with remarkable accuracy; she also organized a mass of research information so that I could evaluate it sensibly and finally write about it. Eva Matuszewski, one of my students, translated reviews, articles, stories, and poems from local Polish-language newspapers to make my analysis of Midwest Polish-American culture possible. Sandra Williamson, my developmental editor, cut, transposed, and streamlined style to make the text more shapely and readable. Kathy Wildfong, the project editor, presided over the process of bringing the book to its material existence with calm efficiency.

The dedication is my short-hand acknowledgement of the debt, both tangible and intangible, due my companion and wife for the major part of my life. As my friend and cherished *intime*, she made the effort glow with belief, even when I had doubts.

INTRODUCTION

This book is about the Federal Theater Project (FTP) and the Federal Writers' Project (FWP) in Michigan and elsewhere in the Midwest, about their encounters with public taste, and the effect those encounters had on their creative work. Several motivations account for its timing and focus. In the summer and fall of 1935, the New Deal government of the United States inaugurated four arts projects under the Works Progress Administration (WPA). Controversy surrounded these projects from the outset. Sympathizers hailed them as a bold experiment in the formation of a democratic art, while opponents attacked them as a boondoggling waste of taxpayer money and an underhanded weapon of New Deal propaganda. The sixty years that have passed since these projects began their short but embroiled histories mark off one of those neat intervals of time that is always a reason for remembering and commemoration. In this case, they also provide the distance needed from a troubling period that provoked intense passions, in its own time and later, to review these experiments with a cool mind. My fairly long career in the Midwest, in-the-bone New Yorker though I remain, convinces me that mapping an accurate image of American tastes and cultures requires some careful study of what happened in the industrial flatlands of Michigan and its sister states. The dazzling lights of the cosmopolitan center and the seductive shadows of agrarian regionalism have, in different ways, made this terrain invisible. Finally, this study is a means of discovering the reality and myth of what many of us whose teenhoods were shaped by the Great Depression remember of that experience.

Two stories of a personal kind illustrate what I believe are typical memories. They embrace some of the problems and themes explored in this study. The first story is about a thirty-year-old Polish-American tool-grinder, whom I got to know in the early 1950s, when I lived in Buffalo. I recall how, one cold March afternoon, he deplored the alienated, fragmented state of human relationships then beginning to characterize the post-World War II era. He didn't describe the state of human affairs in those words or explicitly generalize in that way. He spoke rather in everyday terms about the hard-hearted attitude of the company he worked for. What had set my tool-grinder friend going was the company's treatment of a fellow employee, a rotary drill operator who, after thirty years on the same job at the same place, was finally retiring. What did management do? Nothing, my friend reported. No one in charge, not even the general foreman most closely involved with the drill operator's department, came around to say goodbye or thank him for what he had done for so many years. My friend suggested that the machine the retiring man had worked at in his last years at the plant, since it was worn to his touch and broken in to the rhythm of his movements, belonged more to him than to the company. If nothing else, if not another gift in appreciation or good wishes for the future, the company could at least have given the retiring operator one of the machine's drill bits as a memento. The idea, my friend realized, was unreal, but it made a wry point and reminded him of his childhood in the Great Depression. In that period his father, like the other men in the neighborhood, could never find a full year's work. Employment and layoff had become the rhythm of life, and of course money was scarce. But, like his neighbors, his father always kept some beer in the icebox. When friends or relatives dropped in, he offered his limited supply of beer around, never thinking to keep a hard-to-afford, simple pleasure only for himself. Everybody shared, not only the hard times, but the little they had, and everyone had a good time.

My other story is about the first professional stage play I attended. It happened during the summer of 1937 on the eastside of the Bronx in Crotona Park, where earlier that year Hank Greenberg, trying to stay in shape while recovering from a broken wrist, fungoed fly balls to some teenage kids playing the park's sandlot diamonds. I had the good fortune to be one of those kids. A magical moment. But even more magical was the play I saw that summer, Shakespeare's *A Midsummer Night's Dream*. It played under the stars at the foot of a hillside that curved around the stage like a concave fan and sloped upward for several hundred feet to form a "seeing place," as in the Greek theater. I recall that a huge audience, sitting on newspapers, blankets, handkerchiefs, paper bags, or simply on the grass itself, covered every square foot of the hillside. The younger, more inquisitive members of the audience crowded close to the stage, a cleverly equipped truck trailer opened out to form a proscenium platform with a shallow backdrop. Here the pageantry of the drama unfolded to my wonder and delight, and, as I remember, to that of the audience as well. The drone of sound that issued from it died away shortly after the curtain parted, and this audience of Bronx eastsiders sat as still as it could on a crowded, bumpy hillside that became more and more dampish as the night advanced. When the play was over, it came back to noisy life: cheering, whistling, applauding, and waving handkerchiefs in grateful appreciation of the work the actors had performed. Since then, I have been a devoted fan of live theater, my Crotona Park connection to drama and story. For that, I owe a debt to the Federal Theater Project. The version of *A Midsummer Night's Dream* that I saw was put on by its caravan unit, at no charge, as part of its program to tour the New York City parks on the theory that out there an audience of common men and women existed with a taste for and an ability to feel and perceive the magic seriousness of the stage.

I call these two accounts stories because I am not fully sure that the details which have infiltrated my friend's consciousness or mine are exclusively facts. The problems of those years and the many actions taken to solve them were compelling and dramatic. The fictional embellishments that may have invaded memory are not likely to falsify the truth of two very real characteristics of the period that my stories illustrate and that have been neglected or forgotten in the shuffle of time. Desperate as those years were, not every outlook was drab and hopeless. The crisis became a challenge, not simply for the recovery of prosperity, but something more visionary: to move on to new, more cohesive formations of social life, to accomplish, through a massive involvement of ordinary people, mammoth undertakings in the domains of nature, practical affairs, and cultural activities that the past had not dared on any such scale. In my friend's story, one of those characteristics is symbolized by the spirit of communality he remembered, a spirit of sharing and reciprocal responsibility that enabled an economically beleagured and disfavored group to stay alive and have fun. It represented a human practice of greater worth than the laissez-faire, narcissistic culture of the group in charge or at the top of society. For the artists supported by federal patronage, that spirit and practice of shared fate represented an untapped source of energy and inspiration to be organized and enfranchised for esthetic and social ends.

My own story touches on the other characteristic, that of making the hard times the ground for undared accomplishments. Among the period's mammoth undertakings belong the four WPA experiments in support of the arts. Although they received a very minimal portion of the funds allocated to the WPA, they are unprecedented in the history of modern civil society.[1] There are no ventures of the same kind in Western Euro-American cultures under capitalism to rival them. No ventures of governmental patronage of any kind approach them, not in scope, esthetic aims, or collective methods of creative activity, and particularly not in populism—the attempt to relate the arts to an esthetically ignored section of the social order. Compared with other New Deal projects, they were unusually explicit in making the aim of reaching an audience of common men and women a cardinal principle. They expected to inspire this audience and to be inspired by the energies, culture codes, and experiences that its spirit of communality, as dream or practice, galvanized. For me, that audience, represented on the night of my theatrical initiation by the crowd of Bronx eastsiders, is a palpable part of the made-up world of the stage. They are the flesh and blood performers on the other side of the footlights who fill out the meaning of live theater. Because they were intellectually unsophisticated, they were not burdened by the distancing disadvantage that so often accompanies formally acquired knowledge. They were able very easily, by a wonderful or perhaps naive expansion of mood, to become part of the drama being enacted before them.

How far and how deeply the FTP and the FWP in Michigan and the Midwest succeeded in tapping into this source of energy and inspiration is a major theme of this book. Did these projects work out a relationship with an audience of common men and women that was esthetically and significantly rewarding for both? The problem is complicated by several factors. In the Midwest, the audience the FTP and the FWP were out to attract was an industrial population of varied immigrant and cultural antecedents. To establish an esthetic relationship whose inspirational currents flowed in both directions, the writers and performing companies of these projects had to know an audience considerably unlike the conventional ones generally addressed by literature and drama. Did these projects understand and feel ultimately in the marrows of their being this audience's cultural codes, its daily experiences, its conceptions of reality, and particularly its hard-time struggles and hopes for the future?

The account of my first experience with the stage illustrates the difficulties of coming to know such an audience, of understanding and feeling the parameters of its tastes. I can identify to a fairly exact degree those Crotona Park viewers of *A Midsummer Night's Dream*. They were mostly Italian, Jewish, and Irish laborers: women's-wear operators, men's-clothing workers, furriers; some brick layers, longshoremen, and stevedores; and a sprinkling of others, such as fruit and vegetable peddlers in outdoor public markets, grocery story clerks, and mail carriers. They had jobs, but they were victims of recurring layoffs. Many were foreign-born. A growing number of those under twenty-five were native Americans, but of immigrant parents. Few could boast of being second- or third-generation citizens. Their response to the play, whose language and themes were so different from their own speech and reality, is more difficult to specify. Did they respond to the play's pageantry, its formal strategies, its fanciful plot, its moments of strife and danger, the caricatures and unnatural transformations of the lower orders, or did they respond to a play-world whose fictions allowed them to forget the grim hardships of those depression days? Or simply to the thoughtfulness of an agency that had come to entertain them, whom the world of art had generally ignored?

The various features of this audience which make identification easy are also what make its tastes so hard to fathom. This public shared a common set of immigrant experiences: first, in being manual laborers and, second, in having to construct, within the boundaries of a still alien territory, a relationship to its dominant groups and their sanctioned culture. But thick walls also separated the members of one group from those of another. The traditions stemming from the different national, religious, and linguistic origins persisted with remarkable strength, although no longer fed by native soils. They were the codes that gave them a sure sense of self and an established place in a culturally familiar community, the weapons that each immigrant group used against the defamiliarizing and hence the self-estranging effects of an approved culture whose customs, largely unknown to the newcomers, were confusing and whose power to decree what legitimately belongs to or constitutes culture made it appear as a denigrating, hostile force. But they were also defenses that each immigrant community erected against other immigrant groups, notwithstanding their common experience. They were barriers designed to prevent a diffusion, through experiences shared in a neutral workplace, of the cultural integrity required for an effective shielding against defamiliarization and self-estrangement. These barriers walled off the various communities of this immigrant public from each other. They were used, frequently with ugly chauvinist overtones, by each community to protect itself from a threat in securing jobs, status, and cultural acceptance that each imagined the other immigrant communities posed for it. The illusion had two sources: fear of what is foreign and the frightening images of immigrant groups painted by the established powers of American society.

The tastes, then, of these various immigrant publics are a curious amalgam of contradictory experiences and traditions. The problem of becoming thoroughly acquainted with these tastes would have been uncomplicated if the shared experiences and the exclusionary traditions were related to each other in a simple mechanical way, that is, without each mediating the structure and substance of what the other was and without mediating and being mediated by the American scene as a whole. The exclusionary traditions themselves were altered almost from the moment immigrants set foot on the shores of the new world. They were transformed by the new soil in which they rooted themselves—by the encounter with the dominant culture and by the interaction among the various laboring, immigrant communities. But they also profoundly affected this new soil. The shared experiences, relatively new and not yet fixed by long-standing practice, were themselves being continually modified in response to the multi-national and multi-cultural work force they entailed. Together with the exclusionary, old world traditions, the shared experiences formed a set of American tastes far,

17

far different from the tastes authorized by high culture. Because of its difference from high culture and because of the complex dialectics of the shared and exclusionary immigrant experiences, this amalgam of tastes is extremely difficult to grasp.

The difficulty is a problem of national scope, not an enigma confined to regional studies. The Michigan region in the 1930s is, perhaps more than any other, instructive in this regard, for its industrial and immigrant population represented that difficulty in a particularly intense and typical form. The tastes of the New York audience I have described were made somewhat more accessible to those, such as the federal arts projects, who wanted to know them by the force of the city's chief character, its cosmopolitanism. The power of cosmopolitanism to absorb and accommodate alien codes had a mutational effect on the dynamics of shared experiences and exclusionary traditions. Under that power, the techniques, customs, language, and even some of the modes of perception differentiating the various immigrant groups jumped over the walls separating them, much as genes, under given conditions, hop from chromosomal strand to chromosomal strand.

But in Michigan cosmopolitanism was not a condition of signifying influence. Geography and history did not favor it. Industrial isolationism was the more powerful agency, and it acted to reinforce rather than transform the dynamics of shared experiences and exclusionary traditions. In Detroit, for example, the shared experiences had a far greater sameness than in the cosmopolitan center because it evolved in an environment dominated by the automobile industry. It was the foremost influence on those whom it employed directly as well as those who worked elsewhere. It not only determined the economic ups and downs of other regionally-based enterprises, but also the politics of work—how work was done and what practices regulated the relationship between labor and management. As a consequence of their midwestern milieu, the culture codes dividing the groups were far more cut off from each other, far less able to jump over the dividing walls. The overriding isolationism of the Midwest strengthened the provincialist-peasant history of so many immigrants: on the immigrant side as automatic, ingrained response, and on the industrial side as conscious policy to make managerial control of labor relations easier to execute. Because the Michigan experience reinforced both sameness and difference, it slowed down the process of mixing and jumping over. It was thus far more difficult for the WPA projects to know and feel at home with the tastes of the industrial, immigrant publics. The American diaspora of the midwestern publics makes the difficulty I am speaking of more typical of the nation than cosmopolitan flexibility is: as different groups migrated across the nation, they settled in urban places much more like those in Michigan and the

Midwest than cities along the Atlantic coast, such as Boston, New York, Philadelphia.

The cultural convergences and disparities of these publics make up only one of the factors complicating the federal goal of achieving a two-way esthetic relationship with them. The art professionals recruited by Washington to administer the WPA experiment with the arts—national, regional, and local administrators as well as the on-site performers and writers—constitute another, equally problematical factor. The administrative staffs of the projects and the local performers and writers were always the primary agents in working out the principle of attracting an audience from disregarded publics, for the principle was most regularly articulated by them. Who these administering professionals and local artists were and what experiences influenced their perceptions of art and society make up another theme of this book. These issues are at the root of the question I asked first: how well did the Michigan FTP and FWP fare in carrying out the federal aim of winning an audience of common men and women?

I am convinced by the information on record that the art professionals appointed to conduct the WPA experiment in government patronage sincerely wanted to attract such an audience. But there is no doubt that they were far removed from its work experiences and cultural derivations. As well-educated members of the middle class, engaged full-time in various kinds of art careers, their esthetic and social perceptions were quite familiar and at home with cosmopolitan conceptions of art and society. Yet because most of the administrative professionals came from college theater or small, experimentally-oriented, community-based performing companies and from literary experiences of an analogous kind, they were also deeply affected by agrarian regionalism, much more so than by cosmopolitanism. Although agrarian regionalism is an alternative to cosmopolitanism, refusing above all to share in commercialization of the arts, it does not differ radically from the standards and tastes which cosmopolitanism defines as true or intrinsic culture—what we now call high or dominant culture. Agrarian regionalism is also more socially conservative, particularly with regard to industrial capitalism and the proletariat, which it considers the prime culprits of economic and cultural debasement. Hardly a social or esthetic view to move one toward an association with an industrial, immigrant public. But with the outbreak of the Great Depression, a more radical kind of regionalism began to appear. I call this industrial regionalism, and its major roots were anchored in the soil of the Midwest's industrial-urban centers. As the depression wore on, this tendency became increasingly attractive to the art professionals who later came into federal arts as upper- and middle-echelon directors. It made them more sensitive, at least in theory, to the immigrant workers who inhabited these centers.

The local artists recruited to the projects in these industrial centers had a more miscellaneous background, principally because of the relief function of the projects. To qualify for a place in any of the arts projects, one had to demonstrate need as well as talent. Only ten percent of the placements in these projects were allocated exclusively on the basis of talent, and generally these went mainly to art professionals who already had jobs and were recruited to fill various administrative or directorial posts. No matter how talented an actor or writer might be, he or she had to be out of work to qualify for a place among the ninety percent that remained.[2] Although most personnel came from middle-class backgrounds, a fair number were from the working class. In the Midwest they represented a larger variety of immigrant, industrial cultures than elsewhere. All were victims of the depression to a greater degree than the administrating professionals for whom they worked. They knew more directly, as the industrial and immigrant publics knew, how it feels to be out of work, to be deprived not only of earning a living, but also of being engaged in a productive human activity necessary for survival and self-esteem. But if, on this score, local artists were closer to an audience of common men and women, they were not as consistently so in esthetic perceptions and tastes. As persons interested in the arts, even on a part-time schedule, they were conditioned by the standards of high culture, in both cosmopolitan and regionalist manifestations. The few performers and writers among the local artists who developed their esthetic perceptions in left-wing literary and theatrical groups shared political principles that made them more programmatically sympathetic to a mass audience. But the political-esthetic standards of stylized agit-prop skits or realistic social-problem plays did not necessarily lead local artists to a closer, deeper feeling for that audience's syndrome of tastes. The two leading players in this drama of cultural alliance—the double-coded industrial and immigrant audience and the two-tiered artist-members of the arts projects—met each other as obstacles to a successful outcome at the center of action.

In the wings, other agents played a part in complicating matters: the politicians who, for one or another reason, were involved in the fate of WPA. Although invisible to the audience, they comprised a powerful and troublesome force in clear view of the project members, in particular the professionals administering the actual work and deciding what kinds of plays to produce and what general subjects to write about. The first group of politicians included elected and appointed officials on the national level who were responsible for policy and legislation; in the official chain of command, they were the court of last resort for all the arts projects as well as the WPA as a whole. Second, there were the political bureaucrats at the regional level who were responsible for the day-to-day execution of WPA work relief; as a consequence of bureaucratic inertia, they very often functioned as a de facto court of last resort. Elected and appointed officials at the policy-making level are, it seems to me, always confronted by two problems. One is how to maintain the integrity of a program in terms of what that program is about: for example, in the case of such top New Deal leaders of WPA as Harry Hopkins, an art program with a populist orientation in terms of what art and populism are about. The second involves getting reelected and reappointed. Sincerity toward program and desire for office are often at cross-purposes, particularly in a system such as ours where raising money and support from those who are economically privileged and powerful has always been among the most important requisites for staying in office. The New Deal turned out to be as vulnerable as any other administration to this general bind of American politics. When it came to the WPA adventure with art patronage, the administration's political decisions were governed by a pragmatic dynamics that differed from and often contradicted the dynamics governing the aims of project members concerned with populist esthetics and populist audience relationships. One step down from policy making, at the level of local and state bureaucracy, the problem took on another dimension. The bureaucrats in charge here were not very familiar with the world of art, and they often mirrored the widespread anti-intellectual bias among Americans. They understood so-called practical matters, bottom-line issues of work relief, but they were puzzled by and sometimes hostile to the arts experiments of the WPA.

The New Dealers, who represented the liberal resurgence triggered by the economic crisis of the 1930s, were not the only politicians who made life difficult for the arts projects. The depression also stirred up greatly invigorated right- and left-wing movements, and these complicated matters still more. Far-right and conservative politicians opposed New Dealism as a matter of course. They suspected that the arts projects were a Roosevelt conspiracy to flood the country with liberal and New Deal reelection propaganda. Many of them, in accord with traditional attitudes of religious fundamentalism, viewed the arts projects as dangerously immoral. Moreover, they considered them hotbeds of bolshevik ideas and actions. The glare of right-wing publicity, in newspapers and in Congress, on one or another of these grounds, constantly plagued the work of the projects.

The left-wing movements, however, were generally in favor of the government's program for the arts. Although they frequently objected to the low pay rates and the pink-slipping of project artists, they sympathized with the idea of making the arts more democratically available to the masses. None of the forces to the left of the New Deal—whether trade unionist, populist, socialist, or communist—felt that such a plan was at odds with its principles. The intriguing problem here is how WPA actors and writers associated with communist or socialist thinking affected the esthetics of the

Introduction

Theater and Writers' projects in their quest for a people's audience. Although much has been written about the few disturbances organized by communists and socialists, mainly in New York, little space has been devoted to this problem. Communist and socialist ideologies have always been global views, addressed not only to economic issues, but even more fundamentally to the nature of social relationships and the state of culture. Did the actors and writers who advocated these views have some strong things to say about the plays and writing produced by the FTP and the FWP in pursuit of a mass audience? If they did speak out, did they help or hinder? Were they so caught up in economic issues that they said very little to clarify the social-esthetic character of art and the winning of a mass audience? The far left constituted an eternal problem for the arts projects. To be convinced of this, we need look no farther than, on one side, the watch-dog, Red-menace spirit of reactionary politicians and, on the other, the pragmatic political fears that preyed sometimes (more often than is usually recognized) on New Deal liberals. But the questions I have asked about the left-wing effect on esthetic and social issues speak to a more fundamental problem for the arts projects, and the answers to them make up another key theme of this book.

All the various factors—the immigrant communities, the project personnel, and the various political forces—we have briefly sketched here and which made life a thorny affair for the Theater and Writers' projects were at play across the nation, in cosmopolitan as well as industrial centers. In Michigan and the Midwest, they interacted with each other in the special setting of that area's landlocked isolationism and automobile economy. These circumstances make the region a bellweather of much that is most typical in U. S. culture. How these groups affected each other under the pressure of the Midwest setting tells us a great deal about the way the tastes of different American publics have confronted each other and mediated the forms they have taken, of the way esthetic and political purposes have intruded on each other's territory. This part of the story takes us through the dress rehearsal of what the WPA projects accomplished in Michigan. The performances and literary work the Michigan projects considered professional enough to bring before the public take us through the climax of our narrative. Public performance and published text are in that privileged position not for metaphysical reasons, but because they make up the ground where the audience and the federally supported artists were finally joined in an act that confirms either a cross-fertilizing inspiration or a failed understanding. An evaluation of the works produced by the Michigan FTP and FWP completes this book's story of public taste and government patronage. The narrative takes on importance, in my view, because these public projects ran their course in a crucible of American culture whose industry and population have forged icons and tastes that have traveled far in the United States and influenced American imagination very deeply, farther and more deeply, I should say, than those forged in the workshops of cosmopolitanism and regionalism.

I return for one last reference to my opening anecdotes. In addition to implying the themes of this book, they indicate the angle from which much of this material is gathered. My perspective is from the ground up: what the English historian Christopher Hill has called "the worm's eye view."[3] Readers will recognize in this angle a tendency that has grown quite prominent in social and cultural history. It has not yet made any major progress in literary history, although a recent study by Frederick Brown, *Theatre and Revolution* (1980)—especially the chapters "The Speechless Tradition" and "The Boulevard of Crimes"—shows how valuable it can be for these disciplines.[4] This lack of progress seems unfortunate. No doubt the view from the top down has provided us with a great deal of information. But in an industrialized nation such as ours, operating under capitalism and its system of disparities in power distribution and social relations, the view from the top down primarily focuses on the works of the dominant culture and leaves the cultures emerging among the industrial work force in deep shadows. It leaves the story of American cultural life only half told. Since in any society the works of its various cultures are inseparable from the way each interacts and collides with the others, even dominant culture, seen only from the top down, remains hidden in the same deep shadows. We view it from a single side, as a richly textured surface, but without seeing very far into its deep structures or hearing what its silent omissions, invisibly present, say to us. The perspective from the ground up has its problems, including willful or unconscious neglect. But over and above this is another, perhaps even more intransigent obstacle. The terms we use to designate the status of cultures—dominant, residual, emergent, if we follow Raymond Williams—are clues to it.[5] The cultural records of publics which have no officially sanctioned power are victims of what the dominant culture considers historically important. These records disintegrate, disappear, wind up in obscure, unlikely places. The view from the ground up requires a great deal of digging, with no assurance that anything much will be uncovered. I presume the same is true for social history's burrowings into the story of the births, family structures, economic conditions, religious and political ideas, health conditions, daily habits, and deaths of those who are powerless. For drama and literary history, the discovery of appropriate material is an exceedingly chancy business. Where it has been attempted, the results have been severely handicapped by multitudes of missing parts and enormous disconnections. The risk of coming away empty-handed or at best with heavily filtered results makes the angle from the ground up an uninviting pursuit. This difficulty imposes an obligation on the researcher to be cautious in delineating disenfranchised cultures, particularly where the phenomenon of public or popular taste is concerned. Assuming too much simply courts disaster.

Assuming too much is, however, an easy danger to fall into when it comes to analyzing public taste. At the center of such analysis are two fairly common modes of perception in bourgeois civil society. One of these homogenizes socially differentiated sub-populations and their complexly overlapping and diverging cultural codes with grand abstractions: for example, there is an American public, it has a definable taste, and something we call popular art caters to it. The other mode atomizes sub-populations to such a degree that they vanish in the random play of absolute individuals.

Of the two, it seems to me that the main danger to the study of popular art is the homogenizing mode. A lively and informative study of Post Office murals commissioned by the Treasury Section during the Great Depression is a telling illustration. In *Wall-to-Wall America* (1982), Karal Ann Marling tells the reader that her main theme is popular taste in the 1930s, and she concludes from the murals which the Treasury Section endorsed and rejected that it was a taste for "a pleasing image of an operative cultural myth that made life seem more beautiful."[6] Two issues arise here. The first is the ill-defined nature of the term "popular." The author pays little attention to the distinguishing occupations and traditions of the masses who underlie her notion of "popular"; the term becomes an inclusive abstraction, and Marling derives from it a single dominant taste, the "pleasing image." The second issue is the nature of the evidence she uses—for example, a judge who publicly attacks a mural because it paints an unfavorable picture of our penal system; an editor who objects to the way his agrarian milieu is depicted and editorializes a "groundswell" against it.[7] Such evidence surely proves something about a small-town judge and a small-town editor, but the leap from judge and editor to popular taste is arbitrary. It ignores the many variables in the evidence and overlooks other conclusions that could be derived from the evidence. A different conclusion is, in fact, suggested by Marling's own description of how the Treasury Section staff reacted to the controversies that surrounded the Post Office murals. Where they tried to save the esthetic character of a mural under fire, they eventually appeased the local leaders of controversy. After a few such experiences, they began to appease by anticipation, requesting some artists to ameliorate their depictions of particular environments and history before local communities had spoken.[8] The results seem always to have been in favor of an image that indeed pleases by making life more beautiful than the realities of justice, agriculture, industry, and local history indicated. Since the final word went to the section rather than the artist, and since influential individuals, not the masses, initiated almost all the controversies, it seems reasonable to conclude that the "pleasing image" represented the taste of specific, vested community interests and the political needs of federal officials. It was necessary to pacify local interests to win them as political supporters or, at least, keep them from becoming political enemies. It was also necessary to distract the various publics that comprised the masses from images that threatened the political sovereignty of established power, images those publics might have accepted had they been left to themselves or artists in sympathy with them.

The problems I raise with Marling's interpretation confront us with the dilemma that haunts all conceptions of popular art. Is popular art a genuine response to the inherent tastes or demands of the masses or is it something imposed on them by a highly controlled culture industry and for which a taste or demand is induced by the seductions and assaults of marketing schemes? The control of the culture industry makes it hard to conceive of popular art in other ways. There is simply too much political indoctrination, bottom-line economics, and advertising hype involved. That is why the cartoon image, the Hollywood picture, the narrative themes of pulp and slick magazines, the popular icons that arouse passions or stroke anxieties are not always the best guides to the myths and tastes that reside in the hearts of our sub-populations.

The worm's eye view is a methodological filter against the blurring over-simplifications of homogenizing abstraction. Its willingness to listen carefully for the voices of the masses among records uneven in sound and blurred by channel noise guards against a too naive endorsement of what is generally called popular art and against a too easy acceptance of the icons of popular art as evidence of the esthetic attitudes of the masses. In this spirit, I have tried to use the term "public" in the plural, whenever it was not too awkward, in referring to the American population or the masses, and I have tried to keep in mind the specific features of the subsets of common men and women who made up the masses in the 1930s. In the same spirit, I have selected for especial attention the industrial, immigrant population of Michigan, and I have listened to the voices of local artists employed by the Michigan FTP and FWP. These individuals were at the point of contact where the principle of cross-fertilizing audience and artist could, in the final analysis, be transformed into fact or failure. I shall not assume that the local artists and art professionals responsible for FTP and FWP operations were interested only in the esthetic aims of a self-enclosed art world and were naive about practical politics.[9] Such criticism is so conventionally applied to artists in general that to distrust it for that reason alone seems to me a wise procedure. Neither do I assume that what may be practical strategies for staying in office are effective as political or esthetic strategies for carrying out an art program with a populist orientation. Nor shall I take it as a matter

25

of course that the icons of popular art signify the dreams and myths at the heart of the audience these projects sought to win. That they signify something important about American culture is beyond dispute, but they are too compromised by the commerce of culture to be taken, without some close questioning, for signs of inherent popular taste.

Nevertheless, I must add that it would not do to dismiss altogether the mode of dissolving abstractions and the icons of popular art. The enormous effect that Detroit had on social relationships and cultural practices and on the iconography of popular art in the 1920s and the 1930s and still has makes that a failing of another kind. In *Engels, Manchester, and the Working Class* (1974), Steven Marcus uses Detroit as a metaphor for Manchester, the city he calls the most sensational in England in the first half of the nineteenth century and "the living embodiment of what was happening in and to the modern world."[10] As in all cases of metaphor, what it says about its subject, it says about itself. I don't think anyone will argue strenuously against the view that Detroit's automobile industry means to the 1900s, certainly to the first half of the century, what Manchester's cotton industry meant in its time. The central role of Detroit and Michigan in twentieth-century American capitalism and the typicality of its industrial work force are the main reasons why my focus on government patronage in this area is more than an exercise in local history. The Michigan flatlands is often called the heartland of America for good reason, and a study of what happened there to the FTP and FWP in their quest for an ethnically diverse audience of common people illuminates a very wide horizon of American culture.

The shaping power of the automobile center may be sensed in practice and in product. As far as practice goes, its production techniques—specifically the use of the assembly line, the standardization of parts, and the replacement of craft labor by a work force not required to be particularly skilled—embody two paradigms of modern society: the growth of formularized mass taste (the magic behind mass demand) and the transformation of working people from makers of complete products, as in earlier capitalism, to scientifically managed proletarians, alienated from the product they make because they work on fragments of production rather than the completion of whole objects. As for marketing techniques—that is, the strategies of annual style change, model proliferation, and a hierarchy of models to embody social status—there is in these a reverse paradigm: the growth of narcissism, whose social and personal consequences are an anxious and restless quest after identity through purchased objects to certify individuality and social order, certifications that are continually being swept away by product obsolescence and changing fashions. The product which these techniques produce and strategies sell, the automobile itself, has become a key image in our arts and entertainments, a symbol of the sweet and adventurous life. But for the industrial, immigrant worker who makes cars or whose prosperity and way of life are affected by the making of cars, it also means—in a way more central to everyday life—bitter, hard work, unequal relationships depriving the worker of a sense of worth and control of life's outcomes, and a call to resistance, (as in the sit-down strikes of 1937). Yet because there is a dialectical relationship between the central and inherent tastes and codes of specific publics and the making of industrial capitalism, we will not forget the formularized icons of capitalist strategy, even if they have been so frequently misinterpreted and so frequently considered the measure of mass culture.

Finally, we need to remember that everyday life is carried out within a framework of political economy—for us, within the framework of capitalism—whose tendencies and policies manipulate and disturb all forms of society. The worm's eye view must also take that into account. Leaving out that historical framework, like overlooking society's emergent and residual cultures, produces a tale that leaves much of neglected as well as dominant cultures in shadow. Therefore, before I delineate the audience as well as the members of the FTP and FWP in Michigan, and evaluate the work they produced, I shall describe what I consider the overriding tendency of the arts in modern civil society, some of the reasons for it, and some alternatives that bore directly on the federal art experiments and made them different from other capitalist forms of patronage before and after the Great Depression.

PART 1

**Patronage and the Arts:
From Hegemony to
Counter Choice in
the 1930s**

I

The Arts and Patronage
in Modern Civil Society

THE WPA arts projects were children of catastrophe, the Saturday's children, as a matter of fact, of the massive relief program the federal administration enacted in 1935. The program was a response composed of hope and desperation to a stubbornly persistent economic breakdown. By 1935 it had become clear that the depression was unlike any other in the history of capitalism. It had hurled the American economy down to record lows, lasted longer than any other modern slump, and continued to defy the predictions and strategies of the political-corporate complex which dominated American society. From 1933 to 1938, joblessness ravaged farm and factory workers, running as high as twenty-five percent of the working population and never lower than nineteen percent.[1] The legacy of despair and discontent threatened to erupt in social disorder. As a result, the New Deal administration had to give up the view that quick-fix Keynesian measures, such as the makeshift relief allocations of 1933 and 1934, could rescue the economy from the pit it had stumbled into or tranquilize the pressures of unrest. It still considered the crisis a temporary malfunction of the system, but "temporary" was revised to mean years rather than weeks and months. In the middle of 1935, with less than half its first term in office to go, the New Deal government came up with the Works Progress Administration, a greatly magnified relief enterprise designed to go on for more than a single year. This new response included in its mandate four projects to relieve the condition of unemployed artists with professionally appropriate work.

Although New Deal policy makers had made some attempts in 1933 and 1934 to deal with the plight of artists, they gave it no very high priority. It is hardly surprising, therefore, that making room for the arts projects in WPA came as an afterthought and an incidental part of the other undertakings for which WPA was responsible.[2] The arts projects seemed to be, even to many officials in the administration, an indulgence. Too many millions of ordinary workers—makers of things useful and needed in everyday life—were out of work and restless, and government funds were in too short supply to make public support of the arts a compelling or affordable need. The view taken by the arts community was more sympathetic, but even here there were doubts. The projects were perceived as the offspring of a highly unnatural liaison between economic need and esthetic purpose, and their future was felt to be uncertain. The liaison which produced them generated both innovational possibilities and disorienting dangers.[3] Hesitations and fears notwithstanding, the fact that these projects ran counter to the chief ways of producing art in modern civil society and were allocated $300,000,000 made them an unprecedented experiment in public patronage.

Private Self and World City

From the first appearance in the early Renaissance of settings and relationships which define modern civil society not as new invention but as new capacity to dominate other settings and relationships, the arts have tended to become private and cosmopolitan. Patronage has traveled the same path, being derived more and more from private wealth located in the great urban centers of Western Europe and later the United States. In the Renaissance and the transitional period later on—in France, that is, the *ancien régime* combining absolute monarchy, mercantilism, and the seigneurial system; in England, the Restoration and the compromise with it of the Glorious Revolution—there still remained substantial expressions of art whose assumptions reflected the expectations, values, and tastes of publics whose beliefs and loyalties were shaped by parochial or insular national orientations. There were also substantial instances of patronage that still assumed a stewardship of the arts as an obligation of governors: ruling aristocracies or institutionalized churches. These manifestations of social accord and function are part of a long rule of such practices. But now the space they occupied was invaded more and more by the tendencies of the arts to express either self or individual genius and, therefore, to cut away from the norms of a parochial or insular audience. The tendency of patronage to fall under the sway of capital wealth and individual inclination usually accompanies this takeover of territory. Not, however, until capitalism had triumphed as a system, that is, as the chief mode of production and as the controlling organization of exchange in Europe, and had begun to colonize other marketplaces did the new tendencies conquer the old.[4] But absolute banishment is hardly ever an enforceable prerogative of conquest, particularly when it comes to cultural forms. The best the conquering new tendencies could do was confine old ways of art and patronage to narrow boundaries and distort their growth.

An art that breaks away from the coherence of parochial and insular cultures for the worldly cultivations of the cosmopolitan city and the private landscape of the self may seem caught up in nullifying experiences. But once we see these experiences against the history and typology of capitalism, what appears nullifying is understandable then as the energy of bourgeois life moving the arts toward both the isolated private landscape and the expansive tastes of the globally-oriented city. Belonging to this history and typology is the social atomization closely connected to the way marketplace economy and marketplace culture are organized and manipulated on the grounds of competition, individualism, and theories of free trade. Also belonging to these is the prodigious increase in the population presumed to have no individual personality or culture. The rise of the artist as an alienated creature and the development of the city as a grim, densely packed place of horrors (but also as an exciting crossroads of international competition and exchange) are both linked to the history of capitalism.

After the eighteenth century, the movement toward privacy and cosmopolitanism shows itself in a set of closely related esthetic and economic features. On the creative side, the process manifests itself in the subjective nature of art work. The choice of subject is individual, the impulse of genius, even where the matter selected is a public issue. In finished form, art reflects idiosyncratic, private imagination, presumed to symbolize nothing but itself or non-historical archetypes, or, the reaction to and rejection of public expectations and values. The more the work depends on the inventions of private imagination, the less it seems entailed by province, nation, or class. At the same time, in matter and style the modern artist abandons such restraints for the free spirit of urban bohemianism and the infinite variety of the modern, world-related *civitas*, which is a kaleidoscope of imported and displaced cultures.[5]

On the economic side, the process transforms the esthetic product into what all products of human labor have become, a commodity for exchange. Through the medium of the privately owned publishing house, art gallery, music hall, or playhouse, art appears in the form of a unit of capital freely competing with all other commodities brought to the marketplace—but most intensively with commodities that are, as itself, cultural in kind. The competition is an affair of private individuals, either in the human or the bourgeois corporate sense: sellers vying for buyers, publishers for readers, theatrical producers for theatergoers. The setting for the transaction is cosmopolitan: the political, banking, and commercial centers of Euro-American capitalism. These circumstances cobble the artist into a grotesque, double-natured agent: an artisan—who in some repects resembles the artisans of old but who differs from them in now being a maker of prototypes to be mass reproduced, if the entrepreneurs of the culture industry deem it a salable work—and an entrepreneur, an owner of a commodity which he must sell to another entrepreneur. Although it is not clear what the artist owns, it would seem to be the prototype. But here deformation sets in again, for it turns out that what he owns is a very small part of each reproduced item that makes up the mass going to market.[6]

It seems logical to presume that the artist's share of what the mass-produced prototype is priced to sell for should allow him to practice his craft on a full-time schedule. We know that for most artists this is simply not true. The cost to the artist of producing the prototype is the last thing paid for. In earning the time to work at his art, the artist is constrained by seemingly normal business procedures, and his artistic fate hangs perilously on the whims of the marketplace, of readers and viewers who put down their money for books, plays, and paintings to satisfy private inclinations, not public responsibilities toward the values of culture. The risks involved in realizing the capital buried in an art produced for mass consumption and of realizing thereby the money equivalent of the time needed to work regularly at his craft are the haunting compulsions behind the steady commercializing of the arts and the alienated feelings of our artists. With classical and romantic perversity, our culture still idealizes art as an inspired, noble good, but forces the artist to wait for its marketing and depend for his artistic life on the cool pragmatics of bottom-line accounting.

It is not at all surprising that the artist should be confused about his position. In his relationship to the entrepreneurial reproducers and distributors of his work, the power is overwhelmingly on their side. In this respect, the artist seems little different than the ordinary worker. There is a hands-on quality to the way the artist works, a quality of pride, that is also much akin to the ordinary worker. Yet no matter how much common ground worker and artist share in the face of superior power and in the tangibility of their work processes, the ordinary worker gets back the entire cost of his labor power at one time, while the artist receives it back in bits and pieces and recovers all of it only if book sales, theater admissions, and so on, are sufficiently above the level required to cover the break-even costs. Further, no matter how much he is constrained by the marketing techniques of nineteenth- and twentieth-century industrial capitalism, the artist's method of production is economically anachronistic. His method is artisanal. He is, in other words, a loner-producer. The industrial worker is, to the contrary, a collective producer, working on a single step along with many other workers in the process leading finally to a finished good. In pointing out these differences, my object is not to awaken pity for the artist. His life may be more precarious in a sense, but I doubt that his lot as a person is harder. My

34

point is that the way he works and gets paid back represents another alienating impulse, a socio-economic exception to the norms governing a vast portion of the producing populations of Europe and America.

The subsidies that private wealth has felt called on to make to the arts have established contexts where artists fortunate enough to be funded or commissioned may avoid, for a limited time at least, the caprices of the marketplace and the incentives to commercialize culture.[7] But such private wealth is itself conditioned by cosmopolitan parameters, since it is usually an accumulation that is achieved or ultimately settles itself in the world centers of capitalism. Its underwritings signify another set of private markers for the arts: if not the whims of buyers solicited by constantly changing displays of art commodities, then the self-interested political and esthetic inclinations of individuals and privately managed corporations with substantial socio-economic power.[8]

The political needs of the new order have also played a prime role in the way the arts have moved toward private landscapes and cosmopolitan tastes. In its early history, capitalism appears as the universal champion fighting all the constraints that impede one's ability to develop freely and fully in whatever way he or she wants. When it finally became the organizing form of social and national life, it did away with the feudal and old regime rules and customs that were damaging to itself.[9] These rules and customs covered both prohibitions and obligations, what persons and estates should not do and what they must do. For those engaged in the use of capital to acquire more capital, these customary and legal don'ts and do's were intolerable checks to growth. At the edges of feudal and *ancien régime* power, in the cities where the commodity market had strong footholds and where density and diversity of population made feudal rules difficult to supervise, capitalism got around them with whatever cunning the moment required. But ultimately it had to challenge the feudal and mercantilist orders politically. The constraints which confronted capitalism were not simply an issue of formal political hegemony. They were authorized by established frameworks of conceptualizing the world—by theology in the first place, but also by the content and formal structures of art, philosophy, and science. The authority achieved through these frameworks is, according to Michel Foucault, power's "capillary form of existence." Under most circumstances, it is a more efficient exercise of power, for as an unrecognized, ingrained form of compulsion, it commands compliance as if it were a voluntary offering or a conditioned reflex of the individual and the social body.[10] Therefore, if the politics of capitalism were to produce an authoritative triumph over the old political economy, they had to be directed at dissolving the regulating conformities of feudal culture as well.

35

The political response of the burgeoning bourgeois class to feudal and *ancien-régime* constraints developed quite haphazardly in its early stages. It had little theory behind it, and its strategy was that of naked opportunism. By the late eighteenth century, in parallel with the continued assumption of power by capital over its own form of society, these politics had become rationalized into what appeared to be a consistently logical principle, that of *laissez-faire, laissez-passer.* This principle presumes that when the members of society are free to pursue individual interests without political intervention, society is spontaneously self-regulating. Its members produce for each other, without necessarily knowing it, an adequate quantity of goods and services to fulfill whatever their economic, social, and esthetic demands may be. This is not only a quantitative response, but one that matches in quality every level of expressed need and desire, except as constrained by the limits of human talent and technological advance. Society not only gets what it wants, but also what it deserves and what is maximally good for it. The lever is free competition in a free marketplace, where what the buyer is willing to spend expresses truly the kind of need and desire to be fulfilled. The key premise is that all private selves in the marketplace are equal, have equal competitive opportunities, and discover the competitive slot appropriate to their natural talents and trained skills. Political interference simply upsets the natural logic of such self-regulating performance.[11]

The *laissez-faire* theory behind the political organization of the state is also based on free competitive relationships among private selves who have equal political rights and influence regardless of economic status. Were the state organized on this principle, the political advantage that one individual may achieve over others is neutralized before long and spontaneously by the free working of the system. But since the inequalities of economic status and social privilege are persistent realities, the principle of *laissez-faire* has never been instituted with absolute purity and, where adulterated forms of it have been applied, never equally to all members of society. Even where the rhetoric of law and theory is utterly consistent and chooses not to recognize these inequalities as legally meaningful, the principle regularly bows before practice. It has always been modified by the power of capital over the marketplace and state structure. Wherever capital could intervene to its own advantage, it has practiced non-intervention toward itself and regulation toward others. Although this has surely been the prevailing mode, one should not imagine that it is all powerful. Whenever opposing social groups have been strong enough to compel the state to intercede in regulating the advantage *laissez-faire* gives to superior economic status or in granting concessions to public welfare, it has done so. These various conflicts between forces of unequal power, not the rationalizations of *laissez-faire* theory, are the real parameters of modern politics.[12]

We see this with particular clarity in economic and social affairs, which have never or only minimally been left to self-regulation. But in cultural affairs and art we discover a special case. Here the principle of *laissez-faire* seems to govern practice quite consistently. In the long history of modern political intervention, neither capital power nor the opposing power of dispossessed classes has been concerned to do anything much about culture or art. It is as if these areas of human practice are not star players or should not be in the serious game of privilege and control. The nation-state under capitalist sovereignty has left the arts to themselves, as have the civil and religious institutions identified with the modern state. Since the eighteenth century, with the atrophy of public and institutional patronage, the arts have had to find their destinies where and however they could, and that has been primarily in the marketplace. Such *laissez-faire* politics is again a source of ambiguity for the artist. It appears as a source of freedom. On the lowest, although not unimportant level, it is a casting overboard of the censorship privilege by officialdom. More profoundly, it implies the right of the artist, even aside from governmental constraint, to create whatever he wants to create, to achieve whatever his talents enable him to achieve. But it also appears as a negative sign, a forsaking of the artist as a use value or natural resource to the shark-infested waters where exchange value rules. Rather than lessening the breach between artist and public, it intensifies that alienation and drives the artist more relentlessly toward self-concern and cosmopolitanism.

Keeping the Arts
after Hard Times and Global War

Are there grounds for believing that the *laissez-faire* policy toward the arts has been reversed since World War II? Most Western governments now affirm, in political rhetoric everywhere and by constitutional precept in some European nations, that the state is obliged to promote the spiritual well-being of its citizens and the progress of national culture by supporting the arts. Given the long-standing convention that the arts are the noblest products of human history, the proposition is hardly new. Partisans of nearly all political persuasions throughout modern history have been moved to say something of the sort. But since World War II, rhetorical support for this proposition has reached a fairly high level, and the idea of national responsibility for the arts appears to have achieved legislative and executive authorization.

In continental Europe, where state subsidized and operated art museums, opera houses, and theaters have a fairly continuous history, this commitment attracts attention because public allocations for the arts have become relatively sizable in the post-war period. In Great Britain and the United States, the commitment to the arts is a surprise. For the better part of its history, the United States has been reluctant to patronize the arts, a point made by Lillian Miller in *Patrons and Patriotism* (1966) and also by Dick Netzer in *The Subsidized Muse* (1978). Janet Minihan's study, *The Nationalization of Culture* (1977), deals with the same footdragging on the part of the British government from the late eighteenth century to the outbreak of war in 1939.[13] From time to time, public authorities in both nations spoke, in glowing but always general words, of the state's duty to promote the arts, and their governments contributed money on occasion to particular arts projects to commemorate state events. Yet no administration in either country allocated public money for all the arts on a regular, annual basis until after World War II. Great Britain began to do so in 1946; the United States waited until 1965. Once legislation had been enacted, however, the rise in the amounts allocated was remarkable. In the United States, governmental art subsidies rose from $12,000,000 to $282,000,000 between 1965 and 1975, and by 1981 they had increased still more, although not at anywhere near the same rate.[14]

But in the context of all the monies expended on the arts, specifically private and corporate venture investments, these increases are extremely modest, even insignificant. In 1972 the United States allocated $150,000,000 directly to the arts. This sum represents a mere one percent of all art revenues, $11.5 billion, that year. In 1975 the subsidy represented not much more than two percent. On a per capita basis, the 1975 allocation came to $1.33. If we measure government subsidy against non-profit institutions and forms, the share is still on the small side. For 1972, it amounted to approximately fifteen percent, probably lower in 1975. Government support in the Reagan administration was a grim reversal of these modest subsidies and in the Bush years not much better.[15] The commitment, so new for the United States, is crablike moving backward.

The fact that government subsidy is restricted to non-profit organizations also bears some investigation. The overwhelming portion of this subsidy is granted to high-culture institutions. This means that most public funds for the arts are distributed to institutions controlled by private sources of wealth and located in a few, generally cosmopolitan, national centers. The small share that goes to individuals is awarded mostly for proposals that accord with high culture esthetics and that are carried out through privately- or corporately-controlled institutions.[16]

The limited ratio of these post-World War II allocations to the arts, their number, and the fact that they represent transfers of public funds to non-public or private control make it clear that the *laissez-faire* attitude toward the arts has not been abandoned. The esthetics which government patronage finds acceptable for funding and the transfer of the bulk of public money to cosmopolitan institutions tightly controlled by trustee boards of private wealth reinforce the tendency of the arts toward the private and the cosmopolitan. In the long-run history of modern civil society in the United States, the tendency seems to have become more relentless than ever in the post-World War II period.

2

Counter Choices:
A New Deal in the Arts

THE most opposed alternative to this two-headed drive toward self-re-
flexivity and cosmopolitanism before it came on the scene and after it
disappeared is New Deal patronage. The WPA arts projects were conscious offerings to various American publics whose most prominent features differed genuinely from the private, cosmopolitan characters of the
arts produced under the rubric of free enterprise. Although the WPA assured Congress, the commercial theater, and the publishing industry that it
had no intention of replacing Broadway or conventional ways of producing
literature in the United States, its arts projects pursued a course whose spirit
and effects were the opposite of the arts controlled by cosmopolitan commerce and the dispositions of high culture. The work of these four WPA
arts projects represents, by wide agreement, a government endeavor unlike
anything in the history of capitalism. What makes it so different—an issue
that has never been examined thoroughly—is that there had never been a
patronage so large in scope, so thoroughly organized, well financed, and
long lived. But it is also unlike anything before it, as well as after, in that it
organized itself not as a clearinghouse of funds to private agencies and individual artists but as a series of projects employing artists and guiding them
in the collective production of art, literature, and theater.

The patronage program undertaken by the federal government during
the Great Depression had a rather spastic initiation, coming and going between 1933 and mid-1935 to the fitful tune of one timorous relief act after
another. By mid-1935, however, it had settled down to a steady course
along three lines. One was the program sponsored by the Treasury Department and known as the Section or Section Art. Although it was a response
to the depression, it was not a relief measure. Its story has been most re-

cently treated with verve and insight by Marling. The photography program of the Farm Security Administration (FSA) was not a relief measure either. It is now recognized as probably the most felicitous esthetic fallout of New Deal patronage. But what the New Deal intended by this support was less to sanction an art form than to preserve, in another kind of response to the depression, a pictorial record of ordinary agricultural life. The third of the settled lines, the four WPA arts projects often called Federal One, is clearly a mapping in the relief terrain. Together as well as separately, the WPA projects received a more substantial government patronage than the other two. As a consequence, the term, "WPA Art" became the generic label, as Marling points out, for whatever the New Deal did in assuming an obligation toward the arts.[1] Our concern is with "WPA Art" in the specific sense.

I have already noted in Chapter 1 that the sums of money allocated to the WPA arts projects far exceed anything appropriated by Western European or United States governments before the 1930s. More interesting and surely more informative than money as an index of magnitude is the number of artists supported as salaried employees, the number of arts supported at one and the same time, the duration of years over which they were sustained, and the vast number of viewers, listeners, and readers they attracted. These too far exceed all ventures into art patronage of the modern past.

My figures for artists are from the FTP and the FWP. They provide a fair summary of all the projects, since the Federal Art Project (FAP) nearly matches the FWP, and the Federal Music Project (FMP) engaged considerably more musical artists than the FTP did theatrical artists. In May 1936, 12,372 people were employed by the FTP. Average FTP employment for the four years, 1935 to 1939, was 10,000.[2] The numbers for the FWP are not quite so high, but they are still prodigious, especially since the 1920 census enumerated only 10,499 gainfully employed writers. In November 1935, according to Noam Penkower's research, 4,016 writers, researchers, and manuscript copiers were on the FWP payroll, with over 6,000 by the end of December that year. The FWP average for the four years ranged between 4,500 and 5,200.[3]

More remarkable is that the four major arts were supported by the government on a continuing basis for four years, not only in a single center, but in a regional and local network covering all of the United States. I have pointed out that much of Euro-American art patronage before the 1930s took the form of specific responses to particular public art needs, for example, to commemorate a national event or hero or to decorate a newly-commissioned public building. Responses of this kind required no massive employment of artists or continuing patronage. And once the project was completed, the particular patronage ceased. Where patronage did have an ongoing character, as in the sponsorship of a national theater or opera, it was confined to a single center, usually the capital city, and generally restricted to classical or high culture offerings.[4] The WPA arts projects, on the contrary, were a form of patronage responding to the contingencies of an era and to the cultural needs of an entire nation. The difference between these two responses, one particular, the other holistic, explains why the WPA arts projects entailed unique magnitudes of support in the range of arts, geographical space, and length of time.

Probably no index of size is more dramatic than the vast and various publics the WPA arts projects attracted. FAP attendance figures, one close to the beginning of WPA and the other toward the end, give us a glimpse of how amazing these numbers are. The first set of figures is for seven states, five in the South and two along its border. Although this region had a much lower density of population than the Northeast and the industrial Midwest, from December 1935 to July 1, 1936, nearly 300,000 persons attended exhibitions of FAP work at eighteen FAP art centers and experimental galleries in those states. During that same period, over 56,000 adults and children in those states took advantage of FAP instruction in the arts and crafts. The boldest FAP encounter with the American population occurred in 1940, during National Art Week, a program which William McDonald calls "the greatest mass display of art . . . in the United States." During the last week of November 1940, an estimated five million persons came to view about 15,000 arts and crafts objects on display in 1,600 exhibitions across the nation.[5] If any other single encounter comes close to this, it is surely the FTP production of *It Can't Happen Here*, which opened simultaneously in twenty-one theaters in seventeen cities across the country on October 27, 1936. Over its entire run, according to FTP Director Hallie Flanagan, it played "260 weeks, or the equivalent of five years," in three different languages, English, Spanish, and Yiddish. In New York City alone, it played, in various productions, to over 414,000 people.[6] From 1935 through March 31, 1939, FTP's overall attendance figures totaled 30,398,726. This includes New York City, which predictably outdid every single state where the FTP operated. But even if we consider only the industrial Midwest (Illinois, Indiana, Michigan, and Ohio), we discover an impressive audience: 5,651,456.[7]

Trying to estimate how many readers the FWP reached with its published works is a more difficult matter. Unlike the FAP and FTP, the FWP issued no final report with an accounting of this sort, perhaps because it did not distribute its work to the public. Through a variety of contractual agreements, the FWP relied on commercial publishers to do that. As a result, it could not keep direct tabs on how many copies of a work were printed and sold. Spotty records of printing runs and sales do exist, however, and give us some clue to the magnitude of readers involved.

The numbers are impressive when compared to the beleagured state of publishing in the 1930s. Penkower reports that during that period publishers were happy if they sold between 2,500 and 3,500 copies; he adds that they called a sale of 7,000 "a pronounced success." Publishers who agreed to issue FWP work—the state guide series in particular—had no reason to regret their decision, for the series found a truly considerable readership in all parts of the country. In its first week, the guide book for the small state of Vermont attracted 2,000 buying readers and over 6,000 by 1940. The *New Orleans City Guide* became a local best-seller, reaching at least 10,000 readers by 1941. The publisher of the *Massachusetts Guide* started with a printing of 10,000—and planned another one of 20,000 but a swarm of local politicians became upset by the guide's candid treatment of the Sacco-Vanzetti case, forcing the publisher to revise the book. *American Stuff*, a collection of poems and short stories by FWP writers, came out in a first edition of 5,000, at a time when the usual practice of the publishing industry for anthologies of creative work was to start with no more than 1,500.[8] These extraordinary publisher expectations and sales indicate how well the FWP fared in readership. But it should be remembered that figures such as these, indeed even complete figures were they available, establish only a floor limit of readership. Unlike museum and theater attendance, where each ticket sale represents one viewer, the literary form cannot be pinned down. Each book purchased is very likely a sign of more than one reader.

Finally, if we add to this evidence the equally extraordinary number of FWP works published, we begin to get a full sense of the magnitude of the readership. A selected compilation made after World War II lists over four hundred titles, of which some three hundred are substantial contributions to either United States history or literature.[9] While not all achieved the readership levels suggested by my examples, many did, and a few, the *New York Panorama* for instance, did better. Taken together, the evidence suggests a reasonable estimate of hundreds of thousands and reminds us again how massive New Deal patronage was.

Comparing the WPA arts program to government patronage in the United States after World War II is somewhat more problematical. The two major agencies of contemporary federal patronage, the National Endowment for the Arts and the National Endowment for the Humanities, have a history as federal instrumentalities more than twenty years longer than the four WPA arts projects. Moreover, they support artists and reach audiences in an entirely different way, making accurate judgments about their extent quite dubious. Neither endowment engages directly in producing art objects, plays, or writing, and neither employs artists directly. Each endowment is a disbursement agency, awarding grants through competition to a limited and changing number of individuals and institutions for disparate and changing purposes—for aims, in other words, that are more or less privately determined. Hence, while each now has a longer history than the WPA arts projects, neither has anywhere near their record of continuity in programmatic purpose and performance or continuous and direct involvement with many artists in a common context or work. Nor has either been directly responsible for reaching audiences the way the 1930s projects were.

Even if we deal only with unanalyzed numbers, we find that in no year, no pair of years, and no set of four years has either endowment supported artists in the same numbers as the WPA. If we consider only the most opulent years of these endowments, awards have gone at best to a few thousand people, a far distance from the twenty to thirty thousand supported for most of the four-year period by New Deal patronage. Although it is impossible to compare audience numbers, we can reasonably assume that the disparate nature of endowment patronage very likely makes for a less concentrated, less deliberate effort to reach masses of people. With regard to published works, endowment funding simply does not equal, for any commensurable period, the results of the FWP. Nor is it likely that the total literary output under endowment funding has accumulated as wide a readership, since it tends to be overwhelmingly scholarly or, if imaginative, intellectually self-absorbed.[10]

The cultural and esthetic motivations of the WPA arts projects disclose what size and number are unable to—the bone and marrow, the soul of that numerically unmatched, numerically impressive obligation the New Deal assumed toward the nation's culture. It seems to me the most central motivation, the one that gives definition to the others, is that of being an alternative to the *laissez-faire* attitudes toward esthetic self-absorption and cosmopolitanism. This motive animated the art professionals called on to administer the program and many of the artists who worked in it, and it constituted the general proposition determining the nature of creative work: the populism of artist-audience relationships, and the kind of content deemed worthy for dramatic and literary treatment.[11] These two factors constituted the esthetic side of being an alternative, the side that gave the arts projects texture and reality. The political side of the alternative, its official and legislative sanction within the frame of government, was itself conditioned by a number of qualifications to insure esthetic integrity and open content, freedom from party politics and from governmental censorship. This side of the alternative connoted a logic pointing beyond relief to permanent support, and the projects' art professionals and working artists held fast to a vision of federal patronage as a continuing obligation of government. To that end, they helped draft a legislative bill and agitated for its passage.

44

The motivation to be an esthetic alternative directed the WPA arts projects to a *modus operandi* of creative collaboration, a method of work diametrically opposite to the way the arts have developed in modern civil society. Instead of endorsing the individualistic and self-absorbed aspect of creative work, the projects transformed an army of artists into a collaborative force to produce plays and manuscripts that were truly ensemble creations. The theater, by its nature, is always a form of collaboration. Yet its history under capitalism reflects a continual surrender of company character to the star system, whether the star be a dominating playwright, director as *auteur*, or performer: the company loses whatever standing it might have had as a significant creative force and becomes a frame or backdrop for one or more stellar individuals. The FTP deliberately turned its back on the star system to experiment with ensemble creativity, even in New York City, where it had an enormous pool of talented theater people on its payroll. The simultaneous opening of *It Can't Happen Here* in seventeen cities strikes me as an example on every level of production of the collaborative *modus operandi*. The living newspaper form, for which the FTP is justly famous, is an example of playwright collaboration and company adaptation to local conditions, docudrama writing by central research and editorial committees with the idea that alterations would be made from place to place.[12] The FWP was as deliberate as the FTP in concentrating on ensemble creativity, a feat perhaps more remarkable, since literature seems to be only possible as a production of individual authors. The FWP's state guide series, to take one example, contradicts that assumption. It demonstrates collaborative work, little of which can be attributed to individual authors, of extremely high quality.

For the FTP and the FWP, the collaborative mode meant something more than an ensemble of complementary artists working to produce unified artistic effects. Their esthetic motivations included working closely with the common publics they saw as their main audience. For the FTP, this took a number of courses, the most superficial of which was canvassing audience opinion after each performance. Although it is not clear that the FTP ever used this information to modify its esthetic concepts, it seems to have paid attention to the views it solicited from labor and community leaders thought to represent the common man and woman. Since in many particulars these views resembled audience opinion, we may assume that, in one form or another, they contributed to the populist effects the FTP intended to achieve. The most profound attempt at audience collaboration was the FTP's program to produce plays by local writers immersed in the life and problems of farm-worker or immigrant, working-class communities. The program also called for local companies to stage pageant dramas based on local and regional lore. Although the results of the program were uneven, the best results signify the mutual reward and importance of audience contribution where the FTP was able to establish a close and reciprocal relationship with its publics.

The FWP had a far better record on this score. In fact, few of the literary goals it pursued could have been accomplished without consulting ordinary publics. The state guides, for example, could not have become the fine cultural histories they are without the factual and anecdotal information garnered from the ordinary folk whom FWP writers and researchers interviewed in rural and urban areas. The same is even truer for the pioneer work the FWP did in black and folklore studies and in occupational histories. Dependent on rural and urban workers for the content of these studies and histories, the FWP tried rigorously to safeguard that content against editorial distortion and insisted on working into the manuscripts as much as possible of the language and style of the people interviewed. The program effectively captured the sound and culture of disregarded groups on a scale never before attempted.

The story of these audience relationships inevitably touches on what the arts projects deemed worthy for dramatic and literary expression. We need to remind ourselves, perhaps, that the publics which make up the masses were generally excluded from the usual or dominant forms of drama and literature. High prices constituted one daunting barrier, and place was another. Outside the nation's major cultural centers, the opportunity of experiencing the usual forms was severely limited. But the most telling exclusion relates to the way the usual forms ignored the lives and culture of these obscure publics.[13] If the FTP or the FWP were to make headway with the audiences they were out to win, they had to make their work affordable and available. Each project could keep its prices low because its artists worked at relief wages and, as a federal effort, each could be available in community after community across the nation. But to make their proposed publics a staying, reliable audience, the projects had to portray the lives of these men and women with insight and honesty and in language that caught the sound and style of their speech. The stress these projects gave to Americana is one general fallout of giving serious attention to such lives. In part, the purpose was to discover in the past the meaning of the present; that did not imply simple patriotic glorification, although political leaders and bureaucrats often deflected it in that direction. It implied showing how the sweat and inspiration of uncultivated settlers transformed the United States into an industrial giant and how difficult their lives were made in doing so. The art professionals at the head of local projects as well as their staffs fought hard against trivializing the lives of these hard working settlers that glorification entailed, and they often prevailed in giving an honest and compelling account of their unsung audience.[14]

46

The clearest examples of what the arts projects accomplished in this regard are their studies of folk, black, and ethnic cultures and their collections of life or occupational histories. The FWP is more noted than the FTP for these studies, but similar effects are, nevertheless, deeply engraved in the Theater Project. They are represented in plays and programs created by Theater Project staffs or written by playwrights whom the commercial theater ignored. The project's program for foreign language drama, its black theater sections, its pageant and spectacle presentations, and its living newspapers would have been inconceivable without a sympathetic openness to these unfavored classes and the common life histories of their members.

Such plays as *Turpentine, Big White Fog, 200 Were Chosen, The Tailor Becomes a Storekeeper*, to name only a few from the foreign language program, the black theater, and topical depression drama, are typical of this effort. They dig deep into the folkways, the occupational hardships, and the daunting inter-group relationships of black, rural, and immigrant workers. Among the living newspaper productions, we have *Injunction Granted, One-Third of a Nation*, and *Triple-A Plowed Under*. Docudramas skillfully weaving newspaper headlines and experimental stage techniques into dramatic presentations of current political and social issues, these living newspaper productions capture the voices, styles, and customs of the ordinary folk they are concerned with. The pageants and spectacles, primarily intended to celebrate local events of historical or traditional significance, tend toward patriotic oversimplification. Still, in several there is an attempt to portray features of local common life without euphemistic distortion.

FTP adaptations and translations are also proof of how deeply interested the arts projects were in the residual and emergent cultures of rural and urban workers. For example, *The Swing Mikado*, a production of the black wing of the Chicago Theater Project, transformed Gilbert and Sullivan's work through an original score based on the musical and lyrical idioms of jazz and swing. The end effect is an artful expression, specifically of African-American culture, but also of other working-class and ethnic cultures, since these musical idioms had become an integral part of non-elite culture in the United States. Translations of plays written in English into other languages were only one part of the foreign language program. Although the classical plays of other languages made up the larger part of the program, such translations as the Yiddish version of Odets's *Awake and Sing* in New York and Los Angeles and the Spanish translation, *Esto No Pasara Aqui*, of *It Can't Happen Here* in Tampa, were probably a more convincing sign to immigrant workers of the empathy the arts projects had with immigrant culture.[15]

What the FTP deemed worthy for production was not, however, limited to the folkways and urban styles of the ordinary masses. Also included were classical plays (Marlowe, Molière, Schiller, much Shakespeare, and others), scores of modern plays (Ibsen, Shaw, Capek, O'Neill, Elmer Rice, Susan Glaspell, Maxwell Anderson among them), musicals (a number composed through project staff collaboration), and religious plays.[16] Some of the musicals and more commercially- oriented modern plays were a concession to the view that spells of circuses were needed to make serious drama palatable. Religious drama constituted an attempt at occasional presentations appropriate to community beliefs and celebrations, and they represent part of the FWP desire to give stage voice to the culture of the masses. Of these various additional play categories, the FTP concentrated most heavily on the classics and modern plays that were considered esthetically accomplished and thematically profound. That concentration signified a fairly standard idea that the best of bourgeois theater had universal value and the masses would be vastly enriched by exposure to it. Yet it would be a mistake to overlook the populist intent behind this esthetic motivation or to ignore how unusual the FTP mass offerings of classical and serious bourgeois drama are in the theatrical annals of the bourgeois era. This, together with the work directly connected to the underside cultures of America, reflects the esthetic and thematic break—a rather raggedy break to be sure—of the FTP with the dominant stage forms under capitalism both before and after the 1930s.

The Writers' Project's sense of what subjects it should favor did not include the classical canon or previously published modern works, whether of intellectual depth or light popular appeal. Designed to be a work-relief program using and developing the writing skills of out-of-work writers, it confined itself to original compositions based on primary research, most extensively of local and regional communities and underside cultures. Clearly the Writers' Project deemed the people of these obscure communities and these generally unrecognized cultures worthy subjects of literature and the key to its literary goals. It could hardly have succeeded without an extensive contribution from the common men and women of these communities. The point is self-evident in such special and pioneering work as the Writers' Project's slave narrative collections, occupational histories, ethnic studies, and its collections of folk life materials and urban industrial lore. It is also true for a large part of its major undertaking, the state guide books. The high quality of so many of them as cultural histories and records of material that might otherwise have remained scattered or even been lost is a result of the project's heavy reliance on factual and anecdotal information provided by a host of ordinary folk in rural and urban areas. Where the state FWPs rigorously protected the content provided by these common men and women against editorial distortion and evoked their language and style, they produced outstanding guides, culturally distinguished and vivid records of America's working people.

As the FWP's first collaborative experiment, the state guide series had a time advantage over the project's other undertakings. Eventually a guide was published for each of the forty-eight states then in the Union. The other collaborative undertakings fell short of this accomplishment, in part because they remained auxiliary activities until the guide books were virtually completed. Once the FWP could concentrate on speeding up their production, time began to run out. The first setback came in the summer of 1939, when Congress transformed the arts projects into programs for which the states were basically responsible.[17] Under those circumstances, the cultural and esthetic motivations I have been discussing were largely abandoned. The second setback, World War II, quickly followed. Even before the United States became directly engulfed in the war, the work of the arts projects became a tool of defense, and after December 1941 the FWP wrote nothing but how-to pamphlets for the war effort. In 1943 the arts projects were terminated, ending a form of federal patronage with alternative cultural and esthetic motivations unique in capitalist history.[18] But if much of what the FWP recorded of America's working people, black population, and ethnic groups was never published, what it accomplished with these studies is still impressive and testifies to how strongly it valued their literary worth. Penkower illustrates how much we need to remind ourselves of that accomplishment and how the present still undervalues the worth of those subjects: "The approximately 14,000 manuscripts of folklore, 3,000 ex-slave narratives, and 1,000 social-ethnic manuscripts that were turned over to the Library of Congress project . . . in September, 1940, varied in quality, but they provided a wealth of information for future scholars that has yet to be fully appreciated."[19]

Creative collaboration, reciprocal audience interaction, and high esthetic regard for subordinate cultures represent the truly alternative character of the WPA arts projects. But they were not the New Deal's primary motivations for supporting the arts. The chief purpose for those who pieced together the New Deal, the one they could ill afford to ignore, was economic. The WPA arts projects were initiated as emergency work relief for a specific group of unemployed persons, not as art patronage. Harry Hopkins's well-known retort to silence critics who favored WPA, but not money for artists, sums it up: "Hell they've got to eat just like other people."[20] The economic goal, making jobs for the unemployed until prosperity returned, continued to be the key factor motivating Washington politicians and local bureaucrats, and it illustrates the firm grip the *laissez-faire* principle had on officials in matters of cultural and esthetic affairs.

49

Still, the play of the esthetic and cultural factors guiding the arts projects was inevitable. From the beginning, these factors commanded the attention of the art professionals selected to administer the projects and the unemployed artists who were put to work. The concept of work relief in the 1930s made them inevitable, for it implied the same answer to the question: what kind of work were artists on government payroll going to do? Unlike the premise of those who saw work relief in the narrowest economic sense, as a temporary emergency measure to alleviate suffering and prime the business pump, the more up-to-date theory behind work relief was that people should be put to work on socially needed projects and that setting people to work should help preserve a national resource: the varied actual and potential skills and talents of the millions thrown out of the work by the Great Depression.[21] The first principle implies work benefitting and reflecting the many regions and populations making up the nation; the second implies work appropriate to the experience and specific talent of each worker.

This double-barreled conception of work relief implied for the arts projects a collaborative esthetic enterprise with an inclusive populist content. It became a clearly articulated goal as the projects began to formulate more thoroughly their essential esthetic and cultural aims.

Conservative and Progressive Regionalism

Two other examples from this period, regionalism and left-wing arts, played an important part in the history of New Deal patronage and were themselves oppositional alternatives. Even before the 1930s, regionalism represented itself as a thoroughgoing opponent to the direction of the arts under industrial capitalism, especially to its cosmopolitanism, and the depression afforded it new vitality and increased influence. The depression also gave the arts of the radical left a momentum they lacked in the 1920s. Each saw its own esthetic aims as an antidote to the toxins of interiorization and cosmopolitanism, as the means to rejuvenate and revamp culture.

The revived interest of the late 1920s and early 1930s in regional modes of life had a complex personality, one phase conservative, the other progressive or radical. The esthetic views of each phase were counter movements to the solipsistic, cosmopolitan art of twentieth-century America. In both phases, regionalism conceived of esthetic issues as dynamic phenomena inseparable from the natural setting, economy, politics, and folkways of geographically distinct communities. In its conservative character, regionalism naturalized social organization, establishing geography as the only determinant of production and social order. Conservative regionalism also nationalized the diversity and decentralization of regional life by presuming it to be the norm of American nationhood. Progressive or

50

radical regionalism tended to concentrate on the largely ignored culture of deprived or exploited working populations in diverse regions of the United States. Moreover, its definition of region included what the conservative side rejected, the urban working classes whose ethnic particularity remained instrumentally cohesive.

Among the advocates of regional culture, the conservative view was expressed most forcefully by John Crowe Ransom in the *American Review*. In "The Aesthetics of Regionalism" (January 1934), he proposed that "regionalism is really more reasonable, for it is more natural" than cosmopolitanism, progressivism, industrialism, internationalism, or whatever name may be assigned to nonregional urban society.[22] A region is distinguished by its natural terrain, he argued. Its economy, localized like its geography, is a direct outgrowth of physical shape and natural resources. Hence agriculture is the quintessential economic activity of a region, and the regional city supports its needs. Identification with local geography and the bond linking workers with their locale comprise the soul of a true esthetic. Once succeeding generations of regional populations have worked in intelligent harmony with physical nature, "nature not only yields up her routine concession," according to Ransom, "but luxuriates and displays her charm." The response of regional men and women to this generous overyield of nature is "to represent it lovingly in their arts," and "their economic actions become also their arts."[23] Since in the conservative view, regional economy is natural, it is also conceived to be long-lived and free of crisis, and a region's population is thought to be relatively entrenched from generation to generation. Although tradition is an important feature of the conservative conception of regionalism, no locale is ever an entirely isolated area of self-generating culture. A regional culture imports forms and traditions, but never in a way that displaces the essential relationship between itself and its natural economy. Ransom believed that a region slowly adapts such importations to its own purposes so that ultimately they look and feel "native."[24]

Conservative regionalism saw something quite different happening in the sprawling urban centers of the nation. In the cosmopolitian as well as the industrial city, where trans-regional and international trade is the norm, the chief purpose of economy is to make money rather than specifically useful things for a familiarly known group of people. Moreover, in the making of things primarily to be exchanged for money, production in the industrial city relies more and more on complex machinery. Ransom attacked both money and machinery for the disabling effects they had on goods and work. Money, where it becomes the chief aim of economy, converts things into abstractions, and machinery does the same to labor. Hence, Ransom argued, "the cities of the machine age are particularly debased. . . . They are without history, and they are without region, since population is imported from any sources whatever; and therefore they are without character."[25] The cosmopolitan center, with its purchased forms and traditions from everywhere else on earth but particularly Europe, forges a cultural abstractness and eclecticism that matches the facelessness of its money and the lost personality of its mass-produced product. In the industrial city, where workers are mute auxiliaries of machines, culture barely survives in any form, neither as native experience nor as abstracted, eclectic importation.

The conservative side of regionalism expressed an apparently radical critique of twentieth-century capitalism reminiscent of more left-wing views. But its cold eye on capitalism was a consequence of nostalgia for an earlier arrangement of social classes. Its disparagement of working-class experience indicated, sometimes implicitly but often directly, a rejection of liberal reformism as well as socialist solutions for capitalist ills and underscores its regressive attitudes. Blaming disruptive conditions and the disharmonies of gross inequality on the denaturalizing of regional economies by big-city finance and industrial capitalism, it advocated a return to an order dominated by agrarian forms and interests. Conservative regionalism saw the onset of the Great Depression as a breakdown of capitalism no longer rooted in region, and it felt that regional agrarianism had become historically credible once again. It would not admit that the agrarianism of an earlier period of capitalism, before the invasion of impersonal, regionally unaffiliated big business, had its own built-in logic of disruptive and savagely unjust practices, its own way of denaturalizing and debasing esthetic sensibilities and cultural traditions.[26]

Progressive or radical regionalism had little interest in turning back to older forms of economic life. It deplored big business intrusion for destroying the culture of unfavored groups, such as black and poor white folk. Progressive regionalism wanted those cultures preserved and recorded. It saw the culture of those groups as a history, in a commonly shared natural setting, of unrelieved hardship and frequent conflict, and it wanted to record that aspect of their lives in narrative and drama and preserve the stories about that experience.

To varying degrees, progressive regionalism was suspicious of its conservative counterpart during the late 1920s and 1930s. It suspected that conservative regionalism harbored in its theories parochial solutions and designs to safeguard the self-interest of local ruling elites. Even the mild version of progressive or radical regionalism expressed by Howard Odum and Harry Moore objected to this narrow agenda. As they saw it, conservative regionalism obstructed the path of new national policies (they meant the New Deal) which aimed to solve problems affecting all regions and all sectors of regional population equitably by tailoring federal and regional planning to each other. "Emerging new regionalism," they wrote "offers a better, more workable solution of the problems arising from the complexity of American life." In a very clear example of populist thinking, they fixed on the grave condition of tenant farmers and the need for population and income redistribution as inveterate problems that a focus on sectional advantage obscured and a focus on national well-being revealed.[27]

Militant regionalism stressed to an even greater degree class relationships, inequities, and conflicts in regional life and defined regional more inclusively, making categories of work central to its definition. It included not only rural subdivisions still close to nature by dint of agrarian work, but also urban subdivisions, where commerce and industry made work remote from nature. The severe depression at home and the hostile impasses of international affairs forced these issues to a head, and scholars followed the lead with reevaluations of American history.

Louis Hacker, for example, felt that the frontier and sectional concepts of Frederick Jackson Turner were very wide of the mark indeed. In a 1933 review article, "Sections or Classes?", he argued that "with settlement achieved—that is to say, the historic function of extensive agriculture performed, class (not section!) lines solidified, competitive capitalism converted into monopolistic capitalism under the guidance of money power, and imperialism the ultimate destiny of the nation—the United States was returning to the mainstream of European institutional development." Hacker rejected Frederick Jackson Turner's precept that the uniqueness of America resided in its frontier-sectional structure, and he lamented the prevalence of Turner's theory among American historians for forty years.[28] The political scientist A. N. Holcombe also stressed that class had become more important than section in the twentieth century. Urban industry, he declared, had shattered the rural, sectional dominance of national life. Urban classes now determined party politics.[29] Surely an overstatement, but Holcombe had put his finger on a real shift of political power. Because of these shifts in class relationships, the more radical version of regionalism also saw the urban-metropolitan center as the focal point from which a new kind of region emanates, particularly in terms of culture. "Through its newspapers, theatres, schools, and museums," Louis Wirth asserted, "the city diffuses its culture over a large area."[30]

This heightened awareness of urban class, of the urban working class in particular, was articulated quite effectively in the midst of the depression by the folklorist Benjamin Botkin, one of new regionalism's most consistent advocates. In a 1936 article, "Regionalism: Cult or Culture?", he pointed out how the radical notion of regional life differed from the conservative one. The radical notion he called "scientific regionalism," the conservative one anachronistic, arcadian, and utopian, "a genteel tradition-in-decay-and-at-bay, preaching a theological war between an agrarian god and an industrial devil." But he also criticized certain Marxists, such as Granville Hicks and V. F. Calverton, for their sweeping charge that regional literature is nothing but an escape from the central issues of social reality. Citing two proletarian novels that are genuinely regional in basis, Grace Lumpkin's *To Make My Bread* (1932) and Erskine Caldwell's *Tobacco Road* (1932), he suggested that the Marxist critic who fails to see the part regional folk resistance plays in class struggle runs the risk of constructing an intellectual synthesis of American life that is as mythic as the conservative idyll of agrarian class harmony.[31]

Botkin felt, however, that Marxism, if it were not oversimplified, had an important relationship to the kind of regionalism that embraced neglected folk cultures and exploited classes. Marxism, the disciplines of ethnology and folklore, and the regionalism he advocated made up a four-fold affiliation that marked a turning away from what he called the "literary anarchy" of "pure literature and absolute poetry." Scientific or class-oriented regionalism represented a turn toward "a social and cultural art," a turn toward a revitalizing "literary collectivism." The particularly important esthetic accomplishment of literature based on the urban, proletarian concept of region is the amplitude, wholeness, and rooted personality of its social portraiture. Regional literature restricted to the conservative agrarian concept portrays "limited solidarities." The regional literature that includes city and countryside in a context of diverse, struggling groups, transcends the circumscribed and ultimately falsifying unities of the conservative illusion. "In this regional literature," Botkin declared, "a natural division of labor exists between the provincial writer, on the side of the rural and agrarian, and the metropolitan writer, on the side of the urban and the industrial." He argued that both are needed to achieve a complete portrait of the nation and its folk and to capture the "new technology and mythology emerging alike from our buried cultures and our submerged classes."[32]

The literary output inspired by this new concept of regionalism exemplifies the range of its esthetic orientation. This is true for the early years of revived interest in regional modes of life (before the 1930s) as well as for the years of the Great Depression. Across the nation, the hardships and ways of life of the obscured masses emerged from the deep shadows cast over history by the self-centered, universalizing tendency of the bourgeoisie. As a consequence, while such picturesque occupations as lumberjacking, steamboating, and canaling continued to attract attention, in the late 1920s and the 1930s, other, less glamorous occupations usually associated with highly developed monopoly capitalism, like coal mining, textile work, tenant farming, and the auto assembly line, claimed an increasing share of literary interest. In these kinds of jobs, in the regions where they were performed, in the people who occupied them, this literature discovered a plight crying for attention. It discovered not only a fighting mood of enormous dramatic potential, but an exciting cultural diversity and an invigorating brand of talent and raw energy.

A 1927 anthology called *Songs and Stories of the Anthracite Industry* is an early example. It retrieves for the record a substantial part of the musical and narrative culture of Pennsylvania coal miners. A group of novels that followed on the heels of a series of strikes in the South does the same for the struggles of North Carolina textile hands in 1929: Mary Heaton Vorse's *Strike!* (1930), Grace Lumpkin's *To Make My Bread* (1932), Sherwood Anderson's *Beyond Desire* (1932), William Rollins's *The Shadow Before* (1934). Zora Neale Hurston, among others, covered the customs and stories of black sharecropping communities in Florida, in addition to describing some underground hoodoo rituals of New Orleans' city folk in *Mules and Men* (1935). Hurston's sweep from tales of everyday life to exotic ritual is typical of the new regionalism, whose interest easily ranged from the life and dialect of the Gullah blacks on Georgia's Sea Islands to the songs of everyday work, as in the 1926 collection *Negro Work Songs*.[33]

Songs of protest and traditional ballads revised to suit specific industrial struggles also testify to the range of radical regionalism's more inclusive concept. Here Marxists, particularly in the Communist Party, and their labor-oriented, left-wing allies played a very supportive role. At meetings, rallies, and demonstrations, they helped publicize them and make them popular among a fairly substantial urban middle-class and working-class audience. The repertoires of singers like Huddie Ledbetter and Woody Guthrie come to mind. Writers of a left-liberal mind, like Margaret Larkin, Mary Heaton Vorse, and Loretto Carroll Bailey of the Carolina Playmakers, helped preserve the ballads of the Appalachian mountain folk and the Piedmont tenant farmers whose declining economies had driven them from mountain and field into the textile mills.[34]

Radical regionalism accepted a wide variety of ethnic and working-class fiction. To illustrate the breadth and actuality of literary regionalism, Odum and Moore list for the years 1927 through 1936—along with such commonly recognized regional authors as William Faulkner, Ellen Glasgow, Sinclair Lewis, and Edvard Rolvaag—Albert Halper's novel about Chicago factory workers, *The Foundry* (1934); Langston Hughes's account of the black working class, *Not Without Laughter* (1930); James T. Farrell's *Studs Lonigan Trilogy* (1932, 1934, 1935); and John Steinbeck's story of a California Chicano community, *Tortilla Flat* (1935). In addition to the novels, they cite a series of life-study articles published by *Scribner's Magazine* in 1931 and 1932, including narratives of eastside New York teenagers, a radical childhood in an Italian neighborhood, a big-city lawyer, a Slavic steelworker, and the southern black belt.[35]

Regional magazines of the period also illustrate the new, more sympathetic attention to the rural poor, the urban working class, and the industrial city. Two Midwest magazines, the *Midland* (1915–33) and the *Anvil* (1933–35), are interesting examples. The first reflects the mild version of radical regionalism, the second the strong version. Founded and edited by John T. Frederick, who later became the regional director of FWP for Illinois, Indiana, Michigan, Missouri, and Ohio, the *Midland* was not very political. It sought primarily to be an outlet for midwesterners writing stories, poems, and criticism related to the Midwest. Still, from its early issues on, it offered a fairly steady, if limited stream of stories about small struggling farmers, ordinary city folk, and industrial laborers. Stories of this kind increased in frequency with the onset of the Great Depression.[36] *Anvil* started life in 1933 in a Minnesota cowbarn. Its editors, who had previously published the *Rebel Poet*, came from remote sections where rural workers had already been transformed into proletarians by the invasion of capital investment. Its purpose was to be an outlet for proletarian writers and for "stories from the mines, mills, factories, and offices of America." The stories and poems that appeared in it and its predecessor covered mining life in the Ohio-Mississippi basin, ranch-hand life in Texas, the drought in Arkansas, and growing up black on Chicago's South State Street.[37]

Regional theater supplies still more evidence of the proletarian and urban vitality of new regionalism. In the Midwest, Chicago, Cleveland, and Detroit had left-wing theater groups that stimulated local playwrights to dramatize working-class struggles and politics. Their most innovative stagings were achieved in short agit-prop skits and musical farces, the latter relying on popular and folk tunes for their basic material. The attempt of these groups to reach lower-middle-class and working-class audiences is another side of their more inclusive esthetic practices.[38] Other, less politically-oriented regional theaters wanted to reach out in the same way. At Cornell, for example, A. M. Drummond directed a country theater in the 1920s and 1930s with the aim of developing home-grown plays about western New York and performing for a grass-roots audience. According to the testimony of Robert Gard, himself a director of grass-roots theater in Wisconsin after World War II, Drummond's country theater fulfilled both purposes. "A woman from Buffalo," he writes, "brought her play about Underground Railroad days at Niagara Falls. . . . A machinist from around Rochester brought two scripts about workmen. A girl from the western part of the state brought her play about grape pickers." Standing-room audiences of local people attended quite regularly, many visiting the theater, whose doors were always open, to see what went on between plays.[39] The Carolina Playmakers, under Frederick H. Koch, proved to be one of the most outstanding outlets for plays about local working folk by local writers. In 1931 the Playmakers produced Loretto Carrol Bailey's *Strike-Song*, based on the 1929 Gastonia strike of Appalachian mountaineer millhands. This was only one of several plays the company put on in the 1920s and early 1930s portraying the lives of the region's working people and ethnic minorities— plays about fishermen on North Carolina's Outer Banks, Piedmont tenant farmers and textile workers, moonshiners, blacks, and Croatian immigrants. The playwrights were mostly of local origin, and the Playmakers toured their dramas in the mill towns and rural cities of the state.[40]

Clearly, by the mid-thirties, these two forms of regionalism had become quite active. But had they become tightly-knit schools of thought and esthetic practice or widely known among the regional cultures of the United States when the New Deal administration authorized the WPA arts projects? The answer is no. Both were largely spontaneous responses to common circumstances. Neither had any highly structured organization. Those who identified themselves as conservative disagreed about many issues, as did those who thought of themselves as progressive. Neither had any central or individual funding to rely on as a regular or adequate source of support. Nor did either branch reach very large audiences, particularly not among rural working folk and city-based proles. Conservative regionalism, because of its adherence to the literary standards of high culture, appealed mainly to esthetically-oriented audiences. Progressive regionalism produced works that were less arty, but its reach among country folk and city workers, while considerable by past norms, was never very extensive. As alternatives to the private and cosmopolitan directions that dominated the arts in western civilization, their vigor was unfortunately blunted by scant resources and disorganization. In these respects, they differed from the New Deal arts projects considerably. Government patronage in 1935 provided resources that neither wing of regionalism could boast. It offered a united, planned program with massive, central funding and a nationwide organization—one that could easily be imagined as a formidable rival to the private, cosmopolitan ways of bourgeois culture. Nevertheless, as forceful and clear alternatives already articulated by 1935, these regionalist concepts were a ready-to-hand set of ideas and practical models for the government's own entry into supporting an alternative direction for the arts.

The Regionalism of New Deal Patronage

The influence of these concepts, particularly in the case of progressive regionalism, extended directly into the projects, since a substantial number of the key professionals staffing and advising the arts projects came out of that experience. My examples start at the top: Holger Cahill, Hallie Flanagan, and Henry Alsberg. But as we shall see, the ranks below them were equally—and, in some cases, even more closely—associated with regional culture.

Holger Cahill, the director of the Art Project, started his professional career at the Newark Museum, where John Cotton Dana had made his innovative idea—that American art ought to serve the common man and have an intimate link to everyday life—a basis for museum activities. Before he left Newark to become the folk art curator at the Museum of Modern Art, Cahill had played an important part in organizing exhibitions on two subjects rarely treated in the dominant art world, "American Primitives" (1930) and "American Folk Sculpture" (1931). These regional and democratic influences had a deep effect. He fervently believed that art could flourish only if it had a close connection to a mass audience. Before and after he assumed the directorship of the FAP, he repeatedly emphasized the need for this kind of closeness in the subjects art dealt with and the audiences it sought. Early in 1935, in an essay for *Art in America*, he greeted the federal government's first work relief efforts enthusiastically, suggesting they might heal "the breach between the artist and the public, a breach which has become distressingly evident in the contemporary period."[41] After four years at the head of the FAP, he spoke even more sharply of the subjectivist tendency of the arts over the past three hundred years, their segregation from the ordinary vocations of society, and the dominating role of the private collector. The arts as collective and social in the commonest sense, "as a part of the significant life of an organized community, and of the necessary unity of the arts with the activities, the objects, and the scenes of everyday life," seemed to him a far better way.[42]

Cahill's regionalism is populist rather than conservative and is indicated by the FAP artists he singled out in his 1939 address. One was a seventy-year-old FAP painter from Northfield, Ohio, who painted the low hills, small valleys, and tilled fields of his native area while the farm folk looked on with appreciation and respect. Another was a Boston artist in his twenties, who considered himself "a city dweller" and wanted to record in his work the detritus of slum life: "newspaper, cigarette butts, torn posters, empty match cards, broken bottles, orange rinds, overflowing garbage cans, flies, boarded houses, gas lights, and so on—to present this picture in the very places where the escapist plans his flight."[43] A third was a Chicago painter whom Cahill thought "one of the most brilliant young muralists of the Project" and whose words he quoted as still another sign of the requisite collaboration between artists and common citizen: "Ours is the story of Labor and Progressivism, of Jane Addams and Mary McDowell, of Eugene Debs and Robert LaFollette, Sr., of Vachel Lindsay and Theodore Dreiser, of Haymarket and Hull House."[44] Cahill saw all this as an odyssey, an adventure, and with good reason. He and the other members of the FAP thought that in the farms, cities, workplaces, settlement houses, and traditions of working-class struggle, they were discovering the myth and developing the forms to express it that would inevitably bind them closer to the audiences of whom and to whom they spoke.

Hallie Flanagan is WPA's most dramatic representative of regional experience. Harry Hopkins had asked her twice to take on relief programs for theater people: first in 1934, when theater relief came to little more than a catch-as-catch-can application of bandaids under the Federal Emergency Relief Act of 1934, and again in 1935, after the passage of the Emergency Relief Appropriations Act. The first appeal she turned down, the second she could not resist. Hopkins pressed her to accept the directorship of the Federal Theater Project with these words: "I know something about the plays you've been doing for ten years, plays about American life. This is an American job, not just a New York job. I want someone who knows and cares about other parts of the country." Flanagan saw the job in the same way. A government-subsidized theater in the United States meant to her a network growing out of and responding to "a people's need over a vast geographical area."[45] Having agreed to the job, she was thankful that she had a wide, intimate familiarity with the country. Born in South Dakota, she had lived on an Iowa farm, in a small Iowa college town, and in a country village. But she had also been to school in Massachusetts and had lived in Chicago, St. Louis, and Detroit. Her familiarity and varied experience with rural and city life fit her concept of the Federal Theater Project perfectly. One of the first persons she consulted was a regionalist director of community theater, E. C. Mabie, at the University of Iowa. The plan he drafted for the FTP argued for theater in local and regional centers, "which have," he said, "common interests as a result of geography, language origins, history, tradition, custom, occupations of the people." Both she and Mabie were convinced that only with such regionalized networks and with such specific interests could theater, particularly in the Midwest and West, be genuinely creative.[46]

Flanagan added to the Mabie plan a profound sense of regional and national conflict. Some of the plays she had produced—from original scripts, frequently by students—focused on the discords of contemporary social life. Flanagan's own documentary drama, *Can You Hear Their Voices?*, dealing with starving dirt farmers in Arkansas, is a first cousin in form to the living newspaper for which the FTP later won critical praise. A production of her Vassar Experimental Theater in 1931, it frames the struggles of these farmers between scenes portraying the windy antics of a self-important congressman holding forth on the advantages and disadvantages of the dole and scenes of a lavish debutante ball. The events were taken from actual life. What makes it drama rather than history is the way Flanagan brought the simple but elemental needs expressed in vernacular idiom into direct conflict with political vulgarity and upper-class insensitivity.[47]

Flanagan's sense of class discord surfaced often. One example is the first meeting she summoned FTP regional directors to, on October 8, 1935. The situation struck her as ironic. There they were, the leaders responsible for organizing a populist theater, assembled in the mansion of Evelyn Walsh McLean. By one of those strange twists of history, the McLean mansion had been made the national headquarters for all the arts projects. To Flanagan, it represented precisely what ailed the arts in this country, their conception "as a commodity to be purchased by the rich."[48] While artists hungered for work and the people hungered for music, plays, pictures, and books, the rich buried art in their gilded manorial chambers. She spoke to her regional directors quite openly about a different vision of the arts which she thought more promising than buried treasures, the public theater of Russia. She had studied the new theater of the Soviet Union in 1926. It was, she told the assembled directors, a theater for the proletariat, where company and proletatrian audience were transformed into one another. She proposed that at a time when wealth and poverty faced each other so sharply, when war threatened the nations of the world, the theater they were about to set up had to consciously reflect the changing social order or the new order would leave it, and deservedly so, in the dust of time.[49]

The vast space of her regional conception is charted in the notes she kept and letters she wrote to her husband, Philip Haldane Davis, as she traveled across America consulting with the FTP's resident companies. In every region she saw the stuff of exciting drama and pressed each regional company to find original work by local playwrights about local life. In the project's four years of existence, her theme was that unless the FTP responded fully and sensitively to the dramatic possibilities of each region, this public alternative to a narrowly subjective and privately possessed art would fail. "Sliding down the terrific grades through the Northwest between great crags, gray and purple with dark embroidery of pines," she writes in *Arena*, "I would think where are our mountain plays? The great plains, the cactus and sagebrush, the vast cattle ranges, the rivers blazing with reflections of red and yellow trees, the sheer precipices of brilliantly colored rocks— where were the plays which made you feel the vastness and might of this land?" In contrast to the wildness, the grandeur, the brilliance of the West, she saw a different kind of energy, a different kind of bigness, another, quite ominous coloring in Michigan's principal industrial city: "Detroit as always is big and black, dingy and dirty and terrifying," she wrote to her husband in October 1937. She saw there the same sort of polarization that the McLean mansion symbolized. On one side there were the estates of Grosse Pointe, on the other the River Rouge plant "painted on a smoky cyclorama." Like the West, it struck her as an untapped source of great regional drama: "Any play is apt to seem pallid in comparison with Detroit itself, a cosmopolis essentially dramatic, full of conflict, contrast, and underlying struggle. . . . Being all this and the world's motor capital, this Great Lakes link is a showplace and a place for putting on shows."[50]

In contrast to Cahill and Flanagan, Henry Alsberg, national director of the FWP from 1935 to 1939, had an intellectual experience and background that was essentially cosmopolitan, international, and bohemian. A native of New York City with a law degree from Columbia University, he entered the writing field as an editor for the *New York Post*. After that he spent several years in Europe, first as an ambassadorial secretary, then as a foreign correspondent for the *Nation* and the *New York World*. From 1922 until he joined the New Deal administration in 1934, he centered his life in the art and political circles of Greenwich Village and Provincetown.[51] These experiences, however, did not keep Alsberg from wholeheartedly endorsing the spirit of populist regionalism that electrified the FWP. In fact, he not only endorsed it but did a great deal to make sure that it would remain a fullforce current in the project. Two reasons probably account for this. First, Alsberg had been attracted to socialist ideas in his European and bohemian years. Second, some of his work and friends in the 1920s exposed him to settlement-house methods of dealing with social problems. His socialist ideas were actually of a liberal, welfare kind, not far off the thinking of the settlement-house professionals whom the New Deal recruited for government service, particularly for its relief programs. The settlement-house always emphasized the arts in its work, seeing them as a powerful tool for democratizing American culture and rehabilitating the victims of social deprivation. Although its aims were educational and therapeutic rather than esthetic, it shared something important with regionalism: the desire to stimulate the cultural resources of the common people and reach them in their local and regional communities with their own imaginative work.[52]

I have called these reasons probable, but whatever the explanation, Alsberg's contributions to the populist, regional spirit of the FWP are undisputed. His strongest advocate, William F. McDonald, writes that Alsberg followed a set of principles for the FWP that did much to make it put "emphasis upon folklore; the speech and mores of the common people; stress upon the contributions of minorities, like the American Negro, to the creation of a genuinely native culture; and an accent upon regional, sectional, and local characteristics that in their variety formed a manifold unity that only a decent respect for each could preserve." McDonald's claim is based on Alsberg's approach to the American guide series, still much admired for its magnitude as well as its historical and literary excellence.[53] Various government documents, staff memos, and reported conversations indicate the influence Alsberg had in making the series what it is and later in the undertaking of the FWP narrative studies and cultural research devoted to specific aspects of common life. They show that from his job as FERA supervisor of reports in 1934 through his tenure as head of the FWP, he directed the guide series away from a Baedecker-version of tourist attractions to a well-written, carefully researched history and interpretation of local and regional customs, legends, economic and social traditions, and specific ways of daily life among ordinary people. Although he continually requested that local color be preserved in these accounts, he made clear that he aimed not at quaintness, but at vitality and authenticity.[54]

In the ranks below the director we also witness the influence of regionalist experience. But because the staff below was more numerous and less involved in high level administration, the experience was more widely diversified and more regionally dispersed, hence closer to the sources of inspiration. Of Flanagan's initial appointees to get the Theater Project underway across the country, only two, Eddie Dowling and Elmer Rice, came from the Broadway stage. The others came from a variety of regionally oriented community and university theaters in different parts of the country: in addition to Mabie, people like Jasper Deeter from Philadelphia's Hedgerow Theatre, Glenn Hughes from the Birmingham Little Theatre, and Thomas Wood Stevens from the Wisconsin Players and Chicago's Goodman Memorial Theatre.[55] Moreover, one of the New Yorkers, Rice, had already demonstrated a strong populist inclination in his plays, quite in accord with Flanagan's proposal that the theater had to keep up with the social changes taking place and reflect imaginatively the lives of ordinary people.

In the Federal Writers' Project, the regionalist orientation of its lower ranking members, again more populist than conservative, is quite clear. George Cronyn, the associate director, included among his occupations ranch hand in the Southwest, apple grower in the Northwest, plumber, and anthologist collector of American Indian songs.[56] Joseph Gaer had been an adapter of folk legends before he joined the California relief program in 1934 as chief editor for writers whose work included descriptions of struggling homesteaders and Southern California's racial groups.[57] He became one of the most effective field representatives of the national office in 1935, contributing in the early months to the development of the project in the Midwest, particularly Detroit. Among the regional directors were William T. Couch and John Frederick. Frederick's regional outlook in the *Midland* and the fact that he became the Midwest director for the FWP have already been noted. By the early 1930s, Couch had established a regionalist reputation at the University of North Carolina through his interesting life histories of southern tenant farmers, textile workers, and other laborers occupied in lumbering, turpentining, and fishing. Under his guidance, the first-hand life history accounts gathered by FWP collectors became compelling narratives of considerable literary merit.[58] From the earliest days on, the national staff also included people who had focused on other kinds of folk culture and language: John Lomax on song collecting; Sterling Brown on black history and slave narratives; and Benjamin Botkin and Morton Royse on comprehensive folk and ethnic studies, respectively.

People and agencies outside the arts projects also made proposals from regionalist points of view, exerting pressure on the government to channel its arts support in these directions. The evolution of the American guide series illustrates the point. In early 1934, the Authors' League proposed that unemployed writers be assigned to compiling the history and ethnology of the local areas in which they lived and even, if possible, other communities where no writers were available. That summer, a FERA administrator from Ann Arbor, Michigan, wrote to the national office about his idea for a directory showing travelers "what is worth seeing on the social, industrial, or historical side" of American life. He thought of it as a way of making "our people know America."[59] An iconography program, described in a FERA procedural publication dated October 12, 1934, anticipated the local and regional thrust of the FWP and the American guide series. Primarily a pictorial project, hence the term "iconography," the collecting of images was apparently to be done by writers, who were to work on three subjects: "1) general historical development of a city or local community; 2) economic and industrial development of an era; 3) regional changes which might show phases of Indian life, farming, lumbering or mining."[60]

Among these examples of outside regionalist influence were the independent state initiatives for writers' work relief during the FERA period, that is from 1934 to early 1935, before the establishment of WPA. Connecticut, with funds from its FERA allocation, put volunteer writers and researchers to work on a guide book for the state.[61] Although not as culturally comprehensive as the FWP series, it consituted the first published precedent for the national program. Michigan, also with FERA money, began a program on local histories.[62] Of these independent initiatives, California offers the most dramatic instance. Under the guidance of Hugh Harlan and Paul Radin, the state FERA program launched a writers' project for a series of monographs dealing with San Francisco's Italian community, the Bay area labor movement, the West Coast's migratory farmers, and California's folklore and Indian History. At the inception of the program in early 1934, Harlan had written to Hopkins asking why such a project could not be instituted on a national level.[63] These monographs, universally praised for their historical and literary quality, reflect again, in scope and detail, the insistent and diverse sources of the regionalist and populist spirit streaming into federal patronage of the arts in the 1930s.

Populism and Conventional Politics

The evidence I have cited argues against the idea that President Roosevelt played a large and singular part in orienting federal patronage toward the country's ordinary life, toward what McDonald calls "the honest, if untutored, sense of beauty of the common man" and away from "the garden closes of Greenwich Village."[64] McDonald's indispensible account of the legislative and bureaucratic mechanics of 1930s federal patronage, *Federal Relief Administration and the Arts* (1969), from which a fair portion of my evidence is drawn, impresses the reader with the widespread diversity of regionalist experiences among professional art administrators and rank-and-file artists before and after the New Deal came on the scene. It testifies to how much of the program they initiated and the steadfast role they played in setting up a national, yet locally decentralized set of projects, reflecting and speaking to the sensibilities of ordinary Americans. McDonald's analysis of the milieu that made populism and industrial regionalism central to the close bond between the arts projects and the common man undercuts his view of how important Roosevelt was in the matter. He points out that a double movement in twentieth-century American culture favored the outcome: the twin awakenings of American artists and of ordinary Americans to each other. McDonald finds the sign of these awakenings in the skyscraper, the cinema, jazz, and experiments in poetry and fiction with industrial subjects.[65] We are reminded of Flanagan's own response to the skyscrapers and smokestacks of Detroit and of her experience with or, at least, sympathy for proletarian and farm-labor life long before 1935. Neither she nor her colleagues in the FTP and other projects showed much tolerance for bohemian hothouses or carriage trade. Their lobbying for these projects and their work when they became staff members demonstrate that they always pushed for their populist and regional potentialities and always believed that these potentialities made them a major rival to the private and cosmopolitan dominants of American culture.

I see no reason to assume a necessary connection between the aim of making the projects permanent agencies of the government and artsy, big-city chauvinism. The concept of permanent arts projects does not *ipso facto* contradict regional and ordinary life orientations. For that matter, it doesn't contradict a relief orientation either, since high unemployment among artists is an ever-present structural fact of bourgeois culture. The argument that the public would not accept a permanent federal patronage of the arts is always suspect, since politicians have a tendency to attribute to the fiction of a homogenous public what they fear is the attitude of their political peers. At any rate, nothing in the way the directors, their professional associates, and field artists conceived of a permanent program employing artists (as distinct from dispensing grants) suggested esthetically elite goals directed toward the esthetic needs of artists vegetating in the cosmopolitan enclaves of bohemia. In fact, few of them thought a permanent program would be warranted or could be enacted unless the projects became truly regional and indispensibly integrated with the populace, through the subject matter of their products and their openness to mass audiences.[66]

Unless we are hopelessly bogged down in the conventional common-place that politics is the art of the possible, under which rubric the record shows we get in name rather than substance what we presumably aim for, there is good reason to regard this last conviction of the members of the arts projects as a sign of political sophistication, not naiveté. If the professional at the top and the artist in the field were naive, it was not because they lacked the political sophistication we associate with Roosevelt and his New Deal colleagues, but rather because they had an innocent faith in the relia-bility of the administration. They were naive about the relationship between power and privilege in the American system. Before long that relationship made the president, Hopkins, and his closest associates in the relief program equivocal about the concept of federal patronage and about subsidizing a grass-roots, populist arts movement engaged in representing freely and forthrightly the special sense of beauty and the trying conditions of ordinary life in the dynamics of a stratified society.

The New Deal expressed its economic, political, and cultural views in populist rhetoric, but it never intended to operate programs that upset or deeply questioned the power structure of American capitalism, as a fairly aroused grass roots surely enabled it to do. Nor did the staffs directly ad-ministering the Federal One projects intend in any way to overturn this structure. But they were thinking of free, uninhibited, and accurate repre-sentations of the position of folk and working-class culture in the hierarchi-cal interactions of American society. They assumed that the New Deal was free enough, at least with regard to the arts, from the political imperatives of privilege and power to retreat into accommodation. In assuming as much, they were indeed naive.

They were also naive in not anticipating how perilous a stumbling block the banality and robot-like practices of the city and state bureaucra-cies in charge of WPA operations would be to their populist, regionally dis-persed esthetic. Several factors made this obstacle unusually hazardous. First, there was the problem of organizational authority. The special charac-ter of art, theater, and writing required decisions about the talent of person-nel, subject matter, artistic quality, and the methods required to insure out-put that only professionals from these disciplines or highly knowledgeable about them could sensibly make. At the same time, the line of authority for the WPA, including the specialized projects of Federal One, flowed, as always in governmental affairs, through the standard political structure, the network of local, state, and federal bureaucracies appointed for the task. Appointments were made by the party machines in control at each level of the network. For the most part, the appointments were drawn from party-machine regulars. The arts projects, therefore, had a double set of guardians, professionals and politicians, and they were not compatible. Political appointees were adamant about sharing authority and made decisions that were perhaps practical from a business-management point of view but inappropriate to effective cultural practices. The professional staffs found Hopkins and his top level political administrators unreliable in the contest of authority. Although Washington administrators had the final right of approval, they tended to let questionable local appointments slide in order not to rile state and metropolitan party machines. They equivocated over the issue of how arts projects professionals and local bureaucrats were to share command. Ultimately, Hopkins and his closest political associates came down on the side of local and state political authority.[67] The professional staffs had to get bureaucratic approval for whatever they needed to do to make their projects function effectively as instruments of work relief and grassroots culture.

The incompatibility of these two different administrative staffs, one with professional qualifications responsible for a set of specific, highly specialized projects, the other with standard political credentials responsible for all WPA projects, was even more fundamental than conflicting authority relationships and the way each made decisions. Their concerns were basically out of joint. Since the largest allocations of funds in the WPA went toward manual-labor projects, the politicians in charge had to focus overwhelmingly on work relief in construction. This focus was custom-made for their notions of no-nonsense, practical activities. Cultural affairs, particularly those involving imaginative expression, were not. Political administrations on the local and state levels were at best unfamiliar with these expressions, at worst deeply suspicious of them. Political administrators often found the plays and writings of the projects threatening to the established norms of social and economic privilege. Professional staffs of the arts projects were quite blind to this stumbling block at the outset of their work. They were, however, rudely awakened to it in short order and learned, in consequence, to walk through the bureaucratic mine field more warily.

Naive as these professionals were about how firmly the New Deal high command would fight for an uncensored art program with close ties to the grass roots, and naive as they were about local bureaucracies, it would be a mistake to overstate the effect of these shortcomings. If they were over-confident about how much the political system would allow them to accomplish, they never thought that a populist, regional alternative—in the form of federally supported arts in a marketplace economy—depended solely or even primarily on liberal politicians or the entrenched bureaucracy. They believed that the projects must focus on the people in the communities of America: on stimulating and tapping the regional folk and working-class imaginations; on expressing the joys and struggles of grass-roots culture; and on rooting themselves in a vast, thus far ignored audience among the folk in the provinces and the workers in the cities.

The primacy of this focus to their goals is a political wisdom that conventional politics, limited by its top-down attitudes, simply could not see. What the presumably innocent art professionals and artists recognized was a source of power in the common publics, perhaps the only one that could give the projects a chance to stay alive without sacrificing integrity. These publics were the source of the material and expressive life needed to give the projects the cultural and esthetic character which could make them an exciting contribution to the arts and an indispensible part of the community. This belief in the community down below is, however, a political wisdom of beginnings. How to convert its potential into active energy for the projects proved to be very problematical. How well project administrators and artists understood the imaginative life of the mass publics they were interested in attracting, one of the issues at the center of this work, was ultimately more important to their success or failure than their naive perceptions of how liberal politicians and entrenched bureaucracies functioned.

Since the projects covered such a vast and diversified territory, a uniform understanding could hardly be expected. In some regions, relationships to the communities down below flourished. The South is a prime example for all four projects. Several regions did quite well with folk and occupational histories, particularly inside the rural framework. The region that proved to be most problematical was the industrial Midwest. Here the various publics presented a considerably different set of challenges. It is time now to turn our attention more specifically to that area and particularly to the example of Detroit and Michigan, an area which typifies so much of that region and whose influence as a productive center represents a national economic and cultural force. Although the area's economic significance has been thoroughly acknowledged over the years, its cultural impact has generally been overlooked, except in a negative sense. We have seen how conservative regionalism made Detroit the chief metaphor to demonstrate what it perceived to be the destruction of American art and culture by industrialism. The cosmopolitan Northeast, toward which conservative regionalism also took exception, voiced no such hostility. Its attitude seems to have been rather neutral. But it too rejected the cultural worthiness and impact of the area. Its cosmopolitan chauvinism—or should I say big-city provincialism —blinded it to the art and cultures of the industrial hinterland. Even the present-day upsurge of interest in WPA arts projects themselves hardly extends to the Midwest. Recent studies of New Deal culture lavish a great deal of attention on other regions, such as the Federal Theater in New York or the Theater and Writers' projects in the South.

Is this neglect a reaction to the declining economy of the industrial heartland which we call the Midwest, a reaction to what some economists and sociologists consider the prime example of American de-industrialization? Perhaps so. But however one judges the decline of the Midwest, to think that it is no longer an industrial lodestone is foolish. Hard times notwithstanding, it continues to draw a variety of ethnic and sectional working people (people from other regions of the country) into its orbit. Some newcomers reinforce older resettler groups and some constitute new ones. The migration of large numbers of Midwesterners to other parts of the country in the last decade, with people from Detroit and Michigan very much in the front ranks, often obscures this continuing attraction. The combination of shared industrial experiences and insular traditions that were true back in the 1930s remains at the heart of the tastes and culture of the Middle West, nowhere more tellingly than in the Detroit and Michigan area. The present out-migration may indeed be viewed as another way these tastes and culture exert a wide national influence. The problems the Theater Project and the Writers' Project in Michigan encountered in relating to the disjoined yet united population represented then and does now a microcosm of the national difficulties in maintaining a free, innovative, and profound alternative esthetic, one that addresses and draws sustenance from America's grass roots. How the Theater and Writers' projects worked in Michigan reveals a number of valuable lessons with which to judge present and future policy toward the arts, particularly with regard to the network of cultures that the masses of working Americans shape and form in the crucible of our industrial society.

PART 2

**Neglected Publics for
Federal Patronage in
the Midwest**

3

In the Eyes of the Beholder: Assembly-Line Publics in the 1930s and Before

THE aim of Federal One to draw strength and sustenance from the communities down below expressed an optimism that was and is among twentieth-century artists and intellectuals an unusual attitude, particularly toward the industrial working-class publics of the Midwest. The optimism about the Midwest is a nineteenth-century phenomenon and has long since withered. What Alexis de Tocqueville, for example, saw as promise when he toured the eastern shores of Michigan in July 1831 is no longer possible. He saw a wilderness covered by gigantic oaks and pines. "Still air, cloudless sky," his diary for July 26 reads. "Our canoe glides without making the slightest noise. . . . Immense forests reflected in the water, setting sun shining through and casting its light on the undergrowth." Later he writes of a trek through forest from dawn until evening without having "met a living creature except for some deer and birds." Only the Detroit scene revealed a substantial run of cultivated land and many houses. For Tocqueville, the Detroit prospect was a harbinger. He predicted that in twenty years the forests would be replaced by thriving farms and villages. The people who would transform this midwestern wilderness, he argued, would not be new immigrants, but native-born Americans who had acquired some capital and credit and who, as a consequence of birth, were physically hardened to the rigorous climate of the New World.[1] That kind of American had already moved westward and cleared what little of the wilderness had been tamed. Tocqueville presumed that the same pattern of migration and enterprise would remake the Michigan territory in the next two decades.

The hundred years and more between Tocqueville and us has radically altered what he saw and what he predicted and rendered the optimism underlying the federal arts projects unreal for most observers. The twentieth-century observer witnesses a far different scene and demography. The silent forests, bountiful farms, neat villages have been overshadowed by smoky industrial workplaces. The resourceful, independent American, master of his destiny and humanizer of the wilderness, has all but disappeared. His descendants have become, in considerable numbers, urbanized industrial workers. More dramatic is the fact that since the mid-1920s, the region's work force has been made up overwhelmingly of poor, newly arrived and second-generation immigrants of a kind and from places largely unrepresented in the 1830s: poor peasants and small village artisans from southern and eastern Europe and black resettlers from the American South.[2] Given such an extremely altered environment and economy and such a vastly different populace, literate twentieth-century observers are no longer capable of Toqueville's benign and hopeful view. They are often overcome with a sense of devastation: the industrial scene is a nightmare, and those who toil in its endless factories and mills are transformed by the work they do into anomic creatures, bereft of the ability to feel, think, control, or create.

No other reaction to the twentieth-century industrial scene and new make-up of population seems to have penetrated American intellectual life and imagination so deeply. As we have seen, the political-aesthetic theories of Southern agrarian regionalism reflected it. But its images are also among the most enduring expressions of our poetry and fiction, in both popular and elite literary forms, where they may be discovered from the beginning of the century through the present. A typical contemporary example, especially appropriate to the focus of this study, is the way Philip Levine, a poet steeped in the caldron of Detroit, sees the urban environment:

> In this state, which is not madness
> but Michigan, here in the suburbs
> of the City of God, rain brings back
> the gasoline we blew in the face
> of creation and sulphur which will not
> soften iron or even yellow rice.

And no less by the way, in another poem, he characterizes factory workers:

> The charred faces, the eyes
> boarded up, the rubble of innards, the cry
> of wet smoke hanging in your throat,
> the twisted river stopped at the color of iron.
> We burn this city every day.

Book reviewers and scholarly critics regard such anomic depictions as accurate and empathetic renderings of working people—a sign of the pervasive sense of devastation evoked by the conversion of the natural environment into an industrial workshop.[3]

Considering how widespread this down reaction has been is it possible that the FTP and the FWP were following a fool's errand in desiring to bring all art form experiences to these groups, to benefit artistically from their close contact with unjaded audiences, and finally to produce works that saw them as tough, but undegraded, saw their culture as worthwhile and without need of condescension? There are several ways to answer the question. Although the down reaction expresses a genuine empathy, making it seem quite "revolutionary," neither empathy nor "revolutionary" aura should obscure its stereotyping reductiveness and fatalism, a set of characteristics that, in fact, throws revolutionary implication into doubt. The various expressions of this attitude almost always mark working people as impaired beyond rescue, dispirited creatures no longer capable of effective, common action to change or relieve their circumstances, unable to sustain, much less construct a purposeful culture in defense against or resistance to a dehumanizing system. This reaction is fixed exclusively, although with a sharp eye, on a single destiny open to workers under industrial capitalism: demoralization and utter defeat.

Eric Hobsbawm suggests something more complex and varied. He agrees that vast numbers of workers have allowed "themselves to be ground down." But not all. Some escape into the middle class, although the route in is much more closed than is imagined. A much larger number find some way of rebelling against the brutalizations of an exploiting, money-motivated economy and the chill disregard of bourgeois self-interest. He notes that working people have found a variety of cultural and political strategies to retain their humanity and exercise their own kind of creative energy.[4]

More than we imagine or like to admit, this century-long fixation on the degrading destiny of industrial workers is a reflex of our even longer history of anti-working class bias, ethnic prejudice, and racism. The system of preferences in the United States for northern Europeans over Slavs, Balkans, and Latins, for whites over blacks, and for the bourgeoisie over all other classes has been a powerful tradition in all the decades of this century. It has colored, against reason, knowledge, and will, how a considerable number of American intellectuals and artists perceive the world: liberals no less than conservatives. If nothing else, the way our urban settings have been fragmented into ghettos has almost always excluded the intellectual and art world from a literate, inside knowledge of southern and eastern European immigrants and American blacks, from seeing their lives and cultures as they are actually practiced in community. As a result, the intellectual and the artist remain victims of the tropes generated by the traditional system of biases toward the immigrants who came here after the 1880s and, as always, the black population, even when he or she constructed an image intended to evoke sympathy. The other side of this reflex to traditional biases signifies nostalgia for a Tocquevillean untouched nature, a longing for the resourceful Yankee agriculturalist, for an individualism, out of place in an industrial setting, but appropriate in the uncrowded spaces of the Midwest over a hundred years ago. The bias and nostalgia of the down re-reaction makes its prevalence unremarkable and less of a mark suggesting that the FTP and FWP were foolhardy in their aims.

The sustained hiatus in tropes of degradation or romantic retreat introduced by the Great Depression is a still more telling sign that the quest of federal patronage was not silly. Since both urban and rural workers responded to the economic catastrophe with a difficult collective resistance to the conventional policies and practices of industrial capitalism, it was hard to ignore their vitality. Through a wider range of work, the arts focused on a working people who maintained their humanity in the teeth of a brutalizing set of economic and social relationships, who, in short, took the paths of rebellion described by Hobsbawm.

The arts of the socialist movement provide examples of this more positive view even before the catastrophe of the 1930s. For the most part, the socialist arts tend to idealize their subjects, to portray them in monumental scale. Other favorable perceptions of working people before the 1930s, usually the work of artists outside socialism or only loosely tied to it, stick closer to life-like modes and scales. Lewis Hine is an outstanding example. Through his camera, he captured workers on the job or in their seamy environments; notwithstanding oppressive conditions, indeed as if in response to them, the figures in his photographs appear resistant, deeply thoughtful, intensely alive.[5] Such favorable socialist and non-socialist depictions before the Great Depression are, however, a scattered, minor key. The 1930s transformed them into a major register and compelled a vastly larger number of intellectuals and artists to see and hear immigrant and minority workers with less stereotypically conditioned eyes and ears.

As an institutional form, nothing was more crucial to this transformation than the relief program for the arts which the Roosevelt administration set up within the WPA. Aiming to bring the works of the dominant culture to disregarded publics, the arts projects were motivated by a social-work as well as a humanistic presumption that these made workers' lives spiritually richer and more humanized, less subject, as Terry Eagleton, who questions the presumption, puts it, "to the deadening effects of industrial labour and the philistinism of the media." The projects were, however, as a matter of principle, open to the cultural forms and energies of industrial workers and alive to the new currents stirred up by hardship.[6]

74

The best proof against the idea that federal patronage was embarked on a fool's errand and that the social and ethnic communities outside the cordon of bourgeois occupation and culture were not so degraded as they had been traditionally depicted were these communities themselves. They were alive with their own kind of ritual and creative energies. Various traditions, collectively practiced social customs, amateur and semiprofessional theater could all be found among these predominantly working-class people. They wanted and were able to stimulate, through song, tale, personal account, theater, and festival, a cultural context that gave their lives coherence and signification against the disintegrating onslaughts of an alienating environment. There was such an abundance of cultural vigor and inspiration for the WPA arts projects to find among these publics that a journey into them was anything but quixotic.

The most remarkable evidence of this abundance can be found in the theater and non-dramatic literature of immigrant life. Of particular note in Michigan are the highly active and numerous theatrical companies available to Polish, Finnish, and Yiddish audiences in the 1920s and the first part of the 1930s. These audiences could regularly avail themselves of stage performances in the languages of their ethnic origins without leaving their cultural enclaves in Detroit and the Upper Peninsula. Although black theater was far less abundant in Michigan during this period, it is nevertheless another striking example, given that the black population was still rather small at the time. The left-wing theater, spurred into renewed vigor by the economic crisis, also belongs to this evidence. Its working-class orientation, its frequent presentation of plays about workers on strike, about solidarity between white native Americans, blacks, and immigrants, meant that here too was a stage available to the ghettoized populations of the region. It dramatized their industrial experience in the United States and provided a complement to what they could rely on in their ethnic theaters. The oral and written literature of these publics and the left was never far behind the bustle of theater and served also to produce an idiom and representation of life that reenforced the integrity of their cultures and that prepared an audience for populist innovations.

4

Church, Center, Left:
The Trinity of Polish-American Culture

ALTHOUGH the great swell of Polish immigration to the United States began after 1900, Polish-American theater and non-dramatic literature in the Midwest can be traced back to the 1870s and before. In both cases, the evidence is fragmentary, but compelling enough to show a thriving culture both nourished from below by its working-class citizens and gratifying their hunger for life's representation on stage and in literary expression.

Polish-American Theater in the Midwest

Half-a-dozen articles, Stanley Cuba noted in 1981, are the extent of recorded research on all Polish-American theater in the entire lifetime of the journal most devoted to such subjects, *Polish American Studies*.[1] The information we do have points to a secular origin in Chicago, where an organization of Polish exiles, *Gmina Polska* (the Polish Community Society), appears to have begun its sponsorship of amateur performances in 1873. This sponsorship averaged five plays a season throughout the 1870s and continued into the late 1880s. After these beginnings, Polish-language theater grew with extraordinary vigor. Chicago continued to be the most flourishing center, but by the late 1880s Polish enclaves in other cities maintained highly active stage programs. "Teatr Polski Za Oceanem" (The Polish Theatre Beyond the Ocean), an 1890 essay by Karol Estreicher, a noted Polish bibliographer from Lwow, cites New York, Brooklyn, Philadelphia, and Pittsburg in the East, and Chicago, Milwaukee, St. Paul, Winona, Minnesota, and La Salle, Illinois in the Middle West. Included in Eistreicher's account are two Michigan cities, Grand Rapids and Detroit.[2] Menominee, on

Green Bay in Michigan's Upper Peninsula, also had a group of Polish immigrants interested in Polish-language theater. According to Cuba, the first amateur theatrical there in 1892 moved the correspondent of the *Gazety Polska w Chicago* (The Polish Gazette of Chicago) to write: "the heart of every true Pole genuinely rejoices when he sees his immigrant countrymen fostering patriotism through shared and inoffensive entertainment."[3]

The Polish wing of the Catholic church also played an important part in making amateur theater widely available to the Polish-American population. In a late-1930s article reviewing amateur theater among Chicago Poles, Natalie Kunka claims that the Polish parishes were, in fact, the nucleus of its evolution. There is no doubt that once the parishes began to be patrons of amateur theater, they were a powerful force, quite possibly equal to or even more powerful than the independent dramatic groups in making it a vibrant, widely available part of Polish-American culture. From 1891 to 1915, more than a half-dozen Chicago parishes became theatrical benefactors. And parish-related theaters were still being set up or reorganized for renewed life in the 1920s and as late as the 1930s.[4] Parish theatrical patronage in Chicago typifies other Polish communities in the United States, although that city, as the premier Polish center, pioneered and provided the model for other enclaves, particularly in the Midwest.

With the opening of the twentieth century, Polish immigration changed not only in magnitude but in social character—masses of peasant workers with old-country industrial experience poured in during the first two decades of the century. During this period, the Polish socialist movement also became a sponsor of amateur theater. Although never as significant as the other secular theatrical activities or the parish-supported theater, its efforts were quite far-flung and, to one degree or another, persisted into the thirties. In Chicago we find one socialist company, the Society of the Free Spirit, which very early in the century presented the play, *Kordian*, by the radical democrat and romantic playwright, Juliusz Slowacki. Centering on the 1830–31 insurrection against czarist rule and featuring a Byronic hero —"a neurotic Hamlet" in Czeslaw Milosz's words—*Kordian*'s thesis that Poland's upper class and particularly its religious hierarchy had betrayed the masses in the course of the uprising evoked praise and rebuke. The *Robotnick Polski* applauded it as an instrument of political illumination: "[it] opens the eyes of the masses to the evil and treacherous politics of the Roman Catholic clergy." The *Dziennik Chicagoski* (Chicago Daily News), a close ally of the Roman Catholic Resurrectionist Order, disapproved because, according to Cuba, it feared that such plays alienated Polish immigrants from the church.[5]

After the October Revolution of 1917, a socialist tendency closer to a Marxist-Leninist orientation emerged among Poles in the United States, as it did among other American populations with large proletarian segments, and it also promoted, although less consistently, Polish-language theater. The Great Depression fired up its most fervid period of activity. An early 1935 editorial in Detroit's *Trybuna Robotnicza* (Worker's Tribune) illustrates the point. It reports that although left-wing, worker-oriented dramatic clubs and choirs, including Polish-language groups, were to be found in many American cities, they carried on their cultural work quite isolated from each other, and the editorial called for more cooperation among the groups. Two weeks later the *Trybuna* reported an item from New York City about a Polish-language theatrical group, the *Teatr Siwecki,* which had made a working-class mark for itself in local neighborhoods during the few months of its existence. It had already put on plays—*Rodzina Slepych Szotovzy* (The Blind Brush Worker Family) and *Unemployed*—with skillful staging—and was rehearsing a play about an American worker, called *At Three O'clock.*[6]

In Detroit itself during this period, Polish drama circles and choruses sympathetic to the working class and a soviet-oriented socialism were eager to perform. Secular dramatic groups—less politically motivated or, when political, more liberationist and nationalistic than radical—were, by far, the most active part of Detroit's Polish-language theater. Although rooted in the amateur theater tradition, they had acquired by this time a semiprofessional character, and they were the mainstream of Polish-American theaters. We learn from playbills and newspaper reviews collected by some of the leading stage persons on the local scene that between 1915 and the early 1930s at least eight such Polish theater companies produced plays with a fair degree of regularity.[7] For the most part, they came and went in the wake of each other. But since two of the most active directors and performers, Wladislaw Leskiewicz and Stanislaw Wachtel, seldom worked in one company together, and a third, Stanislaw Stawinski, occasionally set up his own productions, we assume that the Polish enclaves in Detroit could often rely on two or three simultaneously operating groups. One account reports that at one time during this period seven companies were performing for the community, although for how long is not indicated.[8] This figure needs to be treated with some caution, for the papers now available are too haphazard for ironclad verification. It is certain, nevertheless, that in the fifteen to twenty years in question, a fair number of semiprofessional theater groups were performing for Detroit Poles.

The names of these semiprofessional companies or (again to be cautious, because the records do not clearly distinguish) the playhouses they performed in reveal the range of traditional and new country influences at work in the Polish community. Almost every city where Polish Americans set up amateur theater had a group named after the satirist playwright, Aleksander Fredro, and sometimes after other fairly well-known Polish playwrights. Detroit had two circles in the 1880s with playwright names: the Fredro and the Anczyka. The *Teatr Wolna Polska* (the Free Poland Theater), dating back at least to 1916, that is, before Poland had regained its independence, and the *Teatr pod Bialym Orlem* (the Theater Under the White Eagle) reflect the liberationist and nationalist spirit. New country influence is apparent in the *Teatr Lincoln*; it is tempting to speculate that the name of this theater signifies an adaptation of the American struggle for national sovereignty and freedom to the fight for Polish liberation. The *Teatr Ludowy* (the People's Theater), whether taken in the traditional sense of folk, as one Polish-American informant believes it should be, or in the more contemporary sense of the ordinary working masses, reveals two things: first, the social and occupational character of the Polish community, and second, the progressive or populist attitudes carrying weight within it. Two other groups, the *Teatr Rozmaitosci* (the Variety Theater) and the *Teatr Lira*, a musically-focused group, represent theater as sheer entertainment, often in a pop-culture form, with no overriding concern for national liberation or classical literary tradition.[9]

These theaters, however, did not present programs that were exclusively or predominantly restricted to the influences implied by their names. Except perhaps for the *Teatr Lira*, the repertoire of any one of these companies might include musicals, melodramas, comedies, and tragedies; plays from the Renaissance and the nineteenth century as well as contemporary plays; plays by non-Polish playwrights translated into Polish, Polish classical plays, and plays written by Polish-Americans; and themes from domestic fluff to the heroics and betrayals of national rebellion. The *Teatr Lincoln*, for example, presented on one occasion an exotic light opera, *Japonska Herbaciarnia* (Japanese Teagarden), and on another an historical drama, *Turcy pod Kamiencem* (Turkey at the Podolian City of Kamieniec), an account of the heroism and defeat of the Polish and Russian forces by the Turkish army in that famous sixteenth-century battle. The *Teatr Rozmaitosci* illustrates the same diversity. Among its playbills, we find an historical romance, *Trubodurowie*; an operetta, *Wieslaw* (The Vistula), whose action centers around a Krakovian wedding; and *Noc w Belvederze*, (Belvedere Night), about the seizure in November 1830 by Polish insurrectionists of Warsaw's Belvedere Castle, the seat of tsarist authority over the Duchy of Warsaw.[10]

Another guide to the diversity and inclusiveness of the repertoire is Stanislaw Wachtel, a major force in Detroit's semiprofessional theater. His papers include an index of plays for Polish-language theater and a collection of playscripts, some by Wachtel himself and some with a Detroit dateline. These represent the wide variety of material Wachtel relied on not only in his theatrical work in Detroit, where he settled for good in the late 1920s, but in the theaters he conducted or performed in in other Midwest cities with large Polish populations. His index and scripts included translations of Gozzi's *Turandot*, Schiller's *The Robbers*, Gorki's *Lower Depths*, a French comedy, *The Married Miss*, and an anti-Soviet play, adapted by Wachtel from a skit by an unidentified B. Kresow, *Out of the Bolshevik Hell.*[11]

Another equally significant leader of Detroit Polish theater during these years, Wladislaw Leskiewicz, illustrates the point with a different stock of performance materials. His main center of activity was the *Teatr Rozmaitosci*. He had a great talent for composing topical pieces, mostly of a humorous kind, in the form of *rozmaitosci*, which could be either short skits or verse, and *kuplety*, verse in rhymed couplets. One attraction of this kind of entertainment was Leskiewicz's ability, in keeping with the old country tradition of *rozmaitosci* and *kuplety* performance, to compose them extemporaneously in response to audience requests. They dealt with everyday subjects: drinking and prohibition were favorite targets for comic treatment, as were work habits, domestic relations, local celebrations, and political issues. Where they touch on working-class experience, which they do quite often, they are clearly sympathetic in their humor. Those dating back to World War I are often satiric anti-war, anti-German, and anti-Russian commentaries. *Panu Fordowi Do Albumu* (Mr. Ford for His Album) pictures Henry Ford as a fool looking for glory in believing that by taking a "peace" ship to Europe he could convince the warring governments to end hostilities. One from the 1920s or early 1930s, depicting Al Capone and J. P. Morgan, associates capitalism with racketeering and political control. After 1930, depression themes surface. *Buy an Apple* (the title is in English) is a lament by a Polish worker in Polish, set to the Russian melody, *Bubliczka*, over how hard times have thrown him out of his job and home and forced him to sell apples on the street corner. Also in a serious vein are two, *Kweicien w Polsce* (April in Poland) and *Budzi Sie Miasto* (The City Awakens), that provide a grim contrast between the Polish countryside in spring and industrial Detroit.[12] As this wide range of themes illustrates, the *rozmaitosci* tradition in Detroit's semiprofessional theater, although concentrated on entertainment, offered more than escape from the problems of everyday life or world issues.

The secular and parish branches of Polish-American theater were also strongly committed to promoting the linguistic and cultural heritage, yet their motives for doing so differed. The point is illustrated by what each of these segments selected from the categories of plays in the repertoire available to them both and how each used what it had selected. The repertoire was quite extensive, as we have seen, and included the masterworks or classics of partitioned Poland, the stellar playwrights of other nations, popular dramatic forms, and plays about the Polish-American experience by Polish-American playwrights.

Under the linguistic and political difficulties of partition, Poland produced an unusually large group of accomplished literary and dramatic artists who helped maintain the language and who renewed its vitality with considerable invention, writers such as Mickiewicz, Slowacki, Fredro, Anczyc, and later Zapolska and Wyspianski. Some of these artists used the language to reflect a native reality with a view partial to insurrection, to an internationalist ideal in support of other enslaved nations, and to the democratic principles of radical republicanism.

Polish-American theater made extensive use of these literary figures as a resource of cultural replenishment for the immigrant population, but not to the same degree in all its branches. The available plays indicate that the secular groups produced the works of these classic figures of Polish drama more regularly than the parish circles and more regularly selected plays by them about insurrection, upper-class shams and affectations, and democracy. This thematic favoring indicates that in secular theater, from the political exiles of 1848 and 1863 in *Gmina Polska* through the political left-wingers in the 1930s, the flame of militant liberation—that is, the freeing of Poland and the Polish language from big nation imperialism and Poland's masses from upper-class and institutional injustice and mistreatment—was never extinguished.

Secular groups tended also to concentrate more than the parish groups on the stellar playwrights of other nations, for example, Shakespeare, Schiller (apparently the two most frequently produced of this category), Moliére, and Gorki. The translation of these into Polish demonstrated anew what native playwrights had repeatedly proved, the literary sophistication of Polish and its capacity to manage the texts of Europe's most prestigious cultures. The willingness to put on works of this kind represents in another way the non-parochial character of secular theatre. It involved a commitment to dramatic excellence, whatever its linguistic origin, that was akin intellectually and politically to the transnational, free-thinking spirits of a Mickiewicz or a Slowacki.

The less radical secular companies appear to have favored popular forms in the repertoire—operettas, melodramas, and American box office hits, as in a Detroit Polish adaptation in 1929 of *Broadway Melody*—more than the parish or radical companies. Such companies were more willing to put on all sorts of plays, including those that were sheer entertainment.

The last class of plays in the repertoire, works about the Polish-American experience by Polish-American playwrights, is the most important from the standpoint of cultural and linguistic adaptations generated by new world interactions. These plays reveal most clearly how the different branches of secular theater diverged in their conceptions of the liberationist theme and of everyday life among ordinary Polish immigrants. Plays about the Polish-American experience by the more radically Marxist segment of socialist-oriented theater dealt with everyday problems, particularly of inadequate means of subsistence in good times and bad times and with on-the-job class relationships. But they depicted them as systemic inevitabilities rather than reformable abuses. Hence no matter how close they stuck to everyday events, they signified the need for a revolutionary restructuring of society. Although not inclined to the politics of overthrowing capitalism, the other socialist theater groups used theatrical portrayals of everyday life to stimulate audience militancy and political action. Polish-American playwrights connected to the major tendency among secular theaters were equally concerned about everyday life and, in fact, because there were so many more of them, produced a much larger repertoire dealing with that experience. But the plays they wrote were not often as politically explicit as socialist-oriented theater; when they were, they were seldom infused with the same radical or activist resonance.

Although the non-socialist branch of secular theater was a firm advocate of revolutionary action to free Poland from imperialist dominion, its commitment to liberation did not go farther than the restoration of national sovereignty or the extension of political democracy. It did not regard capitalist political economy as systemically precluding true independence and effective democracy for the working masses of society. Hence its liberationist sentiments were not suitable to the social and political dilemmas facing Polish Americans when they turned to dramatizing their new world experience, and such sentiments lost their edge after World War I, with the restoration of Polish independence. The rebirth of Poland transformed the liberationist sense of mainstream secular theater into a different kind of dramatic spirit, a spirit using the drama of insurrection to glorify national history as a stimulus to patriotism. Yet so long as it did not hold that social inequities and abuses were systemic, this liberationist sense could not infuse its dramatization of everyday life in the new world with much more than sympathy. Beset by the depression—which ironically overlapped the last years of vigor for Polish-American theater—the mainstream and socialist stages grew more similar in depicting how social structure affected everyday life.

Did parish theater also shift its emphasis during the depression years to plays depicting the plight of its working-class constituency? Again we are at the mercy of the information now available, and the answer is muddied over. What is clear is that parish theater offered a wide variety of plays. Its repertoire included Polish-language classics, translated works, and also plays about the Polish-American experience, but fewer than its secular counterparts. Its agenda differentiated it from them, for it tended in good and bad times to produce didactic plays appropriate to its institutional character and principles: plays about Catholic doctrine and tradition and about the moral consequences of violating Catholic norms of personal behavior, such as marital fidelity and sobriety.

Polish-American Workers and Theater

Did all this theatrical activity involve proletarian Poles to any significant degree or was it essentially an upper- and middle-class enterprise? The problem here is that, as Fernard Braudel tells us, the great palace scenes are generally better known than the fish market. "In the sources," he writes, "the unusual conceals the everyday."[13] Fortunately in this instance there is evidence, easily overlooked by the palace dazzle of conventional perception, to show that working-class Poles were very much involved, on the stage-side of the footlights as well as in the audience, both early and late, in the history of Polish-American theater. Estreicher notes that "working youths readily [took] players' parts" in amateur theaters organized by enclave societies, and that "he who but yesterday earned his bread with a shovel, today dons a royal robe and crown."[14] In Estreicher's observation, the Polish-American audience, "living wholly by labor and for labor, [understood] perfectly well that the theater affords entertainment and recreation after work, and that at the same time it is a pillar of national sentiment."[15] In later years, into the 1920s in fact, worker-performers were evident in socialist theater. Cuba's study of socialist theatrical activities in Walsenburg, a small Colorado mining city, affirms as much.[16] The size of audiences, for an immigrant population so overwhelmingly made up of laborers, is also proof of working-class involvement. Estreicher reports that in the 1880s as many as one thousand people attended some of the performances.[17] At the end of the nineteenth century and the beginning of the twentieth, parish theater played before equally large audiences and perhaps more, as Kunka indicates. The last editor of *Glos Ludowy*, Stanley Nowak, recalls large audiences, even in the falling-off years of the 1930s, for both left-wing and mainstream theater. What else could those audiences have been, if not mostly working class, he proposes, since that was what, in the main, Polish Americans were.[18]

The record of Polish-American theater, given its sixty-year durability, the range of material it produced, and its widely varied group of performing companies drawing on an immigrant populalation adrift in an alien culture, is extraordinary, particularly in the Midwest. The factors that made it so— durability, range, working-class composition—argue powerfully for the well-accepted proposition that Polish-American theater played a notable part in keeping Polish culture, language, and national aspirations alive, and it remained a bustling cultural phenomenon until the late 1930s, when a complex of factors—the takeover of pop culture by cinema, the hard times, and the decreasing use of Polish by second- and third-generation immigrants—did it in. Its attempt to preserve native language and culture was far from being solely conservative, for it also used both to maintain cultural solidarity against the alienating effects of an oppressive industrialism and to invigorate the community in facing up to its new reality. It clearly refutes the image of degradation so prevalent among America's intelligentsia. At the same time, it bespeaks the wisdom rather than the folly of Federal One grass-roots optimism and specifically analogizes, in creative collaboration with working people and interaction with audience, Federal One's populist principles.

Folk Performance

Because it is something imbedded in the unconscious of everyday culture, an even more reliable resource for the populist experiments of the WPA arts projects was Polish-American folkway performance, in the main also a working-class phenomenon. Largely unwritten, it is much harder to delineate precisely. Fortunately folklorists, in showing how important public performance is in everyday life, have rescued some of the details of unwritten practices from historical amnesia. Oral histories collected by or under the supervision of professional folklorists show that public performance characterized not only religious myth and history, but also the rites of marriage, birth, and death. For example, the traditional marriage celebration modified by new world conditions—as in accounts of the customs still practiced in the 1920s in Salina, a community just east of Ford's River Rouge plant, and in Wyandotte, an industrial suburb downriver from Detroit—was a street drama in several of its features. Although the sacramental part was hidden from public view, the procession of the wedding party to the church, with musicians playing sad music, was performed for all the community to see. The return from church became a procession of community performers, as neighbors, friends, and invited guests, the musicians now playing happy music, marched through the streets to the bride's home. The festivities there also had a theatrical character. The guests sang ballads and folk songs and the older women—harking back to a custom whose meaning they no longer knew, the selling of the bride to the man—told stories about her future and about her husband's generosity.[19] Such informal public performances to dramatize the celebrations of everyday life tend to elude conventional history and criticism and are probably something the performers are not conscious of themselves. Nevertheless, they represent theatrical experience more deeply and ineradicably ingrained in the culture of common life than formal theater.[20]

Oral and Written Literature

The arts projects could also have found reinforcement for their objectives in Polish-American non-dramatic culture, although it is far more difficult to establish the same kind of variety in content and form and the same kind of broad reach into the Polish-American working class for it. This is true of narrative and lyric culture in both its oral and written registers.

I shall begin with the written register because the obstacles here are the more vexing of the two, it being composed and consumed and also affected by the state of public literacy in ways that the oral register is not. Whereas theater is quite obviously collective, from its gestation in rehearsal to performance before a live audience, narrative and lyric writing seems the most private zone of the arts. The visual arts fall somewhere in between. They are not particularly collective at the creative pole, although there are exceptions to this, as in the 1930s when FAP muralists at work on public walls welcomed the views of curious bystanders.[21] At the point of exhibition, however, these arts almost always enter a collective setting, for as visual forms they ultimately require a public forum. Narrative and lyric writing, however, are caught up, or so it seems, in acts that are superlatively private at both ends of the zone in which they circulate, from the pole of creative energy to that of recreative reading. The writer mints her script out of memory and imagination alone in a narrow closet, and each reader revalues alone what the writer has minted. The privacy of consumption is an impenetrable barrier to precise information about audience size and social classifications. Our only resource is the one public moment of readership, the moment of purchase. But, as I have argued earlier, the measure of this moment is terribly uneven. The immigrant community itself had limited resources and skills for sound record keeping. The dominant sectors of American society lost the clues of the public reading moment because they were generally dismissive of immigrant culture and inter-class dynamics and were, for the most part, uninterested in keeping track of immigrant readership or its class distribution. We are indebted for information to the few social workers and demographers who were interested. But as a small group they worked against great odds, and could not produce a body of evidence substantial enough to allow for more than tentative conclusion.

Even more hidden from view are the unpublished narrative and lyric writings of Polish-Americans: letters and notebooks, often from the hands of working-class Poles, hint at a substantial underground written culture. The problem here is not so much the private nature of reading as its availability. The barrier we run into in this regard is in part constructed of attitudes toward language competence. For the largest number of Polish immigrants, education was essentially minimal.[22] Low levels of education did not stop those who could write from recording the story of their American experiences or occasionally bursting into lyric expression, but these writers were filled with linguistic modesty and often lacked linguistic confidence. Hence, it is not likely for them to have left clear signals behind, to have flaunted the fact that they were engaged in the act of writing, whether moved by the need to speak to old friends and close relatives or to see for themselves their own stories and feelings captured in words. And what about the few readers they may have reached? There too linguistic modesty seems to have prevailed. For them, it seems, these letters and notebooks were of interest only for the passing occasion to which they spoke. Not unreasonable then to dispose of them casually and unmarked in attic and family shoebox, where they are most difficult to discover.

Literacy affects the problem in still another way. The peasant and working-class makeup of Polish immigration after 1890 made the distribution of literary skills inversely proportional to the mass of Polish Americans. The minimal education of peasants and workers left a very large majority of them either illiterate or quite dysfunctional in manipulating the basic reading and writing demands of narrative and lyric expression. The most highly skilled readers and writers of this immigrant community were the priests and political exiles. The mythos and lyric of the first tended to be hierarchical, theological, nationalistic, and traditional. The political exiles incorporated nationalism into their writing, as we have already seen, but in the secular, progressive forms associated with enlightened bourgeois thought. Both tendencies filtered down into the underprivileged mass of first- and even second-generation Polish immigrants. But the process of upward infiltration into published writing of the life stories and feelings of the underprivileged mass could only occur through the most deeply hidden dialectics in the interplay between privileged and underprivileged cultures. Not an easy mask to see through when searching for evidence of broad reach or of working-class contributions to variety of form and content.

The difficulties presented by the oral register of non-dramatic cultures are not nearly as complex. The chief problem is its variability. The lateral and generational transmission which is at the heart of its enormous staying power is also the lifeblood of its variation. Two recourses to its past character—recording its voice as it is at a later point and looking at records that transposed its voice into written words in its own time—are both problematical. Its voice in a later period is never its precise tone in an earlier one, not even in a recent past, and transposition into words inevitably distorts its social or collective nature. Still, much insight can be derived from each method, and particularly from the latter if it is a fairly thorough record made with a rigorous understanding of how to minimize distortion. Unfortunately, that is not the case for the Polish-American experience or, for that matter, for most immigrant communities during the first third of the twentieth century. We need to remind ourselves that folkloristics is an infant discipline which achieved wide institutional acceptability and methodological rigor only after World War II.[23] Before then, the pioneer collector of oral culture was the Federal Writers' Project, a sign, of course, that Federal One did make use of the resources of disregarded publics. But most of what it collected became one of the early casualties of the war. Before it could be published and publicly distributed, it was buried in battered files. Those who made written versions of Polish-American oral culture as it existed from 1900 to 1939 had no federally funded project to rely on, no widespread academic support as is now available, and nowhere near the methodological sophistication of present collectors. Could the transposing they did be anything but a record perforated with unreliability?

Despite these barriers, there are clues to the specific character of non-dramatic culture among the mass of Polish Americans. Take for example the record of one Polish-American publisher, Antoni A. Paryski. A leader at the end of the 1800s of a Polish group affiliated with the Knights of Labor, Paryski became the central figure in a network of radically-oriented and anti-clerical Polish language newspapers, primarily in a triangle of cities which included Toledo, Cleveland, Buffalo, and Pittsburg. From his first ventures into publishing, possibly going as far back as 1887, to his death in 1935, Paryski published over two thousand titles and more remarkably yet printed somewhere from five to eight million copies of all the titles.[24] While Paryski was the most successful Polish-American book publisher, there were several others, particularly in the industrial Midwest, whose publishing endeavors were prosperous enough to keep them going for sometime and add substantialy to the Paryski record. So if we apply Nowak's rule of thumb that most Polish immigrants were workers or if we recall that highly educated Poles constituted a small minority of the immigrant community between 1900 and the 1930s, the conclusion that a considerable part of the Polish reading public had to be workers is not farfetched.

The same conclusion may be drawn from the high rate of Polish borrowings from the Detroit Public Library for 1898 and 1914 cited by Sister Mary Remigia Napolska. She describes the general categories of reading to which Polish immigrants were attracted, and they make up a wide range indeed: popular science, religion, travel books, and among the literary arts, drama, poetry, and general literature.[25] For written narrative and lyric, the most popular form appears to be the historical novel. No less than readers in Poland and the rest of Europe, Detroit Poles were particularly fond of the

Nobel laureate, Henry Sienkiewicz (1846–1916), so fond as to support by 1930 a number of Polish-language editions of his works, each running to several thousand copies. The kind of books the Paryski firm published up to the 1930s is again evidence of wide reading-range. The list includes the staple of Polish-American publishing, religious books and prayer books, but also, in keeping with Paryski's political and scientific attitudes, anti-clerical brochures, Polish revolutionary poems, dream books, folktales, and many works of history, poetry, and fiction that were imbued with the ideas of positivism and rationalism.[26]

The novelists on his list indicate that a fair number of readers had a taste for realistic fiction as well as exotic romance. The pre-realist Kraszewski, for example, frequently wrote about contemporary Poland rather than a heroic past in a gothic setting. Several of his novels focus sympathetically and realistically on peasant life; several others address the anachronism and "inevitable decline" of the aristocracy. Boleslaw Prus (1845–1912), whom Milosz calls the most distinguished novelist of positivism and realism and a profoundly humanitarian being, is another Paryski author. Not as militant as some of his socialist friends, he was a thoroughgoing secularist and anti-traditionalist. These views are central to his novels dealing with the role of women in society and the need for Poles to transform traditional social and character traits into modern, enlightened, industrial relationships.[27] Finally, there is the positivist poet, Marja Konopnicka (1842–1910), whose poems and short stories, Milosz says, "are very accessible, even to uneducated readers." Sharply anti-clerical and deeply sympathetic to Poland's oppressed classes, many of her poems are narrative songs about the hardships of wage workers, proletarians, and peasants.[28]

The Polish-American press also indicates that Polish immigrant preferences did not run exclusively or even predominantly to gothic style or retrogressive social theme. For one thing, it was a factionally divided press of complex and bitter differences. Stanislaw Osada classified it into three major groupings: liberal and national, Catholic and national, and socialistic. But the nationalism was not all of a piece. Before World War I, the liberal faction tended to support the Ignace Paderewski wing of Polish independence, and the leftist press favored Jozef Pilsudski. After the Pilsudski coup of 1926, many opposing newspapers swung over to the Pilsudski side. However, some, including Osada, were still strongly opposed, unhappy that the *Sanacja* movement behind Pilsudski tried to make Polonian institutions in the United States subservient to Poland's needs. In Detroit, two of the longest running newspapers lined up on either side of the issue: the *Dziennik Polski* (Polish Daily News) supported Pilsudski; the *Rekord Godzienny* (Daily Record) opposed him.[29] Matters were no less in conflict over the role of the church. Many of the liberal and socialist newspapers were fiercely anti-clerical and against the parish monopoly of Polish-language instruction. Newspaper factions primarily represent the political commitments of publishers and editors, as we said earlier in cautioning against generalizing about public opinion. Hence how sure can we be that the diversity of views represented by Polish-American newspaper factions reflected the thinking of the masses? Quite possibly it did but, if not, since several newspapers in these factions were able to maintain a readership that helped them survive financially for a considerable time, they surely induced a diversity of religious and political preferences in the Polish-American community. Whatever the case, the Theater and Writers' projects would have found a mine of rich advantage and complex confusion.

The Polish-American press also testifies to the diversity of our more direct concern, narrative and lyric writing, particularly the serialized novel. "Polish-American papers," Osada informs us, "reprinted practically all the better Polish masterpieces." They apparently had little respect for authors' rights, serializing work after work without troubling to pay royalties. According to Osada, the same was true for the major Polish-American publishers, who were for the most part newspaper owners as well.[30] Polish immigrant authors writing about new-country experience in narrative and lyric form are also represented in the press. The present-day Polish historian, Andrzej Brozek, labels such work "the literature-for-the-people genre." Generally low in artistic standards, in Brozek's judgment, such narrative and lyric writing demonstrates, nevertheless, the elasticity and vigor of Polish culture in the United States and "Polonia's thirst for the written word."[31] Another scholar, Piotr A. Taras, believes that the quality of this people-oriented literature began to improve in the 1920s. In those years, Polish-American poems and stories in English began to take their place alongside those in Polish, a sign of how thoroughly bilingual Polish immigrants were becoming, without, as yet, losing to assimilation the particular culture they had created out of old-world tradition and new-world experience. In Taras's judgment, this literature-for-the-people speaks of the hardships of immigrant life, difficult work and material circumstances, stressful adjustments to other cultural communities, and the web of everyday values and folk traditions which make Polonian culture different.[32]

My own survey of two Detroit Polish-language newspapers, through translations by colleagues and student assistants who know Polish expertly, suggests that the automobile center of the United States followed closely the pattern I have been describing. Both *Dziennik Polski* (Polish Daily News), a traditionalist newspaper, and *Glos Ludowy* (People's Voice), a daily sympathetic to labor and the communist left, regularly featured stories and poems of well-known old-country writers as well as Polish-American immigrants, whose names, as far as I can tell, mean very little to literary history.

89

According to the colleagues I have consulted, in a judgment that matches Brozek's and Taras's, the writings of the latter group are not particularly distinguished.[33]

As we might expect of a traditionalist newspaper, *Dziennik Polski* did not go in for overtly political fiction or poetry. The poets it published turned their attention on several occasions to the lower orders of society as a burdened, gray mass, but they were not consistently for or against this segment of the population. *Glos Ludowy*, as a leftist working-class paper, offered its readers fiction and poetry of a much more revolutionary or at least militant view. These portrayed the masses sympathetically and looked forward to their emancipation in a near future on earth wrought by their own will and strength. Like other Polish-American newspapers, *Glos Ludowy* reprinted several of Poland's storytellers and poets. Its selection from the pantheon of Poland's literary masters leaned toward writers who supported national liberation favoring workers and peasants and often were committed to militant revolutionary action.

Newspapers were not the only outlet available to Polish-American writers. We have noted that Polish-language publishers in the United States assumed some responsibility for publishing immigrant writers, although we have also seen that Polish-American contemporaries with an interest in Polonian history and culture held them in low regard. The road into print was not always an easy one for them, and some writers issued their own work. Wladislaw Leskiewicz, whose *kuplety* were often performed on stage and were very popular with audiences, is one example. In the 1930s, he subsidized a small printing of them in pamphlet form. His collection of literary and theatrical materials at the Burton Historical Collection contains hundreds of his unpublished poems in Polish. Edward Alan Symanski, another Michigan Pole, is interesting to spend a moment on for two reasons: his poems are in English and reflect the combination of tradition, homeland nostalgia, and contemporary life cutting across the narrative and lyric culture of the Polish-American community. His poem "Immigrant" ("I am so lonely, God!! / here all things are strange / not one warm friendly nod") echoes the sense of loneliness and of being a despised alien. "Black Bread" questions the worth of coming to the new world: were the white loaves, the poet asks, worth the difficulties of steerage, the din of a new language, the machine economy, since "they never stop your hunger for the earth / you left"? That sense of attachment to the earth is again reflected in Symanski's poem "Twilight in a Polish Village." Its nostalgia covers the city, too, at any rate the medieval city of Cracow, "Wearing a jewelled crown / of churches," and is combined with a traditionalist religious feeling. Although Symanski tends toward nature and religious motifs, the industrial experience of the immigrant is the direct subject of two poems. "Steelworkers," a three-stanza ballad, is about immigrant workers who "Are kin to ores / The steel mills smelt, / Their sweat and blood / A new man weld." His other industrial poem, "Kowalski," rules out a favorable interpretation of "new man." A steel-mill hand who works the pits and furnaces yet remembers Poland, Kowalski yearns "to hold a swallow's nest" and, when the mill smoke and roar become too much for him, "Drowns down his grief in alcohol." The nostalgia signifies the immigrant's still-present sensitivity to the witchery and poetry of his former culture, to which, unfortunately "he can't go back."[34]

The following example of underground written culture suggests that neither hard work nor lack of education could drive the narrative or lyric impulse from their souls. A 1909 or 1910 letter from a hotel scrub-girl in Chicago to her village friend in Poland about her life in the United States and how much she misses friend and family ends in unintentional verse:

> The rain is falling; it falls beneath my slipping feet.
> I do not mind; the post office is near.
> When I write my letter
> I will flit with it there,
> And then, dearest Olejniczka
> My heart will be light, from giving you a pleasure.
> In no grove do the birds sing so sweetly
> As my heart, dearest Olejniczka, for you.

Bursting with love for her friend, the papa, sister, and brother she left behind, she writes: "I went up on a high hill and looked in that far direction [eastward toward Poland], but I see you not, and I hear you not."[35] The simplicity of language and feeling expressed in the letter is the heart of its lyric eloquence and differs markedly from the lettered stiffness of Symanski. This naive, untutored idiom tantalizes us with what other riches we might discover in the underground written culture of the immigrant worker, and it represents the kind of material the arts projects had hoped to benefit from by interacting with disregarded communities.

The oral form probably sounds the deepest, most pervasive reach of narrative and lyric culture among Polish workers. This is true for the traditional tales and songs transported to the new world with all the other steerage paraphernalia as well as the new urban lore invented to express the American experience. Edmond J. Dehnert believes that the extreme anti-Polish hostility of the early twentieth century made Polish Americans cultivate traditional culture more intensively than other groups did and made them become more Polish than they had ever been in the old country. Old country ways assumed a major role in their schools and fraternal clubs, where adults "practiced harvest rituals and mock peasant weddings and performed them in costume for each other."[36] Among the many traditional songs that the Polish-American community preserved, wedding songs were the most frequently recreated in and accommodated to this country. Among Detroit Poles it was a particularly important form of lyric culture, where these songs have appeared in thirteen variations and been described in twenty-seven contexts.

No matter how bound to tradition, in passing from small peasant village to big-city industrial life, the Polonian community in the Midwest and across the country created a whole range of new urban rituals. Since many of these had no old-country connections or customary forms of transmission, they expressed them in places that had no parallels in Europe: "Grocery stores and neighborhood taverns became new centers of urban folklife. Tavern keepers and priests became culture brokers and heroes who could resolve the puzzles of language, job hunting, and 'American' culture."[37] A few songs from the new urban experience adopted traditional form and diction for a content concerned with the problems of accommodating to American culture and economy. Sometimes those that follow traditional form employ old-country plots and themes, replacing old-country detail with specific American places and events. New oral delineations of immigrant experience are entirely American in linguistic form and content, but not yet assimilationist. They use Polish and English in combination where the English is policized and the Polish anglicized. An example of Detroit origin is oriented to courtship or flirtations among working-class youth:[38]

Ma Chene i Ferry	(on Chene and Ferry)
Stojala Mary	(standing there Mary)
Przyszedl Joe	(along came Joe)
I wziol ja na show	(and took her to the show)
Spendowal dime	(spend dime)
Miela good time	(have a good time)
oj dana dana	[nonsense refrain]
oj dana dana	

No doubt, a comprehensive picture of culture among the Polish masses is hard to draw at present. A fragmentary record is made more difficult to read by the seclusive tendencies of the written form, by the pliant sensitivities of the oral tradition to time and word, and by the state of Polonian literacy. Nonetheless, the evidence and clues we do have of a vigorous, broad-based Polish language theater and of a wide-ranging, populist narrative and lyric culture in the Polonian community make this much clear: the anomic, blank-eyed, culturally-dead image of immigrant workers conjured up by the artists of dominant culture is quite off the mark. We see clearly, too, that, insofar as the Polish immigrant community in the Midwest is concerned, the Federal Theater and Writers' projects had an undeniably favorable context in which to achieve their twin aims of winning a new, mass audience and discovering among those masses the kind of unjaded, basal experience these agencies thought was needed to inspire theater and writing anew.

5

Finn Halls and
Finnish-American Culture

THE Theater and Writers' projects in Michigan and the Midwest had equally favorable grounds for their aims among the smallest immigrant groups in this region: the Finns and Jews. It is a commonplace of thought that the Jewish immigrant community placed an extremely high value on learning and the arts. Less well known is the dedication of the Finnish immigrant community to the cultural side of their lives. That story is truly amazing.

A Stage for Every Finn Hall:
Pink Finns and Red Finns

The Finnish-American communities across the nation demanded and supported an incredible level of dramatic activity. Although Finns and their second-generation descendants never far exceeded 350,000, nearly every town and city with a Finnish enclave—in the Northeast, the Great Lakes region, the Northwest coast—had one and often more than one Finnish-language theater.[1] Small and large enclaves had multiple theaters, because every secular Finnish association—the temperance societies, the Kaleva lodges, the labor movement, and later on the cooperatives—made theater a function of their hall centers. The labor movement was the most consistently devoted to the stage. Key to the building of its halls was the construction of theater space, which became the heart of social life and political education. Moreover, when the labor movement was divided in the early 1920s into its three major orientations, socialist, syndicalist (IWW), and communist, each felt the need to maintain theater as a magnet to communal life and instruction. During the golden age of Finnish-American drama, from the early 1910s to the mid-1930s, the national estimate for a typical year of labor-hall theater runs to three thousand performances played before a half million people.[2] Incredible figures for so small an immigrant group. They signify a ratio of support unmatched by populations three or four times the size of the Finns in the United States, and they far outdistance anything the Broadway stage could rely on from the English-speaking millions in metropolitan New York.

As early as 1912–14, 107 of the 217 chapters of the Finnish Socialist Federation, an organization which then represented 13,000 members, had ongoing drama clubs active on a year-round basis. Timo Riipa and Michael Karni, two leading scholars of Finn theater in America, remark that with each ideological split in the Finnish workers' movement—the first between the socialists and the advocates of the IWW in 1914 and the second between the socialists and communists in 1920—the number of workers' theaters increased. High on the agenda of each new faction was a hall and a suitable auditorium for staging plays.[3] Hence, as the Finnish immigrant population grew in size, it always had a growing number of labor movement theaters to serve its needs.

But multiplying theatrical companies is only part of the story. Throughout its history, the aims of all labor theater for regularity of performance, turnover of plays, and length of season ran very high indeed. In 1913 the Finnish Socialist Federation of Cleveland required its theatrical group to perform three new plays a month. When the director in charge of theater complained that it was beyond human endurance to stick to such a furious schedule, the federation reduced the pace to one new play biweekly. In Conneaut, Ohio, the Finnish Socialists had made it a matter of constitutional principle by 1917 that their dramatic society produce a different play every three weeks. In Warren, another Ohio enclave of Finns, the socialist theater put on twelve stage presentations during the last six months of 1921. Even in 1930, when hard times, the movies, and language assimilation began to take their toll, the Warren group produced thirteen full-length plays, seven by themselves and six by touring Finnish players.[4] The Finnish People's Theater of Detroit, closely associated with the socialist wing of the Finnish labor movement, averaged two plays a month from October to March in the 1920s and 1930s according to one source of information. Another informant recalls two a month on occasion, but closer to an average of one every three weeks.[5] During those years, both the socialist and Marxist theaters of the Detroit Finns included a summer season at their close-by picnic grounds.[6] The Fitchburg socialists, in Massachusetts, probably hold the record with thirty-six plays in 1925 and again in 1926 and an average of 15,000 paid admissions each year.[7]

95

The examples so far are drawn from the larger Finnish enclaves. Companies in centers with smaller concentrations of Finns could hardly emulate such play frequencies and season lengths. Nevertheless, many of them were quite active, even if theatrical facilities and population size were more austere. One correspondent from Suomi College, who as a teenager during the 1930s had a busy hand in the Finnish-language theater of Mass City, Michigan, writes that every Finnish community in Upper Michigan—places like Hancock, Calumet, Ironwood, Negaunee—had acting groups of long-term tenure.[8] The labor Finns of Ironwood are a typical example of the smaller Midwest enclaves. They were still producing three plays a year as well as choral performances and festivals in the late 1930s when Finnish theater activities were falling off sharply everywhere.[9]

On their side, Finnish-American audiences were equal to what their dramatic companies offered them week after week and year after year. Finnish-American theater performed before capacity audiences. Sirkka Tuomi-Lee, from childhood on a part of labor theater in Minnesota, Ohio, and Baltimore, testifies to this for the several Midwest cities where she and her parents lived and performed as well as for Baltimore.[10]

Irja Mattson Connolly, whose career in Finnish-American theater started in Minnesota and moved from there to Ironwood and Detroit, notes that Ironwood audiences were overflowing and enthusiastic.[11] The Finnish People's Theater of Detroit played to audiences of five hundred to eight hundred people during the twenty years (1924 to 1944) it performed in its auditorium at the Finnish Educational Association Hall. From 1906 to 1924, this theater group moved approximately every three years, each time to a place that seated more people. After 1924, when it finally had its own theater to play in, it had a larger seating capacity than ever before.[12]

Temperance, Cooperative, and Kaleva Theater

Although the three Lutheran denominations among the Finnish immigrants denounced theatrical activity as the work of Satan, this in no way stilled Finnish ardor for theaters. The more secularly oriented associations —such as the mutual benefit lodges and later the cooperative guilds— among which church influence was minimal were hardly inhibited by such denunciations. Nor could the temperance societies, where the views of the church had a more powerful sway, resist the pull of theater. As a matter of fact, the first theatrical activity among Finns in the United States began with temperance societies in Massachusetts.[13] In the Midwest, however, affairs were somewhat different. More than in any other region where Finnish immigrants congregated, the clergy there exercised a powerful restraint within the temperance movement against the stage. The Pohjantanti Temperance

Society of Hancock, Michigan, is a case in point. At the beginning of the twentieth century, its actor members, chafed by the leash of religious leaders, demanded more theatrical freedom, and in 1901 they founded the Jousi Society, among the first Finnish labor organizations in Michigan. Cut loose from clerical influence, they proceeded to program, under the auspices of the new group, a series of very "demanding" Finnish classics at Hancock's Kerridge Theatre.[14] The temperance society of Hibbing, Minnesota, also experienced a split in its ranks over another theatrical controversy. In 1897 the society presented *Kovan Onnen Lapsia* (Hard Destinies) by Minna Canth (1844–97), a well-known feminist and socialist playwright in Finland. When the play aroused the ire of the society's wing of religious and conservative members, its advocates left to establish a new club, with a theater unencumbered by religious reservations. The new club turned out to be a workers' group, maintaining many temperance principles, but adding to them a socialist point of view.[15]

Religious scruples and fears did not constrain the two other important Finnish immigrant associations, the lodges of the Knights and Ladies of Kaleva and the cooperatives. A nationalist federation of mutual benefit societies, the Kalevas were willing sponsors of stage fare and regularly availed themselves of the play-rental service operated by the Finnish-American playwright and director, Lauri Lemberg. Lodges in Michigan and Minnesota were among his major clients. Since not many of the Kaleva halls contained adequate theatrical space, they usually had to rent space elsewhere, and this restricted their production of full-length plays "to special celebrations, fund-raising events and annual festivals." Nevertheless, in the 1920s lodges maintained thriving dramatic groups, and their programs warranted the hiring of paid professional directors. Detroit's Kaleva group continued to produce plays, in its own hall and in rented space in larger halls, until the late 1930s.[16]

The cooperative movement, whose great regional stronghold was the Midwest, was the late entrant in theatrical sponsorship, beginning its career in earnest in 1917. Characteristically, the cooperatives staged didactic entertainments in order to abet their recruiting aims. In the Midwest, this need was fulfilled by two very important play distributors: the Finnish Cooperative Wholesale of Superior, Wisconsin, and the Northern States Women's Coops Guild Drama Department. They supplied the various cooperatives with original scripts, some written in Finnish, some in English, stressing the advantages of the cooperative movement. *Liittyyko Maenpaan Isanta Osuuskauppaan?* (Will Farmer Maenpaa Join the Cooperative?) represents one of the plays in Finnish, and its title indicates the drama's thematic aim. An example of an English script is *A Gala Day in a Cooperative Store.* Its didactic purpose is honeyed over by musical comedy routine and enlivened by

97

a line of chorus girls drawn from the ranks of the local community whose cooperative produced it.[17]

A Working-Class Theater

The only way so small an immigrant population could sustain such a full measure of theatrical activity was tireless effort. The Baltimore group, largely composed of factory workers, is an excellent case in point. Not even the obstacle of a three-shift day at the steel mill, where many of the Finn performers and stagehands worked, could daunt their willingness to give hours to the theater. "There were many occasions," Sirkka Tuomi Lee writes, "when they had to rehearse at midnight at the hall since that was the only time they could all get together." Nor could the demands of youngsters not yet in school keep acting families from theater meetings and rehearsals. Tuomi Lee reports that in Minnesota and Ohio, where her parents were busy acting, directing, and writing for the Finnish-American stage, she went to "endless rehearsals" and, if necessary, slept on benches while the theater folk buzzed away on and off stage in the hall.[18] Another second-generation Finnish American whose family was active in hall theater remembers being brought frequently, nights as well as days, to the Minnesota halls where her parents directed and rehearsed plays. After her family moved to Ironwood, she recalls witnessing other children going through the same experience over and over again.[19]

The Gibraltar of Finnish-American theater, on stage and in the audience, was the working-class Finn. I stress the point, as with Polish-American culture, for it is central to the argument about the grass-roots character of the cultures in which the federal art agencies wanted to carry out their aims. Several witnesses among students of and participants in Finnish-American theater testify that working folk created the Finnish dramatic movement on this side of the Atlantic. "A fisherman's theatre" is what the Astoria Finns created, according to Walter Mattila, and he adds for emphasis: "with a fisherman and fishtown cast." His account cites evidence that Astoria's two main branches of labor theater also included loggers, coal miners, and at least one rock quarry laborer.[20] In the Midwest states, performers and audiences came from Minnesota's Mesabi iron ranges, the Chicago steel mills, Michigan's copper mines, and Detroit's auto plants. Tuomi-Lee informs us that cast members, stagehands, and wardrobe mistresses were typically manual laborers. Her own father had to give up playing the violin because his fingers had grown thick with toil in the steel industry. But steel work did not prevent him from remaining actively engaged in performing for labor association theater.[21]

Frans Syrjala, an active socialist and early student of Finnish-lan-guage theater in the United States, is perhaps the strongest witness for the central role of labor, not only in theater but in Finnish-American culture as a whole. In a 1925 series of essays on labor and amateur theater, he concluded:

> Yes. The little theatre and the Finnish-American culture were created by unskilled laborers, by men and women who worked with their hands to earn their daily bread. That culture was not created by the "educated" Finnish middle class—the clergy and the merchants. . . . The clergy considered the theatre sinful. The merchants were too busy trying to make money to spend time with the cultural aspirations of the Finnish American people. The "educated" middle class was, therefore, left behind [by the working class] both spiritually and intellectually.[22]

The Repertoire

The central role of the Finnish working class and the Red Finns in the theater movement and in creating a new culture on American soil did not limit Finnish-American theater to plays about workers from a political view favorable to a collective reconstruction of society. Although Moses Hahl, one of the leading Finnish-American writers and Marxist theoreticians, and Kalle Rissanen of the Finnish-American Communist stage proposed heavy doses of class-struggle plays that provided sound political education, Eero Boman—a professional director and socialist who served a number of en-claves including Detroit and who supported the idea that labor theater ought to educate—argued that an exclusive emphasis on worker-oriented plays would wear out both actors and audiences. Moreover, the need for theaters to make enough money to be self-supporting and the need to produce new plays frequently weighed in on the side of a more varied repertoire in the labor theater movement.[23]

As a matter of fact, the classics of the nineteenth-century Finnish stage made up the largest part of the Finnish-American repertoire. Some seventy percent of the plays listed in the Finnish Workers' Federation Drama League catalogue, probably the biggest circulator of playscripts, came from this source. When czarist Russia supplanted Sweden as the im-perial power in Finland, it did little to foster Finnish education and indige-nous culture. In the middle decades of the nineteenth century, a spring thaw in czarist suppression of the Finnish language set in and what we call the classical canon of Finland soared into existence with an energy and sophis-tication that could not be grounded even when Russian reaction closed in again under the last of the Romanov imperium. Another important chunk of the repertoire, about twenty-four percent of the Drama League catalogue, comprised European and American plays translated into Finnish. Like Polish-American theater, the drama of the Finnish enclaves transcended endemic nationalism. And like Polish-American theater, in fact to a much greater extent, Finn theater in America included plays about the immigrant experience by Finnish-American writers. They make up six percent of the Drama League list. All these sources fed Finnish-American theater with a wide variety of theatrical genres that fit in particularly well with the federal arts intended programs: historical dramas, melodramas, tragedies, comedies, operettas, folk plays, and musicals.[24]

The plays produced by Detroit Finns illustrate specifically the varied source and generic sweep of the repertoire.[25] Among them we find Finland's playwrights significantly represented. Aleksis Kivi (1834–72), who pioneered the use of Finnish as a language for drama and poetry, was very popular in Detroit, as he was in every U. S. enclave. His farcical *Nummisuutarit* (The Cobblers of the Heath [1864]) and the more serious but still comic *Setseman Veljesta* (Seven Brothers [1870]) offered Detroit audiences a realistic view of ordinary people, done with humor but, according to the literary historian Jaako Ahokas, seamed with a dark underside about misplaced love that threatens to destroy.[26] Another playwright Detroiters enjoyed was Mina Canth, most of whose politically-oriented plays about oppressed women, farmers, and workers were performed regularly by various labor theaters in Detroit. At least three plays by Kaarlo Halme, a socialist and proletarian sympathizer to the left of Canth, were also well-received: *Murtuneita* (The Oppressed) and two one-act pieces, *Ennustus* (The Prophecy) and *Sieman Perinat* (Seed Potatoes), both apparently politically pointed comedies about courtship.

Historical plays by Finnish playwrights also proved to be a welcome part of the Finn theatrical inventory in Detroit. *Daniel Hjorth* (1862) by Josef Julius Wecksell (1838–1907), a native of Finland who wrote in Swedish, was probably the most popular play of this genre. The historical event at its heart is the sixteenth-century civil war between the king of Sweden and Finland, supported by the aristocracy in both parts of the kingdom, and his nephew Charles, backed by the Finnish peasants. This could hardly fail to arouse the immigrant audience, with its strong family ties and its equally strong political sympathies for other dispossessed classes. Another very popular historical drama was *Elinan Surma* (Elina's Death [1891]) by Gustaf Adolf von Numers, a man of letters who wrote in both Swedish and Finnish. The tragedy, embellished by scenes of medieval history, is based on a medieval ballad about domestic jealousy analogous to Shakespeare's *Othello*. Zachris Topelius (1818–98), another Finnish writer at home in Swedish and Finnish, contributed a less ominous play to Detroit's productions of historical drama: *Regina von Emmeritz* (1854), a play which Ahokas calls "light, colorful, historical entertainment."[27]

Musical plays of various kinds, folk plays, and melodramas round out the stock of material which Detroit Finns drew from the homeland canon. The play that Riipa puts at the head of all-time favorites, *Tukkijoella* (The Lumberjacks [1899]), received repeated productions during the twenty and more years of Finnish theater in Detroit.[28] A country play by Tuevo Pakkala (1862–1925), it was set to music by two well-known Finnish composers and has had enormous appeal to sudiences here and in Finland ever since.[29] An example of a folk play in verse is *Kullervo* (1895), adapted by Juhann Heikki Erkko (1849–1906) from a *Kalevala* story about an uprising led by a folk hero.[30] Another folk play by a less well-known Finnish writer combined folk song with lore from Karelia, the eastern part of Finland. One important thing to note from the standpoint of Federal Theater Project aims is that this play, *Karjalan Kannaksella* (On the Karelian Isthmus), was one of many performed outdoors from 1926 to the mid-1940s at the Finnish People's Theater summer grounds at Loon Lake in Wixom, Michigan.[31]

Preservation of homeland culture, the linguistic accessibility of stage material, and the protective armor of a self-created but homeland-based new culture led Finnish-American theater to make plays from Finland the core of its world. Yet it did not ignore the drama of other nations, and these, like the Polish venture in other national repertoires, created audiences who could be receptive to the FTP agenda for classical and popular productions drawn from these sources. Over the active years of production, Detroit's Finnish theaters performed Capek's *RUR*, adaptations of Tolstoy's *Anna Karenina* and *Resurrection*, and Shaw's *Candida*. Viennese operettas—Franz Lehar's *The Merry Widow* and Oscar Strauss's *The Chocolate Soldier*—were also attractions that Detroit Finns could count on regularly. Even classical opera made the repertoire. In the late 1920s or early 1930s, the Finnish Marxian Club staged an outdoor production for children of Mozart's *The Magic Flute* at its picnic grounds near the city. Shakespeare, of course, received his due. Of particular interest is the modern-dress *Hamlet* performed here. First produced in the eastern enclaves, *Hamlet* in contemporary dress was brought to Detroit by Alaric Sandelin, a professional director and actor trained in Finland, either at the end of the 1920s or at the very beginning of the 1930s, when he became the full-time director of Detroit's Finnish People's Theater. It thus predates the FTP as well as Orson Welles's modern-dress *Julius Caesar*. Both outdoor performances and modern-dress stagings are again examples that ethnic publics were credible sources in very specific ways for FTP's aim to freshen theater with new approaches and again show that the FTP indeed had foresight in believing that they were.

Of rather great interest is a small group called the English Studio formed by Detroit's Finnish Educational Association, the umbrella organization for Finnish socialists and workers. Its guiding light was Sandelin, who brought it to life in the early 1930s. Its performers were English-speaking Finns, and its purpose was to make plays written in English part of the Finnish theater movement. Although it was not very long-lived, the group managed to produce at least three plays, two by Upton Sinclair and one by Paul Sifton. The Sinclair plays were *Precedent*, about the Tom Mooney frame-up, and *Singing Jailbirds*, based on a Wobbly strike. Sifton's play, *The Belt*, dealt with a theme close to the heart of Detroit, the oppression of assembly-line workers and their conflict with the auto industry owners.[32] These plays show that as Finnish immigrants in this mid-American metropolis were becoming more at home in English, some perhaps now using it as their primary language, the Finnish-American theater movement attempted to adapt to this linguistic shift in order not lose any momentum once old-world and new-world languages began to vie with each other in later generations.

But its ability to be a presence in the community to the end of the 1930s owes most to its success in honing the Finnish skills of second-generation performers who had been brought up in or with a love of theater. Perhaps the fairly regular supply of plays in Finnish about new-world immigrant life by Finnish-American writers had something to do with this outcome. The Detroit productions of these playwrights span almost as wide a range as the material selected from homeland and other-language drama. These include social-problem plays, some sharply proletarian in outlook and form; comedies, many simply to entertain, but others to make social-political points; and musicals and melodramas, with heavy doses of fantasy. The only major type missing from our shards of evidence is tragedy.

The two most widely famous playwrights among the immigrant enclaves, Felix Hyrske and Lauri Lemberg, had close ties to the left-labor theaters and were frequently produced in Detroit. Hyrske remained faithful to labor themes throughout his career. Lemberg started out as a political dramatist, but in the late 1920s he pretty much abandoned such themes for romantic comedies and musical extravaganzas.[33] Another political playwright represented in Detroit's Finnish theater is Fanny Ojanpaa, who also directed productions in the late 1930s. She wrote many of her plays for young children. One that her nephew, who informed me of it, remembers clearly is *Takapihan Lapset* (Children of the Backstreets), a drama about the appalling life of the poor.[34] Important as political dramas by labor-oriented Finnish-American playwrights were in the Detroit repertoire, they did not crowd out non-political works of immigrant origin. Love plays and musical pieces had no trouble holding their own over the years. Typical is Hilma

Johnson's *Syysromanssi* (Fall Romance), a folk play about autumn love set in an American mining town and called a "laughing pill" in one Finnish announcement.[35] Lauri Lemberg produced a string of musical plays, among them *Haihtuvia Pilvia* (The Fading Clouds), whose music and dance sequences frame an Argentinian folk motif, and *Mustalais Manja* (The Gypsy Manja), a colorful costume piece about gypsy life. "Gypsy" played on several occasions in Detroit, including a 1936 staging by the Finnish Marxian Club at the Diamond Temple.

Finnish-American Literary Culture: Folk and Formal

The fertile soil provided for federal patronage by this vigorous, thematically diverse theater, with its working-class backbone was nourished as well by the space and energy that Finnish immigrants devoted to non-dramatic culture. As in theater, where they were makers as well as observers of drama, in non-dramatic culture they were composers as well as absorbers of the oral and written word. According to one cultural historian, all ranks of Finnish Americans, not the least those who were unschooled workers, wrote thousands of verses of their own, covering "almost any occasion—from birthdays to funerals and from divine invocation to strike advocacy."[36]

The first potential source of inspiration for federal patronage was the rich vein of folk material in the making that non-dramatic culture left available for the Writers' Project conservation program. In oral forms and public representations, mainly at association halls, Finns everywhere in the U. S., including Michigan, expressed old folkways and created new ones. On evenings when plays were not scheduled, hall auditoriums became platforms for storytelling and poetry readings. The associations encouraged members and non-members, young and old, to read poems of their own choosing. These turned out to be of several kinds: new renderings of works by established homeland writers, resurrections or reworkings of folk materials, and recitations of original inventions in song and story.[37] The associations seem not to have made it a matter of rigid doctrine that the tellings and readings reflect their primary organizational purpose.[38] Looking at the verse in print, we discover, however, a fair number advocating temperance and a fair number extolling the virtues of the cooperative movement; if these themes appeared in print, it seems likely that organizational purpose found a voice as well in hall readings. As for the labor halls, Sirkka Tuomi-Lee makes no bones about the fact that the readings there "reflected the radical perspective and the pro-union position."[39] In spite of the rancorous debates over ideology among Finns, the halls seem to have been places for the free play of culture and of its members' lyric and narrative impulses. Members were, however, imbued with conviction about organizational principle, and that deep feeling often broke out as partisan spirit in verse and story. One form of hall reading, the *joukka runoja* (group recital), may reveal more about the associational or collective spirit than anything else. Its chief sound was choric harmony, punctuated at appropriate moments by a solo voice, perhaps to help the audience to that level of concentration demanded by poetic density.[40]

Finnish-American labor songs, which required no special place for their voicing, represent a particularly rich strain of the unlettered Finnish immigrant workers' oral expression. Michigan's Upper Peninsula yields a variety of examples. Some are old-country dreams of a paradise elsewhere and could still be heard relatively unchanged as late as 1947:

> Over nine seas
> I flew to a strange land
> Where the trees are scarlet and the earth is blue;
> There the mountains are butter,
> The cliffs are pork;
> The hills are sugar-cakes,
> And the heather is honey.

Most, however, are transformed to fit traditional tunes and underlying motifs. They express new-world realities for protest and struggle, but not without a sense of life's ebullient joy, as in the following example:

> Dance and leap, you light-footed girl,
> Throw your cares to the wall pegs,
> Dance so that your dancing curls
> And the very floor boards sing.
> . . . .
> Hasten to battle, you light-footed girl,
> It is time for all to arise—
> The dance of the slave has been danced to the end
> It is time to tighten the bow.

Another, a copper country strike song called "Mr. Woodenhead," is an entirely American invention set to the melody of "Casey Jones." It constitutes a deadly jibe at the non-union Finnish-American worker, a "wooden-head" with "furry foot," "a slave like all the rest," who bears without complaint "the backlash."[41]

Written sources of lyric and narrative expression were also a rich repository for the Writers' project. *Nyrkkilehti* was one such medium particularly amenable to the circumstances of the untutored immigrant writer. Its exact English equivalent is "fist paper." Its chief characteristic was its handwritten form. In one place referred to as an unpretentious journal, it seems to have been more precisely an informal sheet of local literary efforts and news briefs. It included essays, poems, and stories by folk in the local community, occasionally with borrowings from other sources.[42] When these were insufficient to use up the columns of the sheet, anecdotes about local personal events—courtship and marriage, broken homes, foul alcoholics, or exemplary youth—were used as fillers. Its homemade appearance notwithstanding, it served an important role in bringing forth and helping local writing talent to grow. From 1900 into the 1920s, *nyrkkilehti* existed in every Finnish-American institution—church, temperance society, labor club. Almost every Finn settlement of any fair size had one and usually more in circulation. In the Midwest, the socialists of Munising, Michigan, sponsored one in the 1910s, as did those of Hancock in Michigan's copper country between 1907 and 1912. We discover temperance society *nyrkkilehti* in Iron Mountain, Minnesota. In Conneaut, Ohio, the workingmen's association turned out one called *Moukari* (The Sledge).[43]

The working-class writer of little education—"Untouched by schooling, / Unguided by learned precepts," as one Finnish-American versifier, Matti Johansson described himself—also had access to printed sources.[44] Newspapers were perhaps the most important of these, but there were also song books, commemorative journals, and periodicals. According to A. William Hoglund, editors welcomed working-class writers, even when the quality fell below those of more substantial learning. The transformation of an old Finnish folk motif, the untutored worker who outfoxes his superior, gave rise to a whole series of periodicals based on that character, and their names are instructive: *Rascal, Rogue, Shoepack*. The writers whose works appeared in these periodicals dealt with the motif in verse, song, and story, recording how this stock figure—sometimes in the guise of old-world peasant, but often as immigrant worker—outwitted the gentry, the boss, the foreman, those in charge.[45]

A last resort in print was self-publication. Eelu Kiwiranta, first a Michigan copper miner and then a farmer, is an example. Using his own hand press, he published his otherwise rejected poems and often left the farming to his wife, traveling the upper Michigan enclaves selling them. According to Hoglund, his poems celebrated love and the countryside against the world of bosses, backbreaking work, and unemployment.[46]

Immigrant writers with more extensive educational backgrounds also had a hand in the creation of non-dramatic culture in Finnish-American enclaves during the first third of the twentieth century. Education here means primarily technical or practical training beyond high school, not the belletristic and humanistic studies of dominant culture, either in the old country or here. Such writers produced a stream of stories, novels, and poems about

105

the American experience. And though educated, they maintained close ties with the unschooled rank-and-file. Included in this more tutored segment are well-known, left-wing writers, such as Moses Hahl and Kalle Rissanen, who wrote short stories and novels that dignified working-class life and satirized anti-socialist attitudes. Aku Paivio is another schooled socialist poet whose works span the years 1910 to 1924.[47] Kolehmainen thinks Paivio expresses scorn for politically naive workers, but I hear in him a voice of sympathetic confidence in the power of a politically awakened working-class:

> If they but knew the wretches,
> The slaves led like children,
> If they knew what freedom is,
> If they could but taste it,
> Like a swift current of water,
> They would rush forward,
> Moving mountains from their path.

In the 1920s, the IWW also harbored many highly trained Finnish-American poets who wrote in English for the Wobblies' *Industrial Pioneer* and hence appealed to a larger readership.[48]

Examples of more schooled writers in the Midwest and whose rank-and-file relationships remained firm are Helmi Mattson (1890–1974), Edith Koivisto (n.d.), and Kalle Potti (1871–1935). Mattson attended a business college and a home economics school in Finland and worked for socialist newspapers in Astoria and New York. A description of her writing in the Immigration History Research Center records that "labor oriented Finns" knew her best for her novels about the class struggle among Finnish-American miners, lumberjacks, and factory hands. She was also well-known by the rank-and-file for her poems, which appeared regularly in the Finnish-American labor press.[49] Koivisto attended *Tyovaen Opisto* (The Work People's College), a left-wing school in Minnesota organized by Finnish-Americans. Besides writing plays, she composed a series of histories about the IWW, the cooperative and temperance movements in Minnesota, and the Finns of Hibbing in the same state.[50] Potti enjoyed a particularly favored place among his compatriots. His *Iloinen Harbori* (The Harbor of Joy [1924]) has been described as an earthy, humorous, and uninhibited novel, filled with memorable portraits of Ashtabula's Finnish dockworkers. A merchant and author after business hours, Potti was apparently not involved in the socialist or labor movements. Nevertheless he seems to have known Finn workers well, getting "most of his ideas and plots," his son reminisces, from "working on the docks for a short time when he [first] came to America."[51]

106

Although the non-dramatic culture of Finnish-Americans had a very clear tendency, what Finnish Americans created was not one-sided, for they accompanied it with moods from the old and colorful, with playfulness and flights of fancy. Fortunately these writers and oralists did not whistle in the dark: their compatriots in America were committed listeners and readers. Not adept readers of English in the first two decades of the century, Finnish immigrants were still able to read extensively in Finnish—not only works by Finnish writers, but Finnish translations of continental, British, and American writers. The publishing industry in Finland produced a steady supply of homeland and translated works to fill the demand by Finnish immigrant communities in the United States for books in neighborhood public libraries, association reading rooms, and Finnish bookstores.[52] In 1923 there were eleven such bookstores involved in importing and distributing both kinds of books. The bulk of these were in the Midwest, in Duluth, Hancock, Ironwood, and Ashtabula. In the catalogue of one of these bookstores, we find two thousand titles, covering almost every field: drama, fiction, poetry, art, music, religion, philosophy. The range of individual authors is also impressive. These include Tolstoy, Dostoievski, Daudet, Balzac, Hamsun, James Fenimore Cooper, Jack London, Charlotte and Emily Brontë, Wilkie Collins, H. Rider Haggard, Hall Caine, Marie Corelli, and of course all the important Finnish writers. It was not unusual for a Finnish workingman in the United States to own "several hundred volumes."[53]

All in all, in terms of theater and non-dramatic culture, we may say of this small immigrant population that, like the much larger Polish-American population, it presented the Federal Theater and Writers' projects in the Midwest and particularly in Michigan a most auspicious situation for audience and inspiration from down below. It was not even a matter of potential, of having the FTP and FWP create out of this a mass audience and inspire populist energy for art, for such an audience and populist-inspired art were already functioning forces in the field.

6

Making and Remaking
Yiddish-American Culture

THE small Jewish immigrant groups in Michigan and the bordering Midwest states also offered the FTP and FWP a favorable context for their creative work and audience objectives. But it differed from the kind presented by the Poles and Finns because of the strong presence of "shtetl" experience and the enormous influence of the Yiddish theater and literature created by Jewish intellectuals in New York City.[1] Like the Poles and the Finns who came to the United States, immigrant Jews were mostly poor and unskilled in the new language, and hence became industrial workers. The way that Jews were dispersed and ghettoized in eastern Europe, however, affected both national identity and the production of culture. And the distribution of Jews in the new world affected the style and content of the culture they produced. Because of its alien status among the national languages of eastern Europe, the Yiddish which eastern European Jews brought over with them also distinguished them from other immigrant groups. And the same is true for the esthetic history of Yiddish as a literary and theoretical medium, from the late nineteenth century through the 1930s.

Provincial and Cosmopolitan Exile

The official discrimination imposed by European governments in the modern era and the always hostile social milieu which surrounded them scattered Jews across the national map of Europe and made them, as a cultural entity, a people of all European nation-states and also of none. For a number of historical reasons, the scattering tended eastward, so that by the nineteenth century the bulk of European Jews were to be found in Slavic and Romanian Europe.[2] The language of daily speech among the Jews of eastern Europe remained Yiddish, not the languages of the nation-states occupying the region. The segregation of Jews from the main rhythms of national life in these areas played a powerful role in this linguistic apartheid. Excluded from native-language school systems, major forms of economic activity, and social life conducted in the national languages; geographically isolated in city ghetto and rural pale (the "shtetl" or small village compounds they were legally confined to); rejected and encapsulated in every regard: they had only their common oppression, their narrowed way of life, and the common language they brought with them from elsewhere as resources for the production of culture.[3]

These circumstances made it difficult if not impossible for Jews to identify with the geography and the nation-states they lived in or the other nationalities whose territories and sovereignty these states had conquered. Nor could they, in any substantial numbers, think of themselves as belonging to the geography of the Mideast under a restored, ancient sovereignty. That was too visionary for the mass of Jews in the nineteenth and early twentieth centuries, beyond memory and contact, beyond historical palpability, although not beyond a profound reverence for an ancient mythos. The sense of place and identity that eastern European Jews had was primarily cultural and provincial, not national. The historical experiences that were most immediately telling to them were the happenings and traditions of life in the rural villages, the "shtetls" of the Russian pale.[4]

In my view, these special conditions—dispersal among many nations yet belonging to none, a curious dialectic of cosmopolitan and provincial exile—account for the great ease and speed with which Jews assimilated American cultural attitudes into their old-country ways and "mama loschen" (the intimate term Jews used to assert the profound place of Yiddish in their lives). Unlike other immigrant groups, where so many had the idea of returning home for good after awhile, almost none of the Jewish immigrants, although they remembered the "shtetl" with tears and love, thought of eventually going back.[5] And although many of them wished Zionism well, no significant portion of them intended to relocate to a Zionist homeland. Home country for East European Jewish immigrants, who had little such sense before, meant this country, a national consciousness, new, firmly embedded, and not tied to a notion of dual citizenship. This process of assimilation and the ease with which most American Jews accepted it had ultimately a damaging effect on the development of Jewish immigrant culture or at least that part of it based on the Yiddish language. Nevertheless, because the collective sense of Jewish immigrants from eastern Europe was grounded in culture rather than nation and because the "shtetl" Jews who came here had achieved a high degree of Yiddish literacy, that part of the culture persisted and the language continued to develop on these shores, even while the new sense of national identity took hold with speed.

New York and Yiddish-American Culture

What helped to preserve the spirit of "shtetl" culture and Yiddish in the scurry of adaptation was the dense New York Jewish settlement in the last quarter of the nineteenth century. By the 1920s, the Jews of New York made up some five-sixths of all those living in the United States, a concentration whose ratio to the city's other inhabitants was considerable. This convergence spearheaded the growth of Yiddish in the United States as a language of daily life and as a literary medium. More secure than its fellow communities in the United States because of density and favorable ratio and more prolific in creative output, the New York Jewish community powerfully influenced how Jewish immigrant culture developed elsewhere. This concentration also made it possible to recreate, particularly on the lower East Side, some of the main features of "shtetl" life: the small shops, the Yiddish-language signs in Hebrew characters, the petty-bourgeois occupations carried overseas and reestablished here, the "chedehs" (Hebrew schools) and little store-front synagogues. But, in substantial numbers, New York Jews had also become proletarians, sweatshop and factory workers, as they had not been to any great extent in Europe and as they were not to any great extent in the provinces of America.[6] Moreover, notwithstanding the safety, familiarity , and comfort of the "shtetl" ambience in the Jewish enclaves of America's largest, most cosmopolitan city, Jewish immigrants moved through this world-city with an ease they could not have enjoyed under pale restrictions in the great cities of eastern Europe. The proletarian transformation and the cosmopolitan crucible of New York shaped a new trajectory for the content and styles of the culture produced by Jewish immigrants.

To fully appreciate the vigor and role of that new trajectory, we have to return to the origins of Yiddish. Although it had been used since the 900s, its principal function, according to Irving Howe, was "as a crutch to make one's way across the treacherous Diaspora."[7] By the 1500s and 1600s, it was increasingly becoming the mother tongue of the Jewish population, and by the 1800s it had become completely so among eastern European Jews. In the course of these centuries, it had also taken on somewhat of a life in writing. After the 1850s, literary Yiddish blossomed as never before, and the first real attempts to regularize Yiddish pronunciation, spelling, and grammar began. The power which transformed it over these hundreds of years from a dialectical variation of Middle High German into a language on its own persisted even under the gathering force of standardization. That power was its ability to be assimilative, to use Howe's word, or fusionist, the word Sol Liptzin prefers.[8] This ability to adopt, adapt, and convert what it had accreted to its own rhythms, sounds, and norms made it a language of astonishing malleability that was still newly forming at the end of the nineteenth century and in the first third of the twentieth.

The history of Jewish literary culture in the United States is intimately related to the dual process that Yiddish was undergoing at this time. The simultaneous phenomena of new formations and standardization were inevitable consequences of the old-world homelessness and the all-nations dispersion of its users and in the new-world sea-change of Jewish immigrants into proletarians, encountering and becoming part of the cosmopolitan kaleidoscope of New York. This simultaneity corresponded to the dual self-consciousness of those who used Yiddish seriously as a literary medium for storytelling, poetry, and drama: experimenting with content, style, and the protean capacity of the language as well as legislating its formal standards. In the new world, all the factors that went into the making of Jewish culture in eastern Europe—the provincial, joyful way of "shtetl" life, the fatalistic view of suffering, the living traditional engagement with the biblical mythos —continued to inform literary culture. But now these factors were transfigured by sweat-shop experience, politically radical impulses, and modernist tendencies closely allied to cosmopolitan esthetic movements.

That transfiguration begins with the pioneer Jewish writers in the new world who portrayed the ghetto and shop life of Jewish workers with anguished realism and framed a political spectrum from anarchism to reformism to socialism. To name only some of them: Jacob Gordin (1853–1909), Leon Kobrin (1873–1946), and David Pinski (1872–1959) in drama; Kobrin and Abraham Cahan (1860–1951) in fiction; David Edelstadt (1866–92), Joseph Bovshover (1873–1915), Morris Winchevsky (1856–1933), and Morris Rosenfeld (1862–1923) in poetry.[9] Their use of literary discourse to represent social problems and political views related to their new milieu became somewhat muffled by the modernist tendencies when "Die Junge" (The Young Ones) soon trod on their heels in 1907. But it was never silenced. It spoke with a loud and clear voice again, at least in the theater, with the founding of *Die Freie Yiddish Folksbuehne* (The Free Yiddish People's Stage) by the social-democratic *Der Arbeiter Ring* (The Workmen's Circle) of New York in 1915. With the surge in communist alignment after Russia's October Revolution, it continued to do so into the twenties, infused with new blood with the appearance in 1925 of the left-wing *Arbeiter Teater Farband* (Worker's Theater Movement), best known under its acronym ARTEF. Even in the modernist tendencies which took over (not necessarily in popularity, I should say, as in the attention they were given by Yiddish and American critics), the echoes of that social voice could not be stilled.

111

Hallie Flanagan and many leaders of the FTP and FWP had known of these developments and were influenced by them when they came to formulate the principles of federal patronage.

Nevertheless, cosmopolitan rather than proletarian influences vectored "Die Junge" movement and by 1919 the "In Zich" (Into Oneself) school. The writers of "Die Junge" rebelled against the moral and political character of the socially-oriented Yiddish writers as well as their frank representationalism and linguistic simplicity. One of the leaders of this first experimental tendency in Yiddish-American literature, Reubin Iceland (1884–1944), described the soul of their interests in this way: "Most deeply satisfying to us were the alien poets we were then encountering for the first time; we learned the most from the Russian, German, Polish, and French moderns. Baudelaire, Verlaine, and Rimbaud . . . Sologub, Bryusov, and Blok, and Liliencron, Dehmel, Rilke, and Hofmannstahl."[10] They preferred late romanticism, impressionism, symbolism, and the cosmopolitan spaces of European and American culture to provincial "shtetl" and proletarian city.

The "In Zich" writers were more thoroughgoing and self-conscious experimenters—with subject matter and stanzaic forms; with metrical and sound patterns to test the range of their incongruities for poetic effect; and finally with disruptive image and tone. They were dissatisfied with "Die Junge" notion that a poem expresses a poet's mood and with that school's stress on the rounded regularities of meter and sound. For the In-Zichists, form and content made up a seamless entity: to express mood without taking into account what kind of form it required or how form in fact created it was to use poetic techniques as mere decoration. From 1919, the year of the founding of the "In Zich" magazine, through at least the early years of the 1920s, they argued against such oversimplifications and produced a body of Yiddish poems illustrating their thoroughly modernist views. Although they called themselves "introspectivists," I think Howe's way of putting it is closer to the point: "fierce individualistic expressiveness."[11] Howe, it seems to me, is on the mark in associating this later group of Yiddish writers with Pound, H. D., Eliot, and Stevens and in concluding that with the In-Zichists, Yiddish poetry put aside its crude folk beginnings to enter the mainstream of modernist poetry.[12]

The Yiddish stage in this country did not go in for the same esthetic theorizing of the arts as the poets and prose fictionists, but it did match them in the conscious effort to establish the Yiddish stage as an art form. And in this New York again led the way. The popularity of the Yiddish theater among Jewish immigrants was manifest from the very beginning. In those early years the main fare consisted of tasteless operettas and "blood-curdling" melodramas, filled with stock characters and predictable actions and the most barbaric Yiddish colloquialisms. They were labelled "shund" (rubbish) plays and have been thought to be attractive to the Jewish masses on the ground of cultural backwardness.[13]

The first major reactions to such offerings came after the turn of the century in the work of several playwrights. Jacob Gordin led the way between 1892 and 1908 with a series of realistic problem plays dealing with contemporary life, including *Yiddishe King Lear*, about a self-sacrificing father; *Mirele Efros*, about a self-sacrificing mother; and a perennial favorite, *God, Man, and the Devil*, about the tragedy of a life obsessed with money-making. Among the socially-conscious anti-shundists was H. Leivick (1888–1962), whose play *Rags*, dealing with Jewish-American life at the bottom, received considerable praise from Yiddish and American reviewers. Other playwrights who contributed to cleaning up "the Yiddish theater of junk" before the art theater came into full force in 1920 included Perez Hirshbein (1880–1948) and Ossip Dymov (1878–1959). Hirshbein, even after his immigration to the United States in 19ll, continued to write lyrical plays about the sadness and joy of "shtetl" life, for example *Farvorfen Vinkel* (Thrown Away Corner), a village-centered Romeo-and-Juliet story with a happy ending. Dymov, whose plays combined comedy, fantasy, and symbolism, set up a Yiddish theater in the Bronx in association with Rudolph Schildkraut in order to produce better plays than the more commercially-oriented managers permitted. These and some others formed the transitional phalanx from the "shund" theater to the art theater movement, which was in full force by the 1920s.[14]

The Yiddish art theater movement depended heavily on the all-nations character of Jewish intellectual life and the cosmopolitan experience of Jews in the New York setting. Chief among the European inspirations were the *Théâtre Libre* in Paris, first under the direction of André Antoine, then of Antoine Gemier, the *Freie Buehne* in Berlin, but above all the Moscow Art Theater under Konstantin Stanislavski.[15] In New York, experimental theaters like the Provincetown Players, the Washington Square Players, and the Neighborhood Playhouse also commanded Jewish attention. The two most energetic organizers of esthetically-motivated Yiddish theater in America, Jacob Ben-Ami and Maurice Schwartz, were well acquainted with these new theatrical events on both sides of the Atlantic. To be free of the commercial pressure for "shund," Schwartz set up the Irving Place Theater in 1918 and Ben-Ami the Jewish Art Theater a year later. Schwartz and his company, which was later renamed the Yiddish Art Theater, lasted much longer than Ben-Ami's group, a fact that made Schwartz's name synonomous with the art movement in the Yiddish-American stage. ARTEF also belongs to this movement and may well be its touchstone of achievement. Under its director, Benno Schneider, it was shaped by a variety of forces: cosmopolitan influences; Jaques Copeau's concept of the "naked stage"; the

Moscow Art Theater; and perhaps most by Vsevolod Meyerhold's futuristic expressionism. Over the years, it achieved a rare and highly respected reputation as a forthright working-class theater of supreme esthetic accomplishment.[16]

In addition to works based on Jewish experience and experimental production techniques, the Yiddish theater staged plays in Yiddish from the established European canon, Shakespeare, Schiller, and so on. Honor for this canon differed little from other immigrant groups. Nevertheless, it fits in with the main features of how the production of Jewish culture in America differed from other groups. Because of demography and its all-nations' consciousness, Yiddish-American culture emerged in a cosmopolitan framework and aspired to high culture norms, although it never could or even sought to shake off its anchor in provincial folk life and the urban proletariat. The advantages it presented for the populist aims of the FTP and the FWP were, therefore, somewhat more problematical than the ones we have documented for the culture produced by Polish and Finnish Americans. The considerable identification with and contribution to modernism, particularly in a cosmopolitan context, could represent a formidable contradiction to the populist impulse of these agencies. As noted in Chapter 2, this contradiction existed within their own ranks; as theater people and writers they had been influenced by both cosmopolitanism and progressive regionalism. Yet experiment and faithfulness to populist themes were also principles of the federal arts projects, and hence they could have used the advantages of this problematical set in full measure while avoiding its dangers. ARTEF was probably an excellent guide, more especially because the art administrators were familiar with and had high regard for the sources out of which ARTEF developed its working-class theater. In New York, the Theater and Writers' projects knew what to do with these advantages and grasped them with firm hands.[17]

Yiddish-American Culture in a Midwest Setting

Because Jewish-American culture in New York was such a thriving affair, for New Deal patronage to have seized its populist opportunities, notwithstanding its cosmopolitan dangers, may have been obvious and easy. But did the Midwest's Jewish-American communities generate an equally or at least a sufficiently vigorous cultural setting so that these projects could easily recognize and take hold of its advantages?

I shall once again take Detroit as the bellwether. The bulk of Jewish immigrants to Michigan chose the auto capital for resettlement. In terms of old-world cultural inheritance—"shtetl" experience, common language, religious tradition, and biblical mythos—they were much like their immigrant confreres in New York. But in three important respects they differed. In Detroit they were an inconsiderable minority; they were not blessed with the same concentration of intellectuals and writers; and they were not, by and large, shop workers, for the bulk of the community was employed in trade. The first two factors explain why the Midwest community had to rely so heavily on New York for its most formalized cultural fare. The third difference was a consequence of Jewish occupational history and the industrial character of the Midwest. Jews who made their way to Detroit were not prepared for its heavy industry. As workers or small businessmen, a large proportion of Detroit's Jewish population became enveloped in the petty-bourgeois world and work of the wholesale and retail trades.[18] If Detroit's Jews had produced a formalized culture out of their American experience, it would not have been anything like the literature and drama which New York's Jewish immigrants made. Since Detroit's Jews did not generate much in the way of formal creative work, they had to rely on a Jewish-American culture formed from a context unlike its own, from a proletarian work-life and a cosmopolitan metropolis. But Jewish immigrants in the American provinces and in New York easily found common cultural ground in their old-world "shtetl" inheritance and in resigned resistance to rejection and harassment.

The Stage from "Shund" to "Shul"

As different as the two communities may have been in their development in this country, Detroit Jews had reasons to welcome the cultural contributions of the New York enclave. This is most striking in theater. Before a home-based Yiddish theater was established in Detroit, the Jewish community there enjoyed a steady flow of travelling companies from New York. In June 1918, a New York company came to Detroit's Lyceum with Bessie Thomashefsky performing in *The Woman of Today* by Zigmund Libin, one of the New York playwrights interested in raising the quality of Yiddish theater with dramas realisticly portraying tenement life and protest. "Shund" plays were also among the offerings of the traveling stage. *Vi a Man Libt* (As a Man Loves), by one of the leading "shund" playwrights Joseph Lateiner, was put on by the Max Wilner company in 1919 at the New Detroit Opera House. Isadore Zolotarefsky's lurid melodrama *The Outcast* was performed in May 1924 at the internationally acclaimed Orchestra Hall, and Max Gabel's *The Great Moment* appeared at the New Detroit Opera House that same month under the banner of the New York company Gabel formed with Jennie Goldstein. New York's art theaters were well-represented. Maurice Schwartz's Yiddish Art Theater played Detroit on several occasions, as early as the summer of 1920, when Schwartz himself performed in three short plays: the classic "shtetl" play *Teyve der Milkiger* (Teyve the Dairyman), by Sholem Aleichem; *The Thieves*, by Fishel Bimko, honored with a premier by Poland's famous Vilna Troupe; and *A Night in the Old Market*, by Isaac Loeb Peretz, one of the European fathers of modern Yiddish literature. In June and July of 1925, Schwartz's company was again in Detroit, presenting two plays in Yiddish translation: *The Seven That Were Hanged*, by Leonid Andreyev, a popular pre-revolutionary Russian playwright whose work reflected the period's pessimistic anxiety ; and *Wolves*, by the French writer Romain Rolland, a staunch advocate of a theater in which "the People itself must become an actor in the festival of the people."[19]

In 1924, under the direction of Moishe Schor, Mischa Fishzon, and Abraham Littman, a home-based Yiddish theater with the power to endure became a reality in Detroit. In its first season, a major success, it produced seventy-one plays and attracted enthusiastic audience support. Called the Yiddish Playhouse over its first three seasons, this group adopted the name The People's Theater when it moved to a playhouse with a larger seating capacity. It remained there in the heart of Detroit's second Jewish enclave, until the fall half-season of 1936. By then Detroit's Yiddish theater had become a victim of linguistic assimilation, economic crisis, and cinema as the popularly preferred dramatic entertainment. In January 1937, Littman announced the leasing of the People's Theatre, where the company had played for ten years, to Detroit's Federal Theater Project.[20]

The Littman company relied heavily on the canon established by New York's Yiddish theater, from "shund" melodrama and musicals to social and literary plays. The company's operating formula is another debt owed to New York. Detroit's Yiddish theater was basically a stock company. A few staff members were from the city's immigrant community, but the balance of the company was filled out by performers from elsewhere, mostly New York, who stayed only for the season. The productions that stimulated the largest audience turnouts featured prominent guest stars from New York's Jewish rialto, Second Avenue.[21] Although "shund" plays dominated the Littman repertoire, over the years the company presented with increasing frequency works that represented innovative and accomplished literary stories probing personal, social, and existential issues. These included Gogol's *Inspector-General*, an adaptation of *Hamlet*, Victor Hugo's *Jean Valjean*, Solomon Anski's *The Dybbuk*, and a wide selection of important Yiddish-American playwrights.[22]

For the FTP's aims of reaching young audiences in venues close to where they lived and being enlivened by grass-roots social drama, the most resourceful advantage of Jewish-American culture in Detroit was the variety of amateur theaters it gave birth to. As in all immigrant cases, the evidence on hand is scattered, disorganized, and pock-marked with huge gaps, but I would guess from it that these amateur groups played a fairly substantial part in the community's dramatic experience, although nothing close to that of amateur theater in the Finnish-American community and not with the same dominant working-class makeup. The most customary and traditional of these amateur efforts were the annual productions of Purim plays, basically reenactments and adaptations of the freedom story of Esther and the Persian Jews. More often than not, these were performed by boys and girls in their teens and younger, and they were sponsored by the entire range of institutional life, from synagogues to secular organizations. Other amateur groups seem more akin to the efforts one finds in all communities: endeavors of enrichment and simple love of entertainment, of histrionics, with no particular anchor in tradition, no political view or esthetic aim, no firm institutional support. For amateur theater with staying power and consciously intended as theater, we can turn to two examples, secular groups sponsored by left-wing advocates who remained closely attached to Yiddish, and Temple Beth El, whose congregation had become linguistically anglicized.

The sustaining force behind secular groups was the "shul" movement. This was a current of considerable energy in the first third of the century, providing young Jewish Americans with a Yiddish education free of religious purpose. It stressed Jewish history and culture rather than providential belief and devotion. In most "shul" formations, the emphasis was also political, for the groups sponsoring them were almost all advocates of labor and socialism. The "shul" movement emerged wherever there was a fairly sizable enclave of Jewish immigrants.[23] In 1912 the Paole or Labor Zionists set up the first school for young people in Detroit. In 1921 the Detroit branch of *Die Arbeiter Ring* (The Workmen's Circle), the largest Jewish American socialist organization, founded its own "shul." A year later this school merged with the I. L. Peretz "shul," a social-democratic ally. Detroit's labor Zionists opened the doors of another school, the Farband Volk Shul, in 1927. And from the 1920s into the 1930s, Yiddish-speaking Jewish Americans who favored Russia's 1917 October Revolution maintained a "shul" called Hirsh Lekert, after a poor Jewish cobbler who lost his life for assassinating a Russian baron. The lone exception in Detroit to these politically oriented "shul" was the Sholem Aleichem Institute, which began in 1927 with an apolitical and non-partisan policy that it retained through the deepest years of domestic and international crisis.[24]

Because these "shul" groups were secular, they customarily included theatrical activity in their cultural centers. From the evidence available to us, it appears that the Sholem Aleichem Institute was the most vigorous sponsor of amateur theater. Under the guidance of one of its earliest directors, Moishe Haar (1898–1966), the Institute supported two theatrical groups. One was the *Kinder Teater* (Children's Theater), comprised of children enrolled in the lower school. For this group, Haar adapted plays and stories from Yiddish literature, mostly by Sholem Aleichem. The *Tealeague* was the dramatic circle of young adults in the middle school. In addition to Haar's Aleichem adaptations, it occasionally produced plays by professional storytellers and playwrights, such as Peretz and Pinski. *Kinder Teater* and *Tealeague* also staged musicals stitched together with old and new Yiddish songs.[25] Since the middle school was actually a joint effort of the Institute, the Workmen's Circle, and the Farband, this theater also touched the young adults of the social-democratic and Zionist "shul" movement. The capacity audiences before which *Tealeague* usually performed indicate that older secularist Jews were affected as well.

The Hirsh Lekert Shul appears also to have been involved in amateur theater. According to the memory of one former student, who himself had performed as a child in several Yiddish plays put on by Hirsh Lekert, the plays were generally short, local adaptations to accommodate the abilities of the youngsters and almost always had a political point to them.[26] Since Hirsh Lekert was so strongly Marxist in outlook, it seems likely that the teen-age and adult groups were similarly drawn to politically didactic stage presentations. The chorus connected with the "shul," the *Freiheit Gesaing Verein* (Freedom Song Club), later became known as the Jewish Folk Chorus. Its repertoire featured working-class, folk, and Red Army songs in Yiddish.[27]

Several other drama groups were closely related to the "shul" movement but not actually affiliated with it. One might call them theatrical coalitions of left-wing, working-class, and secular-minded Jewish Americans who were members or sympathizers of one or another grouping within the "shul" movement. The "Dramatische Gesellschaft" (Dramatic Studio) was a particularly active and long-lived "shul"-related coalition of performers, directors, designers, and theatrical people. It performed regularly in the 1920s and 1930s before a variety of community groups, particularly the "landschaftsman" (regional countrymen) associations of Detroit.[28]

The Arts Society of Temple Beth El was the only amateur theater sponsored by the religious sector of Detroit's Jewish community during the 1920s and the Great Depression. Temple Beth El was the region's first reformed congregation as well as the most linguistically anglicized in the opening third of the twentieth century, and the work of its theater group is the best documented of Detroit's Jewish amateur drama clubs. As a reformed congregation, Beth El did not share the orthodox congregations' views that theater diverted Jews from pious living. For at least ten years after its beginning in 1922, Beth El made the Arts Society an important part of its extracurricular services to the community. Although the actors were primarily drawn from temple ranks, they were directed by a paid professional. The effect of the congregation's linguistic and cultural assimilation may be seen in the character of its performances: works in English mainly selected from the established high-culture canon of Europe and the United States, including Henry Arthur Jones, Bernard Shaw, August Strindberg, Eugene O'Neill, and Lawrence Langner.[29] Among its programs we discover some folk-based and experimental drama. Paul Green's work, for example, is represented and so is a 1923 production of *The Curtain*, an early Hallie Flanagan play.[30] The society's tenth anniversary celebration journal cites a play, *Money*, by the left-wing writer Mike Gold. David Pinski, of the Yiddish-American repertoire, is represented by an occasional play translated into English, although Beth El correspondence at the Burton Historical Collection indicates that it contemplated producing works by Israel Zangwill and Sholem Aleichem.[31]

Verse and Story among Midwest Jews

The salutary context that Jewish-American theater in Detroit presented for the twin objectives of the Federal Theater and Writers' projects was duplicated by the poetic and fictional experience of the enclave. As I have already noted, Detroit's Jewish community was deeply beholden to New York City for the formal part of its American-engendered culture. Included in this debt was non-dramatic literature. The most productive poets and fictionists—and the largest number of them—were located there. New York was also the center for Yiddish-language newspapers, books, and journals and, for that matter, English-language publishing by Jewish immigrant houses interested in the immigrant experience.[32] But these printed forms were circulated with regularity throughout all the larger enclaves, and thus New York poets and prose storytellers were quite available to Detroit's Jewish population. The socialist-oriented *Vorwarts* (Forwards), the best-selling Yiddish-language newspaper in the country, was distributed to outlying enclaves on a daily basis, as was its left-wing competitor, the *Freiheit* (Freedom). Both featured the works of poets and fictionists as a standard service to their immigrant readers. The works of these authors were also quite easy to find in Detroit's thriving Yiddish bookstores.[33] The literary and cultural journals published in New York also found a fair market in the Motor City.

Detroit's Jewish community was thus fairly well exposed to the whole range of sweatshop writers, "Die Junge" school, and the "In-Zichists" of New York, as well as East Coast socialist and communist writers. It also had access to local sources of non-dramatic culture. Although not comparable in numbers or acclaim with those in New York, there were a few Yiddish-language poets of stature in the Midwest. Chicago provided three of particular note: Mattes Deitch (1894–1966), Selik Heller (1894–1970), and Shloime Schwartz (1912–?).[34] Detroit's key Yiddish poet was Ezra Korman (1888–1959), who came to the Midwest in 1924. One of his major literary undertakings was an anthology of Jewish women poets, which appeared under the title *Yiddishe Dichterin* in 1928. In the 1930s, Korman was an active member of the Sholem Aleichem Institute.[35] Midwestern newspapers also exposed the region's Jewish-American enclaves to non-dramatic culture. Like their counterparts in New York, they regularly devoted some of their space to printing short stories, serialized novels, poems, and critical reviews covering a whole range of writers and subjects. The classic Yiddish writers from Europe and New York were well represented, but lesser known authors, some surely of local origin, also appeared frequently, as did writers from other cultural and national extractions. As the largest Jewish immigrant center in the Midwest, Chicago led the way. But in such Midwestern cities as Cleveland and Detroit, newspapers devoted to Jewish-American life, both in Yiddish and English, followed the same principle. Detroit evidence of how the press helped to foster non-dramatic literature during the period between the two World Wars comes from the *Detroit Jewish Chronicle*, the most widely circulated newspaper of that period. The work we find in the *Chronicle* in the 1930s is wide-ranging, but not as eclectic as the *Jewish American* of the pre-1910 period. The poems in the *Chronicle* tend to fall into three categories: religious and occasional poems for traditional holy days; poems concerned with self-identification as a Jew; and lyrical, personal poems with no particular or discernible Jewish content.[36]

Literary evenings also played a part in developing non-dramatic culture in Detroit's Jewish-American community. Moishe Haar (1898–1966) persuaded the Sholem Aleichem Institute to make the Friday evening "Shabat" an evening devoted to literary matters, lectures by noted authors from New York, and poetry or story readings.[37] The Young Men's Hebrew Association was another sponsor of weekday literary programs. "Landschaftsman" groups did not schedule literary evenings on a regular basis, but they quite frequently hosted lectures by noted writers and readings by local talents.[38] The community also fostered non-dramatic culture by keeping folklore alive or developing it anew through oral transmission. Cradle songs, love songs, courtship stories, stories about outsmarting the oppressor were all part of community life. One story in the Folklore Archives at Wayne State University is about a fraudulent businessman's offer for the hand of an old man's daughter. The businessman, placing a bundle of money on the ground, says that it covers up all the dirty things he has done. But the old man blows the money away and points out that the dirt indeed remains. One song in the collection, "Oy Dortn, Dortn, Ibern Vaserl" (There, There, Over the Water), is a nostalgic evocation of "shtetl" pastoralism. Another, reported by a worker as a labor song, is actually a Rosenfeld poem which passed into the oral tradition, illustrating how close the folk and the formal were to each other.[39]

All these modes, the regular and formal, the less regular and informal, the evenings, the oral tradition, and the reprinting of classic writers, manifest a non-dramatic culture that was a lively part of Detroit's Jewish community. As with theater, these represent a fairly thriving Yiddish-American culture in the provinces and the audience, themes, and esthetic practices that the Federal Theater and Writers' projects had in mind for themselves when they came on the scene. Neither theatrical nor non-dramatic culture had the weighty presence in insular cities such as Detroit that they had in New York, but they were thriving features of Yiddish-American culture in the provinces.

7

Black Theater and Writing

WE turn now to my last case of a cultural public that presented the federal arts programs with resources for inspiring their populist principles, the black community. The American South, like the areas the Poles, Finns, and Jews came from, was another border region with a supply of heads and hands needed for the growing industrial system in the country's capitalist heartland.[1] A year or two after the onset of World War I, southern blacks began a mass decamping to major urban centers in the Northeast and Midwest that accelerated in the 1920s and 1930s. Like the Polish, Finnish, and Jewish immigrants, African Americans altered the Anglo and German composition of the North and Midwest, forging a new cultural milieu out of rural traditions and northern industrial experiences. As in the case of these other immigrant communities, the milieu they forged profoundly transformed the dynamics of culture in the industrial heartland—a transformation which, like those of the other groups, had much to do with the progressive regionalism that informed the esthetic and thematic principles of the Theater and Writers' projects.

Of all the resettling groups from the periphery to the center of capitalism, blacks were the most marginalized, oppressed public. Their slave history in the United States and the racist ideology developed by America's dominant culture determined their relationship to all the other publics in the nation and affected every social, political, religious, and economic condition of their lives. Unlike immigrants from the European periphery, who arrived in the capitalist center with languages that defined them ethnically and geographically, black resettlers from the American South came with a version of the language of their oppressors on their tongues. This version was more than a variation of the American English preferred by dominant culture. Through morphological, lexical, and phonemic adaptation, adoption, and blending, it had replaced in use and memory the African languages of their forebears.[2] Unlike Yiddish, which is derived from Middle High German but grew as a language far from its source, the black variation of American English existed alongside and depended for its life blood on the other dialects, including the official one, that make up American English. Racist ideology, of course, classified the black variation as a linguistic disability incapable of creating or supporting a cultural life of any merit, particularly in the literate arts.[3]

Because the black form of American English is a highly and uniquely developed variation, and because cultural racism downgrades it, there was a two-fold effect on the way the black community produced its own brand of culture. Cultural hegemony is an attractive and repulsive force that engenders an impulse for cultural assimilation among ethnic and racially defined minorities as well as disfavored working classes—what some may presume is equality through imitation. But because the premise of cultural hegemony devalues these groups as producers of language and culture, it also drives them to resistance. This resistance is strengthened by the availability of a language different in family connections from the language of the dominant culture. Among African Americans the situation has always been more problematical. Both impulses—to imitate and to resist devaluation—must be carried out in one or another variation of the same language family to which the dominant culture belongs.

The demographic profile of the black population in Michigan and the urban centers of its Midwest neighbors affected both strategies. The earliest migration of blacks in any fair numbers into the Michigan area (and this profile is typical of the Middlewest) may be traced back to the 1850s.[4] The largest movement into the state was of free blacks, mostly from Virginia and Kentucky, but also from New York and other places on the northeastern seaboard. These migrants were mainly artisans and small entrepreneurs of some education. A very few were trained as professionals, in theology, medicine, and the law, although for reasons of racism they seldom found opportunities to practice their professions. Nevertheless, they were more educated than their artisan and entrepreneurial neighbors.[5] The second kind of migration in that early period was made up of slaves in flight along the Ohio, Indiana, and Michigan underground railroad. This movement, significant in terms of the physical hardships and dangers encountered everywhere along the way, was quite small. Moreover, most runaways continued on to Canada.[6] The fugitive slaves who stayed in the Detroit area were fewer in number than the free blacks among whom they settled. Together they formed the area's pre-industrial black community and established the first stable black enclave in the region—the only force at that time with a strategy for creating a cultural milieu for the small neighborhood they were restricted to.

After the Civil War, black migration from the South increased as unskilled laborers and sharecroppers fled economic subsistence made more intolerable by the new brand of racism that followed Reconstruction's betrayal. Far less educated, far less artisan and entrepreneurial than the earlier migrants, they were far more marginalized and oppressed than earlier migrants to Detroit. By the 1880s and 1890s, they had become the major part of Detroit's black enclave, although enclave members who had established the pre-industrial community and their offspring remained leaders of the community. As the entrenched economic force in the community and the most literate in the use of standard American vernacular, these leading families formed an elite guard whose voice registered persuasively within and outside the community. These families continued to be an influential force in the formation of Detroit's black culture for a long time.[7] Not surprisingly, both in the short period before the Civil War and long afterwards, they formed a cultural network in the formal arts patterned after the traditions and high forms of the dominant classes of European and American society.

The Strategy of Imitation

Music, fine art, and literature provide examples of the strategy of imitation at work in the black community. Of these, music was quite probably the most frequently sponsored art form.[8] In the late nineteenth and early twentieth centuries, social gatherings, civic or political banquets and meetings, as well as specifically designed cultural programs which the chief families sponsored or were invited to quite regularly included musical performances. These were heavily tilted toward the vocal and instrumental music of the classical tradition of Western music. Although recitals quite regularly featured gospel music as well, it appears to have been the kind more closely associated with the musical tradition of English Methodism than the folkloric tradition of black spirituals. Although gospel songs in the repertoire came from the crucible of black church adaptation, on these occasions they were performed in a recital context of classical style and form, and it seems likely that their African-American folk residues were diluted in these programmatic settings.[9]

Many of the musicians were the sons and daughters of the leading black families and had been trained in classical conservatories or by classical teachers.[10] One such example is Mrs. Anna Chandler Brooks, whose repertoire reveals the classical character and context in gospel and Western vocal accomplishments in the black community. Called the "Queen of Gospel Singers" by the *Dresden Daily* and acclaimed by Thaddeus Wronski of

124

the Boston Opera Company, Mrs. Brooks included in one of her representative programs ballads and operatic pieces such as "Ave Maria," "Vilanelle," and arias from *La Traviata*.[11] Azalia Hackley is another example. As a performer of instrumental music and a music educator, she pioneered the spread of classical forms among Detroit's black enclave. As a choral director among black youth in the second and third decades of the twentieth century, she also devoted her talents to making black folk songs a vital part of concert programming, not only within black culture but for a city-wide audience.[12]

Through its examples of important black cultural figures and its concept of progress, *The Michigan Manual of Freedman's Progress* for 1915 demonstrates the strategy of designing a culture derived from the traditions and high forms of dominant classes. For the compilers of the 1915 *Manual*, progress obviously meant a measured increase of black achievement in fields and styles valued by dominant culture. With sober pride, the *Manual* cites the cases of Professor C. W. Thompson and Harry Guy. Thompson was a fugitive slave who fled to Detroit in 1854, where he devoted himself to establishing and conducting religious choirs and secular choruses. Sometime in the 1870s, he organized the Detroit Philharmonic Society. The *Manual* reports that Guy was a figure of musical importance in Detroit at the end of the nineteenth century as a composer and arranger for soloists and orchestras and emphasizes that his compositions and arrangements belong to "high class music."[13] The *Manual* includes in its record Richard Shewcraft, a black artist born in Canada but resident in Detroit at the end of the last century and the first years of the twentieth. He was the first "colored" artist to gain a scholarship from the Detroit Museum of Art. He studied with another Detroit black artist, Percy P. Ives, who by the end of the nineteenth century was well enough known to be appointed dean of the Detroit Museum of Art. A portrait and landscape painter, Ives was trained in the European tradition, at the Pennsylvania Academy of Fine Arts, and then for three years in Europe with Boulanger, Lefebvre, and Constant.[14]

Literary clubs were an essential part of the cultural network modeled after the dominant modes of Western art. These clubs attracted interested people, in most cases women, for an evening of programmed music and literary appreciation.[15] The Browning Study Club was organized in 1898 to discuss the works of Browning; it later became the Detroit Study Club, when its readings and discussions grew to include other writers: Chaucer, Shakespeare, Goldsmith, Wordsworth, Tennyson, Washington Irving, Lowell, and Emerson.[16]

Other Midwest cities with black enclaves offer examples of the same organized devotion to high culture. The *Detroit Plain-dealer*, an early African-American newspaper covering events of black life all over the Midwest, reported regularly on literary clubs in Ohio, Indiana, Wisconsin, and Kentucky. A December 1892 item reveals that the Literary Club of St. John's African Methodist Episcopal Church of Frankfort, Kentucky, attended a lecture on John Greenleaf Whittier and that all the members "expressed themselves in high praise for the classical treat." A month later, the paper reported that an entertainment by Toledo's Hawthorne Club included a sketch of Hawthorne by Dr. J. P. Haynes, a harp and guitar duet, and a piano solo. The Pierian Club of Grand Rapids, set up by a group of black women in 1926, offers a most direct and cogent example of a community practice that made it an excellent preparer for Federal Theater Project principles. In addition to lectures and recitals, it presented "dramatic plays in which the direction and acting has been done almost entirely by members." These and similar items covering some forty years confirm that black literary clubs and, we may add, theater troupes throughout the Midwest paid considerable attention to the poetic, fictional, and dramatic canon established by Europe's and America's intellectual leaders.[17]

The strategy of hammering out a black culture that conformed to models favored by the ruling strata also guided the work of individual black writers, artists, and musical performers. The black urban enclaves of Detroit and the Midwest counted among their small populations a fair number of people who were talented in writing, music, and the visual arts. Like the soloists and musicians cited above, many came from the entrepreneurial and professional core of the community. The work of these individual makers of black culture tended to follow, as their social group generally did, high culture standards, and they were supporters of the collective forms that aimed at the same strategy of imitation.

In Detroit, one of the most prolific writers was D. Augustus Straker.[18] He belonged to the most elevated stratum of black enclave life, and his work reveals the complexity of the strategy of high culture imitation, a double-sidedeness that should not be dismissed. Straker devoted his literary endeavors to history and social analysis dealing with the condition of blacks in the Caribbean and the American South. He advocated self-determination rather than annexation by the U. S. In writing about the American South, he confronted the vicious slandering of black character by racist politicians and scholars. His *Reflections on the Life and Times of Toussaint L'Ouverture, the Negro Haytien* (1886) is a particularly bold piece of writing. Issued during the period of post-Reconstruction violence and aggressively remodelled racism, it presents a sympathetic model of black revolution.[19] Straker's language is as formal in the use of standard English dialect as any believer in the superiority of dominant forms could desire. Its tone is always reasonable, and his compositional structure adheres to the rhetorical and propositional logic of the ruling culture of modern Europe and the United States.[20]

But the implications of this book dissent from the racist foundation of that culture. Straker argued that blacks had no desire to overthrow the American system, since its principles, providing they were applied equally and justly to everyone, could only lead to black freedom and improvement. However, he also contended that the refusal to apply these principles equally raised the specter of black subversion. Neither Straker's style nor his political content can, therefore, be regarded simply as capitulation, for his strategy of imitation was used as an instrument to further the struggle for black rights. The strategy in general was an attempt to prove the humanness of blacks in terms of elite culture, but it was offered in battle for full, dignified, equal participation in American life.

The strategy of imitation is also found among black writers not connected to the region's entrenched black families. We have the example of Charles Henry Shoeman, an Ann Arbor writer whose grandfather was a freed black slave.[21] According to a *Detroit News-Tribune* review of his *A Dream and Other Poems* (1899), Shoeman came to Ann Arbor in 1894 from his birthplace, Goshen, Indiana. The year this work was published, he was twenty-three, attending high school full-time, and supporting himself by working in a barber shop "during his spare hours."[22] Shoeman's preface to the volume informs his readers that the poems are intended to be part of the struggle to destroy the obstacles imposed on American blacks by slavery and racism. But struggle is a minor, oblique theme of these verses. The poems are generally traditional in form. They present an equal balance between narrative and lyric modes, and the lyric verses evoke rather conventional moods. Several are cast in southern black dialect. In these poems the metrical patterns are free-spirited—unlike those in standard English, which are stiff and overformal—and the vocabulary and flow of utterances fresher and more natural. But even these dialect poems fall within the boundaries of acceptable local color uses of language and motif. The struggle that shows through in these and in Shoeman's standard language verse is implied rather than explicitly engaged, and consistent with the forms that are a deliberate part of the strategy of imitation.[23]

The strategy of imitation is not profoundly understood if it is viewed as surrender and compliance. It challenged the unscientific and racist concept of innate inferiority, forcing the dominant culture into a corner, where hegemony either applied its own standards of acceptance without discrimination or acted in exposed hypocrisy. Its shortcomings were uncritical acceptance of elite culture as a true test of cultural value and an uncritical assumption that skilled conformance could refute deliberately sponsored sterotypes and misguided attitudes and overcome black oppression.

127

The Strategy of Resistance

The federal arts projects had more resources to draw on for audience participation and inspiration down below from the beat of a completely different strategy among African Americans—one that discovered, as it marched along, its own forms and content in the experience and language of the black American masses. This is the underground text, from the earliest experiences of Africans in colonial America to the present, of whatever directions oratory, oral exchange, song, writing, and art take in the black enclaves of the United States.[24] Its presence and impact on Midwest black enclaves during antebellum years and after are hidden affairs to later eyes because its lifelines are essentially oral and informal; since they were not organized in stabilized institutional structures, they are not very well documented.

Demographics plays an important part also in the apparent absence of innovating culture. Before the defeat of Reconstruction, the numbers of blacks whose imaginations moved and expressed themselves primarily to the beat of African-American folk experience were too small in the urban centers of the upper Midwest to be a reckoned or openly acknowledged cultural force. Afterward, those African Americans who made up the folk masses of the black population began their long and ever accelerating sweep northward, and from that point on, that indigenous beat of culture of which they were the prime creators and transmitters became more audible and visible. With more massive migrations from the South, triggered at first by World War I but continuing during the 1920s and 1930s, the dominating entrepreneurial-artisan-professional segment of the black enclaves of Detroit and Michigan was reduced to a minority of the black population, and its cultural influence was radically diminished.[25] From then on, the working-class component of the enclaves greatly outnumbered all other components.[26] As a consequence, a significant proletarian dimension took hold in Midwestern black culture, but with roots still deeply embedded in the soil of African-American folk experience. This beat of culture, based on the rhythms of folk and proletarian lifeways, became a more open, publicly influential strategy of black imaginative life.[27] Before then, although it was present in all black culture, wherever the strategy of imitation held sway it led an underground life, mediating the representations modeled after the elite forms of Europe and the United States, but as a consequence of its underground status also mediating its own voice.

The prime example of this phenomenon is the church, the oldest, most stable, most centrally organized institution of the North's black elite. Before the organized black church came into its own in the late 1820s as a powerful institution influencing black life, the strategy of innovation was creating

128

religious culture out of southern black folk life. It invented a politically subversive, inspirational music and evangelical rite that fused three elements: the historical narrative of freedom, the Christian narrative of redemption, and the surviving sounds and rhythms of African song and dance as they were remembered in transmission from slave generation to slave generation.[28] These new forms of black folk imagination expressed themselves most frequently in the communal camp meetings set up in the South by Methodists and Baptists to renew religious fervor. In those early years, the Methodist and Baptist denominations, particularly in their evangelical enterprises, were open to all and opposed to human bondage. Hence blacks felt welcome at camp meetings and free to express themselves in their own terms. The new evangelical rite conducted by the black congregants at camp meetings combined the freedom and redemption narratives in the style of exhortation and chant, a framework of performance where a leader or preacher deliberately stimulates the assembled crowd to respond with spontaneous, fervent shouts, declamations of torment, affirmations of released spirit, and joyful predictions of glory to come. Both new forms reflected political subversion and promised deliverance; they also preserved, in the innovation, something of West African sacred conceptions that had continued to survive in the slave diaspora.[29] This music and evangelical rite became the spiritual soul of sermonizing in the formally established black churches that assumed responsibility for the African-American community's religious experience from the 1820s on. But behind the scenes black churches replaced camp meetings and plantation gatherings as the dominant venue of religious expression among blacks, modeling their institutional structures according to the strategy of imitation.[30]

The first independent black churches were Baptist and Methodist, with the Baptist far in the lead. By the end of the first decade of the nineteenth century, the egalitarian and oppositional tendencies that motivated Baptist and Methodist recruitment of blacks in the South disappeared after slave masters and white bigots forced them to abandon integrated church assemblies. The spiritual views and practices of these denominations, their sense of closeness to the world of spirit, their notion of sudden conversion, and their religious ecstasy still resonated with the spiritual views that African Americans retained from their West African predecessors.[31]

Detroit's first black church was established in 1837, when, as a consequence of segregated practices, a small group of black Baptists split with the First Baptist Church to set up its own house of prayer.[32] Named the Second Baptist Church, it continues to exist. The honor of being Detroit's largest black congregation during the last half of the nineteenth century and the first decades of the twentieth belongs to the second black church organized there, the African Methodist Episcopal (AME) Church, whose doors opened in 1839 under the name Colored Methodist Society. Detroit's chief families led in organizing both of these congregations. A third black church, St. Matthews Protestant Episcopal Mission, appeared on the scene in 1846. St. Matthews lasted only until 1864, but it attracted several of the most established black families.[33] Although the AME presumably belonged to a more sedate tradition of evangelical service, the Second Baptist Church also conducted services according to acceptable standards of religious dignity. Their models were the more muted evangelicisms of the settled white Baptist and Methodist congregations, not the unbridled religious zeal of plantation and camp meetings.

The cultural forms created by folk imagination were, nevertheless, irrepressible. The sermons preached at the Second Baptist Church of Detroit after World War II are our resource, following the back construction procedures familiar to geology and paleontology in their quest for the deep time of the past.[34] Tapes of these sermons show that while they follow a highly patterned and dignified routine, they are driven by an extemporaneous impulse that engaged the assembled parish members in the kind of fervent, heartfelt response we associate with camp meeting evangelicism. What we discover in these sermons is a deeply implanted folk tendency toward performance. They begin with a soft-spoken, undramatic telling of a story, usually drawn from the Bible. The story is an exemplum intended to illustrate the central narratives of the African-American church, freedom and redemption. As the telling proceeds, the preacher's style changes, and an emotive intensity emerges. The voice grows in power and reaches a crescendo of exhortation, repetition, near chant. The congregants begin to share in the performance with murmurs of assent, which grow louder, more widespread, more stirring. Then the preacher's voice drops off to a near-whisper, a dramatic technique that brings the assembled parishioners back to concentrated focus. This process of performed storytelling is repeated and repeated until the sermon is concluded and the congregation, or some part of it, files past the preacher.

The sermon preached by Reverend A. A. Banks on February 13, 1955, is typical.[35] Reverend Banks opens his story quietly, almost in monotone, describing Jesus' passage through Samaria to Jacob's Well. The minister remarks that the Hebrews would not associate with the Samarians because their ways were impure—an analogy for the social and political relationships of whites and blacks. Jesus deliberately passed through Samaria to reach his goal and thereby revolutionized social relationships, destroyed racial barriers, the Reverend Banks tells the congregation in a voice whose dramatic intensity rises as he speaks. "A man ought to be free to navigate anywhere in the city." Here is the historical narrative of liberation. But the minister also makes the story an analogy for the deepest and broadest religious commitment, noting that Jesus undertook the journey to Jacob's Well as a pilgrimage of spiritual renewal. If the Samarians were excluded from this quest, as they would be if Jesus had gone around rather than through Samaria, the mission, in Reverend Banks's interpretation, would fail. Fighting for social and political freedom by confronting the issue directly is necessary, Reverend Banks intones. But he also asks, reaching the sermon's highest pitch of emotive oratory, whether such historical freedom is meaningful if it is unaccompanied by the spiritual redemption that comes with crossing over the barriers that cut us off from personal and public religious commitment.

As the story of these two narratives unfolds, one notices in the background of the taped sermon the increasing participation of the assembled parishioners. The event takes on the aura of a performance not by a single voice but by many. The response of the church members appears to be spontaneous but not unexpected. The sermon becomes an antiphony between narrating minister and choric audience. The audience voices disapproval when the minister proposes historical and religious shortcomings and approval when he charts the positive actions and meanings of the story. Both responses are uttered in language drawn either from biblical sources or everyday speech. At first the response is subdued and localized among the parishioners. As the sermon proceeds and the minister himself becomes more emotionally intense, the murmurings spread throughout the assembled churchgoers and increase in volume, but never get out of control. At the end of the sermon, Reverend Banks calls on the brothers and sisters to come up to the altar, shake his hand, praise the Lord, and be renewed in the faith that earthly and heavenly freedoms are only achievable together. Once the filing past the minister is underway, we hear the choir in a hymn, which sometimes edges toward the rhythms of jazz or free spiritual.

The sermon I have described demonstrates how the strategy of imitation presides over the decorum of organized church behavior. It further illustrates how underground proletarian-folk culture inexorably tenses formal ceremony. It shows as well the degree to which performance infiltrated the life-ways of the black enclaves, precisely what the FTP believed it would find among the cultures that were marginal and debased.

But the grass-roots performance and narrative that the Federal Theater and Writers' projects theorized about and wanted to make the heart of practice could be found without much deep-time fancy digging among resettled southern black workers. Among them the strategy of innovation was a far more open matter. In the store-front churches that came to dominate the black enclaves and served the religious imagination of the new wave of resettlers that flooded into the Midwest from World War I on, performance had the uninhibited, fervent character of camp meetings. The accompanying music ran freely to the riffs, the flats and blued rhythms, and the celebratory releases of revivalism. The enormous increase of black working-class resettlers made indigenous formations of culture suffuse the black enclaves more openly outside the church also, in all the pathways of material life and daily custom. The popular forms of entertainments in dance clubs, theaters, the streets; in the night spots where jazz emerged as a dominant mode of music among blacks everywhere, but especially in Chicago and Detroit; in the folk tales, poems, songs, remedies, and general lore which continued to function in daily life—all are testimony to the widespread visibility of innovative, performance-oriented culture based on folk and proletarian creativity.[36]

With the mass influx of the 1910s, twenties, and thirties, black performance and narrative appear as well in institutional settings designed to serve the after-work needs of working-class blacks. Their ever increasing numbers pressured secular and religious organizations to take notice, primarily in terms of such social issues as employment, housing, and health care. The most significant work on these issues was done by Detroit's Urban League, established in 1916.[37]

Care for the cultural needs of resettling black sharecroppers, unskilled laborers, and factory workers ran neck and neck with social issues among the black communities' organized groups. By the mid-1920s old-line churches as well as the newer grass-roots ones, such as the Greater Shiloh Baptist Church, were deeply involved in providing the black population with dramatic and literary clubs.[38] Again the Urban League clearly outdistanced all the others. The split personality of its cultural aims and principles, riven by the strategies of imitation and innovation, is revealed in a League document issued in the mid-1920s. It begins with the premise that Detroit's cultural level is low because of its industrial character. It follows this up with the assertion that a college education is not enough to achieve the level of understanding and appreciation of values that equals culture. Above knowledge, culture requires a high degree "of good manners, of dress, of speech, of cleanliness and appreciation of those things that are noble." Exposure to the arts in all its forms is important, and to this end a variety of visual art, dramatic, and writing groups have been established for blacks. We note two things: that the goal to be achieved is a high culture refinement, and that the effort is directed at raising the cultural level of that segment of the black enclaves who presumably lack the necessary manners, dress codes, speech patterns, and sensitivity to noble things. The service aspect inscribed in this document is a response from the creative side to the pressure of folk-proletarian resettlers, even if the goal is to meet the standards of hegemonic Euro-American culture. The document reports that the members of the art group are not imitating the white world but delineating a distinctive "Negro character." Members of the dramatic groups are not performing plays written by others, but writing and staging material from their own lives. The members of the writers' club are similarly chronicling "those things that they observe."[39]

This document of dual personality undergirded all the cultural projects which made the League the chief player in this work. In 1925 it established the Pen and Palette Art Club, whose membership included disadvantaged young people.[40] The bedrock of its work was weekly instruction in drawing under the critical eye of local professionals, and the capstone of its program was an annual exhibition of its members' work, beginning with a display in 1926 and continuing every year through the 1930s.[41] Its history features two points of interest to the two strategies we have been examining. While it was intended, along with the other cultural projects of the League, to serve the needs of the general community, and while several of the drawings and paintings dealt with the ordinary life of blacks, as it began to achieve a reputation for talented work it became somewhat more interested in prestige than in art for the people. In May of 1928, John C. Dancy, the director of the League, prophesied "that in one year the Club will occupy the most exalted place among Clubs in this country. . . . That is why we can now cut out all driftwood and hold only those who manifest interest in the Art." The second feature is the constant attention of the director to enlisting a variety of notables in the affairs of the club, such as curators from the Detroit Institute of Arts, the leaders of the Scarab Club—a local association of accomplished artists—and Edsel Ford.[42]

Soon after the founding of the Pen and Palette Club, the League added a music school and, what is central to this study, a dramatic club and a writers' group.[43] The dramatic program had wide appeal, attracting to its ranks fairly substantial numbers. For example, in 1929 an average of 110 men and women participated in its work. By 1931 the figure had gone up to 365. In the same year, several hundred children attended dramatic classes.[44] The importance of this last figure for the kind of work the Federal Theater Project intended to do is that formal theater experience had reached not only the adult world but also an audience for the future. The character of the adult Dramatic Club had taken shape in 1930. Dancy described it in September of that year as a performing group that "specializes in Negro Folk plays."[45] The list of plays put on in 1930—*Sugar Cane, God's Trombone, Simon the Cyrenian, Death Dance*, and *Broken Banjo*—confirms that description, although it also shows that Dancy's use of the term "folk" is a loose one. The club performed these mostly one-act plays before black and white audiences at various places around the city: at the YMHA, the YMCA, Harper Hospital Training School, a community center, before the PTA, the Junior League, and students at public schools in and just outside Detroit. These performances were generally well received: the assistant director of research of the Detroit Public Schools expressed his appreciation for the chance to see the plays and noted that they were "exceedingly skillful performance[s]"; a YWHA recreation worker, Sarah Hillel, was equally impressed by the high merit of the series.[46]

These same one-act plays triggered a different response from the Willing Workers Society, a black women's church group engaged in community service work. In a letter to Dancy, the members objected that the plays offered "nothing complimentary nor uplifting to our race." "We feel we have progressed so far in our culture and education," they argued, "that we can afford to forget and erase the vulgar and uneducated elements from our race, especially that part which we present to the other group."[47] This response illustrates the clash between the high culture strategy and the folk-proletarian strategy within the black enclaves. Dancy replied that he had "not the slightest intention of stopping these productions," asserting that the plays are "representative of the best material possible of our Negro Folk Life." His defense of the players was based on both the imitative and the innovative strategies. Six of the nine players are college graduates, as refined as anyone in the Willing Workers, he noted, and do not regret being black. "They are not ashamed to present plays of Negro life."[48]

The Lucy Thurman Branch of the YMCA was another active venue. In May 1935 it presented a version of *Hamlet*, described by the *Tribune Independent*, a Detroit black newspaper, as a combination of "song, dance, and drama." The actors included a young New York City composer, Arnold Johns, in the part of Hamlet, and Robert Hayden, who had previously appeared, the *Tribune* informed readers, in a student production at Wayne College of Eugene O'Neill's *The Emperor Jones*.[49] A version of *Hamlet* with song, dance, and drama performed by local actors is another case of black theatrical ambience that preceded and boded well for the FTP's own experiments with classical fare. *The Swing Mikado* produced by the black section of the Chicago FTP is among the most famous of such experiments.

In the same month as the *Hamlet* version, the Lucy Thurman Branch also hosted a production of *Samson* by a black group called the Personality Players of Detroit. This was one of several black theater groups without specific institutional affiliations that appeared on the scene in those years. Another was the Metropolitan Theater Players, which began life in 1935 and continued to be active into the late 1930s under producer-director Willard Leon Gardner, a local playwright whose dramas included *Ethiopia Had a King* and *Booker T. Washington*.[50] Also active during these years, the Paul Robeson Players often staged work at the Second Baptist Church as well as the Detroit Institute of Arts. This troupe included musical excerpts from Shakespeare and Steven Vincent Benet along with readings and songs from black writing.

134

The theatrical experience of the black community was stimulated by other means as well. Nimrod Carney, a Robeson player, described a very interesting production in the 1930s of *Murder in the Cathedral*, for which the Ebenezer AME Church acted as host. St. Matthews Presbyterian Church is also cited for fostering theater in its halls.[51] In addition to providing space for the Robeson Players, the Second Baptist Church sponsored its own drama group, called the Red Circle. The driving force behind this group was Hayden, who acted as its director. A play of his about Harriet Tubman and the underground railroad, *Go Down Moses*, was produced under its auspices and presented at Cass High School in the fall of 1937 before a city-wide audience. An earlier version, *Let My People Go*, was directed by Hayden when he was a member of the Variety Hour Players. It was performed on a major Detroit radio station in 1936.[52] The Red Circle's outreach to high school students followed in the footsteps of the Urban League's drama group and is another example of how disenfranchised communities prepared the way for and reinforced the FTP's outreach work. Two other stimulants of black theater experience were the Nacerima Club, ("America" backwards), a black businessmen's group that sponsored plays among its activities, and Delta Sigma Theta, a black sorority which motivated black playwrights and productions through an annual competition known as the Jabberwock. The competition was open to all amateur theatrical groups in the city, but it drew a significantly large number of entries from black dramatists and production companies. The first staging of the winning entries was held in 1930, and the competition continued for more than a decade.

Aside from the much larger black enclave of Chicago, Detroit's African-American population was actively engaged in and exposed to more theater experience than any other black community in the Midwest. Enclaves elsewhere in the region kept in touch with Detroit's theatrical doings, and from this we learn of active black theater companies in other middle western cities. In northern Ohio, there are two examples: the Douglass Center Players in Toledo and the Gilpin Players in Cleveland. According to Otho Price, the president of the Douglass Players, Toledo presented black theater with "numerous difficulties" because of its size (presumably he has in mind the size of the black population). Yet it did manage to produce plays dealing with folk and religious themes.[53] The Gilpin Players of Cleveland also stressed the representation of black folk life. In 1931 this troupe produced the play *You Mus' Be Bo'n Ag'in* by Andrew Burris and in 1935 Harold Courlander's *Swamp Mud*. Its 1931 productions were deemed to be more finished than those of Detroit's Urban League players because it had "a settled place to rehearse and produce them." The Gilpin Players named their independently housed theater Karamu.[54] We shall have more to say about the group in the next chapter.

135

Closer to Detroit, in Ann Arbor and Flint, we find manifestations of black theatrical enterprise as well. The Ann Arbor experience is closely associated with the University of Michigan and a promising black dramatist, Doris Price, a graduate student in the play program run by Professor Kenneth Rowe, who later became a local consultant for the playwrighting department of the FTP. In 1932 the university's Department of English and Play Production presented three one-act plays written by Price. They were programmed under the heading "Three Negro Folk Plays" and staged by Detroit's Delta Sigma Theta. Rowe thought one of them, *The Eyes of the Old*, among the greatest one-act plays. Price continued to write dramatic pieces until her death in the late 1930s. *The Weakling*, which her brother Otho finished for her after she died, was produced at the 1941 Jabberwock.[55] The Flint case differs from the Ann Arbor one, not only because it was not academically based, but because proletarians influenced and participated in it. In May of 1931 a vaudeville show and dance, billed as "the biggest affair ever held in the City of Flint for colored people" was organized. Its prime movers were "colored factory workers."[56]

Literacy, Lyric, and Story

The non-dramatic literary experience of the black community in Detroit and Michigan during the 1920s and 1930s did not engender as emphatically as black theater a grass-roots energy that the FWP could tap without reserve. Written narrative and lyric beset us with even greater difficulties than those described in our discussion of Polish-American written culture. Because black communities were (and still are) more ruthlessly marginalized and more extensively and intensively oppressed, the information at our disposal about non-dramatic literature is scarcer by far than in the other immigrant groups I have dealt with.

The few clues we have about African-American literacy and reading habits are helpful but difficult to evaluate. A 1926 survey of Detroit's African Americans examined the issues of schooling distribution, the incidence of newspaper reading, and the size of home libraries. Of the 911 people surveyed about formal education, 81 reported no schooling, 100 had three years or less, 315 between four to six years, 242 from seven to nine years, and 119 from ten to twelve years. Thirty-four respondents had attended college (it is not clear how many had graduated), thirteen professional school, eight trade school, and nine religious school. Sixty-one individuals replied that they could not read and sixty-two that they could not write. If we generalize from this sampling to the entire black population, the schooling and literacy portrait is not nearly as limited as one might imagine. But the sampling is rather small, and the study tells us nothing about how representative it was or if it covered all of Detroit's black enclaves.[57]

The study surveyed one thousand families about their newspaper reading. Although this is a larger sampling, again we do not know how representative it is. But if we generalize from it, we again get a portrait of fairly substantial literacy among Detroit's black population. Of the thousand families questioned, nine did not respond and 105 read no newspapers. Six hundred ninety-five read one newspaper, 168 read two, and 23 read three.[58]

One thousand families were also surveyed about their home libraries. The same families? The study does not say, and again we cannot evaluate the quality of the cross-section. Moreover, our ability to generalize from this sampling is hampered by the number of families, 370, whose response is listed under the category "Not Given" and another seventeen listed under "Unknown"—together nearly thirty-nine percent of the total. The number of families reporting between one hundred to one thousand books in their personal libraries comes to 69, two of which had holdings between five hundred and a thousand. Those families having anywhere from above five to one hundred books at home number 338. The balance, two hundred families, listed one, two, and five books of their own.[59] The study also reports that church libraries and reading rooms were used extensively and that libraries in all the black neighborhoods were well attended.[60] These fragments of information suggest that a fair part of the African-American population found reading something necessary to their lives. What we cannot say is how much of their reading was devoted to narrative, lyric, or other genres.

Newspaper material offers some idea of narrative and lyric expression, although not a very precise one. While the black community supported several newspapers from the 1880s on, seldom was it able to maintain more than one at a time.[61] In the 1920s and 1930s, the single newspaper of Detroit's black enclaves was *The Tribune Independent*, sometimes called *The Detroit Tribune*. The poems and stories published quite regularly in its columns, usually by local or regional black writers, are fairly limited in number, but a sampling from the early 1930s shows varied themes: some deal with love or religious faith, but most focus on the issues of race and economic depression. One regular contributor, J. E. McCall, wrote poems which frequently combine religious, racial, and hard-time motifs. His 1933 ballad "Are You There?" transforms simple anger over the social and economic suffering defended by Christian sensibility into a very strong subversive message. The refrain "Are you there? Are you there?" is a rhetorical address to Christ. The central image for both Christ and the masses is crucifixion by those devoted to the creed of Mammon.[62] Not all the poems of this period have so sharp a political edge. One by John Edward Neely is a straightforward love poem, "Our Garden of Dreams," with no race motifs or allusions.[63] Some other poems by McCall from 1933—for example, "The Conjure Man" and "Hastings Street"—deal rather with local character or local color within the black urban setting, a form of the urban-industrial regionalism discussed in Chapter 2. We may also note that these local character and color poems make no attempt to capture local language patterns.[64] Another example from the *Tribune* is of interest for two reasons: it is one of Robert Hayden's earliest poems in print, and its key image is also found in other black verse of the period, including a poem by Richard Wright. Entitled "Hands," it catalogues various human limbs and the actions they have been made to perform: Simon the Cyrenian lifting the cross; Christ's hands nailed to the cross; Negro hands hardened by work; and lynchers' hands, cruel and trembling with hatred. The poem closes with a panegyric predicting the future:

> Negro hands
> Clenched, striking blow for blow,
> Shaping out of chaos
> and starless night,
> New destinies,
> New dreams. . . .[65]

The poem illustrates again how black journalism provided an outlet for black lyric expression and how hard times and racism led to a sense of a proletarianized black public creating a new social order of high vision.

In addition to local enclave journalism, other outlets encouraged nondramatic literary expression by Detroit and midwestern blacks. We have already mentioned the literary classes and workshops sponsored by several church denominations and community groups. In the 1920s the Bethel and St. Paul A. M. E. churches hosted literary societies as part of their adult educational programs.[66] The Baptist Center, a joint 1935 enterprise of white and black Baptists, conducted classes in reading, writing, and English among its other cultural activities.[67] For the twenties and thirties, the Urban League's memorandum on adult education in the Detroit enclaves lists five literary societies, including two of its own: the Sunshine Club, whose activities are described as social and literary, and the Young Men's Literary and Industrial Club, whose name suggests a reading and writing environment for working-class blacks.[68] Black teenagers found encouragement through black and white newspapers, school competitions in poetry and fiction, and teacher concern, as well as the writing classes organized by the churches, the YWCA, and the Urban League.

The little evidence we can assemble of oral storytelling and lyric expression in the Detroit area reveals that they are rooted in folkloric forms and language, unlike the formal conventionality and idiom of so much of the more learned written efforts. Some of the evidence comes from conservation efforts in Michigan and elsewhere in the Midwest by the region's Federal Writers' Project. The folklore gathering of these branches of the FWP, however, was not particularly thorough, especially in comparison with the conservation work of several branches in southern states. Other more extensive evidence is found in the work of Richard Dorson, a pioneer of folkloric scholarship.[69] Since his collecting and recording are post-World War II enterprises, we are forced to reconstruct the innovative strategies of the past from more recent signs. Our other source of information, the Wayne State Folklore Archives, is the most fragile of all; like the Dorson material, it requires us to speculate backward to the oral narrative and lyric culture of the 1920s and 1930s.

The material from the Archives generally falls into three categories: folk hymns or redemption songs; playful songs or verse, often of wry or mocking humor; and resistance verse. Many of the folk hymns are lead-line songs, where the preacher or choir director sings out one line and the congregation responds. In "If You Live Right," the lead opens with "If you live right" and the congregation follows with "Heaven belongs to you." Subsequently the lead line changes, but the response remains the same—Lead: "Treat everybody right," Congregation: "Heaven belongs to you"; Lead: "Treat your neighbor right," Congregation: "Heaven belongs to you." The worldliness of the prescribed code of behavior is obvious; its unspoken denial of redemption for oppressor and racist belongs to the trickster tradition of vernacular or folk idiom. There are several such signifying hymns in the Wayne Archives, not only of the lead-line form, but also of the kind sung by the assembly as unled chorus. The informants who contributed them to the collection report their origins outside the Midwest and Michigan, usually the South, but recall their use in the Midwest in the 1920s and 1930s. Because they were used in church, and probably most often in the more newly established ones that served the black tenant farmers and proletarians who had migrated from the South in the first third of the twentieth century, it can be said with some confidence that the lead-line and signifying forms of religious lyrical expression confirm the influence of folk idiom and models on imitative strategy and of the long tradition of performance in the everyday life of the black enclaves.[70]

What I call the playful songs and verse are also of southern origin. One example is "Lover's Good-Night." The informant recalled one stanza:

> Cotton fields white in de bright moonlight,
> Now kiss yo' gal' an' say "Good-night."

If she don't kiss you, jes go on 'way;
Hain't no need a-stayin' ontel nex' day.

Another example is "My Fiddle," whose unsounded overtone implies that joy and economic relief could still be cleverly sustained in the heart of oppression. Unfortunately, we cannot be at all sure that any particular playful song or verse had wide currency among Detroit's black population or elsewhere in the Midwest.[71] But given the variety of informants who contributed to this collection, one fair conclusion is that the memory of playful song and verse continued to be an important expressive force shaping the oral imaginative experience of African Americans in the Midwest.

The group I call resistance songs and verse are for the most part also wry, mocking, playful, and southern in origin. Most of those in the Wayne Folklore Archives go back to slave experience. Consider, for example, the first two stanzas of "Promises of Freedom":

My ole Mistiss promise me,
W'en she died, she'd set me free.
She lived so long dat 'er head got bal',
An she give out'n de notion of dyin' at all

My ole Mistiss say to me:
"Sambo, I'se gwine ter set you free."
But w'en dat head git slick an' bal',
De Lawd couldn't a' killed 'er wid a big green maul.

Another example, a work song with a clear theme of protest or resistance, could be from slavery days or the period when agricultural day-labor and sharecropping became the chief means of black exploitation. Its ironic intent is another case of signifying a tactic of deflection:

Oh, the work ain't hard,
the boss ain't mean,
but all I hate
dis cotton ain't clean.

The other stanzas are the same, except that the word "corn" or "field" takes the place of cotton to suit the appropriate situation.[72] Again, it is not clear how widespread any particular resistance song was among the Midwest population. But the newly arrived blacks of the 1910s, 1920s, and 1930s were only a step in time removed from the social and work conditions these songs highlight, and they might be expected to remember, if not any specific songs in the folklore collection, the oral tradition of resistance to which they belong. The language of these examples—quite overdrawn in representing southern black English—and the mocking and ironic register which often accompanies it are rooted in the strategy that took its cues and spirit in creating an indigenous African-American culture from black folk and black proletarian lives.

The evidence I have detailed here of black theater and of non-dramatic culture is a strong showing that the black communities of Detroit and Michigan in the mid-1930s managed to shape a relatively vibrant network of culture which parts of all the segments of the enclaves shared and contributed to. Although under far greater social and economic duress than the Polish, Finnish, and Jewish communities, like them, the black enclaves constructed audiences and creative energies out of folk/proletarian and elite cultural formations that were ripe fruit for the kind of grass-roots program at the heart of the Theater and Writers' projects. The cultures these publics shaped contained a hope and vision that these projects wanted very much to have their work share in.

8

Repertory and Political Theater in the Motown Outland

THE immigrant and black resettler communities described in the foregoing chapters are a diverse cross-section of Midwest publics—diverse in geographic origins, traditions, the magnitude of their resettling populations, and the history of their social and economic oppression—and are typical and representative of other predominantly working-class and lower middle-class resettling groups in the first third of the twentieth century. They are signals that the entire range of resettling groups, by and large ignored or rejected by dominant culture, constituted a favorable and supportive context for the aims of the federal arts projects.[1]

The Federal Theater Project in Michigan could also count on four other sources for trained stage people and audiences. One was the active and well-attended commercial theater that had a long-standing affair with Detroit. Second were the repertory and experimental theaters in the region. One of these had acquired a national reputation in the 1920s and early 1930s under the directorship of Jessie Bonstelle. A third source was university theater, particularly the academic programs, performing groups, and competitions associated with the University of Michigan. Finally, there was Detroit's left-wing theater, which during the 1930s performed at the Detroit Institute of Arts and before working-class audiences in union halls and shop locations.

The commercial theater in Michigan consisted almost exclusively of traveling companies bringing the usual Broadway fare to the outland circuit.[2] It drew the kind of people that commercial theater in New York attracted and cast them into the same role: passive observers or consumers of cultural products fabricated to make money. In this setting, the theatergoer was not exposed to the complex, dialectical engagements that the nation's

142

marginal publics experienced in the bosom of their communities and that the FTP and FWP believed to be the driving stimulants for audiences and creative spirit. The other sources—repertory, experimental, and left-wing local projects with varying degrees of stability—dedicated themselves to different ends. They represented, if not the same cultural dynamics and audiences as the immigrant and black publics, a number of creative advantages for the work of the FTP that went deeper than those afforded by the commercial theater's ready-made, consumer-oriented supporting base.

Repertory and Experiment

The project directed by Jessie Bonstelle was a training ground for performers and production staff. It was essentially a resident repertory company, recruiting its acting and production staffs from local pools of talent as well as from around the country. New York City provided the group with performers of established stage reputations for its lead parts. Accomplished stars—Katherine Cornell, Jessie Royce Landis, Melvyn Douglas, for example—committed themselves to the repertory enterprise for extended stays over part of a season, and sometimes for parts of more than one season. The production staff and most of the actors were on board for the entire season, and many remained with the group for several years.

Between 1910 and 1924, Bonstelle managed a stock company which operated out of Detroit's Garrick Theatre, a venue that Broadway touring companies had first call on. In 1924 the company moved to a site for its exclusive use, the former Temple Beth El, which had been remodeled as a theater and sold to a syndicate headed by a devoted patron of Bonstelle.[3] From that point on until 1928, the company and the building it occupied were known as the Bonstelle Playhouse. In the fall of 1928, Bonstelle worked out an arrangement with Detroit's political and civic leaders to make the company the unofficial but publicly acknowledged theater of the Detroit metropolitan area; the company became known as the Detroit Civic Theater. The depression, which began in 1929, and the growing popularity of low-priced cinema placed the group in great financial jeopardy. It managed to scrape by during these years, however, with offerings that reflected its past adventuresomeness and excellence. The company that Bonstelle had guided successfully for nearly eight years of thriving and trying times at its own site succumbed less than two years after her death on October 14, 1932.

Three features of Bonstelle's resident-theater work would have been important to the FTP. As a resident company, it trained performers and stage personnel, many of whom were still in the region in the 1930s. Several of these later joined the FTP in Detroit, either as part of the allowed staff not qualified for relief or as part of the staff in need of relief. They constituted a head start of trained people familiar with a resident setup, a great help to those in the Theater Project with less experience in performance, production, and the demands of resident structures. But some of the Bonstelle people also turned out to be a headache, because they had star pretensions which were incompatible with the FTP's cooperative approach.

The second feature, even more important than the group's professionalism, was its civic character. By 1928 Bonstelle had developed a plan for a permanent theater "financed, owned and operated by and for the people of Detroit."[4] Another specific civic aim was to give the public "the best of spoken drama . . . at the lowest possible prices."[5] "The best" meant including contemporary popular drama of high excellence in the repertoire, although the emphasis was on the classics and Shakespeare; the plan also made acquainting "the younger generation with the finest of the world's dramatic literature" a particular quest.[6] The "lowest possible prices" meant admission rates "within the reach of all." The company's pricing schedule, $1.50 and $1.00, proved this to be no idle abstraction. Purchasing a book of ten tickets reduced the cost of the first tier to $1.25 and the second to 90 cents, and further discounts were offered to annual subscribers.[7] Moreover, each summer from 1928 to 1932, the company presented a free, open-air production of *A Midsummer Night's Dream* on Detroit's Belle Isle. The Detroit Syphony Orchestra performed Felix Mendelssohn's incidental music to the play as background. Each year thousands attended (over 75,000 in July 1928), apparently greatly delighted by the spectacular union of the two art forms. In 1931 Bonstelle noted that the Belle Isle production had grown from a festival drawing mostly Detroiters into one attracting a statewide audience, and the company had arranged discounted weekend fares with railroad and bus companies to accommodate residents from beyond the metropolitan area.[8] Such free outdoor performances of Shakespeare before large and enthusiastic audiences became a staple of the FTP's Caravan Theater units across the country. The point is not that the FTP took its lead from Bonstelle, but that in Detroit, grass-roots audiences had already been prepared by the Bonstelle Company for outdoor Shakespeare when the WPA arts projects appeared on the scene.

A second bold approach to production by the Bonstelle group was Shakespeare in another form. In March of 1926, when the company was known as the Bonstelle Playhouse, it performed *Romeo and Juliet* in modern dress; one headline among the local reviews read: "Juliet in Flappermood." In May of the following year, it tackled a modern-dress production of *Hamlet*. The twist to this staging is that half the performances were done in contemporary clothes and half in period costume.[9] The dates for these productions show that the Bonstelle group was among the earliest to explore modern-dress possibilities for Shakespeare. Although there were apparently two modern-dress *Hamlets* staged in New York in 1925, the Bonstelle was not very far behind.[10] Orson Welles was a comparative latecomer, although a politically daring one, when his Mercury Theater did *Julius Caesar* in fascist uniform in 1937. Like outdoor performance, modern-dress adaptation provided a ready-at-hand audience in the Detroit region that could appreciate an experimental approach to the arts.

A different aspect of the company's civic character touches on still other aims close to the heart of the WPA projects, dissemination of the arts in the form of service and education. Among the projects the Bonstelle conducted in its theater building were drama classes, a dance school, and a music school for local citizens, with special attention to young people. It also planned to tour hospitals, orphanages, and public schools as part of its community service to educate and entertain the young, the orphaned, and those physically incapacitated.[11]

The third feature of the Bonstelle group important to the FTP was also linked to its civic concept: the relationship between audience and company. Even before 1928, when her troupe became the city's unofficial but premier theatrical institution, Bonstelle had been trying to involve her audiences in the company's work. One means was to ask those attending performances to help select plays for future presentation by marking their preferences among a list of choices presented to them. Another mechanism became known as the "Bonstelle Cross": at the close of each season, company members and audience crossed over the footlights to mingle with each other, the purpose being to promote a more intimate connection between the two.[12] Subscription was a third form of engaging the audience. Before 1928 a Bonstelle subscription meant a paid-in-advance ticket for a season's series of plays.[13] When the company became the Detroit Civic Theater, the plan was to recruit 50,000 one-dollar per year subscribers to fund the group's activities. In addition, an individual contribution of $1,000 or $500 would gain one the title of "Founder" or "Sustaining Member." But the heart of the plan was to win a mass public to support the company. A company play-bill for the 1929 season records 30,000 one-dollar subscribers, surely a show of mass support.[14] These promotional methods indicate that the company's conception of encouraging audience involvement did not go very deep. It comes nowhere close to the profound involvement aimed at by the FTP. Nonetheless these methods fostered some sort of reciprocal relationship, no matter how superficial, between audience and theater, thus easing the FTP's task of interacting with audiences more deeply.

By 1928 the Bonstelle company saw itself in the vanguard of a wide range of individuals and groups across the country that made up what it called the "developing Civic Theatre movement." Letters of encouragement and request for information about the Detroit Civic Theater from around the nation indicated that the movement included not only supporters in the theatrical world, but also churches, societies, clubs, organizations, and municipal governments. Eight city governments wrote asking for the plan being implemented in Detroit, and two sent representatives to interview Jessie Bonstelle. The hope of all was that the movement would eventually produce a national theater like the Moscow Art Theater or the *Comédie Française*. Hence, Bonstelle said, "many eyes are turned toward Detroit and . . . many drama lovers are eagerly awaiting the commencement of the new theatrical season, which will put the plans of the Civic Theatre into operation."[15] Bonstelle's civic theater and the dream of a national theater that it evoked contributed a great deal in the way of concept and a base of support for the coast-to-coast confederation achieved by the Federal Theater Project seven years later.

Throughout the 1920s and early 1930s, a number of other resident-repertory theaters composed of local people—many with some theatrical training and experience—appeared in Detroit, and almost all had some tendency toward civic principles. Although many of these resident groups came and went as enthusiasm and attendance dwindled and deficits grew, several persisted. The Little Theater, with classes in various stage specialities and a school for young people, began its work around 1917; it repeatedly fell on hard times, but survived intermittently until 1931. The Drama League of Detroit, connected to other leagues elsewhere in the country, originated in the winter of 1914 and appeared for the last time in 1929. Another company with an irregular record was formed in 1924, abandoned its activities in 1927, then reopened in an old church in 1928 under the name Detroit Playhouse. In the fall of 1929 it assumed the mantle of the recently closed-down Provincetown Players, particularly as a venue for new American playwrights, and continued to produce plays until 1933.[16]

The academic world also enlivened the little theater and experimental scene, and it too proved to have a bearing on the federal projects. In Detroit itself, Wayne University maintained an extremely active theater program. It included training in stage performance and production and provided an opportunity for both classical and experimental works. The University of Michigan in Ann Arbor supported a vigorous playwriting curriculum in the 1930s under the instructorship of Kenneth Rowe. Among his students were several men and women who became well-known dramatists, poets, and novelists. Some of them became involved in different capacities with the Federal Theater Project or the Federal Writers' Project. Arthur Miller, who wrote his earliest adult plays under Rowe's tutelage, is the most famous. Norman Rosten made a name for himself as a writer of radio plays, which in the 1940s attracted an enormous national audience. Not so well-known, but nevertheless considerable talents, were Kimon Friar and two African-

146

American women, Elsie Roxborough and Doris Price. Friar, who later translated Nikos Kazantzakis's *Zorba, the Greek* into English, worked for some time with Detroit's Federal Theater Project. We have already noted how highly Rowe esteemed Price's three experimental dramas about black folklife. Robert Hayden, who worked for several years with the Federal Writers' Project in Detroit and who preferred to continue with his poetry rather than his prose or drama, wrote the play *Go Down Moses* while studying with Rowe. Others in the university's theater program were Harvey Swados and Betty Smith. While at Michigan Smith wrote a three-act comedy called *Francie Nolan*, a forerunner of her novel *A Tree Grows in Brooklyn*.[17]

Left-Wing Stage: Revolutionary and Liberal

Left-wing theater in the Midwest represents the most important source of grass-roots audience and inspiration for the aims of the Federal Theater Project. It offered an option to audiences excluded by the offerings and high prices of commercial theater, and went to them for dramatic material and attendance with a directness of approach that characterized none of the other alternatives. Moreover, many of its theatrical experiments were direct antecedents of some of the FTP's boldest productions. Although left-wing theater in the United States goes back to the early twentieth century, its most active years began with the early 1930s. It appeared in a range of forms, from stationary theater to IWW soapbox skits—broadly caricaturing the evils of industrial capitalism—to single-time, topical stagings—as in the Paterson Strike Pageant of 1913. The rapid expansion of left-wing theater after 1930 derived from two factors: the dreadful slump that followed the 1929 Wall Street crash and the political energy of the left most closely associated with Marxism and the Communist Party.

Detroit witnessed this impact even in theater not designed to be exclusively political or centered on working-class experience. From 1929 to 1933, the Detroit Playhouse aspired to be the esthetic home for new American playwrights. In those four years, as the nation plunged more deeply into economic disaster, the Playhouse offered an increasing number of works dramatizing the plight of working men and women. These included a play by a former coal miner, Leo Pride, *The Underground Savage*, in the fall of 1931. The local reviewer disapproved of the play, because it was "in the curious modern tradition of violence and despair, showing you how a coal miner goes from bad to worse through strife, murder, and pillage and finally dies a chain-gang convict in the same coal mine where he used to swing a free citizen's pickaxe."[18] The reviewer recognized the ironic coincidence, but seems to have missed the deeper, implicit irony: the subversive analogy that convict and free coal miners are prisoners and victims in one form or another of the same brutal system. A year later, the company offered audiences *Precedent* by I. J. Golden, a play that dealt sympathetically with Tom Mooney, the labor leader convicted of bomb-throwing and jailed for life. The program for this production took pains to note that, however much a propaganda play, it was presented "in accordance with [the company's] policy of producing unusual works of merit." Merit alone seemed not enough to explain the nature of the drama, for the program also reasoned that, because newspaper publicity had so prejudiced the public attitude against the Mooney case, it might be "alleged that conditions did not favor a perfectly impartial trial."[19]

Hallie Flanagan greeted these leftist theater formations with enthusiasm in 1931 and 1932, three years before she was appointed national director of the Theater Project. She applauded the "Marlowesque madness" of founding a theater, without money behind it, that was frankly out to change the world. She also thrilled to the dramatic technique and style of these alternatives, which she described as direct, terse, hard-hitting, and machine-gun-like in phrasing and delivery, and the sharp typing in place of individualized analysis. "When we shall see, as we probably shall during the next year," she wrote, "their street plays and pageants, their performances on trucks, and on street corners, we shall doubtless find them crude, childish, and repetitious. Yet we must admit that here is a theatre which can afford to be supremely unconcerned with what we think of it."[20] Flanagan was prepared for this kind of theater by her study of public theater in the Soviet Union, research made possible by a Guggenheim Fellowship in 1926. She was right about the left-wing theater's early unconcern for the opinions of the middle-class, commercial theater, but premature in judgment about the long haul, for after 1935 left-wing theater paid considerable attention to those opinions.

In the early days of the Great Depression, among the key vehicles for working-class, revolutionary theater were the John Reed clubs. Ideologically they were allied to the radicalism of Marx, Engels, and Lenin, and organizationally to the Communist Party of the United States. The clubs were organized largely because party leaders and friendly intellectuals close to the magazine *New Masses* believed that the crisis of capitalist economy and the suffering it imposed on the masses had radicalized many middle-class artists and produced a flowering of working-class artists. The idea was to form a center where both groups could come together for the benefit of each other, the first to help sharpen skills, the second to impart direct experience of proletarian life. Equally important was to have a center where the talents of both groups could be readily organized to inspire political struggle. The clubs were set up to include artists in all fields—dance, literature, music, theater, the visual arts—and to inspire them with the kind of cultural adventures that Flanagan had observed in the Soviet Union.[21]

Almost all major American cities as well as many smaller ones spawned John Reed clubs. In the Midwest, Chicago, Cleveland, and Detroit were the most important centers. By the fall of 1931, the Chicago and Detroit clubs had already included theater groups among their other art activities. The Blue Blouse mobile company of Chicago was an associate unit of that city's John Reed Club. Essentially an agit-prop company, it took its name and theatrical spirit from the Moscow workers' drama movement founded in 1923 by the Soviet National Institute of Journalists. By April 1933, its busy schedule of street performances, as many as three a night, left no time to write new plays. Since the creation of plays about local class and political conflicts was a central principle not only of the John Reed groups but of most workers' theater companies, the Blue Blouse company called on young laborers and students to take on the job of composing new works for its repertoire out of their everyday experiences.[22] The drama group associated with Detroit's John Reed Club drew fire in 1934 precisely because it had not carried out that principle in the season on hand.[23] In the fall of 1932, the John Reed clubs of Cleveland and Milwaukee formed drama sections. The *Workers' Theatre* for September-October 1932 reports that Cleveland's John Reed Club had recently established a players' circle of youth and was rehearsing an agit-prop play, *Hands Off*, for outdoor performance. Later issues, describing conferences and performances of various Cleveland groups oriented toward working-class theater, indicate that the Cleveland Club also sponsored an adult production unit. The same issue cites a newly organized drama section for the John Reed Club of Milwaukee already in rehearsal on an agit-prop play, *I'll Tell You How to Vote*, for an election event to be held in October. By 1933, if not earlier, a John Reed Dram Group had become active in Youngstown, the steel-producing center of Ohio.[24]

The 1930s efforts at working-class theater are traceable, in fact, to the years before the Wall Street crash and the John Reed clubs. Their predecessors were centered in New York and were the offspring of established artists, such as John Dos Passos, John Howard Lawson, Em Jo Basshe, and Mike Gold. Neither of the two groups they set up, the New Playwrights and the Workers' Drama League, was long-lived. Three other worker theater formations of the pre-depression years had more staying power. In New York, the *Prolet-Buehne*, a German-language group fashioning itself on the *Volks-Buehne* in Germany, was at its beginning in 1925 a part of the German-American *Arbeiterbund*[25] In 1928 it broke with the *Arbeiterbund*, moving to the left under the directorship of John Bonn, a recent immigrant from Germany who had gained his stage ideas from Erwin Piscator and the mobile drama units associated with Germany's left-wing political parties.

Over the next few years, the *Prolet-Buehne* company became the supreme masters of mass chants and agit-prop plays performed with stylized gestures accompanied by rapid fire, declamatory cadences and speech deliveries. Bonn became the leading voice for a complete rupture with bourgeois theater. The aims and techniques of bourgeois theater, he argued, were designed for society's exploiters and could be of no dramatic value to the revolutionary needs of their victims.[26]

Equally important as a committed radical company was New York's Workers Laboratory Theater. Created in 1929 under the urging of some of the people associated with the failed Workers' Drama League, it started out as a workshop training center. It included shop workers and trade unionists as well as professionals with various degrees of theatrical experience, and continued its work well into the 1930s. In its early years it functioned on the principle of cooperation. The ideas of everyone, amateurs and professionals, were considered valuable to all aspects of production: directing, playwriting, and acting. More important, the idea of a division of theatrical labor according to the specialized skills of its personnel was rejected. For example, the company's playwriting committee served not only as an arena where plays might be critically discussed, but where they would be written and rewritten by the panel. It was, at least initially, the ideological counterpart in American drama to the *Prolet-Buehne*, rejecting the work and technical strategies of commercial and canonic theater as bourgeois and serviceable only to the exploiting classes. Hence the Workers Laboratory Theater saw itself as a pioneer in creating new forms for political drama. It was extremely significant in its active years for two reasons: in close association with the John Reed clubs, it led the way toward a national confederation of radical working-class theater groups and, even as it rejected bourgeois techniques and skills, it stressed the need for craftsmanship and careful production.[27]

Immigrant, foreign-language theaters were the third left-wing stage effort before 1929 with the power to stay alive. As my account of socialist and communist stage activities in the midwestern Finnish-American communities indicates, their centers were many and depended on the geographical location and culture of specific immigrant concentrations. In the Midwest, our primary concern, Chicago had several immigrant worker theaters: the Ukrainian Dramatic Society, the Artes Armenian Dramatic Club, the Jewish Workers Club, and a Scandinavian Blue Blouse troupe. In addition to the cited Red Finn stage and the Yiddish Hirsh Lekert group, Detroit's immigrant theaters included the Bulgarian Workers Dram Group, the Jewish Workers Dram Studio, and the *Arbeiter* Agit-Prop troupe.[28]

After the onset of the Great Depression, English-language workers theaters sprouted everywhere, especially in urban industrial areas. Their rapid proliferation led the Workers Laboratory Theater and the New York John Reed Club to urge the founding in late 1931 of the League of Workers Theaters (LOWT) and the journal *Workers Theatre*.[29] This magazine featured essays on techniques, innovations, and cooperative creative methods appropriate to the purposes of a left-wing theater; ran agit-prop scripts for use by all member groups; and kept member groups informed of each others' activities and the formation of new groups. By the following year, the Detroit and Chicago workers theaters felt the need to organize local councils affiliated with the LOWT. The Dramatic Council of Detroit held its first meeting in November 1932 with five companies in attendance—the John Reed Dram Group, the Jewish Workers Dram Studio, the Bulgarian Workers Dram Group, the *Arbeiter* Agit-Prop Troupe, and the Nature Friends Dram Group. In addition, by 1934 the Detroit radical community could boast of an active Film and Photo League. It was sufficiently well-organized and experienced to produce a one-reel film for the Macedonian Workers' Club and arrange for it to be shown elsewhere in Michigan and in Indiana, Ohio, Pennsylvania, and New York State as well.[30]

In Chicago, members of workers theater groups met in June 1932 to plan their part in that year's election campaigns. At the beginning of the next year, the various Chicago groups organized a Workers Theater Council to represent the Blue Blouse groups, the Dram Section of the Morris Winchevsky Club, the Ukrainian and Artes Armenian Dramatic Societies, the Chicago Workers Theater, the Jewish Workers Club, and the Chicago Laboratory Theater. At the conference empowering the council, the member groups decided to produce a mass pageant for the fiftieth anniversary of the death of Karl Marx. Two other groups appeared on the Chicago scene in 1934, the Hirsh Lekert Workers' Club and the Theater Collective of Chicago. Among the many problems the Theater Collective faced was the violent "hooliganism" of local bigots, who physically attacked its quarters because it had black and white members.[31]

Cleveland also teemed with left-wing theater. These included the Youth Branch of the International Workers' Order of 105th Street, a Workers' International Cultural Branch, a Jewish Drama Studio, and two John Reed groups: an adult project under the usual label, the Dram Group, and a young people's project sponsored by the John Reed Youth Branch of Kinsman Road. In March 1933 these groups set up their Dramatic Council and applied for membership in the LOWT. A YWCA Dram Group was also active at the same time, putting on some of the same playlets that other Cleveland groups performed, although it is not clear whether the YWCA group belonged to the Council.

One group whose experience could have been instructive to the Federal Theater Project in the Midwest, especially in Michigan and Indiana, was the all-black company called the Gilpin Players. Although not listed as a member of the national confederation, it had established close ties to other worker-oriented companies in Cleveland during the 1933–35 period. The experience of this group goes back to its founding in 1920. After a three-year apprenticeship of play reading from the canon of Euro-American drama, it began to produce plays about everyday African-American life in the language and folkways close to the articulations of the black masses. This move disgruntled its black middle-class audience. Like Detroit's Urban League, which faced the same kind of criticism and rejected it, the Gilpin Players refused to cave in to these complaints, although it meant the loss of its middle-class audience. The loss proved not to be fatal, for the group made two moves over the next few years that enabled it to win a larger, more engaged audience with different class and intellectual attributes. In 1926 it remodeled an abandoned pool hall into a permanent site and called it Karamu, the Swahili word for "place of feasting and enjoyment." Here it formed a very close relationship with the community, from which it drew a loyal following that came to see its performances and shared regularly in the work of acting, set building, and costuming. Later, with the onset of the depression, it added class-conscious plays to its folk repertoire, producing both kinds of drama from the viewpoint of making what it called "learning by theater" a living part of the community. The new plays in the repertoire added to its neighborhood support an audience of black and white workers and intellectuals from other parts of Cleveland.[32]

The close association maintained by Cleveland's workers theaters and the Gilpin Players is not a solitary case of friendly interaction between blacks and whites in midwestern left-wing theater. The 1930s witnessed a nationwide campaign among leftist theaters to combat the segregation that characterized companies and repertoire.[33] Like other efforts of left-wing theater, this campaign anticipated the federal arts projects' own efforts, mainly in New York and Chicago, to deal with obstacles to blacks in the arts.

Left-wing theater assaulted the barriers first by including plays dramatizing racist oppression and the need for unity between black and white workers struggling against social and economic exploitation. The productions of the Detroit theater group associated with the John Reed Club are typical for the Midwest. In the fall of 1934, for example, the club produced a play, *James Victory*, written by its writers group, about a black man's battle against a false rape charge. It also performed the mass chant "Scottsboro," conceived by the *Prolet-Buehne* of New York. Two years later, after all John Reed clubs had been dismantled, the company produced *Stevedore*, a play about the friendship and comradeliness that black and white dock workers forge out of labor strife.[34]

At the same time, a number of workers theaters assaulted theatrical segregation by integrating themselves. If plays dealing with black experience were to be a regular part of the repertoire, workers theaters had to include black performers. *Stevedore* required the Detroit company to recruit two black actors, Nimrod Carney and Robert Hayden. The company claimed this was the first time in Detroit's theater history that blacks and whites had performed together on stage.[35] Workers' groups in Chicago, Cleveland, Milwaukee, and the Rock Island-Moline-Davenport tri-cities complex also performed locally written plays about black and white workers and hence faced the same need.[36]

Audience was the last factor in the campaign to cleave barriers keeping blacks and whites apart in the theater. Some workers theater units specifically chose to locate where black and white communities adjoined each other and exercised considerable care in attracting blacks and whites to their productions.

The Workers Laboratory Theater of Chicago reveals this three-pronged attack clearly as well as how it fit into the major characterisics of left-wing theater: interaction with audience, the use of drama to intervene directly in issues of conflict, and the making of drama out of actual conflicts still unfolding—"living theater." Located on the border between two of Chicago's south side working-class ghettoes, one white and the other black, the Workers Laboratory Theater brought together a troupe of black and white actors and an audience from both sides of the line. For example, in March 1935 it presented *Eviction*, a play about a black family ordered from its flat for not being able to pay the rent. The Workers Laboratory Theater deliberately chose that work and that occasion because a neighborhood black family, active in left-wing political causes and housed directly across the street from its playhouse, was about to be evicted for the same reason. The company made a special effort to have Irish workers and blacks from their abutting ghettoes in the audience: although the Irish of that neighborhood had the reputation of being racist, they were themselves harried by some of the same problems plaguing blacks, such as rent delinquency and eviction. After the performance, the company engaged the audience in an animated exchange of experiences, underscoring how the blacks and whites in attendance suffered the same hardships depicted on stage and how they needed to oppose together the oppression of any one of them. An agreement grew out of this interaction that black and white members of the audience would unite in an action supporting the about-to-be-evicted black family. People packed the courthouse where the family, charged with disorderly conduct when they refused to comply with the eviction order, was being tried by the authorities.

This neighborhood event also became the occasion for activating the play-making principle advocated by workers theater: one of the Workers Laboratory members, a University of Chicago drama student, began to fashion out of these actual happenings, as they were occurring, a play for the company to stage. The article describing these activities bore the title "The Living Theatre" and lauded the drama student: "Writing into her play the sullen power of two hundred workers sitting in a courtroom for two days—the drama of class struggle ruthlessly outlined before the judge's bench—the excitement of personalities confronting each other over fundamental human values. Could there be a better school for playwrights than such a courtroom?"[37]

These examples demonstrate that left-wing theater in the Midwest had begun the kind of groundwork needed to establish audiences receptive to and sharing in the experiences of black and integrated theater. That receptivity and shared experience is another example among the many we have already offered of attitudes and contexts that were on hand at the end of 1935 when the FTP got the signal to organize. These examples also show that other theatrical concepts of the FTP—community support, cooperation in the theater's actual work, theater actively inserted into the life of the community, use of local events and material for drama—had become part of Midwest theatrical experience through the left-wing stage.

The Cleveland LOWT offers at least one case of left-wing theater, while in the heart of political struggle itself, making current events fare for the stage and the stage a direct inspiration for political action. This particular case is also an instance of going to rather than waiting for an audience, of mobile rather than stationary theater. In the summer of 1933, Ohio left-wing groups and labor unions organized a march to Columbus to pressure the state's capital for relief measures, and members of Cleveland's League of Workers Theaters joined the marching columns. At each stop-over town and city on the way, its members put on skits, fashioned out of actual events, that dramatized current working-class struggles. The skits apparently stimulated audiences to recount their own parts in such events, many of them impassioned stories of hostile police action. The LOWT performers responded to these outbursts with the suggestion that the audiences work up plays based on their encounters with police brutality.[38]

This is another example of what the workers theater groups everywhere called living theater. Such works were largely embryonic, playlets to be exact, but nevertheless drama as political tool fashioned out of current events. Left-wing theater in the United States adopted these dramatic innovations from Russian experiments, in the first years after the October Revolution, with theater as political education for working-class audiences. These overseas and imported innovations, both of which Flanagan and her colleagues in the Theater Project knew about, were the backdrop for their own more expanded and complex docudrama concept called the living newspaper. The FTP has been most widely applauded for this work that put the personally experienced issues of the depression into an imaginative form and had a political impact on audiences.[39] As director of the FTP, Flanagan had a collateral interest with left-wing theater in living theater, but also gained much from its forerunning experiments in that form.

Two other Midwest workers theater productions are worth mentioning in the context of living theater and living newspaper because they indicate how these informed the technical effects they employed. We have already referred to Golden's *Precedent*, the play about the Tom Mooney frame-up. The company that produced it, affiliated with Chicago's Workers Cultural Federation, wove into the author's script a technique it named "The Camera Voice." Written and assembled by its young playwright members, it interpolated commentary and photographs at key points of the drama to clarify "the class significance of this crime [the frame-up] and its relationship to the entire workers' movement."[40] One report of this Chicago version of *Precedent* calls "The Camera Voice" a new technique and implies that because the interpolations represented current conflicts, they established the present significance of the Mooney trial—itself belonging to the decade before. The Detroit group, while it was still connected to the John Reed Club, also mounted at least one play using techniques associated with living theater. In the 1934 season, it produced *Troops Are Marching*, a play about the harsh effects of World War I on workers, who vow to launch a revolutionary struggle against another outbreak of armed hostilities among the nation-states. Quite clearly a cautionary play about the 1930s international crisis and a didactic work calling for proletarian seizure of power to prevent war, it juxtaposes scenes in montage form, using quick blackouts instead of curtain drops to move from montage set to set. Moreover, it combined stylized rhythmic movement with realistic representation.[41]

The depth and reach of these Midwest workers theaters was substantial. The sheer number of such theaters around the nation (from twenty-eight in November 1931 to four hundred in twenty-eight cities by April 1934) suggests a steadily widening reach.[42] As we have seen, the Midwest contributed a good share to these numbers. We have also seen how the Gilpin Players established a rather profound relationship after 1926 with the people of its community and later began attracting an audience from outside those boundaries. We remember too that the Blue Blouses in Chicago cited so heavy a demand for their performances that they had little time to compose new work for themselves. The Minneapolis Labor Players, established in January 1935, reported performing before a monthly average of 2,500 people over a nine-month period, a truly astonishing record for a fledgling company.[43] By 1935 the Detroit group began performing on a regular basis at the Detroit Institute of Arts and continued to do so for more than two years, clearly a sign that it had reached a fairly large audience and, if the place of performance is any guide, one that had a diversified class character.[44]

As the numbers cited in the paragraph above indicate, 1934 was the year of greatest growth for left-wing theatrical groups. They were most numerous and reached their largest audiences in 1935. Circulation figures for *Workers Theatre*, published by the confederation representing the movement, corresponded in growth. In 1933 the confederation changed the name of its journal to *New Theatre*, one of the early signs of a more professional, more inclusive, and less proletarian approach to the stage. This shift in approach was entangled from the first in the aim of the New York Workers' Laboratory Theater to be not only an agitational and propagandistic theater, but a workshop to hone its members' playwriting and performance skills. The inclination toward greater professionalism did not mean at first a major retreat from proletarian plays with socialist themes designed to inspire action. Two years later, however, when the left had hammered out the united-front line for the period, the confederation and its member units all over the country retreated substantially from their original esthetic and political purposes.

A midwestern example of entangled aim is the Workers' Theater of Chicago. In March 1933 it set out "to establish a technically expert, stationary theatre."[45] This did not exclude mobile theater, the key vehicle of agitprop performance which penetrated into the heart of ghettoized, working-class neighborhoods, but it did mean a shift of emphasis. A few months after the announcement, the group had attracted several bourgeois theater people to help it improve technically. At the same time it worked on drawing them closer to the movement through having them study "theoretical books on the class struggle." The information about adding people with mainstream stage experience appeared in the Summer issue of *Workers Theatre*, and this change in the Chicago group's focus was reported with approval.[46] The next issue, that of September–October 1933, now renamed *New Theatre*, opened with an explanation of the revised title and called on left-wing theater in general to recruit experienced bourgeois theater people to workers revolutionnary theater.[47]

As class war and revolution lost their places on the agenda in favor of a united front, multi-class, people's coalition to prevent war and turn back fascism, the romance of left-wing theater with professionals from the commercial theater was accompanied with what the renamed theater units termed politically progressive bourgeois plays. By 1935 professionalist and liberalist views toward drama had conquered the left-wing stage. Even John

156

Bonn, who had been one of the leading voices against bourgeois theater, repudiated his former position. "New theater" had come to mean realism; performance in stationary theater; conventional professionalism; a return to the idea that progressive culture is universal; and the production of anti-fascist, anti-war plays, most frequently by established contemporary writers, in place of works depicting class struggle and revolutionary themes.[48]

Detroit's most enduring theater is a clear case of the process I have been describing. It began as the Dram Group of the city's John Reed Club with the aim of staging short agit-prop plays for workers. In 1934 it became the New Theater Union, combining in that name the change adopted by the LOWT magazine and by the former New York Workers Laboratory Theater, thereby launching its new policy of becoming more professional and performing indoors on a set stage.[49] It abandoned agit-prop for more conventional one-act and full-length plays, often from the inventory popularized by the Theater Union but also by other professional writers. In 1935 the New Theater Union began to present plays at the Detroit Institute of Arts, starting with George Sklar and Albert Maltz's anti-war *Peace on Earth*. The principles outlined by the group in the program for this production illustrate its broader, although still transitional, direction. The focus on plays about social conflict still prevailed, but conflict now applied to actions which affected not only the working class, but the less empowered sections of the middle class as well. This combination of affected classes constituted the new audience the company wanted to win to its theater, which it continued to regard as "based on the interests and hopes of the great mass of working people."[50] Its productions over the next two years, all at the DIA, included Clifford Odets's *Awake and Sing* and *Paradise Lost*, John Wexley's *They Shall Not Die*, Irwin Shaw's *Bury the Dead*, Paul Green's *Johnny Johnson*, and another Maltz play, *Black Pit*.[51] In the fall of 1936, it changed its name once again, this time to Contemporary Theater, which the group felt expressed its purpose more precisely: "the production of plays dealing with social themes . . . and cultural problems that confront the majority of people in our nation."[52] Except for a brief interlude when, in response to the sit-down strikes of 1937, it performed inside the Flint Chevrolet plant and at local union halls, the Contemporary Theater had transformed its political and esthetic character into united-front strategies.[53]

This sidetracking of audience relationships, living newspaper form, and mobile theater to mainstream social plays and stage conventions is important to our study for two reasons. First, it is an analogue of the transformations those projects went through themselves as they temporized with their aims, sometimes voluntarily but most often under duress. Second, it altered the political/esthetic thinking of workers theater personnel for the balance of the 1930s. Hence the many artists who participated in left-wing theater and art groups and later flocked to the federal arts projects in large numbers exerted a far milder and less bold influence on them than they might have if left-wing art aims had remained revolutionary. Nevertheless, as I have pointed out, left art practices of the pre-united-front period did have a strong impact on the Federal Theater Project, particularly in grassroots interplay, living docudrama, and itinerant programming.

Agit-Prop and Revolutionary Modernism

Agit-prop plays, which made up most itinerant fare, have had so bad a reputation and been so misunderstood as formal experiment, that I pause here for a moment to look at them more closely. They were shaped by techniques designed to engage audiences directly in the purposes of the context in which they appeared. Because of their topicality and style of presentation, they contained the germ of the more complex dramatic form, the living newspaper, developed by the FTP. They were generally performed outdoors on a narrow, raised platform, where leftist speakers made fiery addresses after the skits were over. In 1932 many of the skits were about the forthcoming national and local elections, the first presidential campaign since the start of the economic crisis and which included Socialist and Communist Party presidential candidates. They also dealt with other struggles, in support of strikes or against unemployment, racism, and the frequent suspension of civil rights and civil liberties for workers, blacks, and communists. These skits almost always included, in broad caricature, a portrayal of a capitalist who was the direct cause of the topical event being dramatized. The incidents preceding that event were themselves represented in extremely broad strokes. Hence, the themes were explicit and absolutely clear to everyone.

The empirical sketch presented above is a familiar one. It is what people think agit-prop is, if they think about agit-prop at all. And it is that, but only, to borrow an already borrowed term, as "thin description." A "thick description" of it has been neglected because the genre is dismissed as crudely constructed and filled with political clichés. Even early-day left-wing theater people, those who, presumably, would not have been disturbed by its political message, discounted it for its lack of subtlety and complexity, and its amateurism. But I think a "thick description" of agit-prop unveils the tradition of revolutionary modernism. Seeing its aims, methods, and styles in this way makes clearer the bearing agit-prop had on the FTP's aims and techniques.

One of the masks of modernism in theater and literature as well as in the visual arts is to consider politics irrelevant to what makes art specifically art. According to what is most usually considered the esthetics of modernism, to consider politics in terms of a work's thematic content or formal characteristics is to confuse art with other disciplines of discourse. Defining art in terms of a special essence, whose character is always formal and never political, denies that the representations of dissenting cultures and left-wing politics are meaningful to the enterprise of art. This attitude allows the politics of an empowered, dominant culture to be represented in the arts because it pretends not to be there. The politics of disempowered cultures wears its heart on its sleeve and is made to be an esthetic violation. On the evidence of most modernist texts, dominant culture's camouflaged form of politics in art makes it seemingly free of self-interest.

Formal objections to agit-prop also stem from the esthetics of realism and naturalism. The privilege given to realistic and naturalistic representation is related to nineteenth- and early twentieth-century humanism. Based on positivism and empiricism, the objections of this humanism to agit-prop generally embody a liberal political view, but one not at all alien to conservatism and reactionism. Once a united front against war and facism became the political golden calf of good bourgeoisie and laboring classes, those on the left argued against agit-prop from the formal principles and professional standards of realism and naturalism, providing that they represented a benign and progressive account of the human condition. To be kind about the matter, the left failed to recognize the bourgeois character of their objections. But it makes no sense to judge agit-prop by the tenets of elite modernism or of literary humanism. It belongs to a different genre than these, that of revolutionary modernism. It aimed always to make form and substance political and to dismantle the frame separating audience and performance, procedures that distinguished it from elite modernism. Nevertheless, its techniques and formal characteristics—scene changes, use of stage space, and style of delivery—cast aside realistic and naturalistic conventions in a way associated with modernism. But the modernism of agit-prop always saw its conceptual strategies, formal structures, and discourse as thoroughly political. For political reasons, it rejected both the literary decorum of realism and naturalism and the self-reflexive autonomy and opaque discourse of elite modernism. Agit-prop's modernism is parody and carnival. It is intentionally disrespectful and amateurish to mock the canonized forms, but also to make the message unmistakable and disrupt the line dividing message and performance from audience. Through broad caricatures, exaggerated actions, and parodic strategies, it sets out to simultaneously anger and amuse its audience. Its esthetic character needs to be judged according to these elements of discourse and formal strategy and, indeed, according to the effectiveness of its mockery and laughter: angering its audience to action while deflating its paralyzing acquiescence in dominant culture.

Neglected Publics

To identify agit-prop in this way—and this includes other forms of workers theater, particularly living theater and mass chant—is to relate it to the revolutionary modernism that emerged with such energy and distinction in the decade following the Bolshevik assumption of power in 1917. That modernism has been forgotten, partly because the intellectual world of Western capitalism lost knowledge of it and partly because the Communist leaders and intellectual bureaucracy of the Soviet Union rejected it in the next decade for realism and theatrical naturalism.[54] I have in mind the modernism of the 1920s represented by constructivism; the reinvention of opera bouffe along the carnivalesque and stylized lines in Maiakovski; the constructivist, broad expressionism of Meyerhold; the shorthand way of naming objects, events, and concepts ("agit-prop" and "dramburo," for example) in the spirit of rescuing modern language from the irrational residues of its past history and streamlining it for greater usefulness to twentieth-century industrial society; and the mobile political theater in plant and shop.

It is precisely this kind of modernism—with its sense of creating new forms, expressing new social ideas and relationships, establishing new audience connections—that Hallie Flanagan found so exciting in her Guggenheim research in the Soviet Union and admired so much in the early days of workers theater. But it was precisely this kind of theatrical innovation that lost out to the humanist art forms and attitudes that the united-front policy embraced. While my account delineates how left-wing theater in the Midwest and elsewhere generated audiences and approaches of enormous value to the work of the federal arts projects, it is also evident that united-front literature and theater reconditioned those audiences after 1934 to want standard, socially progressive art. Equally evident is that united-front arts policies disposed performers and practitioners who joined the federal art agencies to esthetic views that altered the influence they might have been inclined to exert had revolutionary modernism prevailed.

This is not to say that the aims the art projects began with were Marxist. But they were analogous to much that left-wing theater had made available to audiences in the Midwest through its practices. Their initial aims brought the Midwest projects, and the projects in other regions as well, into conflicts or misunderstandings with the regional bureaucrats in charge of the WPA before whom the projects often retreated. If nothing else, the influence of a politically-oriented modernism on the part of those engaged in the work of the projects would have strengthened these agencies against their own temporizing fall-offs. Those were two problems the projects had to resolve or mitigate to a sufficient degree before they could get to the audiences and tap the inspiration inherent in the favorable circumstances generated in the 1920s and 30s.

PHOTOS

African-American theater group of the 1930s. Robert Hayden, who spent more than four years with the Detroit Federal Writers' unit, is seated second row center. From the photographic collection of Your Heritage House, Detroit.

Costume drawings for the *Macbeth* production of the New York Federal Theater Company. The play was performed in 1936 in Detroit under sponsorship of the local project. Courtesy of the Federal Theater Collection at George Mason University.

The home of an old-time iron worker's family. Photograph by Russell Lee of the Farm Security Administration.

The Snyder family of Manistee County, Michigan, who volunteered to colonize a federally sponsored community in Matanuska Valley, Alaska. The play, *200 Were Chosen*, by E. P. Conkle and performed by Detroit's Federal Theater Group, is based on this 1930s pioneering venture. Courtesy of the Michigan State Archives.

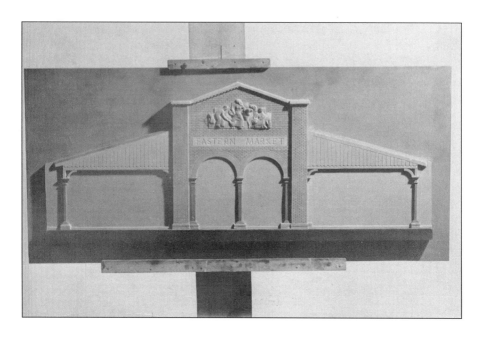

Eastern Market art work by Samuel Cashwan of Detroit's Federal Art Project. Courtesy of the Michigan State Archives.

In addition to fiddling, workers from Iron River made their own fiddles. New Deal federal patronage was designed to focus on this kind of cultural resourcefulness. Photo by Russell Lee of the Farm Security Administration. Courtesy of the Library of Congress.

A scene from Detroit's FTP production of *Anna Christie*, performed March 1938. The players, left to right, are Chester Adams, Courtney White, and Elynor Wylie Hill. Photograph courtesy of Hy Fireman.

A Lano family puppet. David Lano was head of Detroit Theater Project's marionette division. Courtesy of the Museum, Michigan State University.

Peggy Fenn and Ray Rawlings. They had been young apprentices in the Bonstelle repertory group before joining Detroit's FTP. Rawlings left the group for an important role in "The Lone Ranger" radio show.

Detroit City Council hearings into alleged communist domination of the Detroit unit's Federal Theater Project. John Mathews, the standing figure, who made the accusations and discredited himself in testifying, was a professional juggler, one of several vaudevillians assigned to the project. Photograph courtesy of Hy Fireman.

The Lehman Hardison Gospel Singers, part of Detroit's Federal Music
Project. Courtesy of the Library of Congress.

Verner Haldene, the longest tenured director of the Detroit FTP, from early
1937 to the June 30, 1939 shutdown. Photograph courtesy of Hy Fireman.

PART 3

The Politics of Running the FTP and FWP in the Midwest

9

Starting Out from Nowhere:
Artists, Art-Officials, and Super-ficials

THE thunder over official patronage at the end of the 1980s seems fated to shake the art world through the last ten years of the twentieth century. The rage against the federally funded displays of works by Robert Mapplethorpe and Andres Serrano was and remains much more than anger at two particular artists. The attacks by national and local authorities which have followed in its wake beleaguer the National Endowment for the Arts (NEA), the government's contemporary version of art patronage, and cast dark clouds not only over artists who seek national funding, but also over the cultural lives of the various publics that make up the United States. The aim, conscious or not, is control: legislative constraints to govern official patronage and determine art production, and ideological conditioning to regulate the cultural dispositions generated by non-hegemonic publics.

Control over art and culture in such a broad sense may seem to infer a great deal too much from what appears to be an argument confined to the governmental use of taxpayer money. Yet the passions displayed by those wanting to cut federal patronage budgets, use funds more efficiently, or end allocations altogether suggest the far bigger game I propose.[1] These attacks, in the guise of religious orthodoxy and moral outrage against pornography, illustrate the problematics facing an official art patronage that functions within the parameters of a representative political system allied to special-interest privilege, hierarchical arrangement, and social inequality. A representative political system presents an image of equal power relationships between that system and the individuals and publics it governs. Rights and liberties are presumed to be equally distributed to and capable of being exercised with equal effectiveness by all its members and communities. That orientation signifies what official patronage ought to look like: an uncensored, democratic practice. Yet the nature of power relationships within a stratified, special-interest structure establishes privileges, preferences, empowerments, and anxieties about their loss, both within and outside the political structure. And these force official patronage to modify, at times to abandon, the principle of equal rights and liberties in art. Although such abrogations threaten the entire art world, those most victimized are the individual artists, art collectives, and publics whose art forms and subjects fall outside the preferences of dominant culture and conventional political views.

Official art patronage of the Great Depression died more than fifty years ago in the playing out of those problematics. At that time, the problematics frequently donned the masks of anti-communism and fear of sexual representation in art. That patronage received its fatal wound in June 1939, although it was left to draw its final breath three years later, a seldom noticed casualty of World War II.[2] In different historical moments and in different institutional structures, a substantial number of politicians and bureaucrats have found themselves fearful of or ill-at-ease with the arts, often behaving notoriously, as in censorship by the Chamberlain's office in Britain and the Catholic Index. Less obvious but no less related to the same dread and discomfort are bureaucratic routines that assert themselves over lines of authority, priorities of need, methods for carrying out policies intended to make official patronage a reality, and the intent of those policies. At different times, in and out of the official structures of patronage, artists have reacted with principle or panic to these routines and their implications for the free well-being of sponsored art.

The playing out of those problematics in the New Deal era is relatively well documented, better than any other instance of official patronage. But more significant, the problems engulfing New Deal patronage and the way it dealt with them are exemplary and instructive for the present controversy over federal patronage aroused by the Mapplethorpe and Serrano exhibitions of 1989 and 1990. Although the arts projects of the 1930s encountered many of the same factors at work among policy-makers, bureaucrats, and artists as are present sixty years later, they were established to support the arts in a far different way and under a far different organizational matrix than post-World War II patronage. In the first place, they were specific relief projects set up by presidential executive order under an enabling law empowering a comprehensive work-relief organization with a double aim: to alleviate economic hardship and preserve human skills and talents. The arts projects were, therefore, dispensers of patronage both to foster the arts and also to provide hard-up artists, theater people, and writers with temporary relief. But they were not, as the NEH and NEA today, a clearinghouse or way station for the distribution of funds; they were themselves the beneficiaries of funds for the purpose of producing art. They had three responsibilities: employing needy artists directly into their units; formulating the esthetic and thematic precepts underlying the forms and subjects of the work to be produced and the audiences to be reached; and coordinating the actual production of art. The first responsibility cast project administrators in the role of top level bosses, call them super-ficials, of a work force.[3] The second made administrators, who were mostly professionals from the arts or academics from the humanities disciplines, play the part of what I call art-officials. The third responsibility made them functioning artists, usually as directors and stage managers, alongside the rank-and-file of the various units.

The NEA works differently in all these respects. It only dispenses patronage. The funds dispersed are intended to promote the general well-being of the arts through a wide sponsorship of specifically merited private and institutional endeavors. It does not initiate the forms and subjects which its funds may enable. These are proposed by individual artists and institutions, some private and some public.[4] The NEA may affect the nature of the proposals presented to it because it sets up the evaluation process and is the final authority over which proposals are selected and which rejected. It does not, however, affect in advance or formulate specifically or directly what kinds of forms and subjects artists are to work on. Neither does it employ artists, nor function as producing unit. Artists and institutions work out their projects according to their own purposes and needs. The influence of the NEA as dispensing agency is only a factor insofar as any given artist or institution may tailor a proposal to what will presumably find favor with the NEA's evaluating process and authority—and indeed the presumption may be warranted under certain administrations and political climates. Once the patronage is dispensed, the awarded artist and institution are on their own to produce the work proposed.

In the case of federal patronage after World War II, we have a clear triangle: 1) executive and elected policy-makers who determine overall allocations, organizational structure, and general purpose (super-ficials); 2) dispensing agency administrators and evaluators (art-officials) who are neutral about esthetic and thematic precepts; and 3) the artists and institutions (private and public) seeking patronage.[5] From the structural point of view, post-World War II patronage is organizationally independent. The law setting it up spells out its mandate and its autonomy, leaving it free to have art-world peers decide the issue of artistic merit, with the NEA itself the final but largely rubber-stamp arbitrator of peer-selected projects.

In the case of New Deal patronage, the relationships were far more complex. Since it was a dispenser as well as a recipient of patronage, its executive functions were doubly intricate: its art-official side often overlapped with its super-ficial side and, perhaps to an even greater degree, its artist side. One simple example of these conflated, contradictory functions is administrative freedom to modify, when professional exigencies warranted, the formula for all WPA projects—that a minimum of ninety percent of the personnel had to be qualified for relief and up to ten percent only by experience and training to fill creative and managerial posts. In changing the formula to accommodate the esthetic needs of the projects, administrators constantly tripped over their super-ficial and art-official conflations. These are the internal dynamics of the New Deal arts projects.

The projects were also part of a larger organizational structure containing many other work-relief projects. Hence the chain of command, the interpretation of art policy, and the methods for giving objective life to the patronage were far more complicated than in the case of the NEA. Moreover, the constitutional relationships of governmental units in the United States, the different powers reposed by the Constitution in the federal center and the individual states, made the chain of command even more intricate: the arts projects' own line of authority and their artists had to contend with both federal and state orders of authority. This rather complex and divisive organizational setup of executive and bureaucratic super-ficials proved to be enormously troublesome for the arts projects, since it blurred any view of who was ultimately responsible for decision making, what decisions had force, and what policy interpretations should guide decision making.

This complex setup was not entirely disadvantageous. New Deal patronage established art agencies that had their own organizational structures and were also collectives of artists at work. That kind of setup provided one important advantage: a context for rallying resistance to interfering and censoring super-ficials on the federal level or in the regional bureaucracy. But this advantage also proved to be troublesome. The art-official side of a given individual in authority might easily sympathize with and even lend support to organized resistance, but the super-ficial side of the same individual would have to oppose such resistance, especially if it were organized from the ranks of the artists themselves.

The disadvantages attending the varied external and internal dynamics of New Deal patronage were felt everywhere in different ways and with different intensities, depending on the culture and politics of the different localities and regions where the arts projects were operative. Before we turn to the Detroit Theater and Writers' projects as local instance, we should note that the organizational chronology of the Works Progress Administration had the same general effect on all local and regional cases.

Congress passed the Works Relief Act in the spring of 1935, formally empowering the Works Progress Administration. The first job facing Harry Hopkins, who had been appointed head of the WPA, was to devise the federal and state administrative structures that would direct the projects on which the unemployed who qualified for relief would be set to work. When the arts projects were set up later that summer, they were inserted into already existing administrative apparatuses on the federal and state levels. Since the arts projects had their own administrative structure, the lines of authority through which they functioned were confusingly diverse. In May 1936, Flanagan described the difficulties to Hopkins in prose and chart. She wrote that after six months in the Theater Project and a number of field trips across the country, "the difficulty is not so much one of personality as of lines of authority." She found "great confusion" everywhere, "from the arts people" to "district and state WPA administrators and professional and service people."[6] In a chart attached to her letter, she illustrated the mess more precisely. Theater units in the field had to route their responsibilities through two different lines of authority. One went directly to the national director of the Theater Project in Washington, Flanagan herself, who in turn reported to the assistant administrator of Federal One, who reported to Hopkins. But the field units also had to move along an authority line to their direct administrative agency in the states, the district supervisors of the Women's and Professional Projects (the WPA subdivision in charge of white-collar programs). These district administrators were in turn responsible to the WPA district directors of all district projects, who then had to go to two statewide agencies, the state directors of Women's and Professional Projects and the state WPA administrators. The state directors of Women's and Professional Projects also reported to the statewide administrators and had to report as well to the Washington director of Professional and Service Projects (the highest tier of white-collar programs). Meanwhile the WPA state administrators were under the jurisdiction of the WPA field representatives, who reported to the Washington office of Women's and Professional Projects, and from thence to Hopkins.

An example of bureaucratic attitude in this byzantine network of lines is what Flanagan called the New Jersey peccadillo, an offense she found impossible to place in her chart. It illustrates in a chilling way the jealous guarding of authority. The WPA administrator for New Jersey, displaying "some strange sadistic desire," called the Theater Project's state director a "special representative" and would allow him to communicate with the Theater Project's Washington office only through the administrator himself as correspondent and only in third-person address. "We are allowed," Flanagan wrote on the chart enclosed with the letter, "to communicate with our representative in that state only by dumb show."[7] The details in Michigan differ from those in New Jersey. No such prohibition against direct contact appears to have been imposed on the arts projects administrators appointed by the Washington center for the state or for Detroit. Nevertheless, the same maze of authority and unwillingness to let go of power are apparent.

10

The Michigan FTP:
Conflicted Authority and Censorship

I N order to get the Michigan Theater Project started, authorization documents had to be sent from three different sources to administrators at three different points in the organizational structure of the WPA. In a letter dated October 14, 1935, Flanagan commissioned Thomas Wood Stevens, regional director of the FTP for the Midwest, to oversee theater projects in Michigan. At the same time, she informed the Michigan director of the WPA, Harry Lynn Pierson, of Stevens's commission. Four days later, Bruce McClure, the national director of Professional and Service Projects, sent Pierson his seal of approval authorizing Stevens's work in Michigan. Almost a month later, on November 12, Flanagan addressed a memo to McClure and Jacob Baker, the assistant administrator for Federal One, informing them that Stevens was about to start a theater project with fifty people in Detroit at the Bonstelle Playhouse and hence $20,000 should be allotted for six months.[1] Presumably, either Baker or McClure or both authorized the state WPA to release money for the theater project, but unfortunately documents to demonstrate this are now waylaid in the maze. At any rate, Stevens assumed the allocation had been authorized, for at the end of November he was hard at work forming a sponsoring committee of Bonstelle people and exploring the relief lists of theater personnel to meet the project's ninety-percent-need rule.[2] Mrs. McKee Robison, the president of the Women's Committee of the Bonstelle Civic Theater, telegrammed Flanagan on December 27 that the committee had registered ninety experienced, unemployed theater workers who were certifiably eligible for the WPA. She indicated that, according to her understanding, a $75,000 appropriation had been authorized, but the Michigan authorities intended to release less than $30,000 and were holding up the start of the project.[3] Stevens conferred with John W. Stannard, Michigan's acting assistant director of Professional and Service Projects, who agreed to sign the documents establishing the Detroit Theater Project and allocate $30,000, a sum estimated to be able to carry it for four months.[4]

What I have described graphically demonstrates the maze of authority pathways that had to be crossed and recrossed in order to become an effective organization. Money seems to have been a major concern as well as a major way of protecting or at least asserting the primary authority of the WPA state administrators. For example, according to Stevens, Stannard objected to signing for the Detroit unit because "it took too large a proportion of the Michigan allocation and . . . other projects in Michigan might come up which could not be written for lack of funds."[5] But money is a magic that masks, as Shakespeare imagined in verse and Marx in analysis, many things.

Some of the matters it masks can be seen in the second important concern that arose in setting up a work relief theatrical unit in Michigan: the requirement that ninety percent of the personnel meet the need test of relief eligibility. In issuing Stevens the authorization, Flanagan made clear that this requirement had to be the foremost principle in assembling a production unit. Stannard raised the issue in his January meeting with Stevens, implying that there was some doubt about the ninety percent figure for the Detroit unit and claiming that there were more theatrical people qualified for relief outstate. Stannard also implied that Stevens was ignoring a number of requisitions for theatrical assistance coming in from other parts of the state. Stevens, after spending a good deal of time in Detroit going through lists of people to verify need eligibility, found that Stannard could not provide proof of his claims and implications.[6]

What lies behind Stannard's unsubstantiated remarks can only make sense in terms of perceived priorities for a work relief program, negative attitudes toward the work and economic need of art personnel, and state political strategy. Stannard's unwillingness to release money could hardly be limited to the $30,000, for it represented an insignificant proportion of total WPA funds allocated for the state. He apparently believed that other projects not yet conceived would be more worthy of funds than the arts projects. Not surprisingly, his priorities for white-collar work within a relief structure mandated to relieve hardship and produce something of tangible worth did not place art high on the list of practical and value-producing work-relief. Stannard's contentiousness about the eligibility of art personnel also contains an element of suspicion about the qualifications establishing someone as an artist. In the eyes of dominant and popular culture, and in the eyes of political bureaucrats who tend to represent those tendencies faithfully, every artist is manqué—perhaps an artist, perhaps an idler—unless certified by marketplace success. In addition, Stannard's claim that requisitions for theatrical aid from other parts of the state were being unanswered indicates a political concern.[7] The source for these requisitions was the Michigan Centennial Celebration Committee and its influential director. Stevens and Flanagan had already pledged assistance for the celebration, if relief clients suited for the work could be found. Centennial celebrations often speak more to the politics of rural and small urban areas, to the historical pride and patriotism of outstate regions than to the issues current among immigrant and black resettler communities in large metropolitan centers. Stannard's delay of the Detroit-centered Theater Project over requisitions from an agency set up for a centennial performance could hardly be innocent of out-state political inclinations.

The uneasy relationships I have described between the state administrators in charge of all WPA affairs and Stevens continued to plague the new art-officials brought in even after the Theater Project allocation had been released. The ninety-percent rule was a constant irritant. In February 1936 Jack Marvin became project director, and he soon found it necessary to apply for an exception to the formula since there were not enough relief-eligible stagehands in the area to make the company viable. One of the first communications he had with Flanagan was a request to reduce the requirement to seventy-five percent. Although she eventually granted the request, the state administrators were unhappy over an exception not allowed to other white-collar projects or labor projects under their jurisdiction, and from then on they kept an anxious eye on the arts projects' mix of relief and non-relief personnel.[8] They considered work-relief, not culture, the overriding purpose of WPA, and often felt that the cultural projects were incompatible with that end.

State administrators' wariness of art-official intentions, which they assumed placed the needs of art ahead of relief, is exemplified in the problems faced by William Beyer, the Michigan Theater Project's second director, but the first with profesional skills and theatrical experience. Beyer's replacement of Marvin in May 1936 led to a sorting out of art-official and super-ficial functions. Play-producing direction and business/noncreative managerial direction for the Theater Project became two separate responsibilities in the hands of two different project administrators. M. Walter Mountjoy, who came from the Playhouse company, assumed the post of state director. It appears that he owed his appointment to a lifelong friendship with Frederic S. Schouman, Pierson's administrative assistant. His close ties to Schouman became a source of difficulty for the project for two reasons: Stannard and Schouman did not like each other; and state administrators, the national staff of the FTP, and Beyer considered Mountjoy to be erratic and incompetent.[9] Responsibility for play production went to Beyer, a young playwright, whose comedy, *I Confess*, had impressed the Shubert organization. The label for this position was producing director, and it carried the same salary classification as Marvin's more amorphous job.[10]

With Beyer in charge of play direction, the company began in earnest to produce a series of dramas for the community. But trouble with the WPA bureaucracy headquartered in Lansing, Michigan's state capital, soon hindered the production process of the Theater Project. Money and unstable tenure of box-office personnel were the first obstacles to smooth going. In June a change in the theater's business/box-office manager and a mix-up in bonding the new appointee led the Lansing super-ficials to withhold the money required to reopen *I Confess*. When the Lansing bureaucrats were finally convinced to release funds, they sent along what Beyer in a letter to Flanagan called "the overwhelming sum of twenty-five dollars," an amount they doubled after Beyer "raised the roof" with Schouman, the super-ficial who was thought to be more sympathetic to the arts projects. Money required for the Theater Project's operation went beyond reopening *I Confess*. In June the company was also rehearsing its next play, Robert Sherwood's *Road to Rome*, and needed immediately, according to Beyer, $500 for sets and costumes. Lansing would only promise $200 in a week and $200 more later on. Hence the company could not set a date for the play's opening, although it was prepared to do so immediately after *I Confess* had finished its run.[11]

Money and bureaucratic snarls entangled the Theater Project through the summer and into the fall of 1936, but these turned out to be the least of the plagues besetting the project. Far more important was Stannard's entirely unsympathetic view toward Beyer's aims and direction. His first complaint was that Beyer was giving key parts to non-relief and volunteer actors, while letting qualified relief performers stand around doing nothing. Stannard appreciated the difficulty of running a theater where "the relief personnel are not 100% legitimate theatre people" and where a number of the performers are vaudevillians and other actors "who are passé." Nevertheless, the use of non-relief and volunteer actors in a company already exempted from the ninety-ten formula could not be justified. Nor could Stannard tolerate what he believed or understood to be the highhanded or arbitrary way that Beyer deployed his acting personnel. From displeasures voiced by the company's relief members, Stannard concluded that Beyer's favoring of non-project actors had a demoralizing effect. In September 1936, Stannard accused Beyer of casting Sinclair Lewis's *It Can't Happen Here* with a non-relief and volunteer cast, implying with the quip "too much Beyer and too little WPA" that there had been widespread violation of work-relief rules.[12]

Beyer pointed out that of the rather large cast for the Lewis play, only six actors were non-relief, and his inclusion of a volunteer actor for a leading part had been approved in advance by WPA state administrators. A letter from William Farnsworth, one of the FTP's deputy administrators in Washington, supported Beyer's contention. After thoroughly investigating the Theater Project's troubles with the state administration, Harold Stein, director of procedures for the Division of Women's and Professional Projects, said that Stannard's first statements were "quite reckless," except with regard to excessive non-labor costs and poor communication with Lansing. Stein had this to say about the charge that Beyer had mishandled and alienated his staff: "I attended a rehearsal of *Let Freedom Ring* for about an hour and I was greatly impressed by the way Beyer handled his people. They were patently of uneven quality and he was making a valiant effort to give each one the kind of instruction he needed and could understand. Certainly his wholehearted devotion to his work can not be questioned."[13] But Stannard remained down on Beyer, seeing him as "an experimental theatre man" whose commitment to theatrical esthetics did not suit WPA purposes or the abilities of the company's eligible staff. He also belabored Beyer for renting an "abnormally large house," the Lafayette Theatre in downtown Detroit. Stannard added that Beyer has "grandiose ideas of maintaining an entire Broadway Theatre staff."[14]

Stargazing versus Collective Theater

The cost and size of the Lafayette Theatre caused a sharp rift in the ranks of the FTP itself—a rift that signaled major differences among superficials, art-officials, and rank-and-file artists over the best way to get the project accepted as a bona fide enterprise, as well as how to fulfill its theatrical concept. FTP administrators in Washington, the regional command, and those on the local scene began with the idea of securing community support for the company by enlisting the help of prominent citizens. That was Stevens's purpose in seeking the sponsorship of the Bonstelle's Women's Committee. Flanagan thought, however, that Bonstelle sponsorship represented very narrow support and an attempt to emulate the repertory finesse and Broadway orientation of the old Jessie Bonstelle company.[15] She urged art-officials in the local project to seek endorsements from Detroiters outside the theater world, including labor leaders. Following up on this suggestion, local art-officials cultivated support among prominent politicians, religious leaders, and the area's most notable social and civic members. They made some effort to win endorsements from labor, particularly through Frank Martell, the head of the AFL. Although he appeared quite willing to help, he felt that to attract a working-class audience, the FTP would have to highlight plays about issues that concerned them.[16] Elite local support, more inclined to conventional views of theater, pulled the FTP in one direction and labor drew it in another. Far more important is how the art-officials functioned in this unpremeditated tug of war over grass-roots principles.

On the surface, the issue of theater site may seem a mundane, practical matter, but at its heart lies the particularism of the inner dissension—the conflict between cultural populism and cultural elitism reflected in the composition of supporters. The Lafayette Theatre was far too expensive at the standard commercial rates being charged for it, and leasing it was at odds with proper use of work-relief funds. To solve the problem, project administrators came up with the idea of negotiating the rental of the auditorium at the Detroit Institute of Arts. They hoped that since it was a publicly-funded cultural facility, the "city fathers" would be "lenient" in making the arrangement.[17] This would have solved the money issue, but would have relocated the project to another elitist context, one that would probably not be terribly agreeable to a grass-roots audience. Some months later two other alternatives with elitist character were proposed: the Masonic Temple, where visiting opera and ballet companies were frequently booked, and an unnamed site in Ann Arbor, more than thirty miles distant from Detroit. Another approach, which came primarily from the company's progressive and radical members, was to move to a theater that already had grass-roots connotations, either because of its neighborhood location, its modesty, or its connection to such popular forms of entertainment as the motion-pictures.[18] The issue was not resolved until January 1937, when the Theater Project concluded an agreement to perform in the People's Theatre, formerly the home of Detroit's Yiddish theater and at the time a moviehouse located outside the perimeter of Detroit's downtown district in a working-class section not far from Jewish immigrant and black resettler neighborhoods.[19]

The conflict between cultural populism and elitism should not be thought of only in terms of FTP art-officials and work-relief performers. We find the conflict inscribed in the art-officials themselves. In his letter to Flanagan about negotiations for the Institute of Arts theater, Mountjoy reported that after much effort he had won Schouman as an ally in the campaign to establish a summer outdoor theater, in keeping with the free caravan theater concept already being practiced by other FTP units elsewhere. The idea was to have a roofed-over stage at a river-front park, probably Belle Isle—to which the Bonstelle group had drawn large audiences from 1928 to 1932 and which indeed became an FTP center for free outdoor performances in 1937.[20] The Bonstelle connection had another kind of elitist pull that also conflicted with the Theater Project's populist policy. Performers Peggy Fenn and Jay Michaels and set designer Stephen Nastfogel, former members of the Bonstelle theater, became part of the project as non-relief personnel. They believed that professional theater centered around star performers. (Although Jessie Bonstelle had worked hard at developing a grass-roots audience, she still operated the stage side of her repertory group around the star system, augmenting her acting staff each season with accomplished Broadway performers.) Star-system pressures from the Bonstelle-bred FTP members intensified the inner dissension of the group over site preferences. The more politically-oriented work-relief actors and stagehands argued for an equitable and collective distribution of role assignments. In *Arena*, Flanagan comments on this division in the Michigan project: "It took [actors from the Bonstelle theater] a while to learn to work with others less educated, whose work had been in the traveling road show, the tent show, the barnstorming circuit; to learn to find in a common group enterprise a substitute for the highly individualistic theatre they had known."[21]

Red Scare Enflames the Controversy

The heat of this populist/elitist controversy ignited ugly charges of intent to make the FTP a tool for New Deal propaganda and Communist Party subversion. The front-line people making these charges included Stephen Nastfogel, an actor by the name of John E. Matthews, and David Lano, the head of the FTP's puppetry unit. By 1938 the charges had been presented to the Detroit Common Council for consideration, and they received wide notoriety in a *Detroit News* article by a reporter named Donald Slutz, who cited Matthews as the chief source of the charges. One accusation alleged that the company's political aims caused it to be wasteful, inefficient, and amateurish. Another that competent but apolitical members such as Peggy Finn were being penalized. And still another proposed that the company was demoralized because political strategy dominated theater activity.

Tension between professionalist and populist concepts of theater also underlay the general charge that the "FTP in Detroit . . . is strictly a propaganda unit for the New Deal and the Communist Party." There were allegations that on several occasions project workers supported radical legislation, in one instance pressuring the Common Council by packing its chambers and in another participating in a UAW radio program promoting labor candidates in order to attack the automobile companies. A further charge asserted that the company had deliberately produced *It Can't Happen Here* close to election time as a means of winning support for the New Deal. Since Federal Theater Project units in twenty-one cities opened this play on the same evening and continued their runs over approximately the same time period, this allegation implied that the entire FTP was, by design, an arm of New Deal propaganda. The accusation did not originate in Detroit. Its source was multiple, coming especially from the yellow press and conservative congressmen, and it was leveled against all the WPA arts projects, throughout the whole history of New Deal patronage, although most steadily and venomously against the Theater Project.

One charge that clearly indicates the disgruntled motives behind the whole attack was the allegation that Detroit FTP members were pushed aside to make room for three performers imported from the New York unit. Loss of professional opportunity, not politics, enflamed this charge. As it turns out, these New York performers were reassigned at the suggestion of Flanagan, McGee, and the Detroit project's art-officials. They hoped that the New York performers—who all had considerable training and experience in stock, repertory, and traveling theater and even some work in New York's commercial theater—might improve the quality of the acting staff.[22] If anything, the company's left and populist members might have found this move grounds for complaint, because it violated the FTP's grass-roots policy and because it could have penalized them as the less accomplished, less experienced members of the unit more than anyone else. Those who were concerned that the company be more efficient and less amateurish should have found the New York imports welcome additions.

This curious charge seems to be more a matter of tarring the project with whatever might discredit it, particularly on the part of Matthews. Matthews had two quarrels in the project that led to strained, unfriendly feelings. One was with art-officials over his cavalier attitude toward his work with the company and his ham acting. Gordon Fairclough, assistant state administrator of the Michigan Theater Project at the time, commented that "Matthews treated his job here as a joke. He flatly refused to put on his act when ordered to do so."[23] The other was with the project's left-wing members, with whom he was associated at first. He had been an active member of the Workers' Alliance, the union organized by arts project personnel to safeguard project working conditions and resist cuts in project funds. On one occasion he had agreed to be the local Alliance's representative to a protest demonstration in Washington against congressional moves to reduce Federal One allocations. Although he took Alliance money for the trip and indeed started out for Washington by car, he aborted the journey before getting very far. His reasons for doing so made no sense to Alliance members, who took his failure to return the money to be dishonest. From that point on he appears to have become hostile to the Alliance, particularly to Edith Segal—the company's choreographer and one of its leading radicals—and also to the project. Herbert Ashton, Jr., the incumbent Midwest regional director for the Theater Project, lost considerable time from theater affairs investigating the whole matter; he characterized Matthews's reaction to his problems with the Workers' Alliance as a turning "not only . . . against her [i.e., Segal], but the world in general."[24]

175

Slutz, the reporter who publicized the charges and who presented himself as an impartial newsman for an interview with Ashton, was a friend of Matthews, Nastfogel, and Fenn. His article about the event bears an anticommunist tone and evinces hostility toward the arts projects. In addition to Matthews's charges, Slutz also cited the views of three other project members, all critical of radical presence in the project. Two of these were Nastfogel and Fenn, and the third was David Carnes, an old vaudeville actor who reportedly found the communist influence in the FTP disturbing. Nastfogel was far more hostile to the FTP itself, implying that it was so infected with communist precepts that theater was impossible under the circumstances. Slutz quotes him: "I finally quit in August, 1937, because I was sick and tired of the politics on the project." Fenn gave Slutz this more measured account: "I happen to be a New Dealer and I believe the Federal Theater is a worthwhile and interesting project. I do feel that there are individuals in the Federal Theater who are trying to use the project to further their own political ambitions. In other words the fault lies with personalities within the project rather than with the project itself or with project administrators."[25] Ashton, however, was not particularly enamored of her putdown of the group's political personalities and her praise for the project and its administrators. "Miss Fenn, who for some strange reason became involved in this thing," he wrote in his activity report for the period ending July 3, 1938, "will prove to be one of our worst trouble makers inasmuch as she is the instigator of those silly petitions requesting that the New York actors only get the parts that are left over or those which the Detroit people, after reading, did not care to play."[26]

It should be pointed out that, once the Detroit project got over these hurdles of anti-communism and the elitist collision with populist views, none of these fears materialized. Fenn did not go on to cause trouble, neither did she suffer the penalties of competition from experienced and professionally trained New York imports. Nor did the less experienced and less gifted acting staff find themselves discarded by the newcomers. The charges themselves seem not to have made much of an impression beyond their newspaper notoriety, certainly not on Detroit's Common Council and not on FTP art-officials.

Ashton, the FTP's Midwest regional director at the time, considered the charges malicious. While he expected Fenn's professional jealousy to cause mischief, he dismissed the other leaders of the attack even more bluntly. The principal accuser, Matthews, he called a "crackpot" and a liar for maintaining that he was forced to entertain Woolworth sit-down strikers. Ashton learned that Matthews had, in fact, volunteered to entertain them on his own. Moreover, Matthews's claim that project actors had been directed to perform for the UAW was also false. The author of the UAW radio sketch told Ashton that the actors who participated in it were not instructed by the UAW or the FTP to do so and were, indeed, paid for their professional services.

Ashton's bluntness took on a note of xenophobia when it came to Nastfogel. In one communication to Flanagan and her deputy director J. Howard Miller, he wrote, "the Nastfogel mentioned is an alien and where he gets off to butt in I don't know." But Ashton's motivation is less foreign-baiting than it seems, for Ashton had discovered, in investigating the charges, that Nastfogel had not been straightforward with the project about his alien status. Because of congressional constraints, the WPA had to issue directives barring aliens from work-relief projects unless they met certain defined conditions. Exceptions were granted to those who had already applied for citizenship. Ashton informed Flanagan and Miller that Nastfogel had refused four times to sign the alien affidavit and that, although he had claimed otherwise, he had not applied for his first papers until February 1938, the year Nastfogel made his propaganda charges against the project. Coupled with Nastfogel's false charge that two-thirds of every project dollar was being spent for New Deal or communist propaganda—Ashton's careful review of project expenditures from 1936 on revealed the baselessness of the allegation—this subterfuge motivated the regional director to question Nastfogel's right to "butt in" and doubt his claim to have quit the project for political reasons. Caught in his dual function of super-ficial and art-official, Ashton tripped over his own feet. In the legislated xenophobia of the United States (going back to the immigration restrictions enacted in 1921 and reconfirmed in relief restrictions in the hard times of the 1930s), Ashton found a tangle-footed way to safeguard the project against star-system divisiveness and unstable personalities.

This event cost Ashton time and energy he had hoped to devote to matters of play selection, production problems, and other theatrical issues with the FTP staff. In addition, he worried about the effect such a notorious diversion might have on the always tenuous relationships between the Theater Project and the WPA super-ficials in Lansing. "As you know," he wrote in his July activity report to Flanagan and Miller, "when Michigan came into my region, Louis Nims [Pierson's replacement as state director of WPA] nor any of the officials were any too friendly toward the Project." But he pointed out that new achievements—such as efforts to overhaul the project after Beyer resigned and a more modest and grass-roots auditorium had been secured as well as the esthetically and financially successful season that had been concluded under Verner Haldene, the third director—had gained the confidence of state officials. This hard-won backing, after more than two years of hassling and being at cross-purposes with the external bureaucratic structure, steeled Ashton against the internal malice he had uncovered:

"Everybody out here has worked too hard, too sincerely and endless hours to make this thing a success and we are not going to let this Matthews or any of his ilk get away with these charges or hurt this project."[27]

Plays with Bite in the Bureaucratic Maze

These unfounded and distorted charges were a peculiar, perhaps ludicrous aftershock to arts project principles that rejected the showcasing of individual performers and authors and proposed ties to grass-roots sources of inspiration, principles that also implied the presentation of plays with social and historical bite. The objection to *It Can't Happen Here* indicated the discomfort of the internal elitist view over plays with strong social themes. More significant, however, were the tremors of state WPA officials uneasy about the plays planned by the project. The unfriendliness of Nims that Ashton alluded to was rooted in suspicions that the FTP was going to overload the offerings with plays that focused on social and political issues from a grass-roots orientation. Nims had the reputation of being very conservative in his views and tastes and not at all in favor of the arts projects. Nims's disfavor first came up in a January 1937 telephone conversation between Hopkins and Pierson over Pierson's resignation as state WPA administrator. Hopkins wanted to replace him with Nims, but Pierson objected that Nims was impulsive and wanted to "drastically cut those recreation projects."[28] These objections may have held up his appointment, for he did not take over the job until September, when the Stannard-Beyer difficulties were in full swing. These fears were not confined to Nims. Stannard's discontent with Beyer over what he might do with the Detroit version of *It Can't Happen Here* is an example. The Flanagan plan allowed each unit to insert into the script some localizing material to make the play more immediate for local audiences and to finish off Lewis's incomplete script.[29] Stannard was not at all comfortable with a Beyer rewrite. He cautioned William P. Farnsworth, the national deputy director before Miller, to have Flanagan and John McGee check out the final script before allowing Beyer to produce the play. Beyer "is a good re-write man," Stannard wrote, "and has a lot of bright ideas of his own, but I am very much afraid that he is going to take far too many liberties with 'It Can't Happen Here.'"[30] The issue became moot when the national office issued Lewis's completed manuscript to all units.[31]

At the time Beyer was also rehearsing or preparing to rehearse *Let Freedom Ring*, Albert Bein's play about striking mill workers in North Carolina's Piedmont region. The previous May, Flanagan encouraged Mountjoy's proposal that Detroit's unit put on a living newspaper play about the auto industry, but she suggested that someone local write it, since the National Play Bureau headquartered in New York was swamped with other work. She also suggested that *Triple-A Ploughed Under* would be an appropriate play for Detroit. Furthermore, sometime during this period, Fred Morrow, who had taken on the state directorship of the Michigan unit, recommended the production of *Power*, the living newspaper about the relationship of private utilities to the high cost and insufficient supply of energy for common use.[32] But by September this brimful approach to producing plays dealing with social issues was greatly modified. To improve relations between the Detroit theater unit and the state bureaucracy, Flanagan and McGee worked out a revamped plan with Nims, Stannard, and Catherine Murray, the state director of the Division of Women's and Professional Projects, that included attention to Nims's and Stannard's fears of an overdose of plays with social themes. It was agreed that *It Can't Happen Here* would be followed by "a non-controversial play" and then by *Let Freedom Ring*. Social issues were not abandoned, however. In April 1937 McGee proposed that Detroit do three plays: *Let Freedom Ring*; *Altars of Steel*, about management's use of secret police; and *Cradle Song*, which dealt with the birth of Christ and which McGee thought would appeal to the Catholic community. But in October 1937, a year after the agreement with Nims and Stannard, Flanagan made another trip to Detroit to discuss with Nims plans for having the Detroit project tour the state. They worked out an even more modified set of offerings to afford variety "for any audience": comedy (*Boy Meets Girl*, a conventional Broadway romance), tragedy (*Dr. Faustus*), and social play (*Let Freedom Ring*).[33] Bureaucratic fears had managed to scare art-officials away from emphasizing plays that dealt with contemporary social issues.

The 1936 agreement and the additional accommodation made in 1937 did not settle the matter at all. Anxiety over plays with political and social content became a problem again in 1939 with Abner Larned, who had taken over the administration of the state WPA when Nims resigned to return to the business world. After a few months in office, he presented the Theater Project, which had been functioning quite effectively under Haldene, with three demands: that no loan personnel be brought in, no ham acting be allowed, and no social plays be performed. Flanagan was, once again, brought in to work out the project's problems with the state administration. In a meeting that included Haldene and two of Larned's representatives, she pointed out that loan personnel were necessary in order to overcome the problem of ham acting and that the only social plays put on by the Detroit FTP, *It Can't Happen Here* and *Let Freedom Ring*, were the "biggest box office successes and had received no criticism except from the State WPA."[34] But state anxiety overrode evidence of success. Coupled with the fact that by 1939 all the arts projects, the FTP in particular, were coming under the zealous scrutiny of congressional investigating committees for financial mismanagement and subversive activities, this anxiety prevented the Detroit unit for the balance of its existence (only another five months) from performing plays with social and political themes.[35]

The problem over plays that dealt daringly with contemporary issues was not, as one may well imagine, unique to Michigan. The earliest case is the closing down of New York's Federal Theater production of *Ethiopia* because national super-ficials outside the arts projects were nervous that international figures might take offense.[36] The Midwest outside Detroit also had its problems. In Chicago, where Stevens was directly responsible for the unit, *Model Tenement*, a play about a rent strike, ran into trouble. Stevens had worked out a rather conservative program for the Chicago unit, but had followed the Federal Theater Project's policy of encouraging local talent. The result was the rent-strike play written by Meyer Levin, then a relatively unknown author. When the Chicago WPA ordered Stevens to shut down the play, he objected and found ready support in Flanagan. But orders came from still higher authorities. Jacob Baker said: "Listen, Hallie, can we help it if the Mayor of Chicago doesn't like *Model Tenement*? He has the right of censorship . . . . There's just nothing we can do." Levin wrote to President Roosevelt that if his treatment of a rent strike was taboo, then every newspaper that dealt with rent strikes and evictions was treading on forbidden ground. Flanagan agreed, but maintained that the "Chicago project could scarcely enter into an argument with the Mayor."[37]

These disturbances over play form and content and the resulting censorship take us to the heart of the conflicted intentions which reside in a political system that is stratified and privileged according to status and wealth and is also representative and mythologized as a structure of equal individuals. They take us to the heart of the problematics confronting a patronage whose masters are twofold: the bureaucracy which serves the system in general and the art-officials who serve the professed ends for which the patronage was intended. In the 1930s, the mythology of representative democracy and federal patronage generated as one means of dealing with an enormous crisis tended understandably to emphasize the plight, rights, and vitality of publics outside the system's privileged stratifications. On the two occasions in Michigan when plays with strong social content were offered, these publics responded well. But these publics were not involved in the infighting over such plays. The bureaucrats serving the bifurcated system and the art-officials genuinely committed to grass-roots theater ironed out the matter among themselves, while the publics had no idea of what was going on or stood on the sidelines. Why was this so? Possibly because the art-officials, from Flanagan on down, were too timid whenever the issue arose, too uncertain about strategies for an all-out fight, still too caught up in conventional attitudes about power and unprivileged publics to call on them for support, even as they aspired to be a theater for them.

11

The Michigan FWP:
Self-Restraint and the Battle Within

I N the first two years of the Roosevelt administration, attempts at official patronage for writers were less successful than those for artists, musicians, and theater professionals. The nature of writing as a practice and the problem of identifying who was a writer complicated matters. The practice of writing is far less specifically delineated by accrediting apprenticeships or by amateur and professional arenas where experience is acquired than are the practices of the performing and visual arts. Anyone who is literate is potentially a writer. As Penkower puts it, the problem for New Deal patronage was that a writer was "just about anyone who lifted pen to paper."[1] This dilemma pointed to the general condition of apprenticeship in writing, a practice in the acquisition of skills done in private and alone. By contrast, the performing and visual arts are honed to certifying standards in public arenas —the concert hall, the stage, the studio—among collectives of others in the same apprenticeship and under the guiding eye of some experienced performer or artist. The public place and the guiding eye of such apprenticeships establish clearer marks of identification than the room hidden from public gaze.

This more private nature of writing underlies another factor complicating identification. Unlike musicians and actors, who do what they do in concert with others in training and after, writers do what they do alone. Whereas professional musicians and actors are generally employees of orchestras or stage companies, professional writers are usually self-employed and almost always never paid until the job is done and the work sold. So what then constitutes an unemployed writer? Visual artists share the same anomalous employment fate of writers, but they are more recognizable because of the formality and public nature of their apprenticeship. Writers stand alone on both scores.

Not Their Souls: Censorship by Anticipation

But doing what one does in the privacy of one's own space exacerbated the problem of making a place for writers in the federal patronage program. What in the world would writers under federal support write if left to themselves, if they were beyond the range of officialdom's surveiling eye and therefore beyond its control? A 1939 report summarizing the history of the Federal Writers' Project zeroed in on the danger:

> There was no provision for writers [before the WPA]. There had been provisions for musicians, artists, actors—under CWA, FERA. They [the officials in charge of relief for white-collar people] didn't know what to do with them. Writing is so articulate an art and touches so many people and is understood so definitely by everybody and has so many propaganda [potentialities] that it was difficult to have writers without censorship on political, social and moral points of view. We wanted something that would give the widest basis for employment for writers, but at the same time that would not involve their souls too much and also would not involve the Government in censorship.[2]

Mixed with the report's account of providing jobs and preserving human talents is the naive premise, self-delusion shall we say, that censorship is only a formal, legal, regulatory, openly articulated nay-saying. The wish to "not involve their souls too much" is easily seen as censorship through anticipation, censorship before there is anything that requires a direct "no" from super-ficialdom.

The problem of identifying an unemployed writer was resolved to a fair degree of satisfaction within the Federal Writers' Project and to a lesser degree within the WPA lines of authority by using a flexible definition. The project cast its net widely to include librarians, researchers, lawyers, teachers, college students who had been involved with student newspapers and magazines, and others whose work or associational commitments entailed writing of some sort, along with the more specifically identifiable writers of established reputation and unemployed newspapermen.

How to keep any of these souls from having their beliefs, values, and points of view too caught up in what they wrote was resolved by setting a common task for all units, a guide book for each state that described itineraries covering local sites of interest and drew a portrait of each state's economy and history, its accomplishments in art, and its cultural and social diversity.[3] A shared task also made it easier to have the writing done in one common workplace. And since the task was not born out of an individual writer's imagination—in fact, the overriding principle of the state guide books was that authorship was not individual and no individuals were to be named as such—editing advice and approval for all written material came ultimately from the central editorial staff in Washington. The predetermined form and content, the anonymity of authorship, and the procedures for getting individual articles into guide book form effectively quarantined each writer's political, social, and moral viewpoint. There was never any explicit or implicit aim in the Federal Writers' Project to apply the slogan, "free, adult, and uncensored"—an early Hopkins enthusiasm in authorizing the Federal Theater Project.

Internal Conflict

Discomfort over the content of the guides on the part of the state and federal super-ficials in charge of the overall workings of the WPA seems not to have become as intense as it did in the case of the Theater Project.[4] The documents on hand indicate that discomfort over the bias that might creep into Writers' Project content mainly beset the project's central administrators. As in the case of the FTP, FWP administrators in Washington acted out a script, unwittingly or otherwise, based on a confounding, almost totally overlapping set of super-ficial and art-official capacities. Unlike the FTP, the FWP's chief administrators were far less embroiled with WPA authorities outside the project's own structure over political, social, and moral views unacceptable to ruling power and dominant cultural taste.[5] The reason is that constraints on guide book form and matter were promulgated before anything had been produced. Anticipation and production procedures exercised a masked regulatory censorship and seemed to keep writers' souls from becoming loose cannons. The difficulties that FWP units had with state WPA bureaucracies centered primarily, therefore, on conflicts and disagreements over personalities, management techniques, and authority rights.

The Michigan Writers' Project reflects this centering unambiguously and is the common pattern for most writers' units elsewhere in the country. In the first year of operation, the major difficulty seemed to be personalities, particularly in managing the unit. The key figures here were Cecile Chittenden, the first director of the Michigan project, and the assistant director, Mary Barrett. However, it was not until the spring of 1936 that antagonism between the two became disruptive. At the unit's launching the previous fall, enthusiasm and internal harmony reigned. Chittenden and Barrett divided their work amicably. Chittenden devoted herself to personnel, public relations, and organizational matters within the unit and between the unit and the state. Barrett took charge of research and writing, with the authority, granted by the director, to select the researchers and writers she needed. Chittenden, an organizational stalwart for the Democratic Party and former newspaper woman, started her tenure with an enormous charge of energy. In a November 3rd letter to Alsberg, she wrote that "Michigan offers greater and more delightful possibilities than almost any other state for the American Guide and I assure you we are going to make a good job of it." Some two weeks later, again lauding Michigan's unusual qualities, she thanked Washington for its inspiration, adding, "I would rather be doing just what I am doing right now than anything else in the world."[6] Her fulsomeness may be attributed to three sources: a diplomatic desire to ingratiate higher authority; the favorable impression Joseph Gaer, the FWP Midwest supervisor had of the Michigan unit very early on ("Of all the states I visited," he reported to Chittenden, "I feel that yours, so far, seems to be best organized to produce excellent results on our guide"); and Chittenden's New Deal sympathies (she spoke of Franklin Roosevelt as "our 'Man of Great Vision' in Washington" and of this "whole splendid idea of getting people off the relief roles and into employment").[7]

Her bubbly comments about New Deal vision and the concept of employing writers in the Michigan Writers' Project appear in a framework of complaints showing that the early difficulties were between the unit and the state organization. At the heart of her complaints were official procedures and the throng of bureaucratic authorities that had to be consulted every step of the way. "We are still struggling with the countless yards of red tape, mainly wound by various welfare and U. S. E. S [United States Employment Service] agencies with whom we must deal," she informed Alsberg a month after being appointed director.[8] She preferred a more direct, more rapid method of getting the writers work-relief project off the ground. She acknowledged the need and respect for "proper procedure," but felt that the proliferative authorities involved in the process were operating from a self-aggrandizing agenda and needlessly complicating the requisite procedural approvals. She seemed to be particularly grieved with the WPA's engineers, although others did not escape reproof. Explaining the red tape and countless meetings, she surmised that an "inner ring of engineers and personnel officers" had been working to magnify and enhance what they had accomplished in work-relief by "obstructing the advancement of any projects—such as the Writers' Projects—handled by other than their immediate circle."[9]

Chittenden's complaints were probably well taken, judging from accounts of other Federal One experiences with bureaucratic mazes and zealously guarded authority. But her brusque tone and professed directness in doing things foreshadowed something more than a bluntly honest tongue and an efficient managerial technique. When she and Barrett became antagonists, much of it had to do with Chittenden's arbitrary method of managing project affairs, including her disregard for consulting with colleagues. Aggravating this problem even more was her deepening suspicion that her art-official colleagues inside the project and the WPA super-ficials outside it were undermining her authority and the project's domain of work.

The first sign of suspicion appeared in a handwritten letter Chittenden sent to Alsberg from Lansing on November 20. She had gone there because relations with state authorities had been considerably eased, although not enough to temper her sharpness: "We have managed to chisel some 96 workers from the rolls altho everything save tatooing and fingerprinting has been done to them." But she was most upset by what she discovered on her trip about a plan to have the Michigan branch of the National Youth Administration (NYA), under the sponsorship of the Michigan Historical Commission, complete a survey of historical records begun by the commission. As Chittenden saw it, "most of their work is a distinct duplication of the Writers' Project." Actually the plan had little to do with the project's goal of compiling a narrative guide to state culture and places of interest.

Chittenden's insecurities about this plan extended to William Haber, the deputy director of the Michigan WPA. It was Haber, she wrote, still smarting from the delay, who held up "my appointment in Lansing so long." Stannard, who had just been appointed head of the WPA's projects and planning section, also aroused her suspicion because he was extensively involved in the work of the Michigan Historical Association. "He was rather disparaging," she remarked, "of the Writers' Project to me last week."[10] There is no evidence that Haber or Stannard intended to whittle down Chittenden's position or the project's territorial responsibilities; nor is there proof of Stannard's hostility to the FTP. Bureaucrats, of course, did not understand or empathize with the Writers' Project as an art undertaking any more adequately than they did with the Theater Project. But the FWP's informal control over its major program made them a less anxiety-ridden obstacle to bureaucratic point of view.

In the winter and spring of 1936, the matter of what fields of work belonged to the Writers' Project and the Historical Records Survey erupted into a full-scale antagonism, but by then it was predominantly a dispute inside the Writers' Project—between it and the other Federal One units, where many staff members lined up on the side of Chittenden's opponents. As we have already indicated, Barrett was Chittenden's principal opponent inside the project. Jerre Mangione, an FWP writer in New York and later national coordidinating editor in Washington, portrayed Barrett as "a pink-faced former school teacher from Michigan, with silver-gray hair tightly clinging to her scalp."[11] Although his image suggests a woman who is on one hand mild and angelic and on the other contained and perhaps rigid, the record shows her to be a skilled editor, a person of firm principle and as strong-willed as Chittenden.

In the division of labor Chittenden worked out for herself and Barrett, she clearly saw herself as a public relations organizer and the project as an instrument to rally support for the New Deal administration. In a number of documents addressed to Washington, she made much of the fact that her energies were being spent primarily in lining up favorable publicity for the Writers' Project and support for the federal administration among the state's newspapers and club women. However much she was motivated by a commitment to the New Deal's social and patronage principles, it is clear from the style of her reports that she also desired to be a political power broker. The proposal that alarmed her most about the historical survey plan was the $10,000 travel grant included in it. She saw this as a threat to her own desperate desire for travel money: "If I can just get some travel authority, a few good writers and plenty of good typists I have a plan for using club women and newspapers that will keep our project constantly before the public, bring us loads of material and even increase the circulation of the papers that help us."[12] Publicity, easy acquisition of material from a narrow and privileged social stratum, and circulation advantages for cooperating newspapers are the concern here, not the alleviation of need in the framework of conserving and developing talent, not the populism of field work amongst the folk and working populations of the state, not the broad gathering of cultural phenomena for sound historical representation and profound analysis.

Chittenden announced that she was going to discuss the idea of approaching newspaper people with Mr. John T. Bailey, "who is organizing the Democratic Press for Mr. Roosevelt and who is also my director or supervisor in the 8th District" [the southwestern part of the state including the cities of Benton Harbor and Battle Creek]. The Bailey appointment has the earmarks of political more than work-relief and professional motivation. Her description of him when she first mentions the district setup to Alsberg conveys an impression of political opportunism:

> He . . . is a well known man throughout Michigan having only recently called together and organized all the newspapers and periodicals friendly to the Administration. This has not been done before, I understand, and is very significant in this region of dyed-in-the-wool Republicanism. He is progressing very well, indeed, with the Writers' Project. He is very influential

with not only the relief and U. S. E. S agencies but with com-merial, civic and educational groups with whom we must work in the future.[13]

A review of her other district appointments shows them to be a mixed bag: some are essentially based on writing and editorial qualifications and some are marked by the same political considerations that resonate in the Bailey case.

Chittenden was not an odd case in sacrificing principles of patronage to political need. She simply followed practices that were quite common, as we have seen, among top level New Deal leaders—indeed, among leaders of almost all persuasions. She could reasonably assume that within the New Deal structure her aims would be sympathetic to its own, perhaps more mut-ed, but nevertheless quite conventional opportunism. That kind of practice applies more to the New Deal work-relief super-ficials outside the arts proj-ects and even more so to the super-ficials outside the WPA than to the art-officials, such as Alsberg and his Washington staff. While the latter had to be sensitive to conventional political considerations among super-ficials at these other levels of policy-making, they gave first priority to their art-offi-cial functions: to direct an efficient, soundly operating work-relief program that alleviated hardship among artists, conserved and developed their tal-ents, and produced work consistent with broad-based democratic values in forms having professional merit. It is easy to imagine that Chittenden's fre-quently untactful rhetoric and her blunt manner of articulating political stra-tegems made art-offcals and politicians uneasy. New Deal executives pre-ferred candied artfulness to hardball when practical politics took precedence over principle. The relationship between practical politics and program-matic purpose is probably the main variable in the problematics of patron-age. This relationship—whether close or at cross-purposes—is ultimately contradictory, because practical politics (as career and personal power) be-comes an end in itself and program an end beyond itself.

For a short time, the division of labor in the Detroit FWP helped to contain the conflict there between politics and program. As the administra-tor responsible for public relations, the business end of personnel matters, and organizational relationships, Chittenden seemed to be carrying out her job without subverting the program. Since Barrett had been made responsi-ble for writing and research and dealing with personnel, the integrity of the program seemed assured. Nevertheless, perhaps because of Chittenden's high-handed and politically motivated manner, in the early part of 1936 Barrett was assailed by vague misgivings about what Chittenden's direction meant for the future character of the project. In April several events involv-ing the disposition of project writers transformed vagueness into certainty.

She was most upset over Chittenden's discharge of two non-relief writers, Auttie James and Kimon Friar. Barrett regarded both among the project's more talented young writers and therefore a great loss; she was also incensed that Chittenden had dismissed them without adequate notice or termination pay.[14] She considered this summary action a violation of procedures that had been established when the project had gotten underway the previous fall and winter.

One other personnel matter also disturbed Barrett, because it lowered the morale of a number of project writers. It had to do with Clifford Montague, a project member in the Grand Rapids region, who was suspected of violating federal law, regulations, or standards of ethics. What disrupted writer and researcher morale was Chittenden's perceived slowness in resolving the case before its details became known to state officials; FWP staff in Grand Rapids informed Barrett that they had known these details long before that. An internally unresolved issue had become a state and federal matter, and the staff felt unsure whether WPA officials and resource people, such as librarians, would cooperate or trust them with what was needed for an informed guide. By April's end, Barrett's distrust had reached the point that she began corresponding with the Washington staff without informing Chittenden, albeit she was her immediate superior. More significantly, Barrett supported other writers in the project and their allies in the Historical Records Survey who had begun to organize a Writers' Guild; they made Chittenden's dismissal of James and Friar the major grievance of the Guild's first meeting, demanding that the two be properly compensated with severance pay and placed in another Federal One unit.

On her part, Chittenden resisted all efforts to moderate her imperious management style. In fact, an investigation by Joseph Gaer, the FWP's Midwest field director, indicated that Chittenden had become even more high-handed. She retaliated by systematically spying on her staff, recruiting her partisans to attend Guild meetings and report the business transacted there and the names of those attending, and using the information to intimidate both relief and non-relief staff. She interrogated some writers about their lunch partners and asked others about Barrett and the Guild, recording their statements—which they were later asked to sign under notary.[15]

Her hostility toward the Historical Records Survey, her suspicions that it was intended as a means to close down the Writers' unit and deprive her of office, surfaced again at this time. In a letter to Alsberg on May 20th, summarizing a notarized statement by Hannah B. Quigley (a project writer who had attended the first Guild meeting), Chittenden claimed that William Jabine, a Historical Survey writer, had announced that the Writers' Project would be closed down by June 30th. According to her, Jabine had promised those present a job on the survey project if they helped Barrett and himself in the campaign to have Chittenden dismissed from her post. Although Barrett and Jabine, who were dismayed by the pileup of demoralizing events, were anxious to see Chittenden go, nothing in the Quigley statement is at all close to Chittenden's assertion.

In the same letter Chittenden explained her refusal to tell workers and administrators in her unit the reasons for her action and why she was denying them redress of grievance—and unwittingly revealed her collegial distrust and authoritarian view of her position. Insisting that her reasons would be misconstrued out of hand, she argued that she withheld information from them because "after all I am not answerable to any but my superiors."[16] But she also resented interference from those above her in rank. Her Washington superiors, trying to defuse the explosive situation that had developed over her firings of James and Friar, set up further guidelines regarding arbitrary and summary dismissals. In a face-to-face meeting with Gaer, Chittenden denounced them "for clipping her of the authority to remove any person working under her."[17]

The final resolution of this strife was effected primarily by Gaer, Stannard, and Schouman, with the approval of Alsberg: both Chittenden and Barrett were removed from the Detroit unit. After hunkering down briefly and threatening a "red scare," Chittenden resigned from her post and ceased to be associated in any way with the FWP or Federal One. Barrett, however, was reassigned to Washington, where she directed the essays division, the largest editorial section, to the end of the project in 1943. According to Mangione, Alsberg requested her reassignment. In a review of the Detroit troubles, a field supervisor—whom Mangione does not name but who most probably was Gaer—described Barrett as "a wildcat." Intrigued, Alsberg called for her transfer to Washington, asserting that the central staff needed wildcats.[18]

I have told this story in great detail because it so clearly demonstrates that the primary issues in the troubled affairs of Michigan's FWP were clashing personalities, harshly different styles, and opposed managerial conceptions. Principles were unquestionably at stake, but they were principles concerned with labor relationships, project morale, and project goals, not the moral, political, or even esthetic slant of the written work itself. As a matter of fact, the disruptions caused by personality, style, and managerial attitude severely impeded the production of guide material by the staff. Hence there was little slant of any kind in written form to arouse anxieties inside or outside the WPA.

Red Scare among Writers

Political slant, however, did become an issue. The "red scare" threatened by Chittenden appeared in a lengthy editorial on July 25, 1936, in the *Detroit Saturday Night*. This essay attacked the Michigan Federal Writers' Project as a specific example of Roosevelt's intention "to betray this country into the hands of the Lenins, the Trotzkys, and Stahlins" [sic]. Claiming that depression-affected writers were too proud to accept work-relief—which it called "charity"—the editorial alleged the Michigan unit had "filled up with reds, communists and malcontents of every description." It named four people as the "cabal" controlling production of the guide: Arthur Clifford, the editor-in-chief; Arthur Kent, the city editor; Leon Couzens; and Louis Falstein. Not content with "reds, communists, and malcontents," the paper resorted to xenophobic and anti-semitic alarms. It charged that Couzens not only ran for office in 1932 on the Socialist slate, but was "a Russian Jew who had his name changed," and that Falstein was "a Russian factory worker" who had "marched in the Ford Hunger March."

The editorial attack was, of course, anything but reasonable. Its aim was to harm the project. Hence it did not matter that it ignored fact, invoked religious, social, and chauvinist prejudice, and relied on sterotypical anti-communism to malign left-wingers who—as a sober view makes clear—genuinely desired to fight for a more equitable and humanized society, even if they were naive or in error that the political movements they belonged to were the best ways to achieve that goal. It did not matter that the editorial ignored the real grounds for dissension in the project or the possibility that a staff composed of writers with different and often opposing political views could agree about arbitrary management and unjust labor relationships and could work together professionally to produce a guide of high quality, as indeed it did, once the obstacles we have delineated were removed.

Moreover, the editorial's aim was to harm more than the project. So it painted red with a very wide brush. In its attempt to scare, it reached out to state WPA administrators and federal FWP staff. It accused Haber, the deputy director, of attempting to fill openings with "his own socialistic friends." Stannard was no better: he was an Englishman by birth, formerly a *Manchester Guardian* staff member, "very boastful of his socialistic leanings," and "practically dictator of this project." The people on the Washington staff who deprived Chittenden of power were also politically suspect. Gaer, the editorial charged, "is very socialistic in his views," and Alsberg as well as George Cronyn, the associate director, "are also most liberal in their views."[19]

Perhaps because it was so alarmist in tone and illogical in argument, this local red scare, like the one attempting to smear the FTP, withered away quickly. It died after the *Detroit Free Press* picked up the issue on August 17th with a short article, based mainly on the *Detroit Saturday Night* editorial. Chittenden's resignation and Barrett's transfer to Washington brought to a close what proved to be, in the history of the Michigan FWP, the most serious check to the unit's research and writing tasks. A period of peace and re-stimulated productivity prevailed under Dr. Cecil Isbell, an academic from the University of Michigan, who replaced Chittenden as director in July, relieving Stannard of his temporary management of the project.[20]

Peace, Renewed Conflict, and a No-Nonsense Regime

In the brief interim between Chittenden and Isbell, Stannard reorganized editorial responsibilities. He placed Clifford, the most talented writer and editor on the staff in the judgment of Gaer and his colleagues, in charge; Kent and Harriet Culver, a close ally of Chittenden when she was in charge, became his assistants. This arrangement defused the editorial disagreements that were tied to Chittenden's Chamber-of-Commerce approach to the guide. As Gaer put it, the editorial point of view associated with Chittenden's regime was that the guide was to be a promotional advertisement: "Mrs. Chittenden, our State Director, and Miss Culver, whom she appointed as Editor, have obtained the idea that anything which belongs to Michigan must be good. So that workers in a Ford factory, according to their copy, leave work as clean as [if] they came out of a dry cleaning plant and as fresh as the proverbial daisies." Gaer reported that staff writers and editors, particularly Clifford and Kent, resented this approach, and he concluded that this accounted in large part for the friction in the Detroit office.[21] The Washington staff and most of the Detroit project writers wanted the guide to be an accurate, realistic, prose portrait of the state's cultural and social diversity, with a literary rather than an advertising cast to it. The Clifford and Kent conception was not regarded as an unacceptable, left-wing slant. Stannard, who had in this same period worried that the Michigan FTP's repertoire was over-weighted with social plays, felt quite secure in making Clifford the editor-in-charge.

When Isbell took office, he reorganized the district staffs, appointing new district directors to replace his predecessor's less professionally qualified but more politically oriented appointments. These changes enhanced morale in the Detroit and district offices and led to a steady flow of research and preliminary essay drafts for the guide. During his tenure, Isbell raised two issues that he thought prevented his staff from producing work of the highest quality. One problem was the hour-rate basis of payment, which he thought was an unprofessional way to treat writers. He hoped to get Washington's approval to pay writers on a salary basis. Alsberg, however, felt powerless to alter national policy. The second problem had to do with FWP policies requiring authorial anonymity and tailoring all the work to a common style and form. These obliterated author individuality. "Realization on the part of our writers," he wrote Alsberg in the spring of 1937, "that they will in no way be identified with the work for which they are primarily responsible inevitably places a damper on their enthusiasm, and kills that most vital spark in any creative effort, pride of workmanship." It was his view that if hour-rate and anonymity prevailed as policy, the Writers' Project could not achieve professional standing. In these matters, Isbell touched upon the major problematic of New Deal patronage, the dual purposes of the arts projects, and he concluded that without a change in policy "the emphasis must inevitably be placed upon it [the FWP] as a relief set-up."[22] We shall come back to this issue in another context. It is important to point out here that in raising these issues with the national office, Isbell defined his relationship to the Writers' Project staff as a leader advocate, not as a commanding officer.

Isbell's greatly improved staff relationships, the editorial changes, and the agency's steady and increased flow of improved guide essays soon came to an end. The letter pressing for a different method of payment and an end to anonymity was in fact a last-ditch plea. Isbell had resigned, in a letter dated February 23rd to become effective March 15th, to accept the editorship of the University of Michigan Press. Appointed to replace him as acting director was the District 4 supervisor, William F. Young, Jr., one of the people Isbell had chosen when reshaping the districts into more professionally led organizations.[23] Clair Laning, Gaer's replacement as Midwest field supervisor in 1937, was confident that Detroit's accomplished writing staff, especially with the talents of Young and Clifford in service, would now reorganize itself effectively. The change in directorship led to renewed contention and fallowness, however—although the period was in no way as bitter and unproductive as the Chittenden one.

The first scuffle had to do with authority. Clifford, who had been made editor-in-chief nine months before Young's March 1937 appointment, resented having been passed over for the directorship and made his views known to Alsberg and Reed Harris, Alsberg's assistant director for administration. He was disturbed that while he had been in editorial charge of the guide for all of Michigan, Young had supervised only one of the districts. Since presumably merit, not political expedience, ruled administrative appointments, he found it puzzling to have been passed over. He remarked that when he became chief editor, "the Project and the Guide were in deplorable condition," yet under his tenure the situation had completely changed: the office now resembled an efficient publishing house editorial room and good copy regularly made its way to Washington. Moreover, having had more responsibility than Young, he had far greater "knowledge of Project affairs." It was not his intention, he maintained, to belittle Young or call for his removal; he simply wanted to be given a fair hearing. Clifford later suggested that he at least be appointed assistant director.

On the other side, Young felt under siege. On June 18, 1937, he informed Alsberg that he had demoted Clifford to staff writer, returning him to relief status, a move that forced Clifford to seek recertification of need to be eligible for employment. Young charged Clifford with double-crossing Isbell more than once, but cited no specific evidence. And although he asserted that Clifford had not openly dealt with himself that way, he claimed that Clifford had engaged in passive resistance on some relatively minor issues and could not be trusted to maintain the unit's discipline among the writers under his supervision. "The idea of having a bête noire doesn't appeal to me," Young told Alsberg. "I've given him every break in my power so that I might get rid of the distrust I have for him. But I can't shake it off and as long as he's in that position, I'll be uneasy."[24]

Young made his move against Clifford part of his response to a directive from the state WPA and the FWP center in Washington to reduce the size of the non-certified staff. He also demoted a number of other writers, such as Kent, who had been elevated to editorial/administrative posts that did not require need qualification. The directive was issued in order to bring non-certified and certified personnel closer to the ten-to-ninety-percent ratio that had been set for all WPA projects, but Young carried it out by cutting non-certified staff with a battle-axe. As a result, he reawakened staff uncertainty and resentment and incurred doubts among his superiors about his executive competence. Clair Laning, part of the Alsberg inner cabinet from 1935, was appalled at the deep cuts intended by Young. Laning called Young overzealous and his new quota for non-certified people, six in all, entirely unacceptable; it was simply not enough to carry out the guide-book work effectively.[25]

Young never recovered the confidence of the Washington office; throughout the rest of his tenure, people there found his competence wanting, particularly since the unit's guide-book submissions fell drastically from their Isbell levels. In February 1938, Alsberg complained to John Frederick, the state director of the Illinois Writers' Project and also the regional director for the Midwest, that "Mr. Young seems singularly dilatory," that he and Laning were "very dissatisfied with Young's work," and that Young had failed to get public support for the Project.[26] By April, completely distrustful of Young's ability to reclassify people appropriately, Washington had begun the search for a replacement.[27]

The appointment of John Dimmick Newsom in June 1938 got the unit back on track. Newsom, who turned out to be the last director of the Michigan FWP as originally legislated, was an extremely efficient administrator. With completion of the guide at the center of his attention, he insisted on a no-nonsense approach to work. What he said later, when he became the national director of a reorganized writers' program in August 1939, holds for his Michigan tenure: "This is a production unit, and it's work that counts. I've never been for art for art's sake alone."[28] But Newsom was eminently fair in his conduct of business and not self-seeking, and he won the respect of his staff. Although he gave esthetic considerations a backseat to getting work done, he nevertheless appreciated the talents of his staff and, like Isbell, pushed Washington for the right to give his writers written credit if their work excelled. He made a particularly strong plea to have Robert Hayden's essay on Michigan's underground railroad published as a monograph and Hayden acknowledged for this "original piece of research work." Assessing the man who was to become a major American poet after World War II, Newson told Alsberg that "Mr. Hayden is one of our most promising writers."[29] Unfortunately, the Hayden manuscript was never published as a monograph. It probably fell victim to the turmoil the FWP found itself in when it came under attack from the Dies (HCUA) and Woodrum (Appropriations) congressional committees that summer and when the Emergency Relief Act of 1939 imposed severe constraints on the kind of work the reorganized projects were to do.[30]

Writers on Work-Relief Talent

If federal and state supervisors in their dual roles as art-officials and super-ficials—Barrett, Isbell, and Newsom on the state level as well as Gaer and Laning on the federal level—admired the writing talents in the Michigan FWP, the writers themselves were not so sure. Their uncertainty reflects in another way the strange entanglement of New Deal support for the arts under the work-relief concept. My interviews with former members of the Michigan unit, more than forty years after Federal One came to an end, reveal their less sanguine self-appraisals. My informants generally took the humble road, expressing doubts about their individual creative and expository skills. By and large, they thought their FWP colleagues were better than themselves, but except for two or three, they did not regard the bulk of them as particularly talented. One informant reported that two groups, neither of which was very accomplished, made up the great majority of writers on the project: the young people "just trying their wings" and the old-timers, mostly newspapermen some ten to twenty years back, "who weren't going to do a damn thing."[31]

Several informants zeroed in on one young man, Anteo J. Tarini, as the unit's truly promising poet and felt that it would be important to interview him. But when told that many of his former FWP mates thought him to be the best poet in the unit, he demurred emphatically, claiming to have been only a dabbler, not a poet. The true poet in the unit, he submitted, was Hayden. Hayden, himself, however, had a very modest view of his writing at that time. In an interview several months before his death, he said that being on the FWP staff saved his life as a writer, because it meant that he did not have to take on some job that would keep him from writing and because it surrounded him with writers whose abilities were far more advanced than his own. He then singled out, unhesitatingly, the project writer who, in his opinion, was producing work worthy of being called poetry—one could almost hear the name before it rolled off his lips—Anteo Tarini![32]

The self-deference and the criss-crossing evaluation of colleagues that interviews reveal make an amusing anecdote. Still more amusing and also a cautionary reminder to researchers wanting to establish the living truth of a past time is the ambiguity of oral recalls. Oral testimony is shinnying up a greased pole, slipping and sliding as it tries, from a mind-altering present moment, to reach a past cloudy with mists of years ago. The main point, however, is that the uncertain and contradicting judgments about one's own writing ability and about the ability of others is powerfully, if not exclusively, determined by a patronage designed to relieve economic hardship on one hand and to foster art as well as conserve talent on the other. Could high or widespread confidence be expected where untried young writers and past-their-prime old ones—that is, those writers most in need—made up the bulk of the staff? How could the one group learn from the other and the other be recharged with youthful energy, when all were trying desperately to hang on under roller-coaster allocations? Uncertainty and anxiety were rife because allocations were periodically refigured up and down primarily on the rise and fall of the economy and the fickle temperaments of fiscally tight legislators.

Patronage as Work Relief and the Union Encounter

The upper hand given to the work-relief aspect by Congress in deciding annually how much money to dole out for the New Deal's Janus-headed patronage system led to a regularly recurring strife between producing artists, whose jobs were at stake, and administering art-officials and super-ficials. The character of this strife was not the Marxist class struggle, but the usual labor-management dispute over lay-offs, working conditions, and schedules. In 1937 and 1938, conflicts over job cutbacks because of reduced allocations broke out in all the art agencies, but mainly in the Writers'

Projects. "Pink-slipping" in the wake of budget reductions almost always came as double-digit slashes.[33] The contestants were not individuals personally aggrieved with each other, but representatives of the union organized by the writers and artists to protect their jobs, and the managerial staff representing the New Deal administration and the legislative contingencies under which it operated. The art-officials were essentially middlemen in these conflicts, required to administer what government executives (Roosevelt, Hopkins, their super-ficial appointees) and the legislature (through their budget enactments) ordained. Most of them sympathized with the artists' side of the battle; when they were cast into their overlapping super-ficial roles, they were helpless carriers-out of a policy they had little relish for.

By this time Congress, under pressure from its conservative members and a seemingly recovering economy, was bent on paring down WPA allocations. The artists and writers union, first heard from in 1936, had become a fairly well-organized voice of the working members of the various federal art agencies, but it had not become regularly affiliated with an AFL or CIO international. Through a good part of 1937, when more writers and artists were committing themselves to an organized, collective way of dealing with their grievances and lay-off fears, their group applied for a charter from the AFL's American Federation of Government Employees (AFGE). In the months of waiting for their application to be approved, they called themselves Lodge 322, in accordance with the still-retained craft tradition of the AFGE. By late fall, the AFGE rejected their request for membership.[34] In 1938 they continued to be an organized collective under the name Professional Division Workers' Alliance (PDWA). The Workers' Alliance was an independent group originating in New York City and largely inspired by the Communist Party.[35] Workers' Alliances sprang up all over the country in the mid-1930s. Although the drive to organize Alliances came from the left sympathetic to the Party, the various Alliances across the country never achieved more than a loosely federated state. Detroit writers and artists pushed their demands through all of these organizational affiliations over these years, until June 13, 1938, when they were finally absorbed into Local 26 of the larger, more centrally organized United Office and Professional Workers of America, a CIO international.[36]

Through these various affiliations, the Detroit group's membership continued to grow, becoming fairly substantial by December 1937, but never attracting a majority. Nevertheless, the union apparently had the good wishes of most work-relief personnel assigned to the arts projects. The animators of the group, many of them left-wingers, remained pretty much the same as it shifted from one national union to another: Arthur Clifford, Leon Couzens, Stanley de Graff, Louis Falstein, Rebecca Shelley Rathmer, Anteo Tarini of the FWP; Edith Segal, the choreographic director of the FTP, Hy

Fireman, performer and photographer with the FTP; and Maurice Merlin, Barbara Wilson, and Walter Speck of the FAP.

Newspaper accounts of the union confrontations in New York, San Francisco, and Los Angeles paint lurid pictures of radical intent.[37] So did the Dies Committee, which turned its public gaze on the arts projects in late 1938 and early 1939. Among authors of retrospective studies of the era, Penkower attributes a disruptive effect to competition between the Stalinist and Trotskyist wings of the Party and ulterior "red" strategies to achieve recognition from Moscow. In this last charge, he is essentially alone among those who have written concentrated histories or memoirs of New Deal patronage. Mangione, while not denying the presence of communist sympathizers in the projects and their leading role in New York and West Coast union affairs, does not see byzantine plots to enhance reputation in their union activities.[38] Malcolm Cowley's 1938 description of Federal Writers' Project poets is quite on the mark in its lucid detail of the problems and responses of project writers contending with New Deal patronage under work-relief auspices. "They have never been sure," he writes, "of their pay from one week to the next; some whim of Congress or some administrative ruling might abolish their jobs. This situation has led to sitdowns, picket lines, telegrams to senators and, in general, a host of distractions that have prevented them from planning their lives or their work in advance."[39]

The series of demands the Michigan union presented to WPA administrators in the spring of 1937 illustrates the issues that distracted project writers and theater people then and afterwards not only from their development as creative writers, which is what Cowley had foremost in mind, but also from their prescribed task. There were nine demands, all but one of which dealt with job security, wages, or conditions of work. Security was represented by demands to stop further curtailment of WPA projects; increase personnel quotas for the FWP and the FAP; give three months' notice before discontinuing a project; and adopt a policy of two weeks' notice before dismissing anyone. The proposal also called for a twenty-percent wage increase and a workweek of three eight-hour days. As for working conditions, the union called for the right of cultural staff to work at home or other sites outside the project centers if this would be appropriate, and it also urged the state administrator to push for increased material allocations.

The one exception was the demand that FTP plays be freed of WPA administrative censorship. The union asked that FTP employees be granted more autonomy in play selection, that the state administrator be required to call for a hearing by FTP personnel before advising against a play, and that the FTP and the FWP set up a joint committee to assist in choosing plays. Although this issue centered directly on artistic and creative concerns, it is hard to read into a demand for artistic freedom a plot to sneak in Bolshevik ideology.[40] As we have seen, the plays that aroused administrative objections, while exposing social, economic, and political problems, were progressive rather than Marxist.[41]

Other union affairs that went beyond security, wages, and working conditions, and might be seen as a left-wing conspiracy were attempts at displaying art project solidarity with other oppressed segments of society. For example, the union planned to request restaurants in the vicinity of the various projects to serve African Americans and to boycott those that refused. In a show of unity between cultural workers and manual workers, union members organized a dance called "Pick, Pen, Palette Frolic." It also participated in general trade-union demonstrations for jobs, such as the Labor Day march in downtown Detroit's Cadillac Square, where the artists made a "showing with banners" and Tarini spoke with eloquence. The union also organized project artists and writers to show support for striking workers by joining their picket lines.[42]

Rebecca Shelley, a Writers' Project member and at one time head of the folklore program, told me an amusing anecdote, when she was in her nineties, of one such outing by writers and artists to the Flint sit-down strike. A rather frail woman at the time of the telling, tiny in stature, unsure of step but still sharp and focused in mind, she told this story in a quavering voice while nestled in the corner of her couch. One winter day the union rounded up a number of project workers, Shelley included, for a car ride to Flint. As a project member she made $24 a month, leaving her with little money for clothes, and so on this occasion she was wearing a five-cent paper dress. It was a cold and rainy day, and rain fell for the several hours Shelley and her fellow work-relief writers marched round and round the Chevrolet plant where the automobile workers were sitting-in. Pretty soon, she recalled in wobbling tones, the dress was thoroughly drenched and had shrunk halfway up her thighs. Undaunted by this assault of nature on her nickel dress, she kept on picketing, never thinking to retreat from public gaze, modest though she was.[43] Shelley was a life-long pacifist, about whom we shall say more later on; aside from her opposition to war, she professed to be rather uninformed about politics. But her story shows that, during the depression, writers and would-be-writers could be, when called upon, steadfast in solidarity with other hard-pressed segments of the American population. The left-wing leadership could count on devotion to organize auxiliary strike support without being suspected of a conspiracy to take over the federal arts projects for world revolution.[44]

The Detroit union also rallied project writers, performers, and artists behind the efforts exerted by certain senators and congressmen to establish a permanent patronage not tied to temporary relief programs. A bill offered by Representative William Sirovich in 1937 called for a Department of Science, Art, and Literature, with a building to match the new headquarters of the Supreme Court. Another, proposed jointly by Congressman Harry Coffee and Senator Claude Pepper, provided for the retention of all personnel employed by the federal arts projects at prevailing union wages. Both pieces of legislation had the support of the Washington super-ficial/art-official administrators, with the most enthusiastic support coming from Flanagan. She had reservations about the grandiosity of the Sirovich Bill and thought the Coffee-Pepper idea of freezing all arts project employees on the government payroll entirely unrealistic. But she strongly favored the spirit of the legislation: "to enlarge the cultural base of American life by making art the enjoyment and privilege of all the people."[45]

Malcolm Cowley did not think the Coffee-Pepper provision to have artists on the federal payroll so terribly ill-founded. In his view, the 1930s depression had only intensified what had been true for American writers ever since the Jamestown settlement: the overwhelming bulk of them have been driven from the field because they have always "gone without wages." "If we want to have poets in this country," he wrote, "we will have to keep them alive."[46]

From the character of the legislative proposals and the support they attracted at top levels inside and outside the arts projects, we can see that economic issues in the form of living wages and stable federal patronage played a larger part than ideology, content of production, or quality of performance. Flanagan's ideology—that ordinary people everywhere had the right of access to the arts—was hardly more than a commonly held democratic sentiment and in essence economic: WPA-like government patronage, unleashed from emergency and relief, would guarantee a reliable stream of affordable art to all the people.

The rank-and-file in regions where the federal projects had established themselves, including Detroit, responded wholeheartedly to the twin needs addressed by the proposed legislation. Left-wingers in various union branches around the country led the way in this matter, but apparently without trying to supplant the liberal ideology underlying the bills with their own radical ideas. But no matter how warm the response and deserving the legislation (which ultimately failed), this union effort—like others that either were or were not strictly trade-unionist in character—distracted work-relief artists from the craft work that they were intended to perform, as Cowley pointed out.

In Detroit, Edith Segal was the person most deeply engaged in keeping the legislation for a permanent form of art patronage before the union membership. Segal had been accused of selling the *Daily Worker* to FTP members, a charge that neither she nor FTP art-officials ever denied. A left-winger openly sympathetic to communism, she devoted a great deal of time to the Detroit union. But that never seemed to interfere with her choreographic or acting responsibilities, for which she frequently received high praise from the FTP director with the longest Detroit tenure, Verner Haldene. In February of 1938 she was particularly involved with legislation for a permanent federal art establishment. At the February 15th meeting of the union, then affiliated with the Professional Division of the Workers' Alliance, she described the specific provisions of the Coffee-Pepper bill, and formulated plans to enlist prominent people in the campaign to get it through Congress. She also moved that the union and its supporters attend the national conference called for the following month to promote the bill. A week later she spoke about the legislation again, this time proposing that Lawrence Tibbet be invited to Michigan to speak, as he had done elsewhere, in its favor.[47] All of these plans show that Segal never got beyond mainstream strategies to solve the problematics of New Deal patronage.

Mainstream strategies and conventional trade union tactics proved inadequate to cut through the bureaucratic tangle of conflicting authority centers, cultural sensibilities, and practical aims that kept the FTP and FWP in Michigan and the rest of the nation so terribly off balance. Nor were they adequate to resolve the contradiction at the heart of a patronage with bold, populist views of art that had to operate within the contingencies of an emergency work-relief program. Since the staffs of these projects proposed no new liberal or radical strategies for rank-and-file resistance to the destabilizing factors afflicting the projects, we have no way of measuring whether they might have been able to overcome the skein of conflicted issues that constituted New Deal patronage, and we are left with no touchstone to test the ability of politicians and artists to escape the problematics of any official patronage. What we do know is that the circumstances I have described drained Michigan's super-ficial/art-official administrators as well as the writers and theater people under their direction of time and energy and severely handicapped their journey into the brimming cultural resources and inspirational stimuli offered by the unprivileged publics they sought after.

PART 4

**The Making and
Unmaking of Populist
Esthetics: The Midwest
Achievement of the FTP
and FWP**

12

Odd Couplings:
Popular Arts, the Classics,
and Populist Esthetics

N EW Deal patronage, as we have seen, did more than dispense money. It used the funds allocated to it to conserve and develop literary and theatrical talents by employing professional and would-be artists in its own training centers and production units and to make the work produced by these units democratically accessible and responsive to the life and culture of unprivileged publics. That was the side of New Deal patronage directly engaged with literary and theatrical issues and a problematic set different than the one posed by the bureaucratic morass we have just explored. The dynamics of the writing and performance problematic, in the 1935 to 1939 span of the arts projects, was a perplexity caught in a two-step jiggle creatively enhancing on one beat and disruptive on the other.

Key to this two-stepping perplex was a series of specific oppositional factors in the literary and theatrical dealings at the heart of New Deal patronage. The first of these derived from public accountability for tax dollars. Although the federally administered art units and their producing branches focused on the aims of acquiring disregarded audiences and having their own work inspired by the various cultures represented by such audiences, they had to pay attention to quick and successful results measured by audience size and box-office receipts. The anxiety of New Deal policymakers and executives to justify the use of public funds was transmitted to the art-officials directly responsible for the projects at all levels. This anxiety was felt with particular intensity by the Art, Theater, and Writing projects, the ones which most apparently dealt with social and moral ideas and ideologies. Of course congressmen, especially conservative ones, manifested impatience from the very beginning of the venture, and New Dealers in policy-making and executive positions compounded the problem by presuming that ordinary taxpayers might also be impatient or become so at anytime.

But populist esthetics and performance designed to validate as quickly as possible a public investment in art do not always synchronize. The former, with its twin aims of inspiring and winning disregarded publics, moves to a rhythm shaped by circumstances of knowledgeability, transmission, absorption, and creative return. Hence populist esthetics is alien to made-to-order formulas and is not highly predictable, two requisite characteristics for performance measured by rapid results and conventional signs of success. Luck—in the form of already present, concatenated circumstances shaping the rhythm of populist esthetics—may make grass-roots inspired writing and theatrical fare available on short notice; indeed this happened in some regional and local cases. Some of the FWP work in the South on life histories and slave narratives are instances. Foreign language theater in New York, Los Angeles, and Tampa, and black theater in New York, Seattle, and Chicago also come to mind.[1] But luck is not typical of the projects in most other places and not dependable, even in such large centers as New York and Chicago, where creative talent sensitive to unprivileged cultures abounded.

For immediate success, the local writing and theater projects had to rely on more conventional and proven formulas, on the established styles and works of popular and classical literature and theater. For the FWP, this generally meant rejecting style and content that fell outside popular and classical norms to preempt conventionally-minded WPA super-ficials outside the FWP, federal and state legislators, and local newspapers and magazines from objecting and thus delaying guide production.

The quality of writing in non-cosmopolitan regions acted as still another drag on production. Local FWP writers in heartland localities produced many poorly written essays. The FWP editorial staff in Washington had to return copy again and again for revision. That in itself constituted no major drawback, nor was the need to do so at all unanticipated. Administrators at the federal center expected from the outset that writers who met the need requirement for project employment and who lived in places far removed from the major intellectual centers of the United States were for the most part either rusty or green in craft, and thus from the very beginning they laid down principles of conservation and training. The return of essays for revision could have become, indeed seems to be precisely, one of the significant procedures to make those principles a living practice.

But the urgency to produce something that federal patronage could demonstrate as returned value for the public money invested in it often deflected central editing from being a useful learning experience for writers. Washington's editorial commentary tended to routine normative changes, sometimes to imposing a straightjacket of form, and often to being too precise. It seemed to offer little general evaluation that could serve as instructive advice and little editing notation that could stimulate hands-on learning of craft.

The editorial commentary on the architectural essays submitted by the Michigan FWP bears out the point. The earliest ones offer nothing more helpful in the way of advice than this: "The present architectural section is clumsy, especially the handling of functionalism on page 2. The idea is all right, but the execution is poor." "Clumsy" and "poor execution" are not very precise terms. The comments on subject treatment contributed not much more to the possibility of learning. The Washington editor carried on at some length about the inflated reputation and influence of Eero Saarinen's Cranbrook style of architecture. "We should not allow our Michigan people to be pushed around by the shoddy snap judgments and current values of the Cranbrook idea." Abstract handicraft art was too insular, "fussy and modernique," the editor wrote, and of little integrity for depression and industrial America.[2] But how writers might express themselves without being pushed around is no more instructively rendered than what signs constitute clumsiness.

Page by page and line by line editing turned out to be too precise for writers to play around with alternative possibilities. We find among the revisions proposed for an essay on Grand Rapids architecture and furniture-making such entries as: "*Page 4*. L. 4—'a *surprising* number of churches' —State the number. About 200?"; "*Page 6*. L. 12—'only one motion picture in the whole large area'—One motion picture *theatre* probably intended"; and in the same vein, "*Page 18*. 4th line from bottom—'All important buses pass through Campau square'—All important *bus lines* probably meant."[3] Clearly the intent of such revisions is not to teach writers how to be more precise, but to clean up copy and get guide production moving.

A survey of the comments made by Washington on the Michigan labor and black life essays reveals the same editorial approach, general but largely equivocal criticism of style and form and then revision proposals so circumscribed that local writers had almost no leeway in rewriting their essays. The Washington staff frequently voiced a concern that their critical approach would have a demoralizing effect. Sterling Brown, the first person to be put in charge of the FWP's black studies program, wrote Isbell that he hoped his critique of the Michigan essays would not discourage the writer, Clarence Patrick. But believing, as he did, "that the story of the Negro in Detroit and in Michigan is one of great interest," he was "very anxious to see all the drama and truth included in the Michigan guide."[4] Apparently he doubted that the criticism he had made would be instructive enough to be taken positively. As late as 1939, the same insecurity about the instructive value of the critique of the labor essay surfaced in a letter from Alsberg to Newsom. "Criticism of the Michigan *labor* essay, which is being returned to you today," wrote Alsberg, "seems to be a little fruitless." He noted that "a good general criticism" had been made the year before and should be consulted again. Although the resubmitted essay was an improvement over the earlier one, it still had "the mark of a superficial, poorly documented account," and the style needed refining. Alsberg informed Newsom that he did not want his criticism to have a discouraging effect and advised him to consult William Haber at the University of Michigan if he thought it too harsh.

Alsberg, as the Washington editorial staff before, wanted a style that was concise and conformed to standard English. But he was also worried about content that might be regarded as unsupported and injudicious in its sympathies. He assumed—and with good reason, given the dramatic character of Michigan labor in the depression—that its story would have a large audience and receive considerable scrutiny. "Every effort should be made," he pleaded, "to have it a clear factual statement of events. This is especially true of the recent labor history [he surely meant the sit-down strikes], which is the poorest section of the present essay."[5] In May 1939, with the Dies and Woodward committees hot for the kill of Federal One, particularly the Theater and Writers' projects, there was even greater anxiety than in the early days of the project, when the major concern was that non-normative style and content might arouse furies that would hold up production of a Michigan guide.

The fear was not misguided. Nonconforming content often led to outside interference and nonobservance of standard style unquestionably required enormous revision. But the Washington center and local art-officials may be taxed for the delay as well. They displayed too much timidity. Greater confidence in unconventional style and content, in the possible receptivity of grass-roots publics to new ways of writing and new attitudes toward public events and cultures might have overcome or at least defused the force of those fussing over deviations from hegemonic standards. Further, out of anxiety for speed, the Washington center and local art-officials failed to work out an effective program for restoring the old and training the new talents of project personnel. Their procedures were penny-wise but, one may reasonably say, pound-foolish. A sound program of conservation and training would have produced local unit writers capable of quality work, based on their own reacquired and developing craft, in less time, ironically, than the drawn-out process of tedious, uninstructive overattention that resulted from the compulsion to get something done at once.

The felt need for a record of immediate performance interfered with, but did not overwhelm, the populist esthetic of the Writers' Project. Because it was essentially a writing, not a publishing endeavor, and because its assignment was to produce original, although highly controlled projects, the Writers' Project had first to create the material to be published. This material was channeled into studies of grass-roots subjects, neglected or unprivileged publics, and folk cultures. This channelling was an inevitable consequence of a governmental patronage designed for large-scale employment of writers and for all citizens in a market economy governed by private enterprise. What kind of work could such federal patronage do? It could not be allowed to compete, over the same material, with the established professional writing world—which was primarily engaged, as we have seen, in hegemonic forms and issues with tendencies located either in cosmopolitanism or conservative regionalism. Nor could it be allowed to compete with the publishing industry, whose product also generally conformed to the norms and experiments acceptable to the hegemony of privileged culture.[6] Hence, whether it wanted it or not, populist esthetics had to be its lifeblood. Ironically, since a dominating capitalist culture monopolized its own privileged esthetics, it courted its opposite by barring public patronage from private-sector competition.

This inevitable yet inadvertent imposition of populist estheics on New Deal patronage to prevent market competition is not the whole story. For social and literary reasons, New Deal patronage wanted populist esthetics to be the essential principle of the Writers' Project as well as the Theater and Art projects. That want came, as I have pointed out, from the center as well as the outlands. It came from the center, in general, because of the social orientation of the people attracted by depression contingencies to serve in the New Deal administration and, in particular, because of the people appointed to carry out the work of the Writers' Project and the other arts projects. It came from the outlands because of the progressive/radical regionalism of art-officials and rank-and-filers who staffed the outland units, and also because the disenfranchised publics in the rural and industrial provinces offered fertile, lively cultures to seed that kind of orientation.

Even before the Writers' Project officially got underway, a crowd of populist ideas emanated from the center itself, as its personnel struggled to find a professional relief formula that was more than this-month-you-see-it and next-you-don't. But a throng of populist notions also arrived unsolicited from the outlands, where all sorts of people had ideas about professional projects to study neglected publics. In 1934 and early 1935, before the WPA as a whole or the arts projects within it had become detailed, workable concepts, Michigan's Emergency Relief Administration (ERA) had entertained ideas of local histories, ethnic studies, folklore research, and Native-American song and legend collecting. Catherine Murray, the director of the Womens's Work division of ERA in Michigan in those pre-WPA days, had made these known to Nina Collier of Washington's ERA section of

Professional Projects. Murray passed along to Collier the letter, cited in Chapter 1, proposing a series of grass-roots enterprises by people on relief. These ideas came from Bernard Coggan, one of Murray's administrative lieutenants, and covered the collecting of folk songs, customs, games, superstitions, and legends associated with various ethnic communities in Michigan, including its Indian population. These ideas derived not only from a long-time interest Coggan and his wife had in folkloric studies, but from contact he had made with different ethnic publics, among whom he found young people teeming with "varied legends, songs, customs, superstitions, and games" that were "traceable directly to the early home of their parents or grandparents." Coggan was attracted to modern methods of collecting, such as phonographic recording. But because of his contact experiences, he was also partial to having individuals from the community do the collecting without artificial devices, individuals "who could set down the notes as a person sang."[7]

These early-day tendencies toward populist esthetics may also be found among Midwest art-officials responsible for FERA art programs. Nora Crump, who at that time was in charge of Michigan's Wayne County Art Project, spelled out some of the grass-roots work of her group in a December 1934 letter to Arthur Goldschmidt, Washington's acting director of Professional Projects under FERA. She took particular pride in the work, which she called outstanding, because of its enthusiasm and the good-fellowship of the artists she had assembled under the program. She pointed out that the group represented twenty nationalities: Croation, Estonian, Russian, Polish, Yugoslavian, Hungarian, Austrian, German, Swedish, Danish, Swiss, Dutch, Norwegian, French, French-Canadian, Italian, Spanish, English, Irish, and Welsh. The art work her diverse group was doing included folklore illustrated through dioramas, local and state history murals, and oil reproductions of historical subjects.[8]

Coggan's proposal and Crump's account of her group, both seconded by Murray, received a hearty welcome in Washington, as did the proposals from other outlying regions and localities.[9] It is quite clear that Washington art-officials, many of whom were from outlying regions, encouraged populist esthetics from the beginning and that, at the same time, their own commitment was pushed forward by populist proposals and activities from below. The force of this double-headed populist drive was so strong that even when the center faltered, perceiving that political caution and immediate successes were needed, the FWP consistently followed grass-roots themes over its four-year federal tenure.

Its accomplishments along these lines varied greatly from place to place. Some localities produced outstanding work, particularly when the lead was taken by a talented individual or a group of professionally experienced writers, or when the FWP unit was close to disenfranchised publics. The most celebrated cases of project accomplishment as a consequence of talented individual leadership are the Idaho FWP and the Louisiana FWP. The Idaho guide book, crowded with information about Idaho Indians, and *Idaho Lore* (1939), both praised for literary worth, were essentially authored by its state director, the novelist Vardis Fisher.[10] The *New Orleans City Guide* (1938), called a "literary gem" by Jerre Mangione, was written by the Louisiana FWP state director, Lyle Saxon, another one of the few non-eastern novelists appointed to that kind of position. Saxon was also mainly responsible for reworking and rewriting the folk tales collected by the Louisiana staff and later issued under the title *Gumbo Ya-ya*. Considered one of the best folklore collections to come from the FWP because of its authentic flavor and excellent writing, it appeared in 1945.[11]

The best examples of above-standard work produced by collectives of professional writers came from the big centers. The Washington, D. C., guide is one such case. The group of writers assembled by the FWP in Washington, many in leading administrative positions, represented a considerable asset. The collective contribution of this professionally experienced group surely accounts for its high standard in writing and documentary accuracy, but perhaps also for its mammoth size.[12] The Washington guide also demonstrates that collective writing did not forestall individual talent. One of its more compelling accomplishments, the article on Washington's black history and population, is the work of Sterling Brown. Brown's essay is compelling because he was an excellent stylist who never flinched from honestly portraying the harsh injustice suffered by the capital's African Americans in the past and the present. The FWP units in Boston, New York, Chicago, Los Angeles, and San Francisco also benefited from the many experienced writers they could call on. *Massachusetts: A Guide to Its Places and People* (1937) was a collective achievement that received a great deal of praise from a variety of governmental and literary figures. The critic for the *Nation* called its writing "brilliant." It then ran into a storm because of a thirty-one-line entry on Sacco and Vanzetti and what Boston newspapers and politicians blasted as its pro-labor orientation.[13]

The other factor in accomplishing above-standard work—the close ties of particular units and regional staffs to disenfranchised publics—is primarily represented by certain units in the South. Perhaps the best-case scenario in this regard is the oral history work of the North Carolina FWP. Under the guidance of William Couch, who had a great deal of folk collecting experience before he became associate director of that project, interviewers gathered narrative accounts of the daily life histories of agricultural and factory workers, an effort that produced the much-hailed *These Are Our Lives* (1939).

209

The slave-narrative achievement also belongs to this category of ties to disenfranchised publics. Slave narratives were collected in a great number of states. After the FWP passed from federal to state control in the fall of 1939, the unpublished narratives were transferred to the Library of Congress, where a staff under Benjamin Botkin's guidance collated them into seventeen volumes—a priceless collection, much of which is still to be mined by scholars for public dissemination. Indiana and Ohio contributed so many narratives that each of them warranted an individual volume. Only two state FWPs, Virginia and Georgia, managed to publish works using their slave narrative material. *The Negro in Virginia* (1941) is a prime example of how sympathetic orientation and grass-roots ties in the field guided by experience and sensitivity in Washington produced first-rate work. Under careful direction from Sterling Brown, who asked that "truth to idiom be paramount and exact truth to pronunciation secondary," and locally supervised by the black scholar Roscoe E. Lewis, a group of black writers and researchers produced a work of black history reinforced by black slave stories and folklore that was widely accorded the status of a classic for that genre. The *American Mercury* was particularly impressed with its collective composition: "The product of many hands, Negro and white, it is so brilliantly edited that it reads as though it might be an individual work of a singularly competent historian."[14]

13

Federal Writers' Project: Midwest Ups and Downs

B UT distinguished work was exceptional, for the favoring circumstances that led to it were not to be counted on everywhere. Again we turn to Michigan and other Midwest places for the more usual model. The Michigan FWP, like most branches across the nation, hewed to the populist orientation inherent in New Deal patronage with varying intensity. It stuck to its populist guns despite its largely inexperienced writing and research staff, who were quite untrained for the manifold task of discovering, evaluating, and accurately gathering the everyday life experiences, beliefs and customs, tales and expressive modes that signify the heartbeats of unprivileged cultures. Nor were they particularly practiced in the art and science of recovering from mutilation and disregard the history of unprivileged publics. Moreover, the over-the-hill or not-yet-arrived expressive skills of so many of the staff put the Michigan unit to a severe test in rendering such discoveries and recoveries with a dramatic flair that would not violate authenticity. Such circumstances hardly favored riveting results.

The staff's generally progressive outlook fostered an empathy for neglected publics. But empathy is one thing and closely bonded rapport another. Such rapport often inspires a sensitive, imaginative handling of the cultural materials offered from below, as the FWP work in North Carolina and Virginia demonstrates. Writing skills and historical techniques, no matter how advanced, seem incapable on their own of that kind of imaginative leaven.[1] Nevertheless, the work of populist esthetics proceeded, producing some modest success and leaving behind a store of useful material that suggests what could be done and what needs to be done along these lines.

A Guide to Michigan: "warts and all"

The FWP work produced in Michigan in the four major areas—the guide book, folklore, black studies, and ethnic studies—exemplifies, for most parts of the country, how the tangle of factors I have been describing affected specific accomplishments in the populist esthetics aimed at by New Deal patronage. We start with the guide. An unpublished memoir, represented as a novel, provides us with a succinct summary of the kind of guide the Michigan FWP wanted to turn out. Its author, Louis Falstein, includes an account of his interview with Mary Barrett, disguised by the name Myra Kelly, when he applied for a position on the FWP staff. The interview was actually a one-way affair: Barrett's irrepressible conception of the Michigan guide. It was to be "a genuine study" of the state, she said with enthusiasm. "Not only will we include Ford's phenomenal contribution to the science of production, we will also write about the Ford Hunger March—if I have anything to say about it." She summed up the character of the planned work with the phrase "warts and all."[2]

"Warts and all" was, of course, the Washington art-officials' original intention for the guide. The central staff's only dissenter was Katherine Kellock, one of the very earliest proposers of a guide series. Believing that a guide loaded with cultural and historical essays would be boring, she wanted the series to focus strictly on tour descriptions, the chief aim being to attract visitors. While in Michigan and when she was transferred to Washington, Barrett was an enthusiastic supporter of the original intention. In her view, Michigan should produce a guide that was more than a Baedeker clone or a local booster's tract. It was to be honestly gutsy in its treatment of the state's history and culture. The final product, however, tells us that something happened on the way to the forum.

The guide book occupied most of the Michigan FWP's time over the four years of its federal existence, and the work did not get into print until 1941, a record that pretty much matches that of the other midwestern states. Minnesota is the only exception, managing to get its guide book out only a year behind the deadline Alsberg had set. Illinois made it in 1939, Ohio in 1940, and Indiana and Wisconsin, like Michigan, in 1941, four years behind schedule. Those familiar with the scope of the task and the standards demanded for the guides regard Alsberg's publication goal as unrealistic. That most FWP units missed the deadline by several years indicates, of course, the counterproductive effects induced by the politics of speed and caution, staff rustiness and inexperience, and the cumbersome process of editing. The Michigan experience illustrates how hard it was to make headway. Leading the bulk of old-timers with stagnating skills and newcomers with limited practice in the unit were some talented editors and writers: people like Arthur Clifford, who had already established a reputation as a literary prize-winner; Leon Couzens, who came to the project with experience in newspaper and political writing; Louis Falstein, an inexperienced writer who proved to be a capable one very early on; Robert Hayden, who even in those youthful days demonstrated an exact, lapidary style and research diligence; Kimon Friar, who already showed, in addition to esthete affectations, a dramatic and inventive flair for ideas and the capacity to express them effectively. But all that talent could not get up a full head of steam against the contradictory dynamics of federal patronage.

Nevertheless, the Michigan FWP also illustrates the ability of local units, once some of the bureaucratic and personality difficulties were cleared out of the way, to produce a competently written guide studded with information. What the Michigan FWP lost in the process is the gutsiness that Barrett, in the voice of Falstein's Myra Kelly, announced with excitement and determination. In the ups and downs of the bureaucratic snarls, the cautious waverings, and the anxiety-ridden let's-get-something-done spirit that beset it, the Michigan FWP managed to hang on to populist esthetics—but not to Barrett's "warts and all" approach. Her excitement, like the early excitement in Washington, took wing from the promise of doing something original, of seeing the nation and its publics from a new perspective, not from top-down decorum and condescension, but from ground-up candor and toughness. The final version of the Michigan guide retains glimmerings of grass-roots life. Unfortunately, the toughness is gone.

The Cosmetics of Sameness in Structure and Style

The judgment of scholars looking back at the FWP and cultural commentators contemporary with it that the project's greatest literary feat is the guide series is beyond dispute. Even among those most convinced of the need for the FWP, few believed that state units distant from the nation's cultural metropolises and staffed by unknown writers could produce so steady a stream of informed, highly readable works. The series in the aggregate and almost any single volume, viewed without comparison to any of the others, prove the literary impressiveness of the completed undertaking. Examination of the volumes side by side, however, produces a less positive effect. Comparative analysis reveals a uniformity of structural pattern and stylistic/tonal restraint across the series that deprives each volume of the lustre of localized collective personality and hence the spark of discovery that difference could generate.

The Michigan guide is as good an introduction as any to the unrelenting sameness of the series organization. The book is divided into three sections. Part I is called "The General Background" and comprises the cultural and historical essays. Part II is called "Cities" and Part III "Tours." The "Cities" part is itself a series of essays, modeled after the ones in Part I, covering for each major city in the state the substance covered by all the essays in "The General Background." It has, as a consequence, a greater specificity of detail. But because it distributes a much larger range of information in approximately the same space, it also has a greater superficiality— precise detail distributed in a thin layer. The Michigan guide covers seventeen cities in Part II as against fourteen essays in the first part and includes discursive accounts of a multitude of points of interest for each city. Part III outlines specific routes and mileages to place after place and, of course, sites to visit and their exact locations. Because of its greater specificity, Part II occasionlly sparkles with a closeness to grass-roots life and lore that is lost in the generality of Part I. To a far lesser degree, one sometimes encounters a trenchant item among the schema of routes and sites in Part III. The same three-part set up, without significant exception, is true for the Illinois, Indiana, Ohio, and Wisconsin guides.[3]

In each of these the essays which make up "The General Background" deal with the same subjects and follow, with minor variations, the same order. The Michigan guide starts with an essay called "Contemporary Scene," follows it up with "Natural Setting," "Archaeology and Indians," History and Government," "State Development," "Conservation and Recreation," "Social Institutions," "Racial Elements," "Marine Lore," "Artists and Craftsmen," "Literature," "Music," "The Theater," and closes with "The Development of Architecture" (xi). Consider the Indiana guide: Part I begins with "Indiana Today," continues with "Natural Setting," then separates "Archaeology" and "Indians" into two essays, and ends with the same order we found in the Michigan guide, except that the subjects of music and the theater are telescoped into one (ix). The Illinois guide is also very close with respect to subject and order, although its essay titles—"The Illinoisan," "The Land Itself," "Before the White Man," "The Land and the People"— are perhaps a little more striking. It includes a special essay on Abe Lincoln, "Man of Illinois." The order of concluding essays in Part I, which are on the arts, varies little from the order followed by the Michigan and Indiana guides. Unlike them, it starts with "Architecture" and ends with "Music" (vii).

A brief look at three guides outside the Midwest reveals a common plan that is less constrained, less of a straitjacket, and more of a pattern adapted to local materials and writer temperaments. The clearest case is *Idaho: A Guide in Word and Pictures*. It roughly follows the national plan: general essays deal with some of the same subjects as the others—Idaho history; Indian archaeology and history; state topography, economic character and development—followed by a numbered set of described tours. But the entire project does not come in the neat, three-part package that the others do. For one thing, the general essay section leaves out separate accounts of Idaho arts. Why is not known. Also not to be found are special accounts of individual cities. Even more telling is that its second part is more than a tour guide. It comprises sixty-eight pages of invitingly named essays— "Ghost Towns," "Buried Treasures," "A Few Tall Tales," "Origins of Names"—that counteract the schematism of "Tours" with the individuality of local adventure and lore. The kind of independence Fisher manifested in reshaping the proposed format chagrined Washington as much as the publishing scoop he pulled on them. "Obstinate in his insistence on doing things his own way," Alsberg characterized Fisher to Hopkins.[4]

The *New Orleans City Guide* appears to be a less "obstinate" case of reshaping the format that Washington wanted FWP units to follow. It has a three-part structure, but since it deals with one city, the second part obviously could not have the content of the Midwest guides. Part I provides general, background accounts, but is limited to natural setting, history, government, and racial distribution. Part III is our friend "Tours," but these are more variously organized into walking and motor tours and into city and surrounding tours. Moreover, the schematic tour model so common in other guides gives way to a more writerly approach, particularly for such city places as the waterfront and the French Quarter. What stands out is the far greater space allowed for the second part of the guide. Here we find not only highly particularized, informative essays on art, science and education, transportation, social life, and welfare, but lively essays on black cults, Creole cuisine, unusual burial practices, the city's pleasure times of the past, Creole and black folkways, and the Mardi Gras and its connection to the masked revels of past traditions. These essays are often presented as personally observed event, and frequently resort to narrative rather than expository presentation. The cool expository essays and the warm, storied ones mediate and enhance one another in the second section of the *New Orleans City Guide* so that the stability of the former is kept from becoming dull and the verve of the latter from becoming incredible.

The third example of a less uniform structure was produced by the New York FWP. Here we encounter a work of collective authorship, but of quite a different kind than the Michigan guide and those of its companion states. Members of the New York FWP were natives or long-term residents of the United States' largest city and port. They were imbued with and immersed in cosmopolitan orientations, with metropolitan thought and cultural diversity, with metropolitan sophistications, shrewd wit, and the international currents and peoples that swarmed through its streets. For them, the urban and the international were the favored and only significant caldrons of experience. This collective had a set of sensibilities far removed from the national and regional sensibilities of America's provinces. Moreover, because the New York FWP was located in the nation's cultural capital, it had an enormous base of skilled writers to draw from. Its staff was unquestionably the strongest collective of writing talent in the country. This had far more bearing on the style than the structure of the work it produced. Yet because the New York FWP was so strong in writing and because it numbered among its members a few who had become part of the New York writing establishment, it was allowed a fair range of flexibility in composing its work.

Another factor distinguishing the New York guide was that city's wealth of historical and cultural material, its accomplishments in all the art forms, and its places of interest. If these were to be thoroughly covered in a single volume following the structural formula that all branches were expected to adhere to, the guide would have had to be monumental. The New York FWP kept pushing for the right to deviate from the national formula, and the Washington authorities finally conceded. The solution was to allow the New York unit to write a two-volume guide, separating the historical, cultural, and grass-roots essays from the tour descriptions. This kept the unit from producing a monster and also freed it from the space and bridging constraints that a shorter volume structured by the standard three-part plan would have imposed. The first volume, *New York Panorama*, a work of over five hundred pages, is more thorough in its essay accounts than other guides yet is still manageable.[5] While the staff treated many of the same subjects as other units, they used the freedom they had won to divide the subjects into a larger number of essays, which range over the great diversity of New York's arts, publics, and vernacular mannerisms in greater detail.

These examples of uninhibited structure are atypical. They suggest what can be done with a free range of options. But they do not prove that sameness of structure automatically snuffs out the spark of discovery. An interesting subject, even in uniform, may still ignite wonder and new awarenes. However, sameness of structure is at high risk of damping the spontaneity and invention enabling a writer to distill the distinctive drama and underlying processes of a place and its people, especially if it is perceived as command from above. Moreover, an imposed structural sameness discourages most effectively when a writer or collective of writers is not in close touch with the drama and deep processes of a cultural community. The Washington office surely did not want to forestall imagination and may not have been able to anticipate or prevent out-of-touchness. Its gaze, however, was directed not toward those inhibiting possibilities, but toward a fairly high, if not outstanding level of organizational competence.[6]

The uniformity the center required in style and tone is more inevitably paralyzing because style and tone are the source of writing candor, ease of expression, and the contrastive effect that a "warts and all" approach requires. The ready-made formulas that governed all units in these matters were established to insure professional competence in fluency and clarity of expression. But they were also designed to keep writers from being partisan and expressively zealous. In terms of style, the formula demanded direct and unadorned syntax and precise, relatively restrained diction. The formula for tone required neutrality and balance. The good and the bad had to be represented as offsetting, and both had to be modulated. The requisite style and tone were thus in the nature of linguistic cosmetics that shaded warts into inoffensive blemishes and accomplishments into sedately imaged contributions. Ugliness and unrestrained pride were both ruled out in favor of a tame lucidity and gentle flow of words that could hardly raise hackles.[7]

The Michigan FWP observed the constraints of stylistic practice and tonal attitude laid down by the center quite faithfully. The result is a guide that impresses the reader with its surefooted character from beginning to end.[8] The prose is stripped down, moves along at a rapid but easy gait, and addresses the subject directly. The diction is exact, and indeed its precision turns out to be on more than one occasion surprisingly hard-edged. Moreover, the essays teem with information that is transmitted, sentence after sentence, in concrete detail.

The first paragraph of the essay "Music" exemplifies these accomplishments:

A harpsichord at the Detroit military post, imported by a German doctor in 1796, was the only keyboard instrument in the State until 1803, when a piano was transported by horseback from the East by Mrs. Solomon Sibley. Several years later a small pipe organ was installed in Ste. Anne's Church, but amazed and fascinated Indians promptly stole the pipes. (152)

The same kind of directness in sentence construction and approach to subject, a similar compression of concretely detailed information, is encountered in the report on Michigan's literary history:

American writers introduced Michigan to the reading public in early tales of Indian and frontier life. Michigan supplied the background for *Oak Openings* by James Fenimore Cooper (1789–1851), who lived in the State for a short time. A pioneer recorder of Indian lore and legend, Henry Rowe Schoolcraft (1793–1864), first Indian agent at Sault Ste. Marie, provided in his *Algic Researches* the source book that Henry Wadsworth

Longfellow used in writing *The Song of Hiawatha*, which is laid in Michigan's Upper Peninsula. Schoolcraft's book preserved the legends and fables of the Algic tribes, who, in 1600, occupied most of the United States east of the Mississippi. (145)

What we see in these two examples is characteristic of the entire work—an easily accessed and crisp enough style that conveys interesting information not very well-known to the general public and not much better known, because of its local character, to specialists in the various fields covered by the essays.

Each example manifests another feature true for the entire work: the tonal character is neutral or disinterested. The writer, or I should say the collective, stands apart from the subject and assumes an objectivity free of any informing view or cultural experience. For the purpose of transmitting information and for certain kinds of subjects—music and literature, architecture, theater, conservation, recreation, and so on—this detachment may seem appropriate. But even if that is granted, the tone struck throughout is so controlled and detached it conveys minimal enthusiasm and a tight rein on judgment. Let me cite one other example, from the piece on architecture, to demonstrate the point. Although it is one of the two essays assigned to professionals who were not FWP employees, the style and tone are consistent with material composed by the staff.[9] The passage deals with the modern trend in Michigan architecture:

> Of the more conservative modern buildings in Detroit, the Majestic Building, by Daniel H. Burnham, and the Buhl Building, by Smith, Hinchman and Grylls, employ Romanesque forms and details in terra cotta with the steel framework. Renaissance and classical forms enrich the Grand Rapids National Bank, by Williamson, Crow and Proctor, and the David Whitney Building, by Graham, Anderson, Probst and White, in Detroit. A direct nontraditional design marked by geometrical masses and simple planes is the Central National Tower, Battle Creek, by Holabird and Root; this, like Detroit's Penobscot, Fisher and Stott Buildings, employs setbacks for purely aesthetic effect. (171)

"Conservative" and "enrich," already beaten, although not entirely useless words even in the 1930s, represent the level of judgment the essay is committed to taking. No expressive opinion is yielded in the prose about the art-deco effects of the Fisher Building, about the wedding of romanesque form and terra-cotta. We note no particular enthusiasm for the fact that Burnham, Root, and Holabird, those Chicago pioneers in the creation and esthetics of the skyscraper, contributed to Detroit's skyline, or disappointment, if merited, that their work did not measure up to what they had done before. The paragraph is the manner of the essay. The reader is presented with a great deal of information—names of buildings and architects, details of forms and materials—but no more than tranquil evaluation of and feeling for the subject.[10]

Tonal neutrality becomes an acute problem in the essays that are most directly populist in subject, for example, the stories about immigrants, African Americans, and Native Americans. Even if the aim is to set a tone that rules out partisan outrage, expression needs to match the character and historical implication of events, the turbulence, the fears, the strange attractions accompanying such publics when they interact with each other and the ruling culture. The candor and drama, the "warts and all," that the Michigan FWP had hoped for is only possible where manner of expression is appropriately inscribed with the color, garb, and sound of disenfranchised cultural histories.

The problem of neutrality is compounded by that of balance: a studied distance from the life presumably to be captured by the prose is accompanied by a mode of composition that balances factor against factor as if each were of equal force and a zeroing out of true weight. The opening sentence to "Racial Elements" sets the essay on this course: "Michigan's population is noted for its heterogeneous character" (103). It is concise but unengaged, announcing an enumerative account rather than a dialectical one. Each public is presented in separate but equal time, not in their resistant and mediating relationship to each other and to dominant culture. The method is used as well to describe the internal characteristics of a given public. For example, the essay tells us that "Negro life in Michigan is full of contradictions and contrasts" (109). But what we get is contrast, a placing of differences side by side, not the oppositional interactions that contradiction proposes:

> There is the misery of the typical Negro slum district, and there is also the beauty and order of residential areas inhabited by professional Negroes, such as the Conant Garden section in Detroit. There is the quiet, almost idyllic life of the prosperous Negro farmers in Cass County; and there is the flamboyant, "swing-tempoed" night life of Detroit's Paradise Valley, where Joe Louis vaulted to fame. (109)

The "there is" syntactical strategy is key to the balancing here, and it is reenforced by the nominative parallelism of the first sentence and the piled-up adjectival parallelism of the second. But even when the essay moves on to a different syntax in the next paragraph, the balancing is still retained:

Violent repercussions of race prejudice have not deadened the Michigan tradition of justice to Negroes. The Civil Rights Bill, making it illegal to refuse Negroes service in public places, was passed recently through the efforts of Negro State Senator, Charles C. Diggs, in cooperation with white colleagues. Negroes have won a respected place in Michigan industry. Formerly ignored in the labor movement, many are now members of unions affiliated with the CIO. (109–10)

Gone from this paragraph is the indirection of "there is" and the balancing act of parallelism. The syntactical strategy is that of active-verb sentences, cast in active and passive voice, with the emphasis on the former. The last sentence is the exception. But every sentence, including the last, is so regularly shaped in periodic balance that the narrator still appears as an even-handed reporter studiously avoiding the lexical and linguistic strategies of drama and judgement. Lost in dutiful adherence to structural plan and especially to stylistic and tonal formula is a sense of being inside the subject, of being involved with and willing to discriminate among its moral and social differentials, and of a local collective personality in the writing. The uniform and neutral writing also signifies an abstract and neutered writer.

Only one essay among those written by the staff strikes a note against that loss. Its title is "Contemporary Scene," the lead-in essay to "The General Background" section. According to the Falstein memoir, Falstein himself is the essay's author (70). If that is fact, the essay belongs to late 1936 or early 1937, a period before the formulas for structure, style, and tone had shifted from ought-to into command, largely in reaction to Fisher's idiosyncrasies with the Idaho guide. What is different about "Contemporary Scene" is its thematic stand, or at least part of it. Not very far into the essay, the tone sounds less formal and disinterested. The narrative voice accomplishes this by introducing the cliché "easy come, easy go" (4). The choice is deliberate, and its purpose is double: to capture the heedless, the-moment-is-everything character of Michigan history and to indicate an irreverence for, or at least a departure from, the ballyhoo of commercial tour books and the decorum of conventional history. The phrase becomes a refrain for events chosen to support its theme, the cut and run, no-thought-for-tomorrow, of those who denuded the state's forests, the frenzied disemboweling of mineral wealth for the instant profit and work it yielded, the sly but unworkable land schemes to revive the economy after the lumber barons and the mine-raiders had moved on. In addition to being irreverent, it converts the theme of heedlessness into one of inhumane duplicity and treats it with flippant satire. The first example of "easy come" is that of General Lewis Cass's negotiation with the Algonquin tribes of Michigan for the transfer of land ownership. "The general ordered his men to broach a cask of rum," we read, and hours later this "potent bargaining asset" had won for the Americans what the hard way of war with Frenchmen, Englishmen, and Indians had failed to do. "Just one treaty, true, but it was so easy," the point is made. "And it showed the way to more." Here, with a loose formality, is ethical judgment under the guise of pert thrust.

We ought not to overstate the case for "Contemporary Scene." The themes that coexist with "easy come, easy go" tend to defuse these characteristics. The first of these is common to many of the guide books: the state's population cannot be filed in a single slot. We find this expressed quite forcefully, but without rhetorical exaggeration, in Fisher's *Idaho*, and we find it also in the Illinois guide. In "Contemporary Scene" it is offered at the opening with such extreme hyperbole that narrator credibility and discrimination are immediately suspect. What is a Michigander, the first paragraph of the essay asks. It tells us there is no easy answer: "Michigan is unlike any other commonwealth that lies between the two oceans, and the people who inhabit it have been molded by a variety of circumstances that never prevailed anywhere" (3). The claim is large enough in itself, and the second paragraph becomes still more extravagant. "Elsewhere" means more than coast to coast. The far reaches of the world are not too broad to explain how impossible Michiganders are to categorize: "In the Green Mountain State one may point to an individual and say: 'There walks a typical Vermonter.' In Virginia, one may select with ease a citizen who would be recognized as a Virginian in Timbuktu or Vladivostok. Cotton, grain, cattle States, all have developed their types. But not Michigan." This sounds like an unreliable voice resorting to rhetorical flourish to empower what is not there, a deep knowledge of Michigander, Vermonter, or Virginian. The flourish is so exaggerated that it works against belief and makes the immediately following device of satirical judgment under the cover of breezy informality less convincing as genuine, sharp attitude.

The other theme—the up-beat quality of the state and its people—tends to blunt the essay's ethical sharpness and stylistic irreverence, too, because it is a balancing act. That theme also is common to most guide books, and its motivation is political: first, as comment that the New Deal had effectively rescued the country, state by state, from the throes of depression; and second, as compliment that the nation's citizenry had displayed unusual courage and vision in a decade of crisis.

Wise as the narrative is to associate itself with the people of the state and avoid delivering a message from the outside, it cannot overcome the debilitating effect of balanced representation which grows more intense as the essay comes to an end. The final paragraph repeats its earlier refrain: "Easy come, easy go. . . . Well, we know that now. We tried the easy way and met disaster. Now we are on the hard road, but we believe it is a high road. We Michigan folks are proud of what we are doing and the way we are doing it. We want the world to know of that pride, and by it we want to be known ourselves" (12). The final paragraph balances out any ethical fierceness that may have been implied by the earlier tone of the piece. The historical experience is made positive, the good lesson drawn from the heedless exploitation of natural and human resources, from the hodge-podge of state history that is at once the consequence and shaper of its people's diverse nature.

But if the internal character of "Contemporary Scene" tames its attempts to break away from the neutering formulas the guide was expected to follow, the company it keeps with the other essays makes its deviations appear quite refreshing. In contrast, consider the more sober account in "History and Government." It describes Cass as a man of vision, wise and honest, who had a good sense of when and how to act: "He negotiated the treaties of 1819 and 1821 with the Indians, obtaining for the United States title to more than half the lower peninsula, and the treaty of Sault Ste. Marie in 1820, at which was obtained the site of Fort Brady" (46). The essay also goes into Cass's use of rum as a negotiating technique. But two things highlight the differences between that account and the one in "Contemporary Scene." The first comes after an enumeration of Cass's virtues as a leader and statesman who gained regional security for the young nation, and it is presented in an overly formal style: "Cass was not averse to overcoming their scruples [the Indians' unwillingness to give up land rights] by providing them with all the rum they could drink" (46–7). Against the syntax of the sentence, "The general ordered his men to broach a cask of rum" and the story form with which the first account represents the event, it is easy to see that "History and Government" is far removed from satiric judgment.

The second distinguishing note is the absence of the breeziness with which the first account cites the consequence of the event—"and it showed the way to more." In "History and Government," the Cass-Indian negotiation is brought to a close with this point about its consequence: "At Cass's direction many tribes were given military escort to lands further west—the first use of a method that subsequently spelled misfortune to the red man" (47). The main clause here fails to encounter the actuality of the event directly. Two meanings are suspended in it. Taken at face value, "military escort" may signify protected, even honored emigration; taken as euphemism, it may denote forced exile. Since nothing in the essay's language strategies suggests a tongue-in-cheek manner, neither meaning is validated, and both remain utterly opposed and exclusive interpretations. It is equally hard to take the phrase as euphemism, for the essay never deserts its sober and formal tone. Calling "military escort" a "method" and admitting "misfortune" may tip the scales of interpretation. But the final construction is so cautious that neither term is represented as more than inadvertent spin-off. "Archaeology and Indians" confronts the issue more forthrightly, declaring that "the natives were rounded up without benefit of treaty" and calling their escorted removal to Mississippi "forced migration" (31). Yet this doesn't gainsay the fact that all the pieces, individually and as a collection, are consistently cast, as "History and Government" is, in the manner of neutrality and balance.

That fact notwithstanding, it would be off the mark to infer that the Michigan staff, on its own, sacrificed verbal passion and biting evaluation for the comforting strokes of temperate style and attitude. High level administrative political caution and high level administrative compulsion guaranteeing literary competence through a relatively plain style were the catalysts. As time began to run out, falling into step with official precepts was on one side a practical matter. This was reinforced in Michigan when Newsom replaced Young as state director. It will be recalled that Newsom felt the Michigan FWP had to forego esthetic considerations for a matter-of-fact expression to get the guide produced. But still another factor figured in this conformity. Wit, satire, flexibility; the passion, fierceness, and judgment that result from matching language to ethical and social realities—all these require considerable talent and usually demand substantial remaking and revision. It is quite likely that local diffidence over such a difficult demand effectively contributed to the acceptance of Washington's strictures for guide composition. But even so, local collective personality did not entirely disappear. Occasionally warts break through; a gem of folk and immigrant lore brightens up a text here and there; and a hint of the mixed pain and joy, of the humiliation and resistance that constitute the dialectic of disenfranchised publics momentarily marks the text before the dissipative effects of balanced tone and cool style set in.

The page-and-a-half description of the village Seney, for example, is a pure delight of folk sensibilities and humor:

> 'Stub Foot' O'Donnell and 'Pump Handle Joe' met incoming trains, stood strangers on their heads and shook out their loose change. 'Old Light Heart,' who liked raw liver and slept in two sugar barrels turned end to end, eventually lost his toes by frostbite. Whenever he got drunk after that, 'Pump Handle Joe' and his crony, 'Frying Pan Mag,' amused themselves by nailing his shoe toes to the floor. The slickest gambler about the place was 'Wiry' Jim Summers . . . . The local Paul Bunyan was 'Big Jim' Keene, boss of the woods, who ran half a block with a bowie knife in his heart before he died. In the fiercest rough and tum-

223

ble battle in the annals of the village, fought by 'Wild Hughie' Logan and 'Killer' Shea, ears were bitten off and eyes were gouged out, and the men fought until both were exhausted and neither was victor. (560)

In combining names that reflect precise physical perception and tall tales that display whimsical imagination, the Seney account illuminates the sense of 'marvelous realism' that is so often characteristic of rural common-people's culture.[11]

Accounts of immigrant custom in the urban setting of Polish-American Hamtramck and the Polish-American farming village, Posen, are further instances of effectively rendered, ordinary people's culture. The custom highlighted in each case is the old-country Polish wedding ritual, modified by American experience. The Hamtramck rendition captures the revelry and the foreboding inscribed in the ritual: the *gouzko* or bitterness of married life in the "loud clatter of spoons" that greets the breakfast ceremony and the *stodko*, the sweetness of married love in the kiss that comes after (285). The brief details of this episode stand in sharp contrast to the generalizations represented in the "Racial Elements" essay.

The pain of life in the new-world industrial setting surfaces with a short but telling account of how immigrants were jostled together in Highland Park, where Henry Ford set up his first scientifically-managed production lines. The need for workers was insatiable, the "Cities" essay on Detroit informs us. "An acute housing shortage developed. Beds did twenty-four-hour service; necessities were hawked from pushcarts, for want of store space. Rows of jerry-built houses went up. Racial groups were temporarily disrupted, and Irish, Maltese, Syrians, Mexicans, Japanese, Hungarians, and Scandinavians lived side by side. Even more devastating than this description of overcrowding, of living out one's private routines in the street, of threat to cultural integrity is the last sentence marking immigrant life. Its unadorned expression signifies the snuffing out of immigrant human status: "Since many knew only their native language, a cross-mark was a satisfactory signature on a pay-check, and hundreds of workmen were identified merely by numbers" (290). The bridge in that last sentence is between immigrant and worker. But the workers and immigrants described in the Flint essay are anything but nameless and ciphered. The sit-down strikers are rendered as real people facing the difficult task of making their lives more tolerable. The portrait, general though it is, depicts courage, comradeliness, and disciplined resistance to their opponents' intransigence (299–300). These examples and the few others like them that show up now and then are quickly reinscribed in the equilibrium and tranquility of balancing tone and temperate style, but they show that populist attitude retained an ember of life.

The other Midwest guides also exhibit sprinklings of material that resist the domesticating effects of Washington's prescriptions, although their overriding mode of expression replicates the tameness inherent in the constraints: to guarantee work that was reasonably professional and politically inoffensive. The Illinois guide perhaps surprises us more than any other. The Chicago FWP, the state unit that contributed the lion's share, had a far larger number of talented writers than any of the other Midwest FWPs. Its staff included Nelson Algren, Jack Conroy, Martha Graham, Willard Motley, Studs Terkel, and—in its first year-and-a-half—Richard Wright, along with several other skilled writers. Although the idioms associated with them as maverick writers differ from each other because they are derived from a variety of maginalized ethnic and social classes, they are all close to colloquial and vernacular language. One is surprised, therefore, that within the range of formal difference permitted by Washington's plain style strictures, the Illinois guide veers toward maximum formality in many more of its sections.

Examples greet us immediately in the opening essay, "The Illinoisan: His Background." Like the opening essay of the Michigan guide, "The Illinoisan" argues for a citizenry whose character cannot be pigeonholed. But unlike the easy-going manner of the Michigan description, the Illinois argument is marked by extreme formality. Its first sentence is typical of many others in this manner: "He who would describe a typical Illinoisan may well find, after carefully combing the State, that his only valid generalization is that an Illinoisan is one who resides in Illinois"(3). Another is the comment: "Clearly the infusions into Illinois from its very beginning have rendered a symbol for its residents improbable. Yet, since a land can mold its people into a pattern, it is pertinent to examine briefly the profile of the State." The stiffness in the second example comes from fancy diction—"infusions" for black and European resettling in the state, "rendered a symbol . . . improbable" for a population of varying groups and personalities. The Ohio and Indiana FWPs were similarly constrained by Washington's formal standards, but they steered those standards closer to the rhythms and diction associated with ordinary language. On the whole, the Indiana guide is more relaxed, but there are moments when the Ohio guide seems equally at ease. Yet neither of them ever approaches the mild breeziness of that one instance in the Michigan guide.

One is tempted to see in Chicago's extreme formality the hand of the state's FWP director, John Frederick, an English professor recruited for the job from Northwestern University. Its academic flavor is hard to miss. But the Ohio FWP was directed by no less an academic, Harlan Hatcher, then an

English professor at Ohio State University, who became better known later on as president of the University of Michigan. A case may be made that directors with no or only minimal academic experience led to less rigidly formal guides. In Indiana the story writer and folklore performer Ross Lockridge was in charge of guide composition for a short time. None of Michigan's FWP directors, except for Isbell, who served only half a year, was from the university world. The case is far from compelling. Hatcher sticks out as an exception; Lockridge quit early on because he spent more time with folklore than guide direction; and the early life of guide direction in Michigan was terribly unstable. John Newsom, first a military man and then a writer of popular fiction, is an argument in its favor. Once head of Michigan's FWP, he made known that he had little use for academic formality or esthetic flourish; in his view, both marred plain style readability and slowed down the production of the guide.

I have used the phrase "plain style" more than once to summarize the standards applied in FWP units across the country. Plain style is, of course, not to be confused with vernacular or colloquial language. It is, notwithstanding the word "plain," a formal style. For the FWP, the standards included directness, clarity, and precision, but also balance and temperateness. Particularly because they included balance and moderation, the parameters set up by the Washington FWP art-officials defined a range of plain style formality that could run from the academic stiffness in the Illinois guide to the relaxed manner of its Midwest companions. More importantly, these parameters had the effect of taming displays of sympathy and indignation, at whatever end of the formal range the writing was. None of these guides, therefore, can be said to be closer or nearer to populist esthetics because of their degrees of formality. They all share in the same disabling effect. The point is made clearer if we contrast George Orwell's conception of plain style. Orwell was a staunch advocate of directness, clarity, and precision, but also demanded spirit, passion, and indignation, particularly where ordinary people had received mean and unjust treatment.[12]

New Deal Constraints and Ruling Ideology

Contemporary politics and ideological tradition reinforced the disabling effect of FWP temperateness and balance. New Deal politics tamed the proposal of federal super-ficials and art-officials to show the defects of U. S. society, for they quite honestly believed that the programs designed to meet the domestic crisis were working. For example, all the Midwest labor essays end on an affirmative note. Labor militancy and resistance, strike disruption, company intransigence, spying, firings for union activity, and importing scabs were now overcome by the orderly procedures of union recognition and bargaining empowered by New Deal legislation. The essays deliver the same sort of message, and for the same reason, about the plight of the economy, about immigrant experience and race relations. From their perspective, policy has overcome hardship, opened up equal opportunities, assimilated the Other to dominant American culture, and diminished prejudice and discrimination. The mean and the unjust have been brought to heel —and so have spirit, passion, and indignation in plain style.

Dominant ideology also plays a taming part in the largely unconscious, conventional ways it conceptualizes groups and explains events. These unintended conventions appear to be most persistent in the essays devoted to Native American culture and history. The "Archeology and Indians" essay (24–33) in the Michigan guide presents the history of the state's Native Americans from a sympathetic view: they were peaceful until "the penetration of the French and English into the West"; Europeans transformed scalping from a relatively bloodless ritual into a relatively profitable and cruel practice of war; Michigan Native Americans were skilled in garden cultivation, in copper mining, and the use of trephining for medical purposes, yet they suffered terrible deprivation in the early years of the depression. At the same time, the essay uses the terms "savage," "crude," "primitive" to classify them and their practices, and repeats the old saw that they were a scattered population with "relatively impermanent" settlements. We recognize in these latter characteristics the ideology of colonial America and later of the United States. European notions of settling, cultivating, and civilizing justified the disruption of Native-American culture through arbitrary land appropriation, war, and armed removal. FWP writers were not trying to justify this treatment of Native-Americans; what they have to say about Indian copper mining, agriculture, burial practices, and political-juridical customs contradicts the European perception that these societies were "savage" and "impermanent." The residue of colonizing ideology that shows up in the essay indicates that even writers setting out to present a fair, historically accurate account are still locked into racialist traditions.

The other Midwest guides also offer examples of that ideology. The Illinois guide essay that deals with the history of white people in the state provides an account of the war with Tecumseh in the Northwest Territories (the area that is now Illinois, Indiana, Michigan, and Ohio) and with Black Hawk in Illinois itself. It illustrates the clutch-like grip that dominant white conceptions about Indians had on the Illinois FWP writers, particularly in the description of violent conflict. The last battle in the Black Hawk War, at Bad Axe, followed U. S. military rejection of Black Hawk's truce proposal. It turned out to be a ruthless slaughter of Indian warriors, "where then white men turned savage and committed indescribable acts of cruelty, even scalping the Indians" (31). The play of dominant ideology here is in the assumption that white soldiers regressed (turned "savage") to a form of action not natural to civilized man. The irony of adopting a practice, "even scalping," that European colonists paid Native Americans to do on a mass scale apparently slipped past the Illinois writers. Indian practices are represented differently. The essay informs us that after the capture of Detroit, one of the major battles of the Tecumseh War, "the garrison and inhabitants of Fort Dearborn were massacred by the Indians a few miles from the Fort as they attempted to flee . . . " (26). The passage implies butchery, if not cowardice, in the indiscriminate slaughter of those in flight. Even more significant is the implied premise that massacring is natural for Indians. They are not described as turning into anything other than themselves; they are, it goes without saying, savages.[13]

The essays on Native Americans in the Indiana guide manifest a residue of dominant ideology in less stereotypical terms and with minimal references to bloody savagery. Yet the concept "savage" still informs that guide's perception of the indigenous population and relations with people of European stock. "Indians," the essay on the first peoples in the region, describes Indian demography and customs seemingly without the telltale codes of dominant ideology and without the fire of advocacy. But its major theme is that the various tribes and linguistic groups within the boundaries of what is Indiana were all latecomers to the region. They were forced westward in the seventeenth and eighteenth centuries by Iroquois expansion and other demographic pressures, and hence "when the first whites began to penetrate the wilderness west of the Alleghenies, they encountered no Indian groups within the Ohio Valley who could lay certain claim to this vast territory by virtue of long and continuous occupation or use of it" (26). Here is another version of the primitive, namely, a wandering mode of life with no idea of property ownership. The Indiana essay appears to record accurately and in dispassionate language where and how Native Americans lived, their occasional battles with each other and, in the historical essay, their more frequent conflicts with the U.S. army and territorial militia. Yet in its carryover of the Anglo-American imperial tradition, it is aimed at proving that whites, motivated by the desire to establish permanent settlements, advanced into a gap where the Indian presence constituted a problem, not a claim.

Consistent with this ideology is the pride expressed in Indianian homogeneity. Although the guide writers propose that the state's geographically central location, varied topography, and balanced economy make Indiana a "microcosm of the United States"(3), they also contend, unlike the other guides, that Hoosiers can easily be classified. Undiluted by foreign-born stock, these descendants of English, Scotch-Irish, and German pioneers have inherited "the robust traditions" of Anglo-Saxons, and they occupy a happy space in between "polished urbanite" and naive "rustic" (4). A doubtful picture of Indiana even in the 1930s, it was hardly a microcosm of the nation as much as a vanity of the writers consciously or unconsciously in the clutch of the norms favored by the ruling Anglo-American culture.

The piece in the Ohio guide on the Indians of the region is very short, five-and-a-half pages overall, and, except for two instances, it emulates the neutral tone of the Indiana essay. The two instances are aligned in opposite ideological directions. The first is an anecdote peppered with the usual code words associated with the savage and the primitive. The story is about the encounter of Simon Kenton with the Shawnee tribe at Old Chillicothe in 1778. Kenton and two companions discovered a corral of Shawnee ponies and could not resist stealing three of them. Before Kenton could escape across the Ohio River, as one of his fellow scouts did, he was captured and brought back to Old Chillicothe. The guide describes what happened to him: "an infuriated mob of Shawnee men, women, and children welcomed him with cuffs and kicks, and wild shrieks [plain "shrieks," of course, not being enough] for his execution" (13). The "enraged" Indians made him run their "fierce" gauntlet not once but eight times. Fortunately, Kenton, who was a giant of a man, survived.

In contrast to this sense of the savage at work, we discover toward the end of the essay an explanation of Indian behavior in terms of politics, economics, and white treachery:

> Except for marauding expeditions of young men filled with tribal pride and firewater, the Indians generally attacked the white settlements and killed their white captives only because of encroachments, cheating, or unwarranted attacks; for such reasons, for example, as the Moravian Indian massacre in 1782 and the murder of Chief Cornstalk and his son in 1777. The Ohio Indian often tried to be hospitable toward the white man. (14)

"Encroachment" signifies that Indians had strong claims to land, and the reported savaging is mainly on the side of the intruding white settlers. This second exception to the essay's overall neutrality is reinforced a moment later by unequivocating language in the comment that the Indians "had no defense against the land-hungry whites who swarmed into their coveted corn-growing valleys." Sympathy for the Indians is unmistakable. The terms used to paint white character represent a discourse of greed, plague, and ethical violation, with a trace in the word "coveted" of the ethics inscribed in the grand book of Judaic-Christian culture and of irony in that the Christians who "swarmed" across the land, deadly sinners to be sure, used Christianity to justify victimizing the pagan.

229

In this second instance, language breaks through the taming effects of organizational conformity and stylistic and tonal decorum. Finding words to express an indignation that fits the moral duplicity and inhumanity of the events described, Ohio's FWP writers illustrate the difficulty of suppressing altogether the voice of populist esthetics. Another illustration from the Ohio guide is the sentence sequence in "Folklore and Ethnic Groups" describing African-American life. Contesting the black view of Ohio as an "earthly paradise" promising equality and industrial jobs, the article points out that "Ohio has been no heaven for the Negro. The colored man means cheap labor to Ohio merchants and industrialists, and he is kept at manual labor." The point is not balanced out with the politics of a rectifying new historical moment, for the sentence which follows maintains the force of the theme with statistics that subordinate alleviated condition to the circumstances overwhelming the vast majority of Ohio's blacks: "Ten per cent of Ohio Negroes have a standard of living comparable to that of the average white; the other 90 per cent cluster in wretched tenements or are cast out to farm the painfully sterile land on the city outskirts" (81). The rhetoric is less vigorous in implication and passion, but it is unequivocal.

Ohio is not alone in these breakthroughs. No matter how much tighter its formal practice is, the Illinois guide cannot hide the populist impulses of its labor essay or labor inscriptions elsewhere—in the general historical article, for example, as well as the Chicago article in the "Cities and Towns" section. The Michigan guide's references to labor and to immigrant and black populations repress these impulses to a far greater degree. Here and there, however, such phrases as "vigilantes and strikers" and such accounts as the deaths of striking Calumet copper miners and families—where the guilt of the bosses is strongly implied—reveal the underground populism.

It seems reasonable to say, at least of the Midwest guides, that the formulas adopted by the center and followed without significant protest by local units domesticated the guides quite successfully. But, of course, as the examples of exception demonstrate, not entirely so. The problem is how deliberate were these breakthroughs. Were the guide writers at least fleetingly engaged in rearguard action? Deliberate effort to introduce grass-roots sensibilities seems hard to credit. The Midwest units appear to have followed the formulas without significant protest, none at any rate that is documented. Not even left-wing influence, certainly not in Michigan, appears to have been directed at making populist esthetics central to FWP writing. The most left-wing writers on the Michigan FWP—Clifford, Tarini, Couzens, Falstein—seemed more interested in internal union strategies and tactics, in rallying FWP staff members to workers' struggles elsewhere, and in explaining the class basis of international and domestic power struggles than in motivating left-wing esthetic theory and practice.[14] But, as we know, left-wing and liberal writers in the FWP were concerned about those publics that stood outside the universalizing pretensions of Anglo-American culture. At the very least then, grass-roots motivation lived in the underground of their minds and could not be prevented by the straitjacket of organization, style, and tone from unwittingly sprouting a grass-roots esthetic from time to time with varying degrees of passion.

14

Shreds and Patches:
The Unfinished Business of Folklore

POPULIST esthetics was a much more conscious and above-ground practice among rank-and-file staff and art-officials in Michigan and other Midwest Writers' projects in the work they did on slave narratives and studies of ethnic and black life. Although the main work was to get all the guides published as soon as possible, these other projects got underway before that was accomplished. Part of the reason was that collecting material for these studies provided useful material for the guide essays. The other reason was to ready these projects for high gear production once the guides were published. A few units, in fact, made quicker progress with these ancillary projects than with the guides, managing to get some of the results into print first. Several others made sufficient progress to be able to publish studies soon after the guides were finished.[1] But most units took so long to get their guides done that they ran out of time for these other projects. The open hostility of Congress from 1939 on and the war crisis from that point forward killed the Writers' Project, as it had been originally conceived, before anything much of these other enterprises could be made easily available in printed form to the general public.

The Michigan FWP found itself in that bind. Through 1939, 1940, and into 1941, even under the no-nonsense leadership of Newsom, it had to suspend work on these other projects altogether to finish the guide. At that point, as a consequence of congressional disaffection and international crisis, it was transferred to state jurisdiction and became a writing agency for civil defense and the armed forces. The Ohio, Illinois, and Indiana FWPs met the same fate. None but Illinois managed to get more than an item or two of anything resembling folk or ethnic character into publication. For the Michigan FWP, it was *Michigan Log Marks* (1940), a record of their design

232

as well as the story of their use in the frenzied pine harvest of the 1870s and 1880s. Ohio is represented by *The National Road in Song and Story* (1940). Perhaps because of its larger staff of talent, the Illinois FWP was lucky enough to get several studies published that reflected its folk, social, and black research. The longest of these is the 252-page, two-volume *Annals of Labor and Industry in Illinois* (1939–40). Another is *The Cavalcade of the American Negro* (1940), a compilation of materials collected by the Chicago staff and edited by staff supervisor Arna Bontemps, already an accomplished writer of two novels and at work on a third.[2] What hastened it into print was the 1940 opening of the Illinois Diamond Jubilee Exposition. Other Illinois publications coming out of the same populist research resurrected the folk life of pioneer days before and after statehood and the legends and tales associated with Illinois history.[3] All these publications were mimeographed and bound in paper wrappers, a method of publication that underscores the unfavorable circumstances that battered these other populist projects after congressional politics and international history turned against federal patronage.

What makes the slender publishing record truly deplorable is the vast number of materials and personal recollections dealing with folk, ethnic, and black life that FWP units all over the country rescued from time's dissipation. Some units and regions were better at retrieval than others—better than Michigan and its closest Midwest neighbors to be specific. But even so the Midwest units mined an impressive mass of shreds and patches from the publics that few others cared about. In doing so, the writers and researchers of these units probably established their most regular and prolonged contact with these publics and left the future their most telling populist legacy. It is a tattered but great reward, still waiting for researchers to study, stitch together, and make available to the various publics of the nation, including those cultures from which the shreds and patches derive.

In only a few fortunate cases has that mass of material been retrieved for the general public. Those represent the work of former FWP members who were able, after the trauma of World War II, to assemble for publication the materials they had collected and studied in the days of the Project's high moment of populist enterprise. I mentioned earlier *Gumbo Ya-ya*, the Louisiana folk tales compiled by Lyle Saxon and two colleagues and published in 1945. This is one of the earliest cases of a restitching that made recovered materials available in print. An even earlier one may be found in *A Treasury of American Folklore* (1944), in which Benjamin Botkin included some of the FWP folk collection, especially some of the unpublished industrial tall tales that the Chicago staff, led by Jack Conroy and Nelson Algren, had compiled from interviews with steel workers, railroad men, masons, and other proletarians. The next year, using some of the

FWP slave narratives deposited for safekeeping with the Library of Congress in 1943, Botkin put together *Lay My Burden Down: A Folk History of Slavery*. Published by the University of Chicago Press, it represents only a small fraction of the narratives in the record. The New York City unit's black studies had the luck of being pirated from the FWP in 1939 by Roi Ottley, who had been in charge of that program. Ottley feared that the political attack launched against the project in 1939 and the cutbacks that followed meant not only the end of the FWP but also the loss of the black history material so painstakingly collected by researchers and editors who included Ralph Ellison, Lawrence Gellert, Bella Gross, Claude McKay, Richard Nugent, Ted Poston, Harry Robinson, and Ellen Tarry. Ottley eventually gave this material to the Schomburg Collection of the New York Public Library, which published it in 1967 as *The Negro in New York: An Informal History*.[4]

Not until the very end of the 1960s did the world of scholarship shake off the hostile rejection that dogged New Deal and proletarian culture after the onset of the Cold War era. Still, not very many academics have devoted much attention to the mine of non-hegemonic materials bequeathed to the future by New Deal patronage. At best a handful of scholars may be named as those who have recognized the historical and esthetic significance of the legacy. The National Archives and the manuscript division of the Library of Congress have done a proper job in sorting and cataloguing what is in their possession for scholarly and public use. Yet dust, rather than scholars and readers, is the most intimate companion of the FWP folk, ethnic, and black collections. The frosty attitude toward New Deal patronage and the sparse traffic using what had been sorted and catalogued discouraged archivists from going through some million other manuscript items still in their FWP cardboard files and crowded together beyond use in a Maryland warehouse. Not until the 1970s did the situation change, for until then academic researchers were still bound by conventional wisdoms and viewed New Deal patronage and 1930s hard-times culture with disfavor.

The following anecdote illustrates that my image of dusty companionship is not simply a turn of phrase. In the year of a leave under federal grant to do the research for this book, I learned from the assistant director of the manuscript division at the Library of Congress of a load of warehoused manuscript items numbering a million or more and including a horde of Midwest material. But unless I could get the manuscript division director to permit me into the warehouse, there was no way to rummage through the material. The director told me the FWP files were caved in, their metal frames skewed and bent, the drawers impossible to open, and the Library had no plans and no money to process the manuscripts or transfer them to its research headquarters in Washington. They were going to stay in the warehouse indefinitely. But warehouses are off-limits to scholars. There is no insurance to cover injuries that could result from warehouse research— from falling crates, twisted metal-file frames, the dollies and hand trucks one might trip over, from being run down by forklift trucks moving valuable but unavailable and unprocessed collections from one place in the warehouse to another. I pleaded with the director, I said I was willing to waive all rights to damages should I be brained by any of the inaccessible research material. I gave him heavy stuff, in other words, and to lighten up the mood, I jokingly offered to bring my own crowbar to pry apart the FWP files. The director was very understanding and very imaginative; within two weeks he had cleared my way into the warehouse in the company of two manuscript division archivists. When we drove up to the warehouse dock, one of the archivists pulled three crowbars out of the car trunk. My joke turned out to be a tool of scholarship. For three days, we pried and opened, dusted and sneezed, and brought to light manuscript items for Michigan, Illinois, and the other Midwest states that had reposed in darkness and dust for forty years since 1943.[5]

The happy end to this anecdote is that, ever since, all this material, not only for the midwest states but for all the states of the union, has been sorted, catalogued, and shelved for easy access in the manuscript division's present quite comfortable and safe quarters at the new James Madison Memorial Building of the Library. Along with it is another FWP cache of folk and slave narrative records that until recent years was tucked away in a cubicle room almost literally under the eaves of the old Library of Congress building, a room that had been dubbed with librarian fancy the Buzzard's Roost. However, these now more conveniently housed additions like the extensive FWP materials the Library had made publicly available many years before still await the dust-busting of steady traffic.

Collecting and Narratizing Folklore

This review of the work Michigan and its bordering states did in the field of black, ethnic, and folk studies will highlight two of the major issues this book sets out to explore, the successes and shortfalls in populist esthetics of Michigan and the Midwest, and what they tell us about the problems encountered by an official patronage that subsidized work units to conserve and produce the artifacts of grass-roots publics. Of the projects designed to follow the guide series, folklore studies had the longest history. It began, in fact, almost at the same time that work started on the guides. We have evidence of it in Michigan as early as the opening months of 1936, as well as Bernard Coggan's proposal about folklore collecting to Catherine Murray in 1935. What began in those early days continued for the four years of the

Michigan FWP as a branch under federal jurisdiction. The main effort of this work consisted of identifying folk material through interviews of members of different ethnic and racial publics, sorting the material into thematic categories, and narratizing the material supplied by sources.

The interviewing part of this procedure constituted the site of contact between the FWP and the grass-roots publics that its art-officials and rank-and-file were committed to, in principle, as a base for audience and esthetic inspiration. In a few instances, staff members were still close enough to or part of a non-hegemonic public to be a source of folklore information themselves, but this was unusual. Most of them were quite removed from the publics they were charged with interviewing. They generally conceived of their position in one of two ways, both of which put them at a distance from those communities. If they emphasized their professional intentions, they located themselves in the world of writing, where they were engaged in reviving, extending, or developing their abilities under the circumstances of federal patronage. But as I remarked in Chapter 2, that world tended to pull them toward a sense of belonging to an intellectual or creative group rather than a community of folk tradition. If they emphasized their ideology, they located themselves in terms of political movement and social class. Liberal writers and researchers were pulled toward New Deal persuasions and the benign act of harmonizing relations between the middle class and the distressed proletariat. Left-wing staff members were pulled toward the globalizing politics of socialism or communism and international class struggle, in which the proletariat was the prime force.[6] Whether the professional and ideological conceptions of self worked in tandem or separately, the net effect was to distance the majority of the staff from non-hegemonic publics. This is not to indict them with indifference, but to point out that the site of contact was not inside the writer or researcher. Indeed, the kind of sympathies that liberal and left writers displayed in the 1930s tells us that they were very concerned, although unfamiliar, with rural and immigrant cultures.

That unfamiliarity lies at the heart of an important problem that beset folklore studies. When FWP writers and researchers went into oppressed and ignored communities that they knew slightly or hardly at all, they needed to have special abilities to secure the confidence and understanding of the informants they found there in order to make them willing and capable of coming forth with authentic lore. The problem of securing willingness is first one of technical skill. Although personality and sympathy play an important part in winning confidence, gathering information through oral means requires substantial training and practice. The FWP writers and researchers responsible for folklore collecting in Michigan did not have that kind of professional experience. The second part of the problem, making informants understand what constituted authentic materials, is one of conceptual informedness. And here again the Michigan FWP staff lacked professional folkloristic education and experience to make them adept at recognizing authentic information let alone conveying that discretionary power to their informants.

Members of the Michigan FWP were recruited as experienced or potential writers, not as accredited folklorists. Their professional deficiencies in folklore work were idiosyncratic, for their counterparts in other local units were also untrained in the methods and concepts of folkloristics. To overcome this lack of trained researchers, the Washington FWP directors of folklore studies—first John Lomax and then Benjamin Botkin—provided an elaborate set of instructions to local FWP branches about effective ways to make informants well-disposed to talking about their communities.[7] At the same time, the instructions were meant to enable the FWP staff to recognize authentic folk information as well as teach their informants how to do so. Unlike the stylistic and tonal interventions from Washington over guide texts, which had a dulling effect on local unit populism, these instructions worked to sharpen that esthetic. But a quick course in complex professional know-how could not overcome the problem. In Michigan and elsewhere, many of the people assigned to the task floundered, and on-site art-officials repeatedly assigned other staff members to the job in the hope of improving matters. Frequent personnel changes to guarantee adequate work results were intensified, of course, by budgetary induced layoffs. The deficiencies in folkloristic background and rapid turnover being what they were, it is not at all surprising that the folk materials collected in Michigan are quite uneven in authenticity.

Narratizing the material represented another kind of problem. It was an issue of writing rather than professional expertness in a specific disciplinary method and content. In FWP folk studies, narratizing became a required talent, since much of the narrative lore garnered from informants came in summary rather than story-telling form. But even so, as a writing issue, it was more central than folkloristic methods to the aim of conserving and developing the expressive talents of unemployed writers. Still more important, narratizing became entangled in two creative problems. First, as the reader will recall, to allow relief writers to do creative work implied loss of control over what they turned out, something that troubled FWP authorities all along. But it was also perplexing because not much is known about effective apprenticeship to develop creative potential.

Narratizing in folk studies adds its own difficulties to the creative process, for it means recording in words traditions that have in their oral transmission immediate communal and kinesthetic values for tellers and hearers. The narratizing of folklore as a living communal and personal experience

237

requires the writer to be skilled in closing two gaps simultaneously. The first gap is that between the time-past of tradition and legend and the time-present in which they continue to function as useful, affecting modes of addressing the problematical world.[8] The second gap is between hearing and reading with only minimal loss of the story's immediacy. According to Walter Benjamin, story writers, as distinct from novel writers, have found their sources in the lore transmitted from distant lands through oral recitation by homecoming travelers and from remote times in the same way by stay-at-home natives. The best written versions of oral lore over space and time are those that stray "least from the speech" of these "many nameless" returning and in-place native oral tale tellers.[9] The narratizing task demanded by folk studies is among the more difficult creative problems to resolve. But when that creative task is solved and closes the gaps of time, speech, and letters, it goes right to the heart of populist esthetics.

In Michigan and elsewhere in the outlands, the places closest to the rural and industrial lore of interest to the FWP, the work-relief writers and researchers available for folk studies were for the most part rusty and unpracticed. Those few who demonstrated some creative power were unacquainted with the intricacies of how to transform spoken lore into written narrative and still be faithful to its sounded word and its function as a useful and affective present-day value. Washington art-officials did not issue a set of narrative standards for the branches to follow. One can only view this as an act of wise forbearance in the face of considerable uncertainty. The absence of narrative standards seems to have mattered as little in result as the presence of technical instructions to assure authenticity. Some of the writers the Michigan FWP assigned to the task were good at rendering lore into narrative form, but more were not.

Turmoil at the Top

The overall problematics I have just described are amply illustrated by the accomplishments and failures of Michigan's FWP folk studies. Although the first items collected in Michigan go back to March 1936, the banner years for collecting and transcribing material were 1937 and the first half of 1938. Gathering material and transcribing it continued after that—even after the summer of 1939, when the FWP along with the other art agencies were transferred to state jurisdiction—but never with the steadiness of the previous years. A 1940 Library of Congress inventory of folklore manuscripts records that Michigan's 1936 contribution came to more than 348 thematic items totalling 833 pages.[10]

It appears that turmoil plagued the post of folk-study supervisor in Michigan throughout 1936. One reason is that Washington had not yet been given precise conceptual formulations regarding non-guide studies; as a result, the projects had not yet advanced much in practice locally. The three or four staff members with some responsibility for folklore also seem to have been in charge of Indian, ethnic, and black studies as well.[11] Only one of them was specifically placed in charge, and his title was ethnology editor. The other reason is that staff members succeeded each other so rapidly that they made little mark in the undertaking.

The next year, 1937, the delegation of concentrated responsibility began to shape up around the person of Rebecca Shelley. Isbell had approved her hiring and wanted her to take care of folklore. Because she had already done research on Michigan Indians for an historical novel, she told Isbell that she preferred to work on that subject rather than folklore.[12] But in no time she had launched herself into the position with enthusiasm. In a letter to her husband, she spoke of her pride in being named editor of the folklore and folkways section: "the field is endless, ... Michigan has within its environs practically every race under the sun, except the Eskimo. I must know something of the folklore of all the world." The work was, in her view, the equivalent of doing a thesis for a graduate degree, but "to be sure, the essays must be written in popular style."[13] Subsequently, she was appointed, to use her own words, "the Chief Mogul" of ethnology, with responsibility for "the Indian and Negro ethnic groups." But the Negro study assignment, happy as she was to get it, "made me feel queer," she informed her husband. The reason was the high regard she had for her fellow staff member, Robert Hayden, who was then engaged in writing the history of the underground railroad in Michigan: "the young Negro in charge of his own racial survey is very brilliant."[14]

Her zeal was also fired by the helpful and exciting intellectual atmosphere of the FWP and her conviction that Clifford would be a great support as a demanding but insightful editor and an intellectual modernist in the style of Franz Boas.[15] She had in mind the tendency to see folklore in terms of living rather than antiquarian experiences, and this modernist view apparently influenced her collecting work. In April she claimed to have discovered a Potawatomi legend that a woman with five men in her service created the Michigan peninsulas. In her interpretation, the legend bore out the Edward Westermark theory of matriarchy, still modern in the 1930s.[16] In applauding Clifford's modern view of folk studies and citing Westermark, Shelley may seem to have been professionally informed about folkloristics. But at best she was informed only in a layman's way. She admits over and over again to her husband and to the Washington administrators she consulted with that she is unlearned in the field and needs their good advice.[17] From the beginning, she was devoted to the job, as her enthusiasm makes clear, and handled it more and more competently in the months following her assignment. But it is equally clear that, despite her constant struggles to become more professional, that she was not.

Although Shelley's appointment to the post and the ardor with which she undertook it provided a degree of stability that Michigan FWP folklore studies had not had before, her personal history led to an unsettled situation in 1938. She was a pacifist going back to the 1910s, and her brief writing experience was acquired as a polemicist for pacifism. That work included poems, sometimes very long ones, on the evils of war and the wonders of peace. Before the onset of World War I, she had married Felix Rathmer, an alien who had emigrated to the United States from Germany to escape serving in the Imperial Army and had become a machine-shop owner in Grand Rapids. She played a leading part in the pacifist agitation of the day, openly advising young men to resist the draft; she was arraigned for violating federal law and convicted on the charge. On the grounds that she was married to an alien the government took away her citizenship, notwithstanding the fact that she was a descendant of colonial Yankee stock. From that time forward, winning back her citizenship became one of her major endeavors and a *cause célèbre* in the pacifist movement.

With the onset of the Great Depression, she was threatened with the loss of her family homestead, a farm near Grand Rapids, which she later made into a pacifist retreat called Peaceways. To pay the homestead taxes she left her husband, resumed her maiden name, and moved to Detroit.[18] Applying for work relief as a jobless single woman, she received relief certification and became an FWP employee in early 1937. But the problem in folklore studies that developed around her employment in 1937 had nothing to do with pretended marital separation. The hitch was her alien status. As we pointed out earlier, legislative budget-cutting and conservative anti-alien sentiments forced the Federal One projects to adopt a rule against employing non-citizens. In the first week of August, she received a "quit slip" for not being a citizen. Dismissing arts projects people who had been certified as needy merely because they were aliens never did sit well with art-officials. This was particularly true in the case of Shelley, because her status was a matter charged with overtones of violated civil liberties. By mid-August she had her job back.[19] Although she continued to edit folklore material and to be the assigned writer for ethnology, she was no longer clearly in charge of the folklore project.

This anomalous situation continued until 1938. The arrival of Newsom, however, made matters more difficult. The businesslike rigor that he adopted toward the guide forced folklore studies to take second place to the guide's getting printed. Citing his view that there were no personnel on the Michigan FWP staff trained to supervise folklore studies and that he had no time to train anyone for the post, he asked Botkin to approve a postponement of the work.[20] Political indebtedness may also have been a factor in Newsom's failure to resolve the issue. It seemed so to Rebecca Shelley as well as to William Young, the former director who had been demoted to associate director. Shelley had requested, in lieu of her folklore responsibilities, an official supervisory position. Newsom refused, citing a promise to reserve the post for Leila Bracy, an FWP supervisor who had resigned to run for public office; should she fail in the election and decide to return to the FWP, the position would be hers. His word was a bond that made it impossible for him, he contended, to give the job to Shelley. The bond had a short life, however. Newsom dissolved it before the election was held, but not in favor of Shelley. In October Newsom appointed Ralph R. Wayne, a newspaper man who had captured his confidence, to be chief folklore editor. In December 1938 Shelley left the FWP to join her husband, who had taken a managerial job in Houston.[21] Trouble pursued the enterprise into 1939. According to Newsom two crucial events "upset all plans" for folklore work: the quota cuts of January 1939 and Wayne's departure for private employment in March. But of course by March the FWP, as a federally-centered patronage, was close to its end.[22]

Although in pursuing his single-minded aim to complete the guide he shunted folklore to the side, Newsom did not abandon it completely. He maintained an editorial relationship with Ivan Walton, a professional folklorist connected to the University of Michigan. As far back as 1936, Walton had been asked to write an essay on Great Lakes marine lore for the Michigan guide. Newsom got good press from Walton, who had been dissatisfied with the way his essay had been handled by Young: "I had a pleasant talk with Mr. Newsom of your Detroit office a few days ago," Walton informed Alsberg, "and think you have the right man there now." With regard to specific folklore projects, Newsom went along with the collection of Michigan Paul Bunyan stories until the setbacks of early 1939 impelled him to suggest that they be dropped because the narrativized material was not very good in either form or content. On the other hand, he admired the gathering of Polish folk ballads for a book being prepared on Detroit's racial groups.[23]

The Folklore Accomplishment

It is remarkable then, in the face of inexperience, rapid supervisory turnover, and Newsom's low priority for folklore studies, that the Michigan FWP managed to collect 833 pages of folklore items on a fairly steady basis throughout its four-year period as a local arm of federal patronage. The 348 items in the collection were sorted into thirty-three thematic categories, reflecting the directions handed down from Washington about the kind of things writers, researchers, and field workers should be on the lookout for in folk studies. On the advice of John Lomax before 1938, Benjamin Botkin as chief of the enterprise thereafter, and Alan Lomax as a key consultant in 1938, 1939, and 1940, Washington authorities directed local staffs to be alert to the lore of the various ethnic groups that made up state populations. They also named specific categories for attention, including such narrative forms as ghost stories, tall tales, fairy tales, and witches tales. Other categories were superstitions, riddles, medicinal lore, and folk phrases and sayings. Attention was also directed toward occupational and ethnic ballads.[24] These directions were very helpful, but they soon revealed the problem of inexperience and want of professional informedness. Once the Michigan FWP personnel were turned loose to gather material as directed, they went at collecting with great vigor and sent in hosts of stories, cures, superstitions, ballads, sayings, and other items which seemed to them to conform to the themes that had been singled out. Their inexperience and lack of disciplinary knowledge betrayed them into accepting every riddle, every saying and phrase, every cure, every ballad as an example of folklore simply because the folk said it, used it, sang it.

In her third month on the job, Shelley received the following contribution to folklore from a field worker, who called it a ballad. An explanatory heading precedes the verse: "Sent with a box of candy to Sigrid, who is very thin." Then follows the heart of the matter:

> Silken panties I promised you,
> Instead I send these sweets to chew;
> For silk may drape a bottom bare
> But first the bottom must be there.
>
> This fattening diet you will find
> Will help to get you much behind
> When Mae West's size fits like a glove
> I'll send you panties with my love.

The field worker does not name, or at least Shelley does not indicate, the informant, the folk community, or the geographical source of the ballad, but there is no reason to doubt that it came from a folk informant or was sung in some folk community. As a sign of attitude, it reflects the kind of deep-rooted male sexism and sense of female beauty prevalent among rural and industrial folk. As for rhyme and metrics, it fits the ballad formula quite well. But its language, its shallow wit, and particularly the image of Mae West give it away. Shelley did not believe it was an item of folk material, although she had no grounds to pick on it as a verse form: "This," she writes her husband to whom she had sent a copy for divertissement, "is supposed to be ballad."[25]

242

Consider this riddle submitted by field worker William Shaffer, who found it circulating around Greenland, Michigan, in April 1937: "What is the difference between a goose and an author? Answer: It takes many quills to make a goose, but only one quill to make a goose of an author." Surely an appropriate riddle for a bootstrap agency like the FWP, and one hopes Shaffer had a playful intent in submitting it. But it belongs to a series of riddles of the same character that he sent in: "Why are a horse and a coy woman alike? Answer: Because they both 'neigh.'" I think that the collector submitted them all in good faith as folklore items, that he found them in circulation among ordinary people in an ethnic or traditional community, and that they reflect local attitudes—found abundantly in all sorts of folkish contexts. But they do not represent folklore simply because they are riddles in currency among people we regard as folk. They are corny, anti-intellectual, and sexist commonplaces that circulated then and circulate now, in the same old garb and shallow wit, across many social, class, and ethnic lines; they do not resonate with the characteristics of a specific tradition—not in metaphor, not in song, and not in wit.

Collecting items such as these demonstrates the enthusiasm of field workers who lacked the discriminating powers of experience and training. A group of thirty-eight items covering beliefs, customs, magic, omens, luck signs, tokens, and much else among the publics of Flint elicited this end-comment from Shelley: "The above furnishes some bits of folklore, and illustrates also the difficulty of illuminating our field. The worker should be able to recognize not only folklore, but extraneous material as well." Among the material that project worker Natalie Walter gathered while interviewing Flint residents and which she presented with short expository glosses, one finds sayings ("An expression, often heard, for being pleased is the saying 'I'd be tickled to death'"), greetings ("The wish for Christmas is: 'Merry Christmas,' while for New Year it is 'Happy New Year'"), and customs: ("Catholic people always eat fish on Friday, and Jewish people never eat pork"). Surely Shelley would have judged these "extraneous." A naiveté is revealed in this kind of gathering that is typical of many of the field workers: Having been instructed by Washington to be on the lookout for thematic categories among which were holiday folk greetings and rituals, many field workers took the rote forms common to everyone in Euro-American civilization as grit rather than chaff. However, Walter also included a medical superstition, one suffused with old-time occupational folk life that has the ring of authenticity: "A long time ago it used to be said that a horseshoe nail, made into a ring by an old blacksmith, and worn on the little finger of the right hand, would keep the wearer free from contagious disease."[26] But even where items seem authentic, the manner of representation is troublesome. The clue to that manner is the glossing. The field worker puts the ma-

243

terial at a distance, telling us what the sayings, superstitions, and customs are and what they mean. She makes no attempt to recreate a folk context in which they can speak for themselves in an appropriate contextual language.

But not all the researchers and writers who were collecting and writing up folklore manifested these difficulties. Nor were those who did always off-base. Our riddle man, Shaffer, for example, came closer to the mark in a record of local games that captures the flavor of the regional culture in which they were played. "Run Sheep Run" was a game he witnessed in the farmland and copper country of Michigan's upper peninsula. Many readers will recognize it as a version of "Hide and Seek." But it is a version whose very name announces its rural-folk basis. Shaffer explained that the game is played by two opposing groups, whose members are the sheep and whose leaders are the shepherds. Each leader instructs his/her sheep "in the signs to be used in the game," before one side hides from the other. "A word . . . may mean," Shaffer wrote, "that the opposing shepherd and his flock are coming close to their hideout." He then cited some of the signs, which come from the world of agriculture or foods: "(Peaches) may mean run for the goal. (Onions) may mean stay back. (Sugar) may mean go to the right, or any other direction or order the shepherd may deem necessary, in the management of the flock." The object, of course, is to discover the hidden sheep and for the discovering or discovered side to get back to home base first: "if the shepherd thinks his men have a fair chance of getting back to the goal ahead of the opposition he calls out loudly 'Run sheep run'." Shaffer's report lacks narrative representation, but it identifies a bit of folk-shaped local life-ways.

In the field of ballads and songs, collectors did far better in general than is suggested by the "Candy to Sigrid" ballad. These included work songs and shanty songs composed by particular authors. "De Old Shaintee," a lumberman's song, collected by project worker Earl Girard and authored by F. S. Dewey, a former resident of Alpena, is not only a fine example of how well FWP collectors did, but surprising in its persona, that of an old Michigander of French-Canadian extraction looking back to the heyday of lumbering in the state. It is an unfaltering five-stanza dramatization of a present-moment nostalgia in the language of an occupation and a folk community, traces of which may still be found in Michigan. It begins with this stanza:

> I was go upon de Reever, de Reever Tonnere Bay,
> W'ere de saw log use be swimmin' in de long tam gone away.
> I fin' de place w'ere shaintee full of fiddle once and song,
> I smell de pork an' bean again an' hear de breakfas' gong.

and ends with these two:

> An' dere w'ere trees was stannnin' tick as quill on porcupine,
> De golden rod is noddin' and de crawlin' columbine.
> And de loup was no more howlin' at de moon up in de sky,
> O' it mak' de tear go runnin' 'bout de good old tam gone by.

> An' dere I see day rollway place w'ere Dominique Fourshay
> Got smash lak' pancake 'tween de log dat tam dey break away.
> Of dose six mans on rollway gang I'm lef' jes Pierre La Sazhe,
> Dere' no use me in waitin' now for mak' de las' Portage.

If I am right in assuming that Dewey, the name of the author of the piece, is not a French-Canadian surname, the song is remarkable for its bona-fide sound. The metrics extend the ballad form in complexity: structured on a three or four beat half-line, usually followed by a three beat second half after the caesura.[27]

But other songs and ballads, if not as complex, are equally authentic. The log-jam allusion in the Dewey ballad is a favorite motif in the shanty songs that make up much of lumbering lore everywhere as well as in Michigan. It is usually about the death of a close comrade or a young man when the jam breaks. Project worker Bessie Phillips collected one in the Eagle River district, "The Jam on Gerry's Creek," which an old-time lumber man told her was the most popular camp song of all. Woodie Jarvis, one of the more respected FWP writers, collected another version from an informant who told him he had learned it back in 1881 from a shanty-man near West Branch, Michigan. The Gerry Creek log jam apparently touched the hearts of the people in the region as it did in other sections, and the FWP collectors were aware of its impact, for there are several versions in the Library of Congress manuscript files.[28] FWP researchers also scored well in discovering work songs, particularly about Cornish miners, although some of these bear the mark of being watered down by infelicitous rewriting, not by FWPers, but in the transmission process somewhere along the way. The researchers also did rather well with ballads about love, children's games, and local belles.[29]

With other thematic categories, such as sayings, phrases, and lexicon, the results were more uneven. Farmer sayings seem particularly secondhand and uninspired: "Potatoes and other root vegetables bear heaviest when planted in the dark of the moon." Those words do not sound like a farmer's, but a project worker's exposition of a farmer's belief. But this is balanced by sayings that resound with local phrasing and metaphor: "His teeth fit like a saddle on a pig." And workers could sometimes spot a saying that has the phrasing soul of folk language and wisdom. In a comment that gets to the

245

heart of how technological change endangers folk belief, the mother of an FWP informant on the lookout for superstitions remarked, "superstition disappeared with the gas light."[30]

The lexical work of Michigan's FWP is quite good for extractive and outdoor enterprises, work that is seemingly epic in character—mining, lumbering, lake freighting—but a mixed bag for the commerce it was chiefly responsible for, the auto industry. One reason that may account for this difference is that the more heroic manual occupations established the integrity of their traditions under highly insulated circumstances, whereas manufacturing represented the commingling of various publics in a common workplace of national dimensions, immersed in and buffeted by the cultural riptides of city life. Whatever the reason, the vernaculars recovered by FWP members from mining, lumbering, and marine experience are more metaphorically rich and ethnically grounded, particularly where miners are of Cornish descent, and more imaginatively presented for lumbering and maritime life. "The Cornish Miner" ballad referred to earlier is followed by an "Explanation of terms used": Gurt = large, Toad-in-the-hole = a sort of dumpling, Plod = a story.

On occasion, particularly when treating the logging industry and lake shipping, field workers transformed trade jargon into narrative. George W. Phillips sent logging vernacular to the Detroit office in a short story called "The Gunning Blue Butt." His account of how he gathered the material is unclear about whether he made up the story himself or someone else told it to him. "We woodsmen have a language all our own," Milligan, the protagonist of the story, tells the nurse who has asked how he came to get hurt:

> My partner, White and I were loading a sleigh and going fine.
>
> I says to him, "Throw the string around that Blue Butt but not too close to the brouse end." He did as I told him and I gave orders to hoist, and going up is where the trouble started. I saw the blue butt acting up so I told White to "Saginaw" but he gave her the "Stillwater" instead. Well, madam, she gunned, knocking down a skid and me along with it. . . . I'm lucky to be here at all, don't you think?

The nurse, who functions as the receiving and counter character in the story, appreciates Milligan's account of what happened, but is "still very much in the dark" about how he got injured. Phillips provided no gloss of the terms. He was content to have the jargon represented in use through the story. The category to which this story belongs is as unclear as the identity of its maker. Whether it is referential or fictional doesn't matter. Either way, the in-use character of lumbermen's talk here is a function of the narrative form.

The most extensively informative work produced by the FWP about Michigan lumber "lingo" is *Michigan Log Marks*, a mimeographed work between paper covers. Although the result of collective research, its author is identified, which rarely happened under New Deal federal patronage.[31] It focuses in the main on the logos devised by logging companies to mark their logs; they were used to sort out ownership after the booming drives, in which the cuttings of all the camps were floated down river to the mill and trading center at one time. If one were to understand the entire process clearly, the explanation required an account of the drive from beginning to end. Hence the text is not merely a recording of the marks, although those are nicely reproduced in several pages at the beginning and their meanings explained once the text gets underway. It is also a report of how the lumbermen worked to get the logs from camp to river mouth.

Although the work is primarily expository in form, it is peppered with representations of lumbermen's speech. "Riverhogs" (drivers) and "bulls of the woods" (boss lumbermen), we read there, created a language "of folk imbued with a driving virility," "rough and boastful," but also of "generosities." And its influence, the mimeographed publication concludes, still persists in Michigan's culture: "When team work is needed; when men must rise to an emergency; when a word of cheer is worth an hour of whip-cracking, there rises from the lips and trembles in the air the cry of comradely encouragement that got Michigan pine ["out of the woods" and "in the clear" of the jam] to the markets of the world—'Now you're logging boy!' " (10–11, 85–6). With this ending, the work takes this specific lumber lore and lexical world out of a dead past into a present world defined by depression and the impending war to assert an uninterrupted line of comradely collectivity that we recognize as a never lost, but not always obvious populism in the FWP esthetic. *Michigan Log Marks* attracted praise, occasionally from far across the country, when it finally appeared. "This is the sort of thing that future historical writers are going to find extremely valuable," Stewart Holbrook wrote Newsom from Seattle. "I congratulate the WPA for having the imagination to conceive and execute this job."[32] But the work speaks for itself, as the small sample of prose I have cited indicates well enough.

FWP units in Michigan and the Midwest, around the nation for that matter, were less successful with the lexicon of trade jargon. This enterprise represented the influence of industrial regionalism in the FWP. Progressive regionalists such as Botkin argued that by the 1930s many regions in the United States were extensions of core cities rather than the other way round. The basis of the trade lexicon was not "folk" as commonly understood at the time—a cohesive ethnic group of peasant origin with longstanding traditions still living in a mainly rural setting. The deciding factors were social class and industry. The work-place lingo spoken by factory workers was anchored in urban settings for the simple reason that its speakers and the industries they labored in were also. What made collecting trade jargon a part of the FWP's folk studies was the principle of oral transmission. Updated conceptions of what constituted folklore made oral transmission more compelling than the peasant emphasis of past views. But it was (and still is) a double-headed principle: the orally transmitted material had to have come into the present from far enough back in time to make it traditional. This second feature of the principle posed a significant problem for new industries. The jacks of the lumber industry could produce a special language that measured up on both scores. But the language of workers in the automobile and related industries, still relatively recent in the 1930s, could hardly be considered traditional. The poor showing of the FWP in Detroit and nation-wide in compiling a lexicon of industrial trades may be the fault of a jargon that did not have the aura of time in its favor.

Another contributing factor to the meager success may have been the way Washington organized the program. It assigned the various state writing units the task of collecting the jargon of the key industries in the states where they were located. In the Midwest, the Illinois FWP was asked to provide lexical material for meat packing, railroad, and steel. Indiana was responsible for coal mining, granite and glass cutting, and machine manufacturing. Ohio, like its companion states in the industrial heartland, teemed with industry, and its unit was expected to supply the trade language of the industries most closely associated with it: glass, rubber, and machine manufacturing. Michigan's assignment was obvious: automobile and furniture manufacturing in the lead with the machine-making industry not too far back.[33]

In contrast to this assigned state-by-state responsibility, Washington centralized the job of putting the entire lexicon together for publication, placing that responsibility in the hands of New York's FWP. Thus overall control of the material, except for lexical items collected by New York, resided at a disabling distance from the other forty-seven contributing units. When the New York FWP presented the Washington office with a draft of the lexicon, one major complaint was that a complete set of state field notes or an original copy did not accompany it. Not having those prevented a rigorous check of the manuscript. The Washington office, through Botkin, its delegated authority, considered the notes and copy a collection "of great value for deposit in the Library of Congress," as well as a necessary component of publication. After three months of correspondence between Botkin and New York, the whereabouts of these materials remained in the dark.

Colonel Brehon Somervell, chief of the New York City WPA, could find none of them in New York's FWP files and was of the opinion that they had been sent to Washington. On the other hand, Botkin insisted in a memorandum on the matter to Newsom, Alsberg's replacement, that Washington had never received any of the field notes or original copy.

At that point Washington had on hand ninety-three lists of words and definitions representing the industry classifications used by the U.S. Census Bureau. These were seriously flawed. The jargon for some industries was fairly comprehensive, while for others it was quite fractional. Moreover, the lists reflected a tendency, in Botkin's view, "to give a New York flavor to the slang."[34] In the end, these faults, coupled with the absence of field materials, proved too great, and the lexicon never found its way into print. However, the lists eventually made their way into the Library of Congress manuscript division, but not before a long stay in "Buzzard's Roost."

Centralizing the production of the entire enterprise in New York had another bad effect. It wrested from local writers another opportunity to do something on their own. Washington super-ficials and top-level art-officials had forgotten, as before, the kind of patronage the New Deal had said it was engaged in. They shipped responsibility abroad when they might have, out of the principle they themselves had formulated and fought for, kept it at home in order to stimulate and tap local imagination. What might have been the result if local writers were allowed to produce their own lexicon of trades haunts us. Would the Michigan FWP have been able to turn out as capital a job for its factory occupations as it had done with *Michigan Log Marks* had the center allowed the final compilation and writing to remain in local hands?

The lists compiled by the Michigan FWP for the factory trades hint that this is unlikely. A few terms from the auto and furniture lists give the flavor of the material and the problem with it. "Broken glass" is the term for scrap from various kinds of cut-off dies, "big room" refers to an auto plant's repair shop, "dirt-eaters" are metal finishers, "freelance men" are supervisors or service men, "hold that line" is a peremptory command to stop production, "snitch" is a company spy, "slop pail" names the plant washroom, and "speedwrench" is the lingo for socket wrench. None of these terms seems striking in image or inventiveness. In fact some—such as "hold that line," "snitch," "big room," "speed-wrench"—are pedestrian, with relatively obvious meanings even to those outside the auto industry. Occasionally one finds a fairly colorful term or vivid image, such as "pig's nozzle" for the respirator used in paint rooms and "gashouse gang" for heavily muscled riveters, although that was an already well-known label for baseball's St. Louis Cardinals and probably derivative. From the furniture industry we have "piece of goods" to designate an article of furniture, "putty good cabinet maker" in reference to a poor cabinet maker who covers up mistakes with wood putty, "shoemaker" to indicate a worker of the lowest skill, and "knocker" for hammer. These demonstrate no more verve or imagination than the terms culled from the auto list. One elaborate attempt is "russian renaissance," meaning a hurry-up job. A parenthetical note says it is based on punning the word rush and the view that Russia has no noteworthy historical furniture style.[35] It is altogether an overreaching without sparkle.

Comparing terms from factory and lumber industry jargon highlights the point. In the auto industry lexicon we find a rather mild term for foreman, "handshaker." Against it we have the more expressive logging term, "bull of the woods," which we have already met in *Michigan Log Marks*, and the tersely meaningful "push," whose assistant is "side push." "Wood butcher" is a phrase found in the jargon collected for both the furniture and the lumber industries, but in the former it means unskilled worker and in the latter carpenter. In the furniture lexicon, two terms designate young, inexperienced workers consigned to picking up after older workers: "tailer" and "mascot." "Jungle buzzards," that is, loggers, had several terms, according to the collectors, for inexperienced and otherwise so-so workers: "sheepherders," "stiff," "mucker," "hoosier," "sunshine logger." The word "butcher" comes into play also in the jargon submitted for the auto industry, where it heads the list and means to work so hard at a piece-work rate that the rate gets slashed. "Put her in the gippo notch" is the term discovered by the Michigan FWP to convey the notion of shifting into hard work on a piece-rate basis, although the explanation of the term omits any reference to slashed rates.

The unevenness of the trade jargon collected may be charged to the stock of terms the FWP workers had to choose from. Clearly, it lacked the tradition of the more heroic outdoor occupations. Educational Director Davenport of the UAW thought the auto industry too new and too short of skilled workers to have developed much jargon. One letter from Michigan to Alsberg, probably in 1938, on the meager harvest of automotive slang points out that a good deal of the lingo in that industry comes from elsewhere. As one example the writer cites "bull of the woods." It was frequently heard in the auto plants to designate a foreman, but it was in general use in many other occupations.[36] As we know, it comes from logging. This comment hints at the power that the aura of time bestows on oral transmission. The metaphors that the lumber industry had given life to, even if specific to its own occupational environment, could, on the strength of tradition, leach into other trades. But the language of the new factory trades in Michigan had no such power. Aside from the weakness of flaccid metaphor, it had not yet acquired the strength of time to make its particular brand of speech a force inside other occupational boundaries.

250

Blame for the unevenness of the material collected may also be attributed to the FWP collectors themselves. The problem was not that they had no ear or eye for bracing sound and rhythm or vivid picture. The chief obstacle was the collectors' lack of intimate ties to the factory trades. Although requests for auto jargon had been made by Washington in November 1936, Michigan had produced very little midway through 1938, apparently because the staff had no substantial knowledge of whom to go to for advice. Some of that information came from Alsberg, who, ironically miles from the scene, tipped off Newsom to Walter Reuther's home base, the West Side Local; Joe Brown, a sheet metal worker and active UAW member who was interested in plant culture; and Carl Haessler, the managing-editor of the pro-labor Federated Press.[37]

The FWP staff's unfamiliarity with factory trades is brought into sharp relief by the jargon Joe Brown culled, mainly from shop newspapers. How much of the material from those sources came from oral or written origins in the plant is not clear, but it illustrates that auto workers were continually inventing caustic terms for their bosses and for workers who were disloyal to the union. "Canary colored excuse for a man," "feeney [the name of a foreman] touch" or "foney flourish," "fumigated fuss budget," "can inspector" for a supervisor who spies on the "penthouse" (the latrine, many of which were up a flight of steel steps above the production floor), "maggotzine" to describe the company publication *GM FOLKS*—all these were auto-worker inventions that delighted Brown because they expressed indignation and contempt in novel ways.[38] While they may not seem to us as metaphorically rich as logging language, they do express the deep-seated resentment that autoworkers felt over the power relationships that ruled the work process. Resisting emotive energy is rarely found in any of the factory trade jargon compiled by the Michigan FWP. The desire for populist esthetics faced a formidable obstacle in FWP unfamiliarity with the neglected publics of American society.

Collecting ballads and songs and compiling lexicons were tests of judgment, and judgment depended on professional know-how and grass-roots integration. What I have described so far indicates that the workers assigned to the folk studies program were often surprisingly good in judgment and as often rather shaky. But once the judgment was made, good or bad, the project worker had nothing more to do. The ballad, the song, the jargon were already finished products rescued from possible loss or made available to other cultural publics by fixing them in print. If these had been soundly judged, they became good examples, as they were, of folklore and folk-life. If not, whether because of flaws in folklore know-how or unfamiliarity with grass-roots cultures, they constituted bad examples. As a matter of sound research practice, project workers were not supposed to intervene with the oral material furnished by their informants, who presumably came from or lived close by the folk community whose ballads, songs, and jargon they passed on to the FWP. The FWP staff's responsibility was simply to make an exact written copy of the materials that their informants transmitted to them.

Yet the rescuing of stories, tales, and legends made intervention, in the form of written narratizing, a necessity. Although ballads and songs appear in different versions as a consequence of oral transmission, they have formal characteristics that make them not only more easily remembered but also more reproducible as verse and lyrical sequences. Intervention here is a serious violation of integrity. But stories, tales, and legends, no matter how well remembered their subjects may be, are too formally mixed and complex to be reproducible as a narrative sequence except by those few members of the community with storytelling skills. While all members of a culture are performers when it comes to verse, song, and speaking the jargon of their tradition and everyday life, they are mostly audiences when it comes to narrative. Unless a collector of stories, tales, and legends encounters a "griot" of the community, his accounts will lack compelling narrative form. They will tend to be summaries that dilute the real sound of a community's speech. For these reasons, FWP researchers and writers found that the transformation of the oral stories, tales, and legends their informants provided them tested their storytelling talents as well as judgment. It tried their ability to capture, through narrative representation, the communal sound, emotive feel, and significance of the material in its function as affective value in the past and in the present. Under these circumstances, authenticity of storied tradition is a result of written refashionings wherein the retrieved idiom and story lore of a specific folk or public also resonate as affective and effecting agencies still alive in everyday experience.

The record of the Michigan FWP in transposing the unfinished or raw stories, tales, and legends of their informants is, as one might expect, mixed. Sometimes they did a notable job and sometimes a poor one. Two of the most successful transposers were George Meyers and Elena Mitcoff. Whether Meyers acquired or manifested talent to construct and reconstruct narrative before becoming a member of Michigan's FWP is unknown. He was a native Michigander, deeply rooted in Sanilac County, a part of lower Michigan that runs north along Lake Huron to the "thumb" area, and he was connected to the nineteenth-century populations of that region. His material came mostly from Irish and Anglo-Saxon stock, including members of his own family. These informants were descendants of the European settlers who ventured into this rural lake county in the early and mid-nineteenth century. Meyers called those first Northern-European immigrants pioneers. Mitcoff's background differs considerably from Meyers's. Born in Russia, she and her family came to the United States in 1906, when she was three. She lived with her mother and father in a neighborhood of Russian and other Eastern-European immigrants on Detroit's near eastside. As a young adult, even while still part of that immigrant milieu, she became deeply involved with a group of local artists and writers who fancied themselves part of the arts and crafts cult of the 1920s. The folk material she collected and refashioned into narrative when she worked for the FWP in Detroit reflects this mixed experience. As an FWP staffer assigned to the folk studies program, Mitcoff had to seek out and interview informants who knew something about local and old-time settler folklore. But she also supplied the FWP with refashioned Russian stories and legends that she had absorbed from her own culture.

Our best source for Meyers's work is a seventy-page compilation of stories, sayings, local lingo, and customs from the Sanilac area, entitled *Folklore and Folk Customs*.[39] Meyers apparently saw himself not only as a researcher whose job was to pile up disparate items for later processing, but as an author: he framed his researched material within a running expository account that represents a finished work. He began with a three-page preface on the nature of his material, the people who gave rise to the traditions he represents, and the reasons for the dissipation of folk culture. He concluded with a three-page bibliography and a seven-page addendum of two stories—one about a good fairy, the other a banshee—whose locale, he surmised, was Ireland.

From the way he introduces the non-storytelling material of the document—superstitions, proverbs, nicknames, animal calls—it is obvious that he is inclined to narrative. The section called "Dreams and Their Interpretations," for example, starts with an echo of the simplest and probably oldest way to open a story: "Since the beginning of time." It briefly describes the dreams of ancient rullers and biblical prophets, the throngs who flocked to hear their interpretations, and "learned psychoanalysts" who uncover the failings and aspirations implicit in sleep-time fantasy. This short narrative history (28) prefaces three pages (29–31) of locally reported dreams and what they signify. Other sections—such as "Table Manners of the Pioneers" (48–50) and "Courtship as Mother and Grandmother Knew It" (51–55)—embed the collected material in narrative sequences which frequently lapse into exposition. Although Meyers's narrative inclinations are regularly marked in the framework, they do not show off his storytelling skills at their best, for he has a tendency to shift to modes of writing that explain rather than show and echo colloquial speech. His skills are best illustrated by transcriptions of raw and unfinished narrative lore supplied by informants, including ghost stories, drinking stories (some of which turn into hallucinations about ghosts and witches), a tall tale, and the story of a wake. In addition, we find a thoroughly represented account of local customs, material which is not, as such, narrative lore.

I shall illustrate his narratizing talent with his strongest transcription, "The Ghost on the Hill."[40] This is a story about Jim Manion, a postal stage driver, and his passenger, Tom Johnstone, a small-town farmer who likes his grog. In a headnote, Meyers informs the reader of the time of the story (a frosty night in the 1880s), the place (from the Cowan Hotel in Carsonville to the Town-Line Road), the principal characters, and the narrator (himself). Meyers launches into the plot without any narrative ado:

> "Tush! Tush! That's no feat a'tall. Why when I was a young man, I—"

> "You thought nothing of biting spikes in two with your teeth. Am I right Tom? And you did so many times that now you don't have any teeth. Come, let go that strangle hold on Cowan's bar and let's be on our way."

The second speaker is the stage driver, late in his mail deliveries and impatient to be on his way. Tom, pleading the speed of Jim's horses, suggests one more drink: "And what's a minute more or less? Why with a team of hosses like your'n, ya can easily make it up. A touch of the whip and they sprint like the wind." "Not on your tintype," is Jim's reply.

> "If you drink, you drink alone. And you walk alone. I'm on my way. T'is darker than hades, and jes sech a night as the spooks go walking about on the old Catholic Hill. I'm sober and I'm staying that way. If I should meet-up with any of them hill ghosts I'll know it's the real McCoy and not Cowan's cheap grog playing tricks on me."

These examples of dialogue from the first two pages of the story indicate Meyers's ear for local speech. He allows the characters to enact the story, intervening only minimally when Jim and Tom are on the scene together. The story grows out of the dialogue, and where the narrator intervenes, he captions briefly ("and opening the door of the saloon, the irate Jim barged out") what the dialogue has already revealed. The narrator comes on full force only after Tom has been unceremoniously dropped at his farmhouse and Jim is the only character left on the scene. The remaining pages require the narrator to play a major role. Yet Meyers does so in a language that shows rather than tells and that retains the flavor of the dialogue, even as it shifts into standard English: "Gritting his teeth in a rage, the stage driver picked up his whip, snapped it over the backs of the spirited bays and, with a giddap, was off."

Moreover, Meyers maintains the story's suspense by representing the action as something performed rather than observed by the narrator. One example is the moment after Jim's horses come to a screeching halt and cannot be made to move, not by whip or words of endearment:

> What a place to be parked [the words are the narrator's but the thought represented is Jim's]. A panic of fear re-gripped him. The night seemed to be getting darker and the wind—or was it the wind—pierced the inky darkness, moaning and wailing like that of a lost soul. It gave him the creeps, and he thought himself a brave and fearless man. He couldn't see his hand in front of his face, and he had no lantern. He had forgotten to put the lantern in the rig when he left Port Sanilac in the morning. Anxious to discover what was scaring his team, he fumbled in his pocket for some matches. Locating some he proceeded to light one—on the heel of his boot. The wind promptly extinguished it. He lighted another, and another, but the wind snuffed them out as fast as he lighted them. He gave it up as a bad job. Then in a flash! an idea came to him.

For the reader, the flash may be the word "extinguished" the single false narrative step in the passage. For Jim it is the primitive lore that horses can sense dangers that humans cannot. Meyers portrays Jim peering through the front legs of the nigh horse to see what has unnerved the animal: what he saw made him "screech loud enough 'to wake the dead'" and "glued him to the spot." "A white object moved . . . from underneath the horses and walked or floated . . . into the deep ditch on the right." The dialogue, the characterizations that blossom from it, the sustained tension, and the rendered tonal qualities of local speech in the narrative representations of this transcription manifest the strength of Meyers's narratizing skills, as well as their regionalist flavoring.

In Mitcoff's work we find a narrative talent of a different seasoning than Meyers' local gaminess. She combines a voice of cosmopolitan polish with one that represents the language of local or folk cultures. The latter is indirectly represented by the former and appears in dialogue (direct representation) whenever Mitcoff shifts into the purview of the story's characters. In her own voice, the narrator is altogether outside the community the story belongs to or, if related to it, speaks a language that implies a different esthetic than that of the community. The folk tales Mitcoff refashioned for an FWP assignment called "Russian Folklore Transplanted" exemplify the second relationship, connection to a community but occupying a different esthetic stance.[41] The several rural Michigan ghost stories that Mitcoff rewrote, often ones that Meyers had collected and narratized, reflect the narra-

255

tor who has no connection at all to the locality or folk within which the stories circulate. The dichotomy here between narrator and community does not mean that Mitcoff's narratizing skill is flawed. Both kinds of rewritten tales show her facility to maintain an unjarring co-existence between the two voices. In addition, whenever she shifts into dialogue and indirect imitation to represent local and folk sound, she demonstrates an extremely fine ear for the discourse amd esthetic sensibility of local and folk cultures.

My example of Micoff's skills is "The Dancing Ghost of Fremont Township," one of the Meyers stories that she rewrote.[42] Mitcoff arouses reader curiosity at the opening of the story by anticipating the dreadful end, but only hinting at the conflict that led to it: "Had old Van Sickle taken his wife's warning and not invited that windbag Charlie Martin to his logging bee that day so many years ago, Charlie might have been, together with Hendrick, a live man today, instead of the ghost of a dead one"(1). Immediately after this Mitcoff shifts the register and brings Mrs. Van Sickle on stage with the warning: "I tell you Hendrick . . . that Charlie Martin is a bad 'un as ever there was. I kin tell by his little eyes that he's crooked, and his eyebrows come togither over his nose, and that's a sure sign of a terrific temper" (1). Moving between dialogue and narrative discourse, Mitcoff describes how Mrs. Van Sickle, scrubbing the timber floor of their cabin "waved her brush in the excitement of a new thought, and poor Hendrick had to scuttle out of the way as the dirt and soap splattered in all directions"(1). Martin has warts behind his ears, the woman reveals, and Hendrick scoffs at this news with a good-natured laugh: "Ye be full of outlandish ideas, my dear" (1). Mrs. Van Sickle's angry retort is represented through dialogue and an intervening narrator's comment: "'Men with warts under their ears,' she pronounced in ominous accents, her voice edged with certain prophecy, 'are sure to be hanged'"(2). The intervening narrator comment is clearly a different sound, consciously artistic, but it does not disrupt the narrative flow.

Mitcoff is at ease from beginning to end in moving back and forth between her more sophisticated teller's voice and the voice of the community, as her accounts of the logging bee feast (3), Charlie Martin's overbearing drunkenness (3), Hendrick's vain and ill-considered dancing (4), and the conflict which leads to Martin's "uncorking a vicious haymaker to Van Sickle's chin" all bear out. Mitcoff sums up the outcome of the fatal blow in a tongue-in-cheek narrative voice from outside the community:

> The law took things in hand after that, and Charlie Martin looked anything but a champion boxer when he was led to the gallows. Some lovers of justice among the townsfolk who had the good fortune to go to the hanging, took their spy glasses

along to see if they could discern the warts behind the murder-
er's ears. (6)

Yet when Mitcoff represents Charlie Martin's fate after death, his never-
ending ghost dance in the abandoned Van Sickle house, she brings the prose
closer to local sound:

> Every few minutes the miserable ghost threw back his head and
> called "Grande cachet," and went to it, and now it was, "Swing
> your partner," and whirled away to his own calling. Soon white
> foam was on his mouth and his ghost eyes bulged out of his
> ghost's head like balls of fire, and still the fiddling went on
> without mercy, and he danced on and on the dance of the
> damned. (8)

In representing the few townsmen who come by to see if the house is haunted, she stays close to that sound by capturing the phrase commonly used by
local rural folk at the crossroad of two syntactical possibilities. It appears
between brackets in the example: Calmly viewing the frenzied dancing of
Charlie Martin's ghost, they chuckled, "for now they were in a lighter mood
[seeing as how] helpless the ghost was to harm anyone but himself."

It would not do to leave the reader without the final dénoument. The
townsmen who had witnessed the dance returned sometime later and set fire
to the old Van Sickle cabin. Why did they do that? Mitcoff tells us the regions old-timers still alive in the 1930s speculated it was to let the weary
ghost rest. "'For after all,' the broad-minded ones said, 'Van Sickle was
sick and had an ailin' heart even before Charlie struck him'" (9). But the
narrator poses a more important question to end the story: "Where does a
ghost go when his haunt is burned down by an act of human kindness?"

The differences between Mitcoff's and Meyers's style and narrative
techniques are easily seen by comparing her story to his narratizing of the
same ghost experience. Meyers's version is much shorter and shows less attention to dramatizing events than in the story of his that I analyzed earlier.
His language is much more single-voiced than hers and, like the language of
the story analyzed earlier, is a sound from outside the community in narrative as well as dialogue. Incidentally, Mitcoff takes over some of Meyers's
phrasing, such as the "vicious haymaker" and "balls of fire."[43] She increases
the length of the story by employing considerably more dramatized scene
and dialogue and by adding material, like the townsmen spying on the ghost
and the question about homeless ghosts at the end. But as the two versions
demonstrate, while Meyers and Mitcoff differed in how they accomplished
their ends, they were both skilled in the art of narratizing. In this instance of
ghost lore, the palm goes to Mitcoff, but Meyers refashioned other stories in

his collection, and on occasion, in "The Ghost on the Hill," for example, he was equal in narratizing ability to Mitcoff.

Other FWP writers were not quite so sure of touch in refashioning local folk tales and stories as Meyers and Mitcoff. Yet in several instances their work shows a fairly good sense of storytelling and re-echoing a community's language. Project worker Elizabeth M. Wood is worth noting here. Her transcription of anecdotal material provided by O. J. Clemens, the owner of Clem's Cabin Camp, just south of Kewadin and Elk Rapids, is a good example of a well-executed rogue narrative that preserves a bit of local history. It is called "Hi Robinson," after a local character, an "infidel" with a large "cuss" vocabulary who ran whiskey into Michigan by lake steamer around 1860. The story is almost a tall tale, but not quite, for while Robinson's exploits are grossly exaggerated, they are not made unreal.[44]

Also worth mentioning are some Paul Bunyan legends, which in their exaggerations stay faithful to the Bunyan myth and tall-tale genre. Elizabeth Wood's version explains how the legend got started. Two old "Jacks" would meet and begin a boasting fest:

> The conversation would start something like this. "Peers to me I seen you somewhares before." "Wa-a-ll, peers to me I saw you somewhare before. Say! Did you ever work for Paul Bunyan?" "Sure (swells out his chest), I worked for Paul the winter he had his camp up whare the little Gimlet empties into the Big Auger." "By gosh! That's where I seen you, I was there the same winter. Yep. Remember that was the winter of the blue snow. By Gar! That was some snow. Do you remember Babe, the blue ox? He sure was some ox. He measured seven axe-handles between the eyes." (2)[45]

A departure from Wood's traditional telling is one by project worker J. A. Marshall. He cleaves to the tall-tale character of the legend, but transfers Paul Bunyan to the mid-1930s. Although Bunyan's feats are of a traditional magnitude, they include support for the WPA, the Civilian Conservation Corps, and the Public Works Administration. The third example is again traditional and purports to be a newly discovered Bunyan story: Paul hit a staple a glancing blow, which flew off and, before losing its force, cut a perfect three-mile line around a forest surrounding a pasture he was fencing in. The ten-inch long, two-inch diameter staple of bar iron may be seen, a closing note advises, if "disbelievers of the story, kindly drop around to Camp Sidnaw, Kenton Ranger District".[46]

The last two tales are not nearly in the same league with Meyers's and Mitcoff's and not even as good as Wood's Hi Robinson story. But taken altogether, the narratizing work of the FWP staff in Michigan shows that it

258

had a considerable aptitude going for it. The talent, uneven and random in practice as so much else in the FWP, reveals once again the play of an esthetics close to grass-roots culture that added sparkle to the shreds and patches of its folk-studies enterprise.

15

Neglected Publics:
Ethnic, Black, and Social-Class Studies

THE problems of producing well-written studies of neglected publics based on material gathered from direct contact with them were pretty much the same as those afflicting folklore studies. Here too time and political reaction were enemies. As with folklore, FWP interest in immigrant and African-American cultures and in the working lives of field and factory laborers showed up very early on. But it was not until April 1938 that Alsberg cleared the way for a national consultant on ethnic and social studies. The guide book project had progressed enough and the uncoordinated local and regional efforts at gathering material about neglected publics had bogged down enough to make such an appointment feasible and necessary. The post went to Morton W. Royse, a sociologist, who had written a dissertation on European minorities and was on the government payroll in Puerto Rico. A dynamo of energy, Royse threw himself into the work, traveling cross-country to accelerate and guide field work. The result was that a considerable inventory of material accumulated quite rapidly. But at the same time that Royse was charging up neglected-publics studies, Congressmen Dies, Woodrum, and their political allies mounted their bloodiest attack against the arts projects. By June of 1939, fifteen months after Royce's appointment, reaction was successful in short-circuiting the populist impulses of these projects by getting congress to decrease their allocations, dismantle their federal structure, and disperse their administrative and esthetic authority among the states. This victory of reaction left the FWP with little time to finish any of its various auxiliary projects and particularly hard-pressed to solve the problems of organizing, editing, and putting into effective written form the vast amount of material that Royse's direction and vitality roused local units to collect.

260

Organizing, editing, and writing were problems in their own right that would have been difficult to cope with even without a shortage of time. In these matters, as in folklore, one of the major issues was that the rank-and file members of the FWP were not experts in social studies. For each of these functions, they needed to learn a great deal about recognizing authentic material and about techniques appropriate to social studies. Temperament as well as time interfered here, for Royse's intellectual disposition leaned toward collecting and statistics, not sorting and expression. He admitted the need for editor-writers to provide the training that could bring the material to a finished stage.

In the early part of 1938, the even more bedrock issue of what the FWP wanted ethnic-social studies to be like required some clearing up. Were they to be studies of ethnic and social-class contributions to a presumably seamless American culture and of individual immigrant success stories in business and the professions? Or academic ethnography and ethnology, scientifically statistical and comparative? The latter was impossible, if for no other reason than that the expert training required to carry that out could not be acquired in the FWP under any circumstances. The contribution and success-story approach proved less intractable. Several such studies had already been made in scattered project units, as in Massachusetts with the Albanian and Armenian communities and in New York City with its Italian and Jewish populations.[1] But above all, the academic character of ethnology and ethnography were not in keeping with the spirit of populism, neither as luminous representation coming from inside those communities and individual lives nor as clear, unaffected writing with popular appeal. And the contribution and success frame of reference did not fit in with the attitude and range of cultural, occupational activities that FWP populism wanted to materialize.

Royse and Botkin, who had been made folklore consultant in place of John Lomax a month after Royse's appointment, formulated their own concept of neglected-publics study. These publics were to be seen from the "human angle" and their particular cultures treated as considerable and coherent structures of human experience, no less worth studying than the contributions made by their individual members to dominant American culture. They fought for an approach that rejected the condescending view that immigrant achievement meant doctors, lawyers, and wealthy businessmen. "We assumed that every individual contributed," Royse informed Archibald MacLeish in 1940, "whether he slung a pen or a pickaxe."[2] Royse and Botkin agreed with Alsberg that the lack of a staff trained in the social sciences could actually be a great advantage for an approach firmly centered on a public's everyday people. Alsberg proposed that these studies be carried out by FWP researchers and writers who were familiar with the language, the traditions, the daily life of the groups they were assigned to investigate, and who could, because they were community insiders, easily get the information required. These attributes, he believed, would enable them to come up with the language to make these studies resonate with the soul of the groups and lives represented, and attractive to a large readership.

Language here would have two functions. First it had to have the directness and lucidity that we looked at in discussing "plain style." FWP editors, but in particular Alsberg, never surrendered that ideal. Second it had to render with fidelity the sound, cadence, and idiom of the vernacular spoken by the neglected publics being represented. Coming from the ground up, from the heart of a given neglected public, is surely a great, but not a guaranteed advantage for transposing rhythm and idiom into writing. Having an attentive and discerning ear is an advantage beyond doubt and can make up a lot where close connection is tenuous or altogether missing. Researcher and writer rapport is of course essential. To get first hand information from inside the community—that is, to get community informants to speak in the manner they use when addressing their group peers—requires a context that inspires confidence and easeful interaction.

The national consultants, backed by Alsberg, issued guidelines to local units to help achieve that framework of mutual respect and relaxation. And quite a few FWP members achieved excellent rapport with their informants, generally by working hard at it. A few were acute and careful listeners. But only a handful had the kind of informed insider connections that Alsberg thought would turn the non-expert character of the FWP staff into an asset for ethnic and social studies. In the Chicago FWP, Nelson Algren, Jack Conroy, and Studs Terkel had good ears and were able to make themselves natural members of the scene. In New York there was Ralph Ellison, who spent hours listening attentively in Harlem bars to put his informants at ease and to make himself an accepted part of the action.

But the outstanding example is the team we have already mentioned that W. T. Couch put together in directing the FWP life histories project in North Carolina. Several of the FWPers who interviewed the storytellers and composed their final copy from the extensive notes they had taken were full-fledged members of the publics they worked with. But whether they were insiders or outsiders, they got their informants to speak unselfconsciously; they all seemed to have sensitive ears for hearing and recording the sound and phrasing of their informants' vernacular. Couch banked on that in defending the book that is based on these story collections. He challenged anyone with doubts about the authenticity of the stories in *These Are Our Lives* to read them carefully: "If he does, I am convinced he will agree that real people here are speaking."[3]

Couch and Royse did not get along too well, for Couch believed that Royse was too concerned with statistics. Furthermore, he disagreed with the Roysean notion of trying to represent the soul of whole communities. Couch firmly believed that the best one could do was discover the soul of an individual, hence his uncompromising commitment to life histories. Royse, and Botkin as well, had no objection to them; they did what they could to stimulate their collection. Royse, however, considered them to be only one feature of ethnic and occupational studies, the main work of which, he believed, was to illuminate and bring group experience to life.

Nevertheless, on the issue of authenticity, it seems to me, there was no disagreement. Although these studies, group and individual, were angled to the lived, everyday side of immigrant and labor experience, one key yardstick for all of them was authenticity geared to factuality. There was an uneasiness that human angle, the desire to give face, flesh, and blood to the studies, and the narrative demands of life history might favor literary over focus. While literary highlighting would not disturb the reproduction of authentic vernacular—indeed it could well enhance its achievement—it might be in conflict with an authenticity that gave full measure to the facts of the case. That concern briefly appeared when Harold Rosenberg proposed to compile a group of occupational stories that the ethnic studies program had gathered, to be called "Men At Work." For Rosenberg, the chief thing about the collection was that it represented the first time that a group of writers, all from the FWP, put their craft to making "literature out of the human activity in field, factories, ships, and mines of the United States." The ground rules underscored the requirement that each writer had to "have seen the work done, or perhaps have done it himself." But they were free to use any approach that would be appropriate to the material and the storytelling. Literature, not sociology, was uppermost in his mind when Rosenberg selected material for the manuscript, as his preface clearly indicates; this was duly noted by the American Council on Public Affairs, which had been asked to sponsor the manuscript's publication in 1942 by the last head of the Washington-based FWP editorial staff, Merle Colby.[4]

But since the 1939 restructuring overwhelmed the FWP and the war finally nailed down the lid, the high expectations for ethnic and social-class studies came to very little. The potential threat of literary verisimilitude and dramatic effect to sociological authenticity became moot. Art-official guidance to better plain style skills suffered less from restructuring and dispersal, because it had a headstart in the guide book program. That was not the case with honing acute listening and rapport techniques. The mass of life histories and slave narratives that the FWP accumulated and a few other studies of the program that years later materialized in print indicate what might have been accomplished. Mangione suggested "that the series of books envisioned by Royse and Alsberg would have revealed the nation's soul more tellingly than the Guidebooks."[5] Since Royse and Botkin made the urban industrial region and immigrant publics the heart of the enterprise, perhaps Detroit and the Midwest best illustrate this lost opportunity: Is there in it some glow to warrant the kind of optimistic hindsight reflected in Mangione's speculation or is that whistling in the dark?

Work, Pockets, Ritual Eating: Some Midwest Adaptations

The story's plot is bare bones. Not very much of the work done was published, and the manuscript legacy is a shadow of the record left for folklore, life histories, and slave narratives. Along with the FWP units across the nation, those in the Midwest had been solicited, even before Royse and Botkin appeared on the scene, to start work on the various projects intended to give a more thorough, inside sense than the guides could of the lyricism that hovered, unrecognized by cosmopolitan elitism and bourgeois conventionality, in the everyday lives of America's neglected publics. Exchanges between Washington and the Midwest region indicate that plans were underway among the various units for contributions to national and local manuscripts on group and individual labor experiences, on immigrant populations, on pocket communities—that is, unusual, sometimes exotic, and isolated populations—and on the social character and significance of communal and ritualized foodways.

The Ford hunger march mentioned before as part of a warts-and-all approach is simply an early 1936 sign from Detroit. Correspondence in 1937 between Alsberg and Young, after he became director of Detroit's FWP, alludes to the ethnic research being conducted on Michigan Lithuanians. In two or three letters, Alsberg urged that accounts be done of such pocket communities in the state as the House of David and Michigan's "Pennsylvania-Dutch" descendants, the latter to be part of a one-volume narrative of Amish, Mennonite, and Dutch Reformed cultures in the United States.[6] There are also documents from 1937 about the part the Michigan FWP would play in the "America Eats" volume that Washington had proposed, assigning final editorial responsibility for each region to the regional center, Chicago in the case of the Midwest—with Lyle Saxon of Louisiana as general editor.[7]

After becoming the national consultant for ethnic-social class studies, Royse proposed that Detroit take on the job of producing a work on the sit-down strikes of 1936 and 1937. To this end he sent Newsom an outline of the ground to be covered, the whys and the wherefores that account for emergence and vitality of these strikes, and the arguments against their use.

Included in the document was advice on manner and type of account, stressing plain style and narrative. The evidence cited here suggests that other obstacles than lack of attention caused the legacy in print and manuscript of the Midwest to be such a bag of bones.

Chicago, of course, since it was not only the nation's largest inland industrial complex but also second city in cosmopolitanism, had the best record. Its staff of front-line writers—Algren, Conroy, Dunham, Sam Ross, Terkel, Wright, for example—had managed to get into wrapper print and manuscript a considerable amount of work on Illinois labor, as we mentioned earlier: a number of stories and radio plays on work, and a well-organized account of foodways running from the near Midwest across the plains states. Contributions to the foodways narrative came from writers in the individual units of these states, but the main job of assembling the material and revising it for uniform style fell to Algren. The manuscript that Algren produced reposed in darkness for many years, became available to scholarship in the early 1980s at the manuscript division of the Library of Congress, and finally reached hardcover publication in 1992 with Algren designated as the author.

The other Midwest states have almost nothing to show in print, even in mimeographed wrapper form, and far less in manuscript. Ohio did some work on working-class Akron as a rubber town that triggered Harlan Hatcher, the state's FWP director, to charge that Royse put too much stress on statistics. The Indiana FWP left behind an interesting pocket's manuscript, "The Creole (French) Pioneers at Old Post Vincennes." Michigan's FWP had been expected to tell the story of labor's struggles with corporate industry and to help in composing an auto industry living newspaper, but what remains in manuscript form for ethnic and social-class studies is a poorly written and sketchy account of the German immigrant community.[8]

These scant remains, nevertheless, provide us with enough clues to make some educated guesses about the political/esthetic problematics governing populist oriented studies of immigrants and laboring people and about what might have been accomplished if such studies had not been so curtly disrupted.

Rosenberg's "Men at Work" anthology is a telltale work for the Midwest, because FWP writers from there are so heavily represented. Of the thirty-four stories planned for it, eleven were listed from Illinois and Ohio.[9] It is tempting to presume that such a large representation, nearly one-third of the whole, reflects the highly developed industrial character of the area, but two things make us hesitate. First is the absence of work-stories from the industrial centers: Detroit, Indianapolis, Milwaukee. Second is the remark in Rosenberg's preface to the anthology that most writers chose to submit stories about industries that were midway between the artisan work of the past and the mass-production work of the 1930s—stories about mining, lumbering, sheep and cattle ranching. We have no idea how many stories were submitted. We know that the choices made from the material submitted were reviewed by Rosenberg chiefly, but not exclusively, with literary character in mind. That may explain why eight of the eleven stories from the Midwest came from Chicago. That city had on its staff a much larger crew of talented writers than the provincial cities of the region; indeed, it was second or third in talent resource only to New York. One staff member in particular, Jack Conroy, had considerable experience in novel writing and in editing left-wing literary magazines. But he had also vagabonded around the Midwest from one factory job to another, which meant that he could also fulfill the other standard at work in the esthetic problematic of populism, that of authenticity. Literary ability and intimate familiarity with the work and workers, not the Midwest's industrial character, appear to have had more to do with the large number of selections from that region.

Two Midwest stories in the collection illustrate different balances between the literary and authentic. The first, by Conroy, is a genre piece, a tall tale, essentially focused on the humor and the drama of its fiction (1–4). The tale and the exaggeration rather than the work being performed have the upper hand. Yet that is not to say that the work is incidental, for the worker language Conroy uses gives the narrative form its muscular texture and cultural resonance. Hence while the story is highlighted for its entertainment, by sophisticated indirection it is a dense subtext of everyday working-class life, in this case railroading. Conroy's storytelling maneuvers illustrate his knowledge of railroading speech and his stylistic skill in materializing it in written form. "The Boomer [locomotive fireman] . . . didn't stint the elbow grease; he wore the hinges off the fire door and fifteen pounds of him melted and ran right down into his shoes. He had his shovel whetted to a nub." This is a discourse of exaggeration, suitable to the tall tale that the Boomer's "sooner hound" can outrun any railroad train, freighter, or passenger express, but it is exaggeration that rings with fidelity to railroading speech.

The opening lines of the story are an effective weave of clichés that inform us of the picaresque character of work: "A boomer fireman is never long for any one road. Last year he may have worked for the Frisco, and this year he's heaving black diamonds for the Katy or the Wabash. He travels light and travels far and doesn't let any grass grow under his feet when they get to itching for the greener pastures on the next road or the next division or maybe to hell and gone on the other side of the mountains." In the fast pace of the story, Conroy heaves many black diamonds from railroading talk at the reader. "The roadmaster [who hired the Boomer] got mad enough to bite off a drawbar." He's angry because he lost the bets he made that the Boomer's dog can't keep up with the train the boomer fires up. "'I'll fix that sooner,' said the roadmaster, "I'll slap the Boomer into the cab of the Cannon Ball, and if anything on four legs can keep up with the fastest thing on wheels I'll admire to see it. That sooner'll be left so far behind it'll take nine dollars to send him a post card.'" In all this, there is a flavor of occupational speech that impresses one as the real stuff. It shows off Conroy at his imaginative best in choice of metaphor and idiom and his ability to put us in touch with working-class culture.

But Conroy effectively puts us in touch with that culture through the tall tale itself. One of the chief aims of the tall tale, as we have observed, is to entertain. But entertainment is not always an end in itself, and amusement is caused not only by exaggerated event. In this case the value of entertainment is drawn from scatology, but a scatology in the service of the roguish contempt of the working-class picaro for the boss: not only the immediate supervisor but the corporation as a whole. Looking out from the cab of the Cannon Ball express, the roadmaster, who cannot see the sooner, believes that the dog has been lost in the dust, and himself the winner of the bet. But no, says the Boomer, looking out himself: "He's true blue as they come! . . . Got the interest of the company at heart, too. He's still with us." The roadmaster can't see the dog, explains the Boomer, because "we're going so fast half the journal boxes are on fire and melting the axles like hot butter. The sooner's running up and down the train hoisting a leg above the boxes. He's doing his level best to put out some of the fires. That dog is true blue as they come and he's the fastest thing on four legs, but he's only using three of them now."

The portrait presented through this narrative structure and the discourse that materializes it is hardly that of a worker culture degraded by its condition of work and everyday life into anomie. The occupational language is vigorous and colorful; the humor is sharp in exaggeration and overtone; and the attitude is one of clever underground resistance to and contempt for the overlords of work. It solves whatever conflict there may be in populist working-class studies between literary and authentic representation. Because the genre is fiction, the issue of authenticity engages representation, not fact.

The other story is by Chester Himes, who was a writer with the Ohio FWP in Cleveland. Called "The Shipyards Get a Welder," it is cast in quite a different mold (1–8). Its telling is realistic, its description of the work process straightforward, and the language is standard, albeit plain style idiom. The drama of the story is that of the perseverance needed to achieve a skill that allows one to have a stable occupation. The hero of the story is a former New York hackie, who uses a hefty part of his last $93 for tuition and a train ticket to Cleveland, where he will be enrolled in the country's leading welding school. The dingy atmosphere of the school, the long hours of training, and the motley crew of students and instructors turn the hero off, and he thinks of going back to taxi driving. But he sticks it out and gets the welding certificate for "a job in uncle's shipyards," where, he thinks with pride, he will help "build a two oceaner. No more hacking. Spark Taylor . . . was a guy with a trade." The story may be considered an anti-picaro tale, a story that counters the vagabond road, as symbolized by hacking, with the solid, unmoving space of skilled work. Himes probably wrote this piece less as an occupational life history in the mode of Couch's *These Are Our Lives* than as a contribution to war preparation—the key responsibility of the FWP after its 1939 transfer to state authority. That would also account for its standard, plain style discourse.

In addition to the story line, Himes describes at some length the nature and process of welding. This description is interesting since it presents welding as an attractive work, vital and stunningly colorful. Himes's plain style here has a poetic quality to it.

> The white-hot juice jumping from the end of the rod to bite a crater deep into the metal, melting the rod to fill the crater as it moved in its series of 'C's', was a live vicious thing, a concentrate of light and heat so intense that it seemed as if light itself had been captured and dried and powdered and driven through the end of the melting rod with unbelievable force to form a spitting, frying arc. So whitely hot that in ordinary atmosphere it showed blue beyond white, the tiny arc filled the asbestos curtained booth with a blue-white brilliance that splashed on a naked eyeball like a handful of lye. Through his shield, however, the arc was cunningly toned to a tiny stream of lightish green with a pale aurora about it; a flashlight in a green fog.

Himes also represents the act of welding as a fusion between work and worker:

> He alone could taste the weld; he could feel it in his fingers and his nerves and through his brain. He could smell-hear-taste-feel the heat-light-frying-itching-weird operation. It lived in him and he in it; and he could go away in it, alone in it. And there would be only the vicious, leashed, blue-white heat concentrate of the spitting arc in all the world, controlled and manned, guided and steered, ordered and made to fuse two metal plates by the almost ridiculously gentle motion of his wrist.

268

The act of welding fills the narrator of the story with a sense of power that cab driving, "even when he was new at it and was learning to make his way among all the cluttered facts of the city and its people," never had.

Himes is exceptionally good at conveying what the process of welding is like, how it looks, smells, and feels—in other words how work and worker, like welded metal, become one. The particularization of a specific occupation becomes symbol for all work processes that require skill and leave the worker on his own with the work and absorb him in its transformations. There is no doubt that Himes knows the work he describes and is adept at etching its qualities with precisely tooled prose. But it seems less a delineation, less an echoing of working-class language and culture than a profound and genuine personal response to a magnetic kind of work. This response makes the political/economic moral of the piece—helping the nation in a world engulfed by global war—a minor key to the subjective subtext: mastering the loneliness and uncertainty of a drifting work with a work where to be alone is to exercise the power of transforming raw material into an esthetic experience and finally into another state for industrial or everyday use.

The issue is not whether Himes had that subtext in mind, but what the discourse discloses. Himes's lapidary description latches on to something significant about the problem of work for the working class in a hierarchical structure of economic ownership and power. It also manifests the early writing talent of Himes, who after World War II went on to write several novels in which the effects of racism on African Americans and whites is compellingly dramatized. But in Himes's story, effective though it is, the soul of working-class culture is incidental. Along with Himes's later development as a novelist, it proves the great service the FWP performed in providing young, economically hard-pressed writers a haven in which to sharpen their craft. But it is not a firm ground from which to infer or speculate how great the achievement of an unhampered ethnic and labor studies program might have been.

The standoff here between two relatively accomplished stories as signs of how successfully these studies could have pictured everyday life and thus revealed the human features of neglected publics is indicative of the other stories in the Rosenberg anthology. Some do evoke the bone and muscle, the mind and heart of these publics at work, and some do not. Another problem is that the collection represents the creaming off of the best work stories available, at least in Rosenberg's and his colleagues' judgment. The authors of these stories represented the best talents among members of the FWP. Were talents of that calibre also to be found among all the local units? The answer to that question has already been broached: "no" in some centers and "not in the same numbers" in others. We have noted that Detroit could boast of several quite good writers, although only Robert Hayden proved in his later accomplishments to be the equal of Algren, Conroy, Himes, Terkel, and Wright. And we know that some, such as Elena Mitcoff and George Henry Meyers, produced folklore material that demonstrated narrative know-how. Hence while level of talent might have been an obstacle, that in itself cannot account, at least in Detroit, for the blank in producing work stories.

Work stories, which require specific creative literary skills, are not the only measure of what might have been possible. The "pockets" program is another test. Because of its nature—group portraits of exotic or isolated cultures within or alongside the massive publics that made up the mainstream mosaic of American life—the pockets program made less of a demand on narrative know-how and could presumably tap into a larger pool of competent writers. Unfortunately, as I have already observed, there is little to go on. The Michigan FWP did not carry out Alsberg's suggestions about the House of David and Michigan's Dutch community or discover other pocket groups to study.

Only the Indiana FWP produced a pocket manuscript of sufficient scope to be of help to us. The manuscript's five preparers, as they called themselves, worked at the Vincennes office (District 5) of the FWP and titled their account "The Creole (French) Pioneers at Old Post Vincennes." The parenthetical insertion is intended to make clear that these Indiana Creoles were mixed-blood descendants of early French colonizers and the "Indian maids" many of them had married. After a brief foreword explaining the etymology of "creole" and two chapters on the colonizing history of the area by the French under Louis XIV and Louis XV, the manuscript turns its attention to the everyday life and cultural practices of Creole Vincennes. Of the 246 pages that make up the manuscript, 156 (Chapters 3 through 5) are "an intimate picture of [Vincennes] Creole life" replete with festivals, songs, customs, superstitions, and stories. Chapter 6 deals with communication and social life between various Creole villages and, hence, adds more to the intimate picture, although most of it is devoted to those contacts under French and British rule. The last two chapters, 7 and 8, deal with Indiana's Creoles in American revolutionary and post-revolutionary days, their part in winning the Northwest under George Rogers Clark, and their nineteenth-century marginalization and loss of communal certainty. The heart of the manuscript is thus framed on one side by a history of origin and on the other by an account of decline.

The practices and artifacts that make up a major part of the manuscript's portrait of the Vincennes Creoles overlap with the folklore program. These materials are not, however, presented as discrete examples of folk life and lore. The focus is rather on the coherence of Creole culture in everyday life. The folkways are represented as an important but thoroughly integrated part of that thriving whole. The focus then is much more like Lyle Saxon's in his running account of New Orleans' street life.

That is not to say that the manner of the Vincennes manuscript parallels Saxon's honed writing style. Not at all, for the copy is quite raw and unfinished. It is pencilled through from one end to the other with excision, rewriting, and editorial suggestion. Moreover the tendency of the preparers, almost inevitable when presumably exotic or strange community is under view, is to go heavy on local color and quaintness and to over romanticize the Vincennes Creoles. Nevertheless, there are places in the manuscript where song, lore, daily practice, ritual occasion, and speech seem to be convincing representations of Creole life. They hint that the manuscript preparers listened well and could transcribe skillfully. Unfortunately, the hobbled writing and the exotic emphasis form an obstacle to conviction, stranding readers between what seems in many instances a preconceived notion of Creole life that forces the details to fit its needs and what seems in others to strike the real sound and spirit of that community. Still it is a legacy of some value, possibly the door to the Vincennes Creole soul for future studies, since it is a repository of vernacular and folkways strewn with hints and implications about the relationship of a specific Creole pocket to Creole pockets elsewhere as well as the process that transforms their common ground into local version.

The "America Eats" manuscript for the Midwest is a foray into the area's regional and immigrant foodways. As we know, it was intended to be part of a single volume covering the eating customs and rituals of the entire country. Other FWP manuscripts slated to be part of this program, from Utah and Montana, for example, have been preserved in the FWP holdings at the Library of Congress. The one from the Midwest is of particular importance because it covers an entire region. The foodways information for the manuscript came from many of the localities in the region, and the manuscript version is extremely well written, most likely because Algren was responsible for the final arrangement and copy. The 1992 hardback issue is based on a manuscript Algren had in his possession; it is almost identical to the manuscript in the FWP collection at the Library of Congress. The major change is a new recipe section that has been added to the running text and recipe addendum of the late 1930s.

Excluding the recipe list, the 1930s text, typewritten on standard letter-size paper, is composed of three parts numbering eighty pages. The first two parts deal with the Indian contribution to Midwest foodways, the eating modifications introduced by French and British colonizers, the food customs of Midwest pioneer days, and nineteenth- and early twentieth-century public picnicking festivals. The inclusive historical period dictates an em-

271

phasis on pioneer and rural-agricultural population. The last twenty-one pages deal with Midwest foodways heavily influenced and practiced by the region's immigrant settlers.

The unequal division between pre-industrial foodways and those derived from Indian, French, and English interactions, on one hand, and those that are urban, industrial, and derived from southern European, Jewish, and Slavic immigrants, on the other, is symptomatic once again of endowing remoteness, rugged adventure, and rural tradition with superior value—an attitude that may also account for the different representations we find in each division. The sections that make up the bulk of the text, "The Buffalo Border" and "Festivals in the Fields," consistently represent eating occasions, food preparation, service customs, and consumption mannerisms as social and cultural practices; the last section, "Many Nations," does this far less often.

From time to time this last section inserts into its representation the larger context and meaning of community foodways, but it tends to slide toward compiling with some detail foods favored by the different late immigrant populations. Typical of this section's representational procedure is this: "Favorite foods of the Cornish people, who came from Cornwall, England, and who settled in large numbers in Michigan to become miners, are safferen buns and cake, meat pies made of beef, mutton or pork, and pasties. A pastie is a mystery until you open it." What follows is a detailed description of how a pastie looks, what is in it, and how it is made, but the mystery of its significance to the heart of the Cornish miner, who has made this old-world working-class dish a particular Michigan heart-warmer, is not revealed. The "dobas torte hails from Roumania," "Germans introduced sauerkraut," "macaroni is the basic food of South Italy, and polenta that of North Italy." "The most popular Polish contribution to the Middlewest is *kielbasa* ." These citations are fairly standard introductory rhetoric, and to a large extent they are followed by the pattern of the "pastie" example, rather than a discussion of the part these foods play as traditional residue in new-world experience.

There are exceptions. In "Many Nations," we find an account that relates the Serbian tradition of barbecued lamb to the taboo of slaughtering lamb before St. George's Day and to the Serbian guerrillas who resisted Turkish domination. It explains to us the currency in the 1930s among midwestern Serbs of the Serbian saying: "The Saint George's Day when guerrillas meet" and their going off to a wooded area in the spring, as the guerrillas of the past did, to feast on barbecued lamb. Here we have representation that shows how food sustains and symbolizes communal solidarity and political memory. In Libertyville, Illinois, Serbian barbecued lamb celebrations encounter an American infiltrator. While older Serbs eat *zeljanica* filled with *palatchinka* (pancakes and cottage cheese) and the traditional barbecued lamb covered with green onions, they witness with dismay their American-born children wolfing down hot dogs and cold soda. The hot dog is pictured in this account as an enemy against which barbecued lamb "is waging a losing fight." The reader is not at all sure that the writer sees the irony in his account, that of a new domination to supplant a customary eating event that commemorates a struggle against an old domination. An example of this kind concretely shows what collaboration between informants from various places in the Midwest and the final editor could accomplish in uncovering a community's soul in food. It suggests that the informant or informants are in this instance reporting from inside a group rather than from bookish fact gathering. But, unfortunately, this account is not the order of the day for "Many Nations." It belongs to a few other exceptions in this part.

That this manner of representation is far less exceptional in the first two sections explains another difference between them and the "Many Nations" section. Absent entirely from the third section are the frequent fragments of song and verse that appear in the two preceding sections and that are commentaries, often with wry intent, on traditional lower status cuisine and social eating. These fragments contribute to the greater consistency these parts maintain at revealing cultural practice and meaning. They represent shifts into a narrative procedure that Gérard Genette calls scene—that is, uttered or dialogued expression.[10] The effect of scene is to make a general feature of story or culture more lifelike. One fragment is a comment about Kansas ash-cakes and Kansas boys, who crave them. The ash-cakes are dreadful and the boys rude lovers:

> When they go courting they take along a chair
> The first thing they say is, "Has your daddy killed a bear."
> The second thing they say when they sit down
> Is "Madam, your ash-cake is baking brown."

The fragment resonates with sociological, political, and anthropological significance, for its comedy allies food with sexuality and gender discrimination. But the manuscript explicates none of this and leaves readers to their imagination.

This repeated move into scene of the first two parts is not, however, a sign that they follow storytelling procedures in stressing foodways as cultural practice. Whatever there is of that is minimal. Mostly the account is summary and general, rather than particular and individual, as it would have been in a narrative mode. Here, for example, is a description of Michigan foodways when the rugged days of lumberjacking and farming featured big breakfasts, house-raising feasts, donation parties (eating events that combine potluck and potlatch conventions), and turkey shoots:

> Kitchens were accordingly huge in proportion to the ones which city-bred generations know. Much of rural family life was conducted in the country kitchens. Breakfast was generally served about 6 o'clock in the morning, and the meal was barely over before the women plunged into the business of preparing dinner. Dinners too were lusty affairs: From the cellar came squash, rutabagas, cabbage and some canned fruit and pickles. There was fresh corn so recent from the mill that it had not yet become infested with weevils. A roaring wood fire in the stove that stood high on floor legs, with an apron as a resting place for an iron spider, was the axis around which revolved the kitchen program.

The description gives a very good idea of the homeyness, abundance, and radiating heart of the house that binds everything and everyone together with warmth and the comforting odors of cooking, but none of it is presented in story form. "Kitchens," not a specific kitchen, is the rhetorical center of this summary discourse.

The song fragments that appear in this Michigan contribution strike the particularizing notes that are missing from the summary:

> Come an' see what yo' get
> On yo' breakfast table:
> Ram, ham, chick'n 'n mutton
> Ef yo' don't come now
> You won't get nuttin'

Or the one that closes out the generalizing rhetoric describing Michigan turkey-shoot suppers and dances:

> Sugar in the gourd
> Honey in the horn
> Balance to your partners
> Honey in the horn.

This recourse to singulative or direct narrative tellings occurs frequently. There are five such examples in the eight pages devoted to pre-industrial Michigan. But they do not outweigh the effect of summary telling.

The last part of the manuscript includes no song or verse and few of any other narrative devices. And of course the tendency to summary is even truer for it. The theme that presumably unites the three parts is that of "many peoples, yet one people; many lands, one land." As statement about landed status and citizenship that may be true, but as a comment that cultures fuse in this promised land it illustrates sentimentality and wishfulness. It may explain why, although there is material that arouses interest in the manuscript, and the lucid lean writing sails along, it is on the whole rather tame and does not engage anything that resembles a soul behind the foodways. This lack of engagement is most apparent in the treatment of industrial immigrant cultures. Like the Creole manuscript and "Men at Work," "America Eats" flashes with what might have been accomplished, but not enough to make us all that sure.

Time and hostile politics, as we have seen, were enormous roadblocks. The limited number of good writers in midwestern FWP units outside Chicago were a factor. But more important in the end is that FWP writers, whether modest or good in talent, as several were in some Midwest centers, seem not to have been deeply familiar with neglected publics. Our review of immigrant and resettled publics in Part II is proof that they offered a great deal for FWP research and a wonderful opening into the everyday lives of ordinary people. Those opportunities, had they been seized even in part, would have made the FWP writers aware that the melting pot notion was wishful thought. They would also have provided materials for imaginative representations that could reveal the inner dialectics at the heart of our diverse publics that made the nation a mosaic rather than a stew.

Very little of the labor and immigrant material now available provides evidence of that kind of inside knowledge. Detroit's FWP has been noted as a center with a fair complement of talented writers. And so I take my case from there. None of these writers seems to have turned out anything demonstrating an intimacy with neglected publics, with their idiom or work-a-day worlds. Falstein of the Michigan staff worked at Ford's River Rouge plant for some time before joining the Detroit branch of the FWP, as he tells us in his autobiographical novel. But his account of that experience has none of the linguistic or cultural resonance of working-class life that we found in Conroy and none of the work-process precision and subjective vibrancy that we found in Himes. Nor did the other writers of talent—Clifford, Mitcoff, Tarini, Cousens—produce anything indicating deep familiarity with Polish, Finnish, Yiddish, or other immigrant cultures. Perhaps they were too immersed in editing, rewriting, and reassembling the material that other, less competent staff writers provided for the state guide. But it is hard not to suspect that the entire staff, talented as well as undistinguished, failed to enter empathetically into labor and immigrant experience and to see the work that working-class people do—when they themselves were engaged in it—not as a temporary way station, but as a permanent factor in everyday existence. Trying as all the other obstacles were, that failure is the most likely reason for the bland, superficial representations of immigrant and labor culture.

Slave Narratives and the Underground Railroad

The Midwest branches of the FWP did far better with their contributions to black studies. The two manuscripts out of Chicago cited earlier—*The Cavalcade of the American Negro*, with Arna Bontemps as the chief rewrite person, and the never fully realized project on Chicago's black cults by Katherine Dunham—are examples of excellent research into African-American experience. Although Alsberg complained after attending a Chicago conference on work-in-progress that Dunham spoke about the "cult" project in the psychological jargon then fashionable, the Library of Congress manuscript is relatively free of professional patter and marked by wry, sometimes pungent vigor. The title she assigned to the manuscript, "Revolt in Green Pastures," and the chapter heading for Marcus Garvey—"The King of Sheba"—are signs of that, as is the strong language indicting racism for cult-group appeal.

Chicago researchers and writers also left behind a wealth of material on black migrations to America's second city that Bontemps and Conroy assembled for publication in 1945 under the title *They Seek a City*. Richard Wright and another Chicago writer, Kitty Chappelle, were made responsible for drawing a picture of Chicago's black performing arts. Wright came up with a fairly flat, seven-page report on playwrights and their plays. Chappelle, on the other hand, wrote most of the 312 pages on file. She covered African-American dance, poetry, theater, and film, paying special attention to Oscar Michaux, a black movie pioneer, whose twenty-five photoplays include "Mississippi Rainbow" with music by Shirley Graham.

The less cosmopolitan centered Writers' Projects in the Midwest also contributed remarkable work. I have in mind particularly Indiana's and Ohio's FWP slave narrative collections and the manuscript on abolitionism and the underground railroad composed by Robert Hayden while he was on the FWP staff in Michigan.

Nationally, the FWP made collecting slave narratives one of its most urgent enterprises. It realized from the beginning that those who had been slaves and had first-hand knowledge of the culture that blacks had created in the claws of chattel servitude were rapidly disappearing. In the 1930s the South still represented the most abundant source of former slaves old enough to remember the late days of slavery. The FWP's national administrators made interviews in that region the highest priority. But twentieth-century migrations north and west meant that many African Americans with stories to tell about their lives under antebellum and wartime bondage could be found elsewhere in the nation. This was particularly true of the Midwest. In the first place, it had been the conduit for three of the four major routes fugitives traveled in their flight to northern free states and Canada. In the second, as the nation's main industrial lodestone in the 1920s and 1930s, it drew a substantial number of black share-croppers and laborers eager to escape the South's economic and political bourbonism. Therefore, the FWP center, backed by Sterling Brown and Benjamin Botkin, gave this heartland of American industry a fairly high priority in the enterprise of collecting individual stories about life in bondage, as they did indeed with black studies in general.

The mass of material collected in the Midwest indicates how well justified that priority was. The results, however, were not at all even throughout the region. One might think that Michigan or Illinois would have yielded the most abundant narratives. Michigan had been the northern terminus of the underground railroad and had that gigantic magnet of attraction, the auto industry. Illinois had Chicago and the steel industry. But, in fact, FWP researchers came up with a scarecrow's yield. Robert Hayden recalled some months before he died that one of his FWP colleagues, "Alfred Stevenson, went around and collected old slave narratives." Their whereabouts, unfortunately, are not known at present. The state units that did the most remarkable job in collecting slave narratives were Indiana and Ohio. Perhaps having larger rural segments close to the boundary with the South was more productive for slave narrative collecting than being an underground railroad terminus and locus for heavy industry. Whatever the reason, the FWP units in these states stored up a vast number of slave narratives. Their inventories were so large that the final assembly for publication of the slave narratives turned over by the FWP to the Library of Congress assigned one volume for most of the stories that the Indiana and Ohio units had accumulated, another, in share with Alabama, for still more material from Indiana, and small sections for Indiana and Ohio in two others devoted to a miscellany of states. No other Midwest FWP unit east of the Mississippi River is represented in the forty-two volumes thus far published.[11]

But aside from quantity, what catches our attention in the Indiana and Ohio contributions to this scholars' treasure for the study of slave culture, history, and narrative strategies is the skill and rapport of the interviewers, most of whom were women. The renditions of the stories the ex-slaves told convince us that these FWP researchers and writers were able to establish the kind of confidence required to draw out of their old, minimally educated informants the inside voice of experience.

These renditions take two forms. One is direct voicing of the storyteller. Of course, without electronic taping equipment, this representation had to be a reconstitution based on interviewer notes and memory. And the interviewers almost always resorted to orthographic notation to render ex-slave speech. Nevertheless, the reconstitution has an authentic ring and the orthographical procedures, even when heavy-handed, still allow the voice to

277

be dignified, reflective, and often tinged with heart-rending implication: "When I was a little gal" [old Aunt Katie recalls], "My mammy had to spend so much of her time at humoring the little white chilluns that she scarcely ever had time to sing her own babies to sleep. Old Missus and Young Missus told the little slave chilluns that the stork brought the white babies, but that slave chilluns were all hatched out from buzzard's eggs, and we believed it." The capital letters in the represented direct voice belong to the interviewer and are a less painful example than "we believed it" of how racist ideology injures the human psyche.

The second form combines narrator (interviewer) and direct voice. It often inscribes ex-slave speech in narrator discourse, rendering it as indirect voice. Yet, to the credit of the interviewers, these accounts do not sound false or artificial. One example is the Hoodoo Doctor tale. The Indiana FWP researcher, Anna Pritchett, tells us at the start that "this story of the 'Hoodoo Doctor' was told me by a man, who knows all the persons concerned . . . and [had as a boy] taken part in the ceremony." What follows is the teller's voice reprocessed in her own: "When the doctor came, he asked the wife of the sick man to give him a piece of clothing her husband had worn. . . . The doctor took this piece and formed a little man, put the form in a bottle, poured a clear liquid over it, gave it to the wife and told her to put it under the doorstep." The two passages are stylistically indistinguishable, although the first declares itself Pritchett's own and the second inscribed, indirect teller's speech. At any rate, the charm does not work, and we hear in the inscribed, indirect telling that the ill man's son "was sent with the charm to a nearby stream. He cast it in the water, and did not look back as he too was very anxious about his father's health. After nine days, the old man was entirely well, but the Hoodoo doctor had died." The summary is Pritchett speaking, but clearly something based on what the storyteller had told her: "The family firmly believed the current of the stream was too strong for the Hoodoo doctor to combat, throwing the 'spell' back to himself and the 'spell' killed him." If the reader wonders why this tale, which seems like folklore, is included among slave narratives, it may be helpful to remember that strong Creole influences were present in Indiana in slave days. The story was offered by the ex-slave informant not as lore, but as something that he had actually witnessed in those last days of slavery. The conclusion is simply an attempt to explain why, on the basis of an old cultural belief. The two voices of the story, the narrator's and the indirect teller's, work together, perhaps because of the scrubbed style of both, to give the story a straightforward, unconcocted sound.

One other feature of the Indiana and Ohio slave narrative collections that makes them a trove for scholarship is their large number of songs. Indiana outdoes Ohio in this respect. The songs may be found embedded in the recorded personal accounts or by themselves as items offered the interviewers by the ex-slave informants. In the embedded form, they function as chorus to the experience remembered. By themselves they tell a story of the pains and hardships and also the love that affected the whole community of slaves.

We have said that the FWP, while it emphasized the gathering of slave narratives, also stimulated the study of African-American life across a wide range of experience. Robert Hayden's manuscript on the anti-slavery movement and the underground railroad in Michigan is an example of that encouragement and of what could be accomplished by a talented writer for whom the subject was part and parcel of his culture and history. There is no question with Hayden about his insideness in Detroit's African-American community. From his familiarity with the streets of Paradise Valley, a major black ghetto, where he "grew up in a folk milieu" with his foster parents, to his connections with Detroit's first black congregation, the Second Baptist church, which helped nurture some of his early literary ventures, he was intimately acquainted with the internal dynamics of black culture. Although the historical and research nature of his writing assignment put Hayden at a distance from those dynamics as they worked in the contemporary scene, his insider's knowledge enabled him to inform the work with a perspective from the side of the Other that was cool, but firm in its understated passion.

The two fullest versions of this work, one of sixty-three pages in the Library of Congress and a later one of eighty-five pages in the Bentley Historical Library at the University of Michigan, are almost exactly the same. Although both manifest the same scholarly control, the few rephrasings and expansions in the latter add vigor and punch to the perspective. There are also a number of shorter versions by Hayden and some by other black members of the FWP done before the assignment was completely thrust into Hayden's hands. As a consequence, this material is a wonderful invitation for scholars to examine not only Hayden's development of the subject and improving skill, but also the differences between controlled vigor and raw commitment. But whether we look at the Library of Congress typescript, "Abolition and the Underground Railroad in Michigan," or the Bentley type-script, "The History of the Negro in Michigan," we have in Hayden's work an excellent case for what could be accomplished in black studies when art-official priority, individual talent, and knowledge of a community from the inside reinforced each other.

All that brings us back to Mangione's fond speculation that labor, ethnic, and black studies, had they been unimpeded, would have given us more of the soul of the country. As our study has demonstrated, on all three scores—as well as liberal super-ficial insecurity and reactionary hostility—there were ups and downs. Art-officials encouraged, but often miscalculated about what would help individual talent prosper. Liberal insecurity meant that in the political trenches of election and reaction, super-ficials faltered, at times rather badly, when art-officials and rank-and-file writers needed them most. And although the neglected publics of the United States were astir with cultural spirits that were invigoratingly different from the elite, mainstream of the arts, neither art-officials nor rank-and-file writers found a way to consistently tap those energies.

Free to Write the Imagined

There was one other way besides folklore, life histories, and expository studies of neglected publics for the FWP to capture the soul of a nation: that is, through fiction, poetry, and essays that federal writers did on their own time. Hopkins's ultimately abrogated declaration that New Deal patronage would allow the Theater Project to be "free, adult, and uncensored" did not, even in his early enthusiasm and intent, extend to the Writers' Project, as we have seen. Project time was restricted to assigned common tasks whose general concept and guidelines had been established by the art-official and super-ficial heads of federal patronage in Washington. Before he died, Robert Hayden claimed those assigned tasks constituted the most important problem that staff writers had to face in expressing their views: "a good deal more could have been accomplished . . . if each writer had been free to work creatively and work in his or her own particular idiom and style." But, he added "the Writers' Project was not conceived of as a project that would permit each writer to go his or her own way and to do his or her own creative work." Looking back, Louis Falstein doubted that anything more could have been achieved even if more freedom had been allowed. In his view of Detroit's needy writers, the older hands on the project simply wanted to collect paychecks and the younger ones had talents too immature to produce anything of merit.

FWP art-officials and such outside writers as Cowley, while realistic about staff giftedness, were anything but dim about what relief writers could achieve in fiction and poetry, and they sought ways the FWP could promote rank-and-file creativity. For art-officials those ways could not take over project time, which had to remain sacred for working on the common tasks worked out in Washington. The end products of those tasks, by the rules set up for New Deal patronage, automatically became government property. And that, not so incidentally, posed another obstacle to freely created imaginative writing. Art-officials provided, first through the FWP itself and then through the pages of several literary journals, outlets that encouraged federal writers to use their own time for writing the imagined. Those outlets offered two inducements: a public airing for private-time composition and individual rather than patron ownership of the work produced.

The first of these avenues began as a 1937 call from Henry Alsberg, as National Director, for contributions created on private time to be published by an as yet unsecured sponsor. To carry out the plan, a three-tiered apparatus of state, regional, and national editors was set up. In Detroit, Anteo Tarini was appointed state editor. His announcement of the plan urged the Michigan staff not to feel inhibited about the kind of material to be submitted. In the first place, the intention was to produce not an "arty-arty" book, but a down-to-earth one about modern American life. In the second, all submissions would be sent on to the national board of editors. It was his view that Michigan should be able to make a "vital contribution" to the final result.[12] The response to Alsberg's call, although generally ignored by the Project's best writers, was voluminous and excellent enough to win the support of a sponsor and make possible a book-length anthology of selections, *American Stuff*, published in August 1937. Excellent did not mean the polished style or rarified subjects of high culture (Tarini's arty-arty or what Alsberg called "the echo of the higher aestheticism or the delicate attenuations of emotion"), but the drama and gutsiness that evoked the American scene "as it appears from the roadside ditch, the poverty-stricken tenement or shack, the relief station." There is little doubt that in Washington and the hinterlands, Alsberg and Tarini, for example, saw in the private-time creative writing of FWP staff members another way of expressing, as Alsberg put it in the foreword to *American Stuff*, "a solid passionate feeling for the life of the less prosperous millions."[13]

Tarini's hope that Michigan would have a dominant presence in *American Stuff* did not materialize. We are left with no way to gauge from this in-house effort whether the FWP writers of the "motor state" could evoke in imaginative writing that deep feeling for neglected publics that Alsberg lauded. Only one writer from the Michigan unit, Robert Hayden, was included in the anthology. Was his the only manuscript submitted from Michigan among the hundreds that poured into Washington from across the nation? The archives offer no answer. For the entire Midwest, only one other FWP writer made it into the anthology, Richard Wright of the Chicago unit. His contribution was indeed a brilliantly expressed passion from shack, roadside, and tenement, "The Ethics of Living Jim Crow," which later received larger recognition as the opening to *Uncle Tom's Children* (1938) and the seed that grew into *Black Boy* (1945).

The Hayden selection, "Autumnal," is quite different in tone and engagement. An early poem, it moves throughout to the rhythms of dirge; if it is meant to evoke the pain of the oppressed, it does so allusively. The season it focuses on glows with beauty, but is the mask of death, and one of the key metaphors of the poem is the hunted deer: "the buck lying stark / In a snare of blood." The lines of the next stanza, "gold his body / And scarlet his breath," reimage the slain deer but also delineate the appearance of Autumn, whose beauty disguises the season's final effect: "Medusa trees / And hollow skies." Extending the gold-his-body image from nature, either as buck or season, to society, we have an historical and social allusion that suggests African-American experience and the rapacity that lurks behind the presumed harmonies of American society. But the mood and allusiveness of the poem quiet the feeling and make it remote from ditch, shack, and tenement. The closest it comes to gutty passion are the closing lines:

Who rends the flesh
Shall come to grief,
With broken hands
Bind the poppied sheath
And bear it homeward
To the harvest tune
Of winds that rock
A bloody moon.

But if the passion grows tougher with this end, it is still constrained and moderated by its slow rolling tone and indirection.

It would be interesting to discover how many poems Hayden submitted for consideration. While Hayden worked for the FWP, he managed to write the imagined, he recalled, no matter how drained he was at the end of a day working on his prescribed project. In his FWP years, he composed a large enough body of poems on non-project time to produce his first published book in 1940, *A Handful of Dust*. In it, we find several poems that engage African-American experience more directly and expressed it with a much more aroused passion than the one published in *American Stuff*. With the evidence on hand now, we do not know if Hayden offered these for consideration or if the national board of editors turned them down, even though these poems were cast more vigorously in the creative mode the board admired and wanted to encourage.

The success of *American Stuff*, in the flood of material it attracted and in sales, led the national office to consider an independent magazine (Tarini thought it would appear monthly) under the same name as the anthology. But nothing came of it. However, the national administrators were able to convince existing literary journals to open their pages in 1938 to the afterwork imaginative writing of the FWP staff. The journals generous enough to do so were *Poetry, New Masses, Direction*, and *New Republic*, but in each case only for a single issue. Still, those single opportunities attracted a substantial number of submissions, deemed worthy enough in the cases of

Poetry and Direction to fill a complete issue and of *New Masses*, its literary section. Although the poems and stories published came from all over the country, the weight of representation fell to the east and west coast writers. Not even Chicago, with its wealth of talent, made much of a difference to this overbalance, and the contribution it made is hardly gripping. No one from Detroit, which also numbered some very competent writers, made it into the roster of any of the issues these journals set aside for the FWP. As a result there is little of an after-work creative nature from the Midwest in published form that tells us very much about how well FWP writers from that region, composing out of their imagination, could illuminate the soul of the streets and backwash neighborhoods of America.

It is not at all far-fetched to presume that in this genre indeed there may have been a loss. We have evidence before and after the FWP that writers could represent insightfully and vigorously through verse, drama, and fiction America's neglected publics. I have already alluded to some of Hayden's early poems. Arthur Clifford, who impressed local and national art-officials with his writing abilities, twice won Avery Hopwood awards for drama. The first, a 1932 winner, is *1789: A Mass-Play*; in my judgment, this is an outstanding example of his ability to make a large canvas take seriously the neglected orders of modern civil society. My other example is Elena Mitcoff, whose brief stint with the FWP resulted in some first-rate narrative re-renderings of folk tales. She left the FWP when she won the 1937–38 Avery Hopwood major fiction award for *A New Life*, a chronicle novel about a Russian fugitive and his family who emigrate to the United States to escape the terror following the 1905 Revolution.[14]

Clifford's play is politically radical and experimental, using mass chorus techniques and cubist stage arrangements to intensify the issues at stake and disrupt conventional dramatic and historical attitudes. The "mass" in the title has a double reference: to the choric character of the play, of course, and then to the protagonists of the play, the neglected orders who rise up against their oppressors. The "1789" of the title is a point of origin. The action, the issues of oppression, the costumes, the mood of the protagonists are transformed as the plot tracks out the course from the French Revolution through the October 1917 overthrow of capitalism in Russia and beyond to the onset of the Great Depression. While the power relationships and the abusive treatment of the masses are rendered in the broad sweep we described in our analysis of agit-prop, the taut and sinewy language that Clifford sheathes them in guards against parody and, in keeping with choric sonority, makes those relationships and treatment essential factors of an epic historical movement. On the other hand, he disallows a sentimental closure, victory against oppression. The play ends in uncertainty, as the twentieth-century capitalist is seen against a shadow-play backdrop of a

283

guillotine and a crucified Christ, while the chorus of torso-naked workers wearing red trousers chants: "From his fingers drip the wires of our destinies" (IV, 6). The play is an impressive expression of indignant insight into the difficult lives imposed on our neglected publics; in my opinion, it deserves present-day production.

Mitcoff's novel is impressive also. While it is fixed on the fugitive family, it recreates a convincing picture of Russian immigrant life in the Midwest. It succeeds in portraying the conflicted state of the father, who is riven between his old-country socialist beliefs and his adaptations to American culture, with emphasis on his modest success as a businessman-mechanic, which in the course of events brings him up against the contorted ethics of American capitalism in the form of bootlegging. The story belongs to the immigrant parents, particularly the father Anton, but an incidental companion conflict is the growing Americanness of the younger generation. One daughter, Kitty, becomes a writer and enters a bohemian arts-and-crafts world whose values are quite different from old-world tradition, the father's socialist convictions, and new-world middle-class convention.

Two last events signal that the father finally resigns himself to being not a hero, like Napoleon, or a revolutionary, like Lenin, or a foot-soldier re-emigrant to the socialist Soviet Union, like his first partner Ponasock (362), but an American resident and shop-owning mechanic. His resignation is symbolized by the citizenship papers he files for and the cutting off of his handlebar mustache. But his resignation is not solely defeat: when Anton's wife Anna sees his shaven upper lip she notes that his mouth is not weak, just sensitive, "as it will always be" (444). Mitcoff's narrative handling is conventional, but as we know from her folk-tale transformations, she is an able storyteller. That is evident in the novel, particularly where old-homeland ways of life and Russian radical ideals rub up against new-world ways and cultural values. The story is told in clean, precise language, which electrifies the tensions and contradictions at the heart of a specific immigrant experience, as it also illuminates the general dialectics of all alienated, neglected publics.

Not long after Mitcoff left the FWP a youthful heart illness took her life, closing down a promising literary career that she had carefully nursed through her association with Paul McPharlin and the arts-and-crafts movement and later through the writing milieu and practice that the FWP made possible.

Two other Detroit writers are worth brief citation as examples of this after-work spin-off in writing the imagined. Rebecca Shelley Rathmer, who wrote a great deal over her lifetime but thought of herself as a pedestrian writer, took stabs in her after-work efforts at composing a novel based on her own and her husband's depression years' struggle to maintain her inherited homestead. Her idea was to write a story that would interest Hollywood and make lots of money—her American fantasy for overcoming hard-time crisis. Although she tried to enlist the influence of the Michigan versifier Edgar Guest, she didn't get very far with the enterprise.

Louis Falstein is an instance of the priming power of the FWP that led someone with limited skills (Falstein had a rather modest view of his abilities while with the Detroit Project) to become a professional writer. It is also a case of the FWP's failure to help someone with a direct connection to immigrant and working-class culture—Falstein had come with his family from the Slavic pale and had worked in Chicago and Detroit factories—to center on and express with vigorous intensity the structure of those experiences. What resulted from his role as an FWP writer and his after-work association with other FWP writers were two novels, a non-fiction work on Sholom Aleichem, and a collection of essays he edited on the fate of Jewish doctors in Poland. One of his novels, *Face of a Hero*, enjoyed a rather favorable reception when it first appeared. It is a realistic account of daily life in a B-26 tactical bomb squadron during World War II. The title is ironic, for the story strips military flying of its mythic glamor and, without under-representing the war dangers, characterizes the actions of the crew as generally rather pedestrian. The novel is a competent performance by a writer who flashes no great gift but who has learned to do the job well.

It is hard to say whether the FWP's Midwest writers' attempts to compose the imagined offer more support for an optimistic prediction of what might have been accomplished in revealing the soul of mosaic U.S.A. There are hints from the region, sometimes fairly mighty ones in the drama, poetry, and fiction that were the spin-offs of work done on non-project time or produced before and after FWP tenure. But there are not many, perhaps because non-project time was a cramped and flagging-energy time. Even those are not powerful enough to redress the basic weakness, at least of ethnic and labor studies, of not discovering, under difficult bureaucratic and internally divided art-official and super-ficial policy, how to get inside the thriving cultures of neglected publics or of not recogizing that they were thriving.

16

Smoky Cyclorama:
Putting on Shows in the Midwest

HE reader will recall that Hallie Flanagan saw Detroit as a drama in itself and a place for putting on dramas. She knew Detroit, having visited
over the years an aunt and uncle who lived there. They owned Melville
House, a residence and school for foreign-born factory workers, "Poles,
Hungarians, Macedonians." This "factory district of Detroit," she wrote to
Harry Hopkins on December 26, 1933, "like our small Iowa towns in a different way, made up the very backbone of America." During these visits she
watched in terror as an appalling drama unfolded. The actors were the
shabby and bleak men without jobs crowding Melville House and the surrounding streets. They were growing to hate the "status quo" more and
more every day. Terrified as she was by the stoked-up bitterness, she did not
blame the men, but asked why they hadn't acted more resolutely:
"Watching the waste and terrible contrast between rich and poor, I often
wondered why they didn't smash up Ford's factory and die splendidly instead of gradually."[1] She told Hopkins that the relief program he was administering in that first year of the New Deal government had restored some
measure of hope to the neighborhood's unemployed.

The Flanagan letter points up three issues that we have been concerned with: the mighty heft of neglected cultures in the structure of U. S.
society; the drama of worker-immigrant struggles; and the ambivalent nature of federal patronage. Flanagan was not at all aware of the divided implication she expressed when she applauded Hopkins for his role in raising
the level of hope. To reduce economic idleness and the aimlessness and use-
lessness it induced were to her, as it would be to anyone with strong communal attitudes, good things. To replace idle free time with a theater willing
to inspire and be inspired by worker-immigrant culture was also a good

286

thing. But relief as a safety valve for reducing rebellious pressures threatened to subvert both itself (pressure gone, no need to be humane) and a patronage that wanted to be free and uncensored, that wanted to enrich and be enriched by neglected cultures. Over the course of events, as the bureaucratic and super-ficial disease we analyzed earlier demonstrates, federal patronage suffered most because Flanagan and her art-officials all over the nation were forced to play both sides of the work-relief street. The game hurt all the more because the rank and file under them were politically and esthetically unsynchronized.

But if Flanagan was unaware of the ambivalence built into relief as safety valve, she understood that the un-headlined worker-immigrant publics had become the American scene and how important they were to federal theater. On her travels as national director to the troubled Midwest units, wherever she found diverse immigrant populations, she saw enormous advantage. In Gary, Indiana, the "flame-colored clouds" pouring from the mills, she settled hopes on the Hungarian, Czech, Norwegian, Swedish, Finnish, Italian, French, and Magyar children of the city's steel workers. The ten-member FTP there produced a wide range of plays, including "unique . . . folk plays and dances in which different racial groups introduced their customs and cultures to each other."[2] In Minnesota, the Danish, Norwegian, and Swedish immigrant communities supplied a storehouse of relief-certified actors, 165 to be precise, for the Minneapolis unit, which looked forward to an extensive program of Scandinavian classics. This great opportunity was blown out of existence before the group could get started because state bureaucrats were frightened by a Minneapolis newspaper story claiming that the WPA had brought in a fan dancer to entertain men working in the Civilian Conservation Corps (CCC).[3]

To visit the Milwaukee unit was to walk into a miniature America. Its performers, technicians, stagehands, tailors, ushers, and box office staff came from "German, Polish, Croatian, Jewish, Irish, Italian, French, Bohemian, Spanish, Russian, Danish, and Norwegian" backgrounds. The immigrant communities of Milwaukee refuted the skeptics back in New York who predicted that no amount of scouring would find enough theater people in heartland America. But this kaleidoscope of advantage failed when the local FTP adopted a little-theater approach to programming. In Flanagan's view, this was another example that the success of Federal Theater depended on local units encouraging and doing plays by local talent about local matters and thus becoming "a functioning part of community life."[4]

Only three Midwest projects hung on for the full term of Federal Theater history. They were the region's other smoky cycloramas: Illinois, Michigan, and Ohio. The Chicago Federal Theater unit is, of course, atypical. Its cosmopolitan character and fund of professional theater people made it more like New York and California. The work of Theodore Ward in the Negro unit provided an unusual neglected-publics leaven. Chicago's most well-known production, also a home-based creation of the Negro unit, is *The Swing Mikado*. Its importance as populist esthetics lies in the imaginative way the group remade Gilbert and Sullivan in the style of jazz music and dance. Its flamboyant costuming transformed the imagined exotic Japanese dress in a fitting, but particularly American way. Its entire creation was an extremely collective one that made it difficult, except in the case of design, to mark any individual for credit. The play itself became the star, attracting one of Broadway's premier impresarios, Mike Todd, who wanted to be its Great White Way producer. As government property, however, it could not be transferred to private hands. The FTP brought the show to New York, where it had only a brief run; by that time Todd had mounted a glitzier version called *The Hot Mikado*. The Peoria project's long tenure is a surprise. The few productions from the national repertoire that it mounted were of some quality, but no one on the national staff felt very proud of the "old standbys," to use Flanagan's phrase, which it favored. Ohio had two units. The one in Cleveland scored highest with the community in the series of children's plays it put on. Cincinnati's FTP opened to hostile reviews by critics who believed that federal patronage meant propaganda and partisan politics. But during its three years of life it converted them to cheers: "If your uncle's venture in show business," a reviewer for the *Cincinnati Enquirer* wrote, "produces no more than this on the artistic side, it stands justified."[5]

The Detroit FTP's durability and the fact that, in the course of its troubled tenure, it managed to stage twenty-five major productions are remarkable. When it was first set up, Flanagan complained that the unit's original sponsor, a committee of former Bonstelle administrators, did not reflect the many-sidedness of the city. Moreover, its elite theatrical esthetics were not suitable to the varied character of the acting staff and the "common group enterprise" being planned. Flanagan also felt that the program it wanted to carry out, a duplicate of the old Bonstelle repertoire, would not be attractive to the many sub-groups of Detroit. She set to work on broadening sponsorship and producing plays that would integrate the unit with the city's less advantaged publics.

Flanagan was not alone in working toward these ends. When the FTP first got underway, Gerhardt Lindemuller of Grand Rapids, on WPA advice, wrote Flanagan about the possibility of setting up a workers' theater in western Michigan. The local trades and the labor council, he said, were eager to have a group that performed plays about workers' lives and union problems and that reached out to workers and union locals by touring nearby towns.[6] In May 1936, M. Walter Mountjoy, then the state director of

FTP, asked "why not dramatize the obscure beginnings of the automobile industry in this city, the repercussions and final effect on our economy and society?" That was one of the earliest proposals for an auto-industry living newspaper. Flanagan responded why not indeed, but she noted that it would have to be written by Detroit's FTP, perhaps with the help of local FWP writers. At the same time she suggested to Mountjoy that *Triple A* would have wide appeal in Detroit and that Detroit could become more of a community thing by doing local plays. The play *Prizefighter in Detroit*, she told Mountjoy, "made me visualize what could be done with the strength and cruelty and humor of Detroit."[7] By September 1936, Beyer had written a union play, probably because Flanagan had thought he should, that roused John McGee's enthusiasm. In the spring of 1937, McGee himself proposed that Detroit stage plays close to the concerns of its working publics: *Let Freedom Ring* or *Altars of Steel* instead of the religious *Cradle Song*.

The process of trying to get the Detroit unit to do its own plays, plays centered on local history, and to become an integral force in the community continued to the very end. Verner Haldene's February 1939 report informed J. Howard Miller that the Detroit unit planned to do a living newspaper on Father Gilbert Richards, an educationist and spiritual leader in early Detroit, a man whose work among the common people was much respected by everyone and revered by local Catholics. And he cites, among the many bookings intended to reach out to the community, an afternoon performance of *The Merry Wives of Windsor* before a large audience at the Hungarian Potofi Club.[8]

But we should not make too much of all this. A community-anchored theater as a collective rather than star enterprise did not mean for Flanagan one that exclusively programmed ethnic and working-class themes. Nor did art-officials in the field lean in that direction. Some administrators and directors were less concerned with populism than filling houses. They believed in tempering social drama with entertainment. Some were convinced that light fare was all that provincial federal theater could do because a large number of players came from vaudeville, circus, and burlesque venues. The national plan, moreover, called for a varied repertoire of classics, religious plays, and light comedy, as well as innovative social drama, partly as a way of calming super-ficial and bureaucratic anxieties and partly out of a social-worker attitude that the lives of neglected publics needed to be enhanced by exposure to a wide swath of theater. Usually the best and most experimental social dramas came from the center. While this was a decided benefit to local units, it reduced the necessity of relying on local playwrights writing about the bedrock of America in their own backyards.

At any rate, when we turn to the record of plays produced by the Detroit project, we find nothing that came out of the neglected publics' lives and industrial issues seething behind the smoky cyclorama that Flanagan saw as the dramatic, essential Detroit. What strikes us is loss here, for there were local writers in the area whose talents could have been easily enlisted. In the first place, there were a small number of writers, trying their fledgling wings on skits and sketches dealing with current issues, distributed among the four neglected cultures described in Part II. University theater and writing programs in Ann Arbor were a source of several others. Arthur Clifford, whose play we examined in the foregoing chapter, was one of these, and he was particularly close to home as a colleague in the Writers' Project.

In the program for *Let Freedom Ring*, an Albert Bein play about southern textile workers, we discover two others from the FWP, our old acquaintance Falstein, using the name Lewis Falls, and Maxine Finsterwald. Detroiters both, according to the program notes, although only Finsterwald was a long term resident, they had written a play about a Wisconsin milk strike that had been "first presented in Detroit." The local FTP supplied this programmatic information because Falls and Finsterwald had taken their title, *My Country 'Tis of Thee*, from the first verse of "America"—as had Bein and the authors of two other plays of interest to the FTP, the social drama *Sweet Land* and the political satire *Of Thee I Sing*.[9] Finsterwald and Falls had also written a play about the 1933 Ford Hunger March that deals with how the murder of four marchers by Ford service men affect the internal relationships of a black and a white family. In 1945, Finsterwald, using the pen name Maxine Wood, returned again to black and white family dynamics, this time focusing on the racial hostility that accompanied the famous trial of Dr. Ossian Sweet, a black Detroit dentist, for allegedly murdering a white man. *On Whitman Avenue* was produced by Canada Lee and Mark Marvin, lasting for 146 performances at Broadway's Cort Theater.[10]

One other local writer, the play reader for the company, ought to be mentioned. Kimon Friar had, in his association with the FTP, also expressed the desire to do a play about the auto industry. That he could have done something creditable with this subject may be judged from his remaking of Marlowe's *Dr. Faustus* for production by the Detroit FTP. This remake had two production runs, one in July 1937 at the People's Theater and a free one outdoors on Belle Isle in August, the only Detroit occasion that imitated the caravan theater of New York City. Both the paid and the free productions drew capacity crowds, received glowing praise from audience and press, and filled the company with deep satisfaction.[11] But Friar was never called to do anything else for the FTP.

The quite regular request for a living newspaper on the auto industry and the equally regular support, especially if it could be done by local writers, never led to the involvement of these already practicing local playwrights. Nor does it seem that Washington made its living newspaper research and writing staff in New York—which had been collecting clippings, statistics, and historical accounts of the industry and Detroit—aware of the Detroit FTP's interest in and resources for such a docudrama. The puzzle here is that in 1937, with Mary Heaton Vorse as the driving force, Vorse, Josephine Herbst, and Dorothy Kraus enlisted auto-workers in an effort to do a living newspaper on the sit-down strike. On one occasion in January 1937, Morris Watson, the supervisor of the living-newspaper division in the New York FTP, came to Flint, and Vorse immediately enlisted him in the project. Watson, to make the most of the short time he had, turned the play, which came to be called "Strike Marches On," into a series of spontaneous worker responses to topical newspaper and management items. In her papers, Vorse reports that, on the date set for performance , the strike was settled, and Pengelly Hall, the union's headquarters in Flint where "Strike Marches On" was scheduled to be shown, became a bedlam of celebration. In order to get into the hall, she and the performers had to climb the fire escape. Moreover, she had to rip sheets from her hotel bedroom for costumes.[12] Despite the fact that auto drama was going on before everyone's nose, including a leading FTP art-official engaged in the living-newspaper office, the New York material and the local talent never got together.

But if no advantage was taken of what Detroit had to offer in the way of dramatizing at firsthand the lives of neglected publics and highly conflicted industrial affairs, the local FTP revealed the mark of populist esthetics in the kind of plays that it produced in the middle years of its history. The first two plays the company put on, Ferenc Molnar's fantasy *Liliom* and William Beyer's comedy about true confession contests *I Confess*, got the company off to a shaky start because of unpracticed handling of props and lighting equipment and because neither the fantasy nor the comedy had that trenchancy of event that local audiences could feel strongly about. In fact, when Flanagan reviewed the results, she expressed the hope that Detroit could come up with plays that were more socially incisive.

The company turned in that direction with the next one, *Road to Rome*, Robert Sherwood's satire on Hannibal's invasion of the Italian peninsula. The theme of the play is mildly anti-war. But Beyer and the company's designer, Stephen Nastfogel, had in mind to sharpen the message or make it more timely by having the Carthaginians appear in Ethiopian dress and the Romans in black shirts. Although the state's WPA super-ficials quashed the idea, the turn had been made. There followed a string of plays dealing with the dangers of fascism, the depression, labor strife, and the horrors of war. After the New York company came to Detroit with the Orson Welles and John Houseman version of *Macbeth*—which itself represented a powerful social theme because its cast was all black and the setting and costumes were recast into a Haitian context—the Detroit company participated in the national program of presenting *It Can't Happen Here*. Again state super-ficials became nervous. They suspected that Beyer would advertize the show with posters depicting national reactionaries or overseas fascists hung in effigy. The fear was groundless, and although no sensational publicity appeared, the Detroit production, one of seventeen simultaneous showings, attracted a substantial audience. Of those queried after the curtain came down, almost all expressed highly favorable opinions of the theme and the performances. The local newspaper reviewers were less uniform, but liked what they saw: some felt that it was too propagandistic, and some faulted the acting.

Around the Corner, directed by Herschel Mayall, one of the company's actors, opened the 1937 season. This play by Martin Flavin dealt with the depression from the angle of the rancors it induced in family life. E. P. Conkle's *200 Were Chosen* dramatized the experience of the pioneers recruited by the government, mostly from a Michigan farming community, for colonizing Alaska's Matanuska Valley. In later years, Fred Morrow, who had become the Michigan state supervisor of the FTP, said he disapproved of putting on this play because it was too depressing. But other Detroit art-officials did not see it that way. Verner Haldene, who had by then become the unit's director, had a comment placed in the playbill that voiced the populism of the company: "Unlike the commercial theatre, which selects its productions solely from a profit-seeking standpoint, the Federal Theatre chooses its play from a social angle." "Just as these last frontiersmen are making history," the comment concludes, "so is the Federal Theatre recording it."[13]

The two most forceful social plays offered in the spring of 1937 were Sidney Howard's *Paths of Glory* and the already mentioned *Let Freedom Ring*. The playbill for *Paths of Glory* pointed up the play's strong opposition to all armies; it sought to win the audience to a fair viewing by reproducing Howard's 1935 preface to the work. "I do not for a moment believe that our audience found "Paths of Glory" dull. They found it painful, of course, but audiences do not necessarily shrink from pain. It made them angry, however, and there exists, I am certain, a prejudice against paying out money to be made angry." The Detroit FTP did not shrink from the risk of anger. An anti-war companion to the Howard play that spring was a one-night showing of Aristophanes's *Lysistrata*. *Let Freedom Ring* also had a labor play companion in October 1937, Arthur Miller's first dramatic piece —an Avery Hopwood award winner—*They Too Arise*. Miller structured this play around a dramatic situation he was to come back to with more effect in *All My Sons* and *Death of a Salesman*, the conflict between a son and a father—in this case around the father's anti-union maneuvers and the son's working-class sympathies. A product of Kenneth Rowe's playwriting class at the University of Michigan, it had a short run in Ann Arbor; probably through the recommendation of Rowe, who was an FTP consultant, the Detroit company, sponsored by Hillel, put it on for one performance at the Jewish Community Center. A second run of *Let Freedom Ring*, at the Cinema Theater, shortly after the Miller production, closed out the streak of socially oriented plays.[14]

It should not be imagined that the streak was entirely unbroken. Interspersed with these dramas were other kinds of plays, the comedies *Boy Meets Girl* and *The Spider*, which was also a mystery, and the religious plays *Cradle Song* and, for Christmas holiday, *The Little Crib*. But the heart of 1937 were the plays that dealt with timely political and social issues. In the following year those took a very minor place in the output of the Detroit FTP. In accordance with the national plan for 1938 to have the FTP do a cycle of O'Neill and Shaw, the Detroit company put on *Anna Christie* and *Arms and the Man*. There followed a series of comedies until June 1938, when the company ceased production because it had no theater for showings and it was being considered for reorganization.

In October 1938, the Detroit FTP undertook its last major social-issue production, the living newspaper *One-Third of a Nation*. The company made an all-out effort with this play, perhaps the most heralded living newspaper turned out by the national FTP. The experimental and the social were welded together for this production. James Doll, who had replaced Nastfogel as art director, designed a functional-abstract setting. It "was complete departure from realism," Doll wrote in his report. His design dispensed with elaborate imitative structures and kept the stage in total darkness. This made a virtue out of the lack of mechanical equipment, for it allowed the action to be shifted quickly by spotlighting to different levels of the stage and different actor groups. Dance movement also became a part of the staging. Modern abstract stylized movement was emphasized, according to the company's choreographer Edith Segal, to provide the script with the economy it demanded. Some minor changes were made locally to bring the housing issue closer to home. The experimental features apparently worked beautifully with the theme, highlighting by pace and sharply-focused lighting the drama of immigrant experience in the slums and ghettoes of urban America. The audiences were thrilled by the event: "be sure to let us know when you do another play like this"; "we've got the Federals to thank for an evening of unique entertainment"; "they've got a steady customer from now on"; "the conditions the play brings out made me sick"; "housing, who would have thought it could be the basis for so wonderful a stage production"; "so that's what a living newspaper is." The comments tell the story, the riveting character of social drama, when conceived with an imagination unconstrained by political inhibitions or dramaturgical conventions.[15]

Chrysler and Ford locals filled the huge Lafayette Theater, which the company had leased for this production. Labor leaders greeted the performances and the theme with enthusiasm and said that with more plays like *One-Third of a Nation*, there would be no problem finding a working-class audience—and for Detroit that meant audiences of neglected publics. The 1937 string of social-oriented plays had been heading Detroit FTP toward that port, and with *One-Third of a Nation*, it had found its mooring. Unfortunately, the end was too near and local energies too frayed or timid, still too reliant on national programming and plays rather than local writers near the backbone of America.

The last major play offered to Detroit publics, *The Merry Wives of Windsor*, demonstrated once again that the Detroit FTP had matured as a company. While the trajectory of its production history shows that it did not solve the most pressing problems of populist esthetics, it also demonstrates that a common enterprise in a provincial context rather than a star system is capable of very good and sometimes outstanding work. *The Merry Wives of Windsor* no longer had a theater to play in, but through spot bookings in churches, civic centers, and high schools, it reached a fairly large number of Detroiters, particularly students. It could boast some song and dance of local origin, but they were the swan song. It was an appropriate last production. The mammoth vision, the populist esthetics with which all the projects began ended in Detroit with Falstaff fallen to caricature.

CONCLUSION

The grand vision and from-the-ground-up esthetics of New Deal patronage are for our own time old-fashioned and naive. They are indeed often artistically scorned. As a form of sponsorship that sets theater people and writers to work on a massive scale in contrast to a system that assigns awards in a competition judged by creative peers, New Deal arts patronage has no place in our present cultural agenda. Artists are simply not interested in it, even though their commodity-craft status in a strife-ridden marketplace forces them to need subsidy. Since the end of World War II, the government has frowned on mammoth programs in the field of culture, particularly if they are of a collective nature. Whether a particular administration's disposition is liberal or conservative, it has tended to contain and cut back on whatever remains of such projects, preferring to funnel its subsidies to individual artists and independently run institutions or groups.

Still the sixty-year period of revisions and forgettings that succeeded the culture of the 1930s has not been able to suppress entirely the sense that New Deal patronage deserves some respect for what it accomplished. Several scholars, digging among the ruins, have discovered its artifacts and been surprised at its invention and merit. Their work gravitates toward the most highly active centers of the federal arts projects, New York, Chicago, Los Angeles, San Francisco, and the most outstanding accomplishments— no matter what their source. The more their work advances, the more reasonable it seems that this past adventure into government art patronage has some bearing on the present privatized view of the arts among artists and federal funding agencies.

The unusual form and populist motives that inspired federal patronage in the 1930s were, from inception, in contradiction to the work-relief auspices through which that patronage worked. The unparalleled character of New Deal patronage also put it at odds with the history of patronage in modern civil society, both before its own life began and after its demise. Its populism suggested that many neglected publics of the United States could

295

be its creative inspiration and power against an unfriendly historical framework and its politically conflicted agency. At the source of work relief execution, New Deal patronage found bureaucratic misunderstanding and distrust of cultural projects: a nervousness about dangerous ideas slipping into writing and theater as well as doubts about the practical value of art's patronage. Against the promise held forth by the thriving cultural lives to be found among neglected publics, history, politics, and bureaucratic disfavor were all destabilizing factors to which the super-ficials and art-officials most directly responsible for the arts projects responded with divided souls: steadfast principle at odds with the need to compromise. Against themselves in their dealings with conservative politicians—who were out to get them—with liberal politicians—who were more interested in getting reelected than carrying out principle—and hard-headed bureaucrats, super-ficials and art-officials revealed their slender ties to one source of potential power: the down below ethnic and worker cultures that their populist esthetics addressed. The relationship to those communities where populist esthetics functioned well accounts for much of what the writing and theater projects accomplished and, where it was loose and distant, for their failures.

My goal in this long journey through the history of patronage, the cultures of neglected publics, the political and bureaucratic embroilments that assailed the starting up and maintaining of the projects, and finally the analysis of what these projects produced is to see all of this through the Theater and Writers' projects in the Midwest, with emphasis on the Michigan projects. That setting is more provincial and industrial, more highly ethnic and working class in population—and therefore more reflective of the mosaic that constitutes the backbone of American culture—than are the more distinguished cosmopolitan centers. The cultural influences of these diverse publics have spread far and wide, especially after World War II, as their sons and daughters migrated in increasing numbers to other industrializing sections of the nation. Though I have concentrated on a single region, my aim has been representative. The problems of federal patronage in the depression years, of political and bureaucratic encounters, and of relationships to neglected publics differ in this region from the cosmopolitan centers and bring us closer to the essential dynamics of this unconventional governmental patronage. But the cosmopolitan voice is loud and drowns out what the workings of these heartland Theater and Writers' projects have to tell us about the place of a different, more representative past in the cultural affairs of the present. The key to the current budgetary constraints on and esthetic/moral controversies over cultural production, it seems to me, can be found in what the Midwest projects did and did not do, in the divided soul they manifested, and in their failed relation with the publics down below.

296

One final question remains. Does the way federal patronage worked in the Midwest suggest that present governmental subsidies should be reconstructed along the lines of the 1930s? The accomplishments of the Theater and Writers' projects in Michigan and the Midwest cannot be ignored in finding an answer. The failures and the reasons for them do not necessarily say "no," for they could be lessons that teach us how to use more imaginatively a patronage devoted to collective production as well as to ward off more effectively the endemic tendency of government to intrude and control where it is incompetent. The key to imaginative use and effective defense against the officialness of government patronage is, as I have argued, the ties that writers and theater people have to neglected publics. The accomplishments and failures of the Midwest projects have a great deal to teach us about finding a genuine way into the heart of those cultures. They represent the ticket to more than defense. They constitute the ticket to thematic originality and linguistic innovation. If we have regard for the different place that neglected cultures have in the hierarchical structure of our society, they could suggest how to free ourselves from the dominating political grasp of cultural norms and elite fashions. One is tempted to say "yes" because mammoth support for the arts also guarantees stable creative frameworks for artists through ongoing collective programs drawing on the energies of all our cultures, and this seems to be an indisputable good.

But intrusion makes "no" come to mind once again. Where the money is, there is control. Where money is a matter of political decision, there is the jealously guarded right to control, usually on the specious ground of protecting the taxpayer. Where politicians and bureaucrats are the ultimate policymakers and administrators, there is the danger of know-nothingism and narrow-minded belief. That is why I used the term "endemic" above. Moreover, the art-officials who are in charge run the risk of becoming institutionalized and compromising. The threat is real in a society such as ours, where anxieties over what art might inadvertently or subversively do runs high and the elite view of the "other" is low.

Writers and theater people are still so much in the grip of an ideology that stresses the private and the cosmopolitan they feel threatened as individuals and creative persons by the thought of working in a collective setting under government financing. But has creativity ever been an individual matter or is that a blindness imposed by the history of the arts under capitalist modes of production, a blindness to tracks laid out by modern civil society toward privacy and cosmopolitanism? Is there greater freedom to be creative in running along that alienating pathway where the marketplace gods have overwhelming power than in the bosom of unpretentious welcoming cultures?

Conclusion

A "yes" or "no" answer is really not imperative. Every past is a challenge to the present not to become too comfortable with itself. It seems to me that is most true where that past tears up what had preceded it, as federal patronage, against itself as it was, had done in the 1930s, and where the present, whatever its new fashions may be, imitates what has been torn up. The unconventional side of New Deal patronage, mammoth undertaking and the vision of populist esthetics, and the dialectics that worked its way out in the Federal Theater and Writers' projects of Michigan and the Midwest urge themselves upon us in the present struggle for the future of American culture and art. Among the low, the neglected, and the Theater and Writers' projects in the industrial heartland, there may be answers for the willing eye and ear.

NOTE ON DOCUMENTATION, BIBLIOGRAPHY, AND ABBREVIATIONS

For book, article, and unpublished dissertation references, endnotes cite authors' last names and, where necessary, short title designations. The selected bibliography provides the complete information for this shorthand. Endnote references to manuscript material use the abbreviations in parentheses before the entries under Manuscript Collections. The selected bibliography and, when applicable, endnotes use the below listed abbreviations for libraries, archives, and special collections:

AAA	Archives of American Art
ALU	Archives of Labor and Urban Affairs
BHL	Bentley Historical Library
BHC	Burton Historical Collection
CU	Columbia University
DIA	Detroit Institute of Arts
DPL	Detroit Public Library
FDR	Franklin Delano Roosevelt Library
GMU	George Mason University
IHR	Immigrant History Research Center
ISH	Illinois State Historical Library
LC	Library of Congress
MSU	Michigan State University
NA	National Archives
UM	University of Michigan
UMI	University of Minnesota
WSU	Wayne State University

NOTES

Introduction

1. This is one gauge of how unprecedented are the employment figures for the FWP. In 1935, it had 2,381 on its roster; at its peak in 1936, it had 6,686; and in August 1939, 3,366. These figures prompted the writer of the report in which this information appeared to say "with justice, the Federal Writers' Project was the most notable adventure in writing ever undertaken in this country." See file labeled Writers' Project, A Brief History of the FWP, 1939, FWP. See also ch. 1 and 2 for more details.
2. Executive Order 7046, 20 May 1935 established the 90–10 ratio; WPA Administrative Order 35, 26 Nov. 1935 authorized an exception under justified circumstances of a ratio up to 75–25 for the arts projects. McDonald 173–4.
3. Hill, World Upside Down 14.
4. Frederick Brown 41–131.
5. Raymond Williams 40–2.
6. Marling 3.
7. Marling 63–8, 107–12.
8. Marling 95–6, 174–5, 263.
9. For such an assumption, see McDonald 238–9.
10. Marcus 3, 253.

1. The Arts and Patronage in Modern Civil Society

1. Galbraith 173; Peeler 2; Michael Bernstein, "Why the Great Depression Was Great," 33, in Fraser and Gersfee. Galbraith, using government statistics, writes that the unemployment rate was 25% and 13,000,000 were out of work in 1933 and that the rate was 20% in 1938; Peeler also cites 25% unemployment but adds that 25% more were underemployed; Bernstein gives a "decennial average of 18 percent" for the entire period of the 1930s.
2. McDonald 122–32.
3. George Biddle expressed one of the earliest positive views and certainly the most influential. See Biddle letter to President Roosevelt 9 May 1933, Hop-

kins Papers, File PPF 458 Biddle, FDR. Also Hilda W. Smith memo and attached proposal to Aubrey Williams 13 Mar. 1934, CWA Administrative Correspondence RG69. Henry Seidel Canby voiced grave reservations. Canby, "Should Writers Go on Salary?" See Penkower 7. The *Washington Post* held that national subsidy for the arts would hinder rather than help on the grounds that "luxury and ease" handicapped creative work. See Magione 48. Eva Le Gallienne, a friend of the FTP for the most part, initially expressed terror at the idea of government subsidized theater. See Flanagan, *Arena* 40.

4. Braudel 1:556–8, 3:620–8. Hill, *Reformation to the Industrial Revolution* 282–5.

5. One of the most complete descriptions of the city and capitalism is in Braudel 1: ch. 2 and 3. For a conservative view of the dense packing of population, mass personality, and creative alienation see Ortega y Gasset 49–53, 157. Foucault sees the eighteenth century as a break with the epistemes of the world before the ideological triumph of capitalism. In *Birth of the Clinic* (1973), *Discipline and Punish* (1977), *Madness and Civilization* (1965), and *History of Sexuality* (1976), Foucault argues that new epistemes—centered on the private person as locus of disease, guilt, aberration, and deviation and sharply different from those of the past—came to govern medicine, criminal justice, mental pathology, and human sexuality with the dominance of bourgeois culture in the eighteenth century. Eagleton deals with the same process in the arts in *The Ideology of the Aesthetic* (1990).

6. Poggi 21–5, 30, 84–96, 272. On the last page cited, Poggi offers Arthur Hopkins's view that New York theater in the 1920s depended on the "choice of a few New York producers" who based their decisions on what "appeals to their taste, preferences, and understanding."

7. Examples are Yaddoo, founded in 1926 and located among the natural splendors of Saratoga Springs, and MacDowell, founded the same year and as idyllically sited in New Hampshire. The first is known as the Yale and the second as the Harvard of art colonies. The MacArthur Foundation, whose five-year awards to individuals are known as the genius awards, is of a more recent vintage.

8. For instance, the Guggenheim Museum, fathered by Solomon Guggenheim and housed in the building designed by Frank Lloyd Wright—Solomon's choice for the job—and its collection largely determined by Peggy Guggenheim's taste for surrealism and abstract expressionism; the Museum of Modern Art, the invention of Abby Aldrich Rockefeller, Lillian Bliss, and Mary Quinn Sullivan, backed by the elitist notions of Professor Paul J. Sachs and the tastes of collector John Quinn; the National Gallery, the museum that Andrew Mellon supported with large sums of money and, at its birth, with his more classical collection art. These are perhaps the most obvious examples, but by no means the only. See Davis Part III, ch. 6 "King Solomon's Museum" and Part IV, ch. 6 "Peggy in New York: Ernst, Pollock and the Art of This Century," and Lynes ch. 1. Lynes, 200, discusses Sachs's view that a museum should house elite artists for the benefit of the public. Davis's style is so consistently

flippant and mocking that it borders on prejudice and diminishes credibility. Still his account provides the essential facts of how private wealth patronizes the arts according to its own preferences.

9. Perhaps the most famous polemical account of this historical process is the one made by Marx and Engels in "The Manifesto of the Communist Party"; see *Collected Works* 6: 486–7; see also Febvre 44–69; Braudel 2: 504 and 3: 625–6.

10. Foucault, *Power, Knowledge*, 96.

11. Braudel 2:224, 400–1, 516.

12. Braudel 3:38, 47–50.

13. Larson 37–41, ch. 3, 222–3; Lillian Miller 221–30; Netzer ch. 1; Minihan xi, where she claims that it was only after World War II "when Parliament at last made an extensive commitment to Art," and 243–9.

14. The figures in Netzer ch. 1 are for federal, state, and local subsidies.

15. Netzer 3 (Table 1–1), 9, 12. The NEA budget for 1994–95 tells the dismal story most graphically. The supposedly art friendly Clinton administration and Congress cut the allocation by $4.7 million to $174.5 million. Jane Alexander, the present chair of NEA, says that the endowment has experienced a devastating "reduction of 46% in funding since the late 1970s," *New York Times* 6 Jan. 1994: B1 and B4.

16. A survey of the NEH and NEA annual reports bears this out. See for example the NEH Tenth Annual Report (for fiscal 1975) 63 (private donors) and 85–138 (awards). California, District of Columbia, New York awards are typical; the NEH Sixteenth Annual Report (for fiscal 1981) 13–261. For NEA's elitism, see Netzer's chapter on the kind of institutions and individual projects to and for which grants have been.

2. Counter Choices: A New Deal in the Arts

1. Marling 5.

2. Flanagan, Arena 435. Mathews viii, 297.

3. Penkower 62.

4. See Arian ch. 3 "Elite Domination of the National Endowment for the Arts"; Netzer 183–5; Miller *Patrons and Patriotism*, 90–102; Minihan x–xii, 59–61, 141–6, 243–9.

5. McDonald, 479. Cahill in *Art for the Millions* 39 and chart on 40.

6. Flanagan, *Arena*, 127, 129, 383.

7. Flanagan, *Arena*, 434–5.

8. Penkower 135, 139, 174.

9. Mangione includes the bibliography compiled by Arthur Scharf, "Selected Publications of the WPA Federal Writers' Project and the Writers' Program," 375–98.

10. Any of the annual reports of the NEH gives one a good idea of how the Endowment works and its main intellectual tendencies. The Endowment shifted markedly to elite concentrations after the Reagan administration was in-

stalled. But even under the more liberal auspices of the Carter years, its populism was overshadowed by its elitism.

11. Cahill's speech of 28 Oct. 1939 for John Dewey's eightieth birthday celebration, reproduced in *Art for the Millions* as "American Resources in the Arts" 33–44 is a typical expression of that populism, see especially 43–4; see also Flanagan, *Arena* 45–6: FAP Manual Oct. 1935, 1, RG69; Mathews 32.

12. Flanagan, *Arena* 115–29; Brown and O'Connor 59–86. Ira H. Kastner, "Writing the Living Newspaper," Living Newspaper File, RG69.

13. Critical views, the productions of commercial and experimental theaters, and the fictional canon confirm this exclusion then and now. F. R. Leavis's *The Great Tradition* will do for the past and the concentration on elite works by structuralists, post-structuralists, and deconstructionists, no matter how revolutionary they presume themselves to be, will do for the present. A canvas of plays presented on Broadway and by little-theater groups in the 1930s and now also makes the point. The best-seller lists of the 1930s and now, the canon that continues to be taught at universities, and the present debate over that canon underscore the exclusion of these publics. Cultural elitists such as Alan Bloom, William Bennett, and E. D. Hirsch advocate exclusion. But the cultural expansionists, arguing for representation of female, ethnic, and African-American works, for which, in my view, they are to be applauded, do not as critics or imaginative writers go to the heart of the experiences of the majorities that make up obscure publics.

14. See Mangione 270 on Botkin's prescription for avoiding paternalism, nostalgia, and aristocratic dilettantism and Penkower 75–8 on combating boosterism.

15. See Flanagan, *Arena*, for new productions translated into foreign languages, 389; for Negro drama, 392; and for standard foreign language drama, 422–7.

16. Flanagan, *Arena* 380–433.

17. The Emergency Relief Act of 1939 put the final stamp on this transfer, but a reorganization plan approved by President Roosevelt and advocated by Col. Francis H. Harrington, who had become head of the WPA after Hopkins had become secretary of commerce, initiated the process of dismemberment. McDonald 309–11, 313; Mangione 329–30; Penkower 209.

18. McDonald 320, 691; Penkower 237.

19. Penkower 154.

20. Mangione 4.

21. Hopkins 173–8 and 183–4. See Hopkins's comments about putting men and women to work who "would help build and improve America" in Flanagan, *Arena* 25, 27–8.

22. Ransom 293–4.

23. Ransom 297.

24. Ransom 302.

25. Ransom 306.

26. For other expressions of these ideas see Davidson and Warren.

27. Odum and Moore 367.

28. Hacker 110.

29. Holcombe 11, 13–4.
30. The Wirth quotation is from Odum and Moore 405.
31. Botkin, "Regionalism: Cult or Culture?" 183–4.
32. Botkin, "Regionalism" 184–5.
33. Odum and Johnson collaborated on an analytical and descriptive account of workaday songs, which included a substantial number of examples.
34. Larkin "Ella May's Songs," *The Nation* 9 Oct. 1929, 382–83; mss. of the Bailey play are available at the Philadelphia Library and at the University of North Carolina library. Ms. Bailey was kind enough to have UNC send me a copy of the play. My paper, "Theater of Action: The Great Smokies on the Picket Line," presented at the American Folkore Society Meeting in San Antonio, 21–5 Oct. 1981, analyzes the ballads in Bailey's and other plays about the Gastonia strike.
35. Odum and Moore 185–7.
36. The *Midland*, Iowa City: 1–20, 1915–33. See also book on the *Midland* by Riegelman.
37. See Conroy and Johnson, where Conroy's "Introduction" expresses a radical regionalism opposed to the ultra-left Marxism of Philip Rahv and the dogmatism of Alexander Trachtenberg of the U.S. Communist Party. His brief against these two, who later became bitter enemies, had its origin in the short-lived merger with *Partisan Review* that Rahv and Trachtenberg forced on *Anvil*.
38. See for example Chicago Workers' Cultural Federation and Finnish Workers Theatre and their audiences, *New Theatre* Mar. 1934: 22; also Chicago Blue Blouses and their street corner performances, *New Theatre* Sept. 1934: 28; also Cleveland People's Theatre and their performances before AFL locals, *New Theatre* Oct. 1935: 30; also how Albert Maltz influenced the Contemporary Theatre to reach out to workers on strike and the group's weekly plays for the auto workers union, *Theatre Workshop* Apr.–June 1938: 105 and 107; and finally Mogill interview on performing *Waiting for Lefty* inside the Flint plant where the sit-down strikers were and later at local union halls.
39. Gard, *Grass Roots Theater* 36–7.
40. Spearman 12, 16, 29.
41. Cahill, *Art in America*, 43–45.
42. Cahill 34 in Francis V. O'Connor, ed., *Art for the Millions*.
43. Cahill 41 in O'Connor.
44. Cahill 42 in O'Connor.
45. Flanagan, *Arena* 20–1.
46. Flanagan, *Arena* 23.
47. In 1931 *New Masses* published the script of *Can You Hear Their Voices?* It is also available at Vassar College Libraries, Special Collections.
48. Flanagan address to regional directors 8 Oct. 1935 1, Special Collections, GMU; Flanagan, *Arena* 43.

49. Flanagan address 8 Oct. 1935 2–3; Flanagan, *Arena* 45–6. Flanagan address to regional conference in Washington, D.C. 13–4 Mar. 1936 1, Conference Reports HFD.
50. Flanagan letter to Hopkins 7 Nov. 1937 HH, FDR; Flanagan report to regional directors May 1936, 7, HFG; Flanagan report to regional directors 8 Jan. 1936, RG69, WPA General Subject Series; Flanagan, *Arena* 159, 282–3.
51. McDonald 663–5; Penkower 19.
52. On the social-work influence see McDonald 7–9. Hopkins himself is the best advocate for the social-work point of view presented in the text. See his *Spending to Save*.
53. McDonald 665.
54. McDonald 694–5; see as one example addressed to a specific state project on folklore collecting guidelines Alsberg letter to Egbert R. Isbell, Director of the Michigan FWP 12 Aug. 1936, RG69, State Series.
55. Flanagan, *Arena* 42–3.
56. Mangione 59; McDonald 667.
57. Mangione 62; Penkower 16.
58. McDonald 678; Penkower 152–3.
59. RG69, CWA Administrative Correspondence; McDonald 658.
60. RG69, FERA Procedural Publications, "Preparation of Iconographies" 12 Oct. 1934.
61. McDonald 78; Penkower 23.
62. Nora Crump, Wayne County Art Project, to Arthur Goldschmidt, FERA acting director of Professional Projects 27 Dec. 1934, RG69 FERA State Files.
63. McDonald 650, 659.
64. McDonald 239.
65. McDonald 341.
66. Bills for a permanent, non-relief art program were introduced to Congress in January 1937 by Representative Sirovich and jointly in January 1938 by Representative Coffee and Senator Pepper. See Flanagan's criticism of them and her view that only a strong theater with a grass-roots following were required before one could speak of a permanent government art program of the kind represented by Federal One, *Arena* 325–9.
67. For an excellent discussion of lines of authority, see McDonald 106–12.

3. In the Eyes of the Beholder: Assembly-Line Publics in the 1930s and Before

1. Tocqueville, *Journey* 134, 141–2, 143, 339–40; Democracy in America 281.
2. Thirteenth Census of the United States (1910), Supplement for Michigan 618, 623, 673; Fourteenth Census of the United States (1920), Michigan 8, 33, 36, 52, 65–9; Fifteenth Census of the United States (1930), Foreign Born White Families by Country of Birth of Head 84–5, 129–31; Sixteenth Census of the United States (1940), Characterisitics of the Population 53, 88, 162–5. The

pages cited show the statistics of this change for the Midwest and its major cities.

3. Philip Levine, "Coming Home," in *They Feed* 21 and "Rain Downriver," in *Rose* 65.
4. Hobsbaum, *The Age of Revolution* 200, 204–16.
5. See Trachtenberg for background on Hines and the character of his photography 171, 203–4, 217–30.
6. Eagleton, *Literary Theory* 34.

4. Church, Center, Left: The Trinity of Polish-American Culture

1. Cuba, "Polish Amateur Theatricals" 24.
2. Estreicher 34–6.
3. Cuba, "Polish Amateur Theatricals" 29.
4. Kunka 67–90.
5. Cuba, "Polish Amateur Theatricals" 34–5; Milosz, 235.
6. *Trybuna Robotnicza* 5 Jan. and 19 Jan. 1935.
7. Programs and reviews Box 3, SL; Playbills and Programs Box 1, SW.
8. "Biography of Stanislaw Zenon Wachtel" by Estelle P. Wachtel-Torres, Box 1, SW.
9. For Detroit theater, names, see Strumski 36; All the theater names come from Programs and Reviews, SL; credit for their precise rendition in English goes to the archivist Benedict Markowski of the Burton Historical Collection.
10. The plays mentioned here are from the list in Programs and Reviews, SL.
11. Index of Plays Box 1, SW.
12. Published Humorous Verse and Kuplety Box 5, SL. For the translation of these and almost all of the other Polish literature in this chapter, I am indebted to Eva Matuszewski.
13. Braudel 1: 547.
14. Estreicher 32.
15. Estreicher 36.
16. Cuba, "Polish Amateur Theatricals" 41–2.
17. Estreicher 32.
18. Nowak interview.
19. For the extent of the variations of wedding songs and rituals see the foreword by Edward J. Dehnert in Pawlowska xviii. For the actual songs sung in the processions, see Pawlowska 171–83. For a description of the wedding procession to and from church and the celebration at home, see file 1962 (14), Polish-American Coll., FA, WSU.
20. Geertz 216, 450.
21. For one example of collaboration between artist and viewers in the visual arts see James Michael Newell, "The Evolution of Western Civilization" in O'Connor, *Art for the Millions* 60.

22. There was only a small percentage of educated and professional men among the newcomers, i.e., the immigrants who came after the 1880s, according to Napolska 5.
23. Dorson, *Folklore and Folklife* 1–5 and Part II: 405–532 and Goldstein, whose work is all about the methods for establishing modern folk studies as a scientific or empirical discipline.
24. Olszyk 58–59.
25. Napolska 8–9.
26. Olszyk and Taras.
27. Milosz 291–303.
28. Milosz 318–20.
29. Olszyk 20–1.
30. Olszyk 37.
31. Brozek.
32. Taras 48.
33. Frank J. Corliss, director of the Polish program in the Department of Germanic and Slavic Languages, WSU expressed this view to me in conversations over a two-year period in the mid-1980s.
34. Symanski, *Fallen Stars* 18, 24.
35. Thomas and Znanieck, 1:311–3.
36. Dehnert foreword to Palowska xiv.
37. Dehnert foreword to Pawlowska xiv.
38. File 1982 (31), Polish-American Collection, FA, WSU.

5. Finn Halls and Finnish-American Culture

1. Timo Riipa, "Finnish Immigrant Theatre in the United States" in Karni 278–9.
2. Syrjala excerpt in Hannula 195.
3. Charles Jay, a member of Finn Marxist theater in Detroit in the 1930s, cited the figure of 107 theatrical groups in a letter to me 30 Mar. 1981; Syrjala excerpt in Hannula 190; Hannula 191; Riipa in Karni 284. Niitemaa 124 (fn.3).
4. Kolehmainen, *From Lake Erie's Shores* 208.
5. Jay letter; Valma Lehtela Duletsky interview. Ms. Duletsky supplied me with programs of plays, in some of which she performed in the 1930s.
6. Jay letter; Archie W. Brown (Ojanpaa), a young Finnish actor in the Finn Marxist theater of Detroit, letter to author 14 Apr. 1981.
7. Riipa in Karni 282.
8. E. Olaf Rankinen, chaplain, Senior Americans Center, Suomi College, letter to author 9 Feb. 1981.
9. Irja Connolly, daughter of actors in Ironwood Finnish-American theater, interview.
10. Tuomi-Lee, "Stage Recollections" 4, 7, 12.
11. Connolly interview.
12. Jay letter.
13. Riipa in Karni 280.

14. Holmio 3:511.
15. Karni, "Finnish Temperance" 163–74, but especially 171.
16. Riipa in Karni 280–1; Viola Pudas letter to author 30 Feb. 1981.
17. Riipa in Karni 281.
18. Tuomi-Lee, "Stage Recollections" 10–11.
19. Connolly interview.
20. Mattila 4.
21. Tuomi-Lee, "Stage Recollections" 15.
22. Syrjala quoted in Hannula 193.
23. Hoglund, "Finnish Immigrants" 144; Riipa in Karni 278, 284.
24. Riipa in Karni 283.
25. The information about Detroit comes from the playbills and handwritten expla-
    nations thereon sent me by Charles Jay in a letter dated 2 July 1981 and other
    playbills contributed by Valma Lehtela Duletsky. The Brown letter to me also
    proved to be a valuable resource.
26. Ahokas 73–85.
27. Ahokas 48–54, 110–22, 138–9.
28. Riipa in Karni 283.
29. Ahokas 134–7.
30. Ahokas 141–3.
31. Duletsky comment in playbill for the 1942 performance of this play.
32. Jay letter 30 Mar. 1981.
33. Riipa in Karni 286.
34. Brown letter.
35. Playbill for *Syysromanssi* performance in 1947 at Detroit's IWO Lodge 3820.
36. Hoglund 30.
37. Tuomi-Lee, "Stage Recollections" 12–3; Ross 70; Hoglund, *Finnish Immigrants*
    33–4.
38. Riipa in Karni 278; Kohlemainen, *From Lake Erie's Shores* 113, 263–4.
39. Tuomi-Lee, "Stage Recollections" 15.
40. Tuomi-Lee, "Stage Recollections" 12.
41. Johnson 333, 334–5, 341.
42. Hoglund, "Finnish . . . Letter Writers" 29.
43. Kohlemainen, "Finnish . . . *Nyrkkilehti*" 105–6.
44. Hoglund, *Finnish Immigrants* 30.
45. Hoglund, "Finnish . . . Letter Writers" 25.
46. Hoglund, *Finnish Immigrants* 31–2.
47. Hoglund, *Finnish Immigrants* 144.
48. Kolehmainen "The Inimitable Marxists" 397; for the IWW poems, see for ex-
    ample Tanne 8, and also Sophie Sjoman 18. Prose is represented by Knuuti.
    26–8.
49. Biographical brief to Helmi Mattson Papers 2–3, IHR.
50. Biographical brief to Edith Koivisto Papers 1–2, IHR.
51. Kohlehmainen, From Lake Erie's Shores 264–5.
52. Hoglund, *Finnish Immigrants* 45–6.
53. Antero Riipa 5–8.

6. Making and Remaking Yiddish-American Culture

1. Howe and Greenberg, *Poetry* 2, 12, 15; Lifson, *Yiddish Theatre* 42–8; Liptzin, *History* 79–82; Madison chs. 7 and 8.
2. Weinreich 3–4; Rockaway 51; Meltzer 5.
3. James Miller ch. 1, en. 13; Gross 97–9; Sachar 75, 78–86; Samuel 57.
4. Howe and Greenberg, *Stories* 5–12, Lifson, *Epic* 15–6; Wisse 14–20.
5. See B. Rivkin comment cited in Howe and Greenberg, *Poetry* 18–9.
6. Howe and Greenberg, *Poetry* 17–8; Sachar 373–81.
7. Howe and Greenberg, *Poetry* 4.
8. Howe and Greenberg, *Stories* 21; Liptzin, *History* 1. The major work on Yiddish and proof of what Howe and Greenberg as well as Liptzin say is Weinreich.
9. Liptzin, *Flowering* 131–48; Madison 141–7; Wisse 11.
10. Iceland citation is in Howe and Greenberg, *Poetry* 26.
11. Howe and Greenberg, *Poetry* 41.
12. Howe and Greenberg, *Poetry* 43.
13. Gordon 70.
14. Lifson, *Yiddish Theatre* 63, 254–5; Lulla Rosenfeld 332–6.
15. Lifson, *Yiddish Theatre* 265–7.
16. Lifson, *Yiddish Theatre* 432–83.
17. Flanagan was very familiar with ARTEF, as she was with workers theater in general. ARTEF had translated Flanagan's *Can You Hear Their Voices?* into Yiddish and produced it in the early 1930s, a rendition that in fact displeased her. See Flanagan, *Dynamo* 109–10.
18. Rothschild 6–8; Meyer 114, 121–5; Rockaway 32.
19. James Miller 40–5; Frederick Brown 290.
20. James Miller 127.
21. James Miller 48–50.
22. James Miller App. III.
23. Rosenshine 9–11.
24. Garvett 8.
25. Mogill telephone conversation 14 June 1986.
26. Irving Kroll telephone conversation 14 June 1986.
27. Genser telephone conversation 14 June 1986.
28. Moishe Haar Memorial Foundation Circular, Reading Room File, BHC.
29. BE Box 260, Temple Arts Correspondence 1926–29, Playbill 27 Mar. 1928; Box 278, 10th Anniversary Celebration of Temple Arts Society.
30. BE Box 278, Fifth Performance Program 23 Apr. 1923.
31. BE, Box 260, Temple Arts Correspondence 1926–29, Isaac Gilbert letter [n.d.] to members of the Arts Society.
32. Madison 75–89, 107–28; Wiernick 394.
33. "The Ghetto" 11–2.
34. Lipitzin, *History* 461–2.
35. Liptzin, *History* 462. It is worth noting that Korman produced and edited an anthology of Yiddish-American women poets in 1928. See *Yiddishe Dicterinim*.

36. See for example, Philip Raskin, "A Chanuka Poem," and Edith Hartman, "Realization," *Detroit Jewish Chronicle* 4 Dec. 1931: 1 and 4. The Burton Historical Collection has an almost complete run of the *Chronicle*, and my conclusion about the subjects covered is based on a review of the newspaper through 1934.
37. Rosenshine 12–14. Haar phone interview. Moishe Haar Memorial Foundation circular, Reading Room File, BHC, DPL.
38. Bolkosky writes that the landschafstman groups called their irregular efforts cultural meetings 63–4.
39. Jewish Folklore 1945 (22) and 1952 (46), Jewish Folk Songs 1962 (64) in FA, WSU.

7. Black Theater and Writing

1. Hobsbawm, *Industry* 35; Age of Empire 16–18. Montgomery 83, 378.
2. Dillard chs. 3 and 4. Smitherman *Talkin and Testifyin*, 409–22.
3. Of course the array of regional, ethnic, racial, and class dialects of American English is another example of internal heteroglossia, that concept of "intense struggle" within a national language which Mikhail Bakhtin has clarified for us and which he says is "inseparable from social and ideological struggle." Bakhtin 66–8.
4. A small black community existed in rural Cass County as early as 1830, one of the northern stops of the Underground Railroad, see Katzman 13. *The Michigan Manual of Freedman's Progress* for Detroit, compiled by Francis H. Warren, records the presence in the Michigan territory as far back as the late eighteenth century of a "black man who was very pious" and indicates that by 1861 there were "about 500" blacks living in Detroit (34). See also "History of Slavery, Abolition, and the Underground Railroad" 21–3, File Folder Michigan Underground Railroad in Michigan, A871 FWP. This 63-page ts. was written by Robert Hayden as an FWP writer; it is also available at BHC and BHL.
5. See Katzman, 14–5, 128–9, 158. Katzman notes that there was also an influx of transients and drifters. But the two migration streams I am speaking about were stable and permanent in resettling and therefore had an impact on the formation of black culture in Detroit.
6. See Katzman 14ff., who notes that after the Civil War some blacks recrossed the border to Michigan to become residents of the United States again. For the underground railroad, see Katzman 40–1 and the Hayden work cited in en. 4.
7. Katzman 61–74.
8. Katzman, 136. The phrase is taken from a headline in the *Detroit News-Tribune*, 27 April 1902.
9. Program of Musical and Literary Entertainment at Second Baptist Church 14 July 1887, Robert Shewcraft File, Box 104 HRS; the Henrietta Literary Club of Toledo programmed, among other events, quartets and solos, *Detroit*

Plaindealer, Toledo affairs and Notes 23 Dec. 1892; the Hawthorne Club, also of Toledo, is listed as having performed a harp and guitar duet and a piano solo, *Detroit Plaindealer*, Cleveland Department/Toledo Topics 3, Feb. 1893. See also Katzman 160.

10. Katzman 160. Davenport gives an inkling of the commitment to classical music among Detroit's black elite in discussing Azalia Hackley's background, see ch. 1.

11. For an example of repertoire see Programme, Musical and Literary Entertainment at Second Baptist Church 14 July 1887, Box 104 HRS.

12. Davenport is the best account of Hackley's various contributions over the years to black folk, choral, and classical music.

13. Warren 296, 298.

14. Warren 298; Richard Shewcraft File, Box 104 and Burton Research File 1, Box 103 HRS.

15. According to Katzman 152–3, many of these emphasized social activities over literary substance. But the evidence cited in the text reveals that Katzman overstates the case.

16. Handwritten paper on the tenth anniverary of the club April 1908 Folder 3, "History of the Detroit Study Club" ts. May 1949, "Looking Backward" ts. 19 Mar. 1948, "The Founding" ts. 18 Mar. 1938 Folder 2, all in Box 2 Lillian B. Johnson Collection BHC.

17. *Detroit Plaindealer*: Milwaukee Notes 21 Nov. 1892; Cleveland Department, Frankfort Notes 23 Dec. 1892; Cincinnati Department, Chillicothe Notes 13 Jan. 1893; Cleveland Department, Toledo Topics 3 Feb. 1893. The newspaper did not number its pages. Microfilm copies of this hard-to-find paper (18 – 18) are available at BHL. Mss. holdings of the Burton Historical Collection, *Michigan Association of Colored Women* 10, 22, 25, 27, Mss. Holdings, BHL. *Detroit Free Press*, Jan. 17, 1879, 1:2, V. 44, No. 127.

18. Among others are Robert Pelham, Jr., "able editor and writer" and short story writers Walter A. Stowers and William H. Anderson, Robert C. Barnes Supplements File p. 65, Box 103 HRS; Also Laura S. Haviland, *A Woman's Life Work* (1881) in Bibliography File, Box 103, HRS.

19. The racist feelings that had been latent for more than a decade returned in force after the abandonment of Reconstruction (1863–77) and were refurbished on new ideological grounds and justifications. Foner 587–98, 609–10. Straker himself cites the works, "The Leopard's Spots" and "The Clansman," of the southern writer Thomas Dixon, Jr., who mixes "ten thousand lies" to "poison the minds of the Anglo-Saxon race towards the Negro," *Negro Suffrage* 13.

20. Colonel Sylvester Larned of Detroit wrote in support of Straker's 1888 book that it "bristles . . . with an armament of logic and fact" 15. Larned's military metaphor reveals his background. The structure of logic and content of fact name Straker's style, but also demonstrate that Straker was a lawyer, one of the first black attorneys in Detroit. A letter from Frederick Douglass to Straker, which also appears in the 1888 book, praises the work for showing "your literary ability, your knowledge and experience" 13.

21. Shoeman, note to poem "Lydia" 31.
22. *Detroit News-Tribune* 1 Apr. 1900: 18.
23. See for example "Lydia," a narrative about Shoeman's aunt, 31–40, "Man's Curse On Self" 15–8, and "The Eagle" 13–4.
24. See Gates 44–47, 68–70, 92–94, and 104–5; Morrison 1–34. The article is based on Morrison's Tanner Lecture on Human Values 1988–89, University of Michigan, 7 Oct. 1988, in which she argues not only that African-American mass culture is the subtext for African-American literature but that it is also the subtext for the dominant canon of American literature, as the subtitle of her talk implies.
25. From 1880 to 1910, Detroit's black population more than doubled, increased more than sevenfold from 1910 to 1920, almost tripled from 1920 to 1930. See *The Negro in Detroit* 3. This study includes figures for every decade from 1850 to 1920 based on the Thirteenth Census of the United States, Abstract of the Census with Supplement for Michigan 595 and for Detroit 618; the Fourteenth Census of the United States, State Compendium, Michigan, for the central states 2 and Detroit 52; the Fifteenth Census of the United States: 1930, Population, Volume III, Part 1, Alabama-Missouri, for Michigan 1115 and Detroit 1183.
26. Fourteenth Census of the United States, IV, 1920, Occupations 345, 347, 349, 355, 357, 359. Fifteenth Census of the United States, XIII, 1930, Occupations by States 788–805.
27. It does not become the fully accepted, the clearly main strategy of black culture until after World War II, more precisely until the 1960s and the advent of the Black Arts Movement. By then it has been transformed by the folk experience of urban life. But that urban folk experience had already affected black imaginative work in the 1920s and 1930s. Some prime examples are Langston Hughes, such playwrights as Hughes Allison, Hall Johnson, Theodore Ward, and Richard Wright. By then, the black communities of the North and Midwest had become predominantly industrial, which is to say not only that they had become part of the industrial labor force but also victims again, this time of industrial unemployment and racism. The pre-industrial elite population is mostly a memory. What remains of it—in terms of cultural influence, community leadership, and political power—is a respected, but supplanted trace. On African-American culture after World War II, see Baker, *Blues* 3–16, 140–59; Callahan 256–64; Gayle, see particularly essays by Addison Gayle, "Cultural Strangulation and the White Aesthetic" 38–45; Larry Neal, "The Black Arts Movement" 257–74; Ronald Milner, "Black Theater—Go Home" 287–94; Clayton Riley, "On Black Theater" 295–311; Addison Gayle, "The Function of Black Literature at the Present Time" 383–94.
28. Epstein 187–8, 217–32, 243–50, 252–60; Lawrence Levine 26–9, 136–49.
29. For the character of black exhortation and response at camp meetings, see Epstein 197–9. Spencer cites some examples of preacher chant and parishioner response from the 1920s and later, but connects this type of sermon to antebellum precedents xiii–xiv, 10. Slave masters were fearful of camp meetings

and religious gatherings of blacks away from their watchful eyes or those of their hired supervisors. Their fears soared after experiencing black insurrection or discovering insurrectionary conspiracies at the hands of black preachers, as in the cases of Denmark Vesey and Nat Turner, Epstein 194–5, 229–32.

30. Bradley 33, 34, 50, 90.

31. Sernett 38–41, 98–99, 149–61, 167, 169–70; Bradley 25, 34; Sobel 159–68, 205, 211. For the way African religious views and Baptist and Methodist views were compatible or fed each other in evangelical practices and in religious song, see Sobel chs. 1, 4, and 6; on other aspects of these influences, see Lawrence Levine 20, 22, 39.

32. Special Report of the Clerk of the First Baptist Church, Miscellaneous Materials, BHC; See also "History of the Second Baptist Church" by Nathaniel Leach, BHC.

33. Katzman, 19–20; see also Second Baptist Church, Records of AME, and St. Matthews Church HRS, BHC; " Detroit Bethel African Methodist-Episcopal Church, Historical Sketch, 1841–1927," BHC; *History and Directory of the Churches of Detroit* (1877) 232.

34. Gould 43.

35. Tape 12, "Broken Barriers," BTC.

36. Jazz, of course, became the dominant musical mode of American culture in general and is now recognized far and wide as the most important if not the only major contribution originating within the borders of the United States to world music. Any number of studies attest to this, going as far back as Locke, especially chs. 9, 10, 11, and 13. See also Stearns parts 4, 5, 6, and 7.

37. Thomas 316. John Dancy, who led the Urban League for over forty years, became its second director in 1918, Thomas 318.

38. Outline for the Adult Education, ts, File 2, Box 1 DUL; Reverend S. D. Ross and Miss Eubanks, Church Committee, of the Greater Shiloh Baptist Church letter to John C. Dancy, Urban League Director 1 Feb. 1933, informing him that the Church sponsors a "Melodramatic Club," General File, February 1933, Box 2 DUL.

39. The Cultural State of Detroit, ts, n.d., File 19, Box 1 DUL. My assumption that the document is from the mid-twenties is based on its inclusion among files in Box 1 from that period and on internal evidence: the description of the arts groups indicates a less elaborate program than is true after 1927, especially for the art and dramatic activities.

40. See letter from Spellman Lowe, a Pen and Palette member and exhibitor for several years, to John C. Dancy 18 Nov. 1933, File 35, Box 2, DUL. Lowe had to join the C. C. C. in order to help his family during the Great Depression. He writes, among other matters, how little time the work leaves him for his art.

41. Dancy 20; "Constitution of the Pen and Palette Club," ts, File 16, Box 1, DUL; See also "Minutes" of the club, File 16, Box 1 DUL; "Art Exhibit A Suc-

cess," ts, 30 Mar. 1926, File 16, Box 1 DUL; see also programs of the Third, Ninth, and Tenth Annual Art Exhibits, Cultural Products File, Box 49 DUL.

42. Dancy letter to Miss Phyllis Johnson 17 May 1928, File 23, Box 1 DUL and the Minutes referred to in preceding note.

43. Dancy 158–9.

44. Report of the Urban League Community Center, January 1929 to January 1930, ts, General File, January 1930, Box 1 DUL; Report of the Urban League Community Center, January 1930–January 1931, handwritten in ink, General File, January–February 1931, Box 1, DUL.

45. Dancy letter to Mr. Jack Petrell, Recreation Director of Industrial Mutual Association, Flint, Michigan, 6 Sept. 1930, General File July–September 1930, Box 1 DUL; in April 1931, Dancy delivered a lecture in which he noted that the Dramatic Club repertoire consists of "entirely negro [*sic*] folk plays," Dancy Lecture 8 Apr. 1931, ts, General File April 1931, Box 2 DUL.

46. W. G. Bergman letter to Dancy 9 Mar. 1931 and Hillel to Dancy 24 Mar. 1931, General File March 1931, Box 2 DUL.

47. The Willing Workers Society, Detroit, Mich. letter to Dancy, 10 Mar. 1931, File 10, Box 2 DUL. There is a long history of such attitudes. Foner points out that an 1866 issue of the Mobile Nationalist, a newspaper founded by free blacks, argued that freed blacks should "put away 'nigger' plays and songs" in favor of the "plays and amusements [of] . . . free men and women" 101.

48. Dancy letter to the Willing Workers Society 11 Mar. 1931, File 10, Box 2 DUL. Anne Sprague, an officer of the League and the educational director of the Detroit Community Union, also expressed reservations about presenting plays that depict what she called "bad characteristics," even where these are represented equally among whites as well as blacks. Theatregoers, she held, "are liable to remember them black after the play," letter to Dancy 5 Nov. 1929, File 29, Box 1 DUL.

49. *Tribune Independent* 18 May 1935: 7, Reel 1, Microfilm 605 BHC. Also listed with the other players is Melba Grimes, to portray the dance. It is not clear that she is to perform as a dancer in the play or after it. That a composer played the lead may be a clue that the play was conceived in a new way—if so, an exciting possibility for the FTP. Of course, the reference to song and dance may simply have been an allusion to Ophelia's mad scene.

50. The Metropolitan Theatre Presents Eulalia Gaines, Detroit Drama File, Vertical Files, EAH; Copy of an eight-page program of the "Booker T. Washington" play, provided me by the generosity of Josephine Love, director of Your Heritage House, Detroit. The program includes information about Gardner and his work.

51. Carney and Du Plessis presentations.

52. History "The Sands of Time," the 25th Anniversary of the Second Baptist Church's Cultural Committee Brochure, Detroit Churches File, EAH. This brochure provides a list of productions, which include *Murder in the Cathedral*, "Ethiopia at the Bar of Justice" by Reverend Edward McCoo, "The Oneness of Mankind" by A. Lecik. "Tall Oaks, from Little Acorns Grow,"

the 30th Anniversary brochure, Detroit Churches File, EAH; the *Detroit Tribune*, 4 Sept. 1937:11, Reel 1, Microfilm 605 BHC.

53. Price letter to Dancy 5 Mar. 1935, General File March–April 1935, Box 3 DUL.
54. Andrew J. Elliot, Director of Boy's Work, Goodrich Social Settlement, Cleveland letter to Dancy 23 Feb. 1931, File 9, Box 2 DUL; Harold Courlander File, EAH.
55. Program of "Three Negro Folk Plays," General File March–April 1935, Box 3 DUL; Jabberwock Folder, Titles File, EAH.
56. Jack Petrill, Recreation Director, Industrial Mutual Association of Flint, letter to Dancy 20 May 1931, General File May 1931 DUL.
57. *Negro in Detroit*, Section 2, 17.
58. Ibid., Section 7, 19.
59. Ibid., Section 7, p.20.
60. Ibid., Section 7, p.8.
61. The first newspaper in Detroit published and edited by blacks, the *Popular Era*, appeared on 31 May 1879 and lasted until November of that year. The *National People*, the next black newspaper, began publishing in April 1883 and ended in July of the same year. On 16 May 1883, the first issue of the *Detroit Plaindealer* was printed and continued to appear thereafter for the next twelve years. It was succeeded by the *Detroit Republican* in 1900, which lasted until 1906. These were weekly newspapers. Only after the 1880s was the black community able to support newspapers for a long term. See Woodson 82–3; Detweiler ch. 1 and 58–9; Warren 93–4. On the way the press opened its pages to both professional and amateur black poetry, see Detweiler 110–3.
62. *Detroit Tribune* 14 Apr. 1933: 18, Detroit Tribune Microfilm 605, Reel 1, BHC.
63. *Tribune-Independent* 9 June 1934, Detroit Tribune Microfilm 605, Reel 1, BHC, DPL.
64. "The Conjure Man," 3 June 1933: 8; "Hastings Street," 30 Sept. 1933. See also McCall's "The New Negro," 6 May 1933; 8 and "Gethsemane," 10 June 1933: 8, all in Detroit Tribune Microfilm 605, Reel 1, BHC.
65. *Tribune Independent* 14 June 1934: 3, Microfilm 605, Reel 1, BHC; see also the McCall poem "The New Negro," whose closing couplet reads: "With soul awakened, wise and strong he stands,/Holding his destiny with his hands," *Detroit Tribune* 6 May 1933: Microfilm 605, Reel 1; Wright, "I Have Seen Black Hands," *New Masses* 26 June 1934.
66. "Outline for Adult Education," File 2, Box 1, DUL.
67. *Detroit News* clipping 30 Mar. 1935, Negroes in Detroit Miscellaneous File, BHC.
68. A typed report January 1925, General File, Jan.–June 1925, Box 1 DUL.
69. See particularly Dorson, *Negro Folktales*.
70. For "If You Live Right" and other lead-line hymns, see Religious Folk Music File: 1969 (125), Sharon Ann Harris, collector; also Southern Baptist Negro Spirituals File: 1966, 12–15 (137), Michael Babitch, collector, Arlethia Smith, informant; Yates, Negro Songs: Notebook 51A, 1953 (41), Mrs. Luvenia Thomas, informant. All in FA.

71. "Lover's Goodnight" and "My Fiddle," File 1950 (23) FA.
72. "Promises of Freedom," File 1950 (23); "The Work Ain't Hard," Notebook 51 A, 1953 (41), informant Mrs. Luvenia Thomas; FA.

8. Repertory and Political Theater in the Motown Outland

1. Of immigrant groups from southern and eastern Europe, other examples of similar cultural developments out of traditional and new-world experiences affecting grass-roots theater and writing, I note also the Italian-American, the Hungarian-American, and the smaller Croatian-American communities. The cultural dynamics of old-world traditions and new-world experiences are in many ways the same for the German-American experience and in many ways they are different. German-American migration goes back farther in time, and the German-American community is less massively industrialized. Although large numbers did enter the factory work force, German-American immigrant workers made up, to a much larger extent, the upper echelons of labor. See the following sources for a beginning about these publics: Beynon, D'Angelo, Kistler, "Michigan's Italian-American Heritage," Re, Russell, William Thomas, Vismara, Wichorek.
2. See, for example, Meneghel, Rodgers, Rudick.
3. "The Bonstelle Playhouse Will Be New Civic Center for Detroit Public" by Richard Lawrence; Dean 136, 150.
4. Playbill for *The Marquise*, 28 May–10 June 1928: 3, JEB.
5. Playbill for *Midsummer Night's Dream*, Summer 1931: 3, JEB.
6. Playbill for *Are You a Member*, 12 Nov. 1928: 15, JEB.
7. On ticket policy, see Storey and Gillis 9.
8. Stark, "Shakespeare, Mendelsohn"; *A Midsummer Night's Dream* playbill 7–12 July 1931: 3, JEB; for attendance in 1928, see Bonstelle Civic Theatre Calender with quotations from Jessie Bonstelle, 1933: 2, JEB.
9. Stark, "Juliet in Flappermood," a review by George W. Stark, Detroit News 18 Mar. 1926. Jessie Royce Landis played Juliet; Donald Cameron, Romeo; Melvyn Douglas, Mercutio. On *Hamlet,* see "Summer Plans at Bonstelle," *Detroit News* 4 Apr. 1927 and the review by Shaw. Melvyn Douglas played Hamlet and Gale Sondergaard, Gertrude.
10. Playbill for *The Elephant Man* 1979–80:19; Review "Hamlet Modishly," *New York Times* 8 Sept. 1925.
11. Lawrence.
12. Dean 107.
13. Lawrence.
14. *The Marquise* playbill 5; *Are You A Member*, playbill for 12 Nov. 1928: 15 and "The Detroit Civic Theatre" announcement for 1928 season, 9, both in JEB. For the 60,000 claim, see Storey and Gillis 10. The *Are You A Member* playbill does speculate that by the next season 60,000 subscribers is a likely achievement, but the available evidence does not nail down this figure as an accomplished fact.

15. "Detroit Civic Theatre" 3, JEB.
16. For the three groups cited, see *Club Magazine*, December 1927: 17; vertical files, Detroit-Little Theatre; Vertical Files, Detroit-Drama League, especially items covering the 1914–15 and the 1929–30 periods and specifically "Detroit Drama Needs A Barn" 1 Jan. 1929 and "Drama League Formed Here" May 14, 1930, both clippings from the *Detroit News* (the information in this file folder indicates that the Drama League also serviced the community with classes of various kinds for adults and youth); "Beyond Broadway" a 1931 booklet in *The Detroit Playhouse*, a bound volume of programs and announcements; all in Department of Music and Performing Arts, DPL. At the suggestion of the New York Theatre Guild, the Playhouse changed its name to the Detroit Theatre Guild. Later it became the the the Detroit Guild Playhouse (1929), then the Detroit Playhouse again (1930), and finally the Detroit Community Playhouse (1933). For this history of names, see Detroit Playhouse in the Music and Performing Arts card catalogue, DPL, and for reviews of Playhouse productions under these different names see vertical files, Detroit-Playhouse, Department of Music and Performing Arts, DPL. The vertical files of this DPL department contain information about many other resident groups over these years; to name a few: the Artisan Guild Players, Drury Lane Theatre, Restoration Arts Theatre.
17. See Kenneth Rowe collection in Rare Book Room of the Graduate Library at University of Michigan.
18. Detroit Playhouse Program, Twenty-third Production, 2 Oct. 1931 in the playbill collections of the Department of Music and Performing Arts, DPL. Review by Russell McLauchlin, *Detroit News* 3 Oct. 1931, Scrapbooks of the Detroit Institute of Arts, AAA.
19. Playhouse program for *Precedent* 14 Nov. 1932, Program Collection, Department of Music and Performing Arts, DPL.
20. Flanagan, "A Theatre is Born" 915.
21. For an account of how the John Reed Club became the producing and performing group of the earliest attempt after the crash at establishing a left-wing, workers theater, see Jay Williams 40. Also see Ira Levine 82, 87, and 196 (n). For one account, not entirely sympathetic, of the founding of the John Reed clubs see Aaron 213, 221–30; also Cowley, *Golden Mountains* 135–46.
22. For the best account in English of the Soviet Blue Blouses see Stourac and McCreery 30–76; also Innes 23–4; on the Chicago Blue Blouses see *Workers Theatre* Nov. 1931: 38; on its association with the John Reed Club, Samuel, MacColl, and Cosgrove 278, fn. 13. On the heavy schedule, *Workers Theatre* April 1933: 9.
23. *New Theatre* Nov. 1934: 24, Box 1 HF. By mid-1934 *Workers Theatre* had been rechristened *New Theatre*. The political and esthetic reasons for this name change will be discussed later in the section. Under either name, the journal is available in many major libraries.
24. For Chicago, see *Workers Theatre* Nov. 1931: 38; for Detroit, *Workers Theatre* Dec. 1931: 27; for Cleveland, *Workers Theatre* Sept.–Oct. 1932: 22, Apr.

1933: 9, 10, and July–Aug. 1933: 17; for Youngstown, *New Theatre* Nov. 1934: 24; all in Box 1 HF.

25. Carol Poore, "German-American Socialist Workers' Theatre, 1877–1900," 61–8 in McConachie and Friedman. Fn. 1 cites some sources for the German Volksbuene. See also Friedman, "A Brief Description of the Workers' Theatre Movement in the Thirties," 111–20 in McConachie and Friedman and especially 113–4.

26. Jay Williams 36–7; Ira Levine 5; Piscator 59–66.

27. Jay Williams 37–42; Ira Levine 89–92; Friedman, "Workers' Theatre Movement of the Thirties" 113–4; Samuel, MacColl, and Cosgrove 266 (this source gives 1929 as the breakaway date in contradiction to the 1928 dates accepted by all other sources); Elion Box 1 HF.

28. *Workers Theatre* Mar. 1933: 15, Box 1 HF.

29. Jay Williams 44–6; Ira Levine 89; Blake is an important source on the scene.

30. *Workers Theatre* Mar. 1933: 15; *New Theatre* Feb. 1934: 23; both in Box 1 HF.

31. *Workers Theatre* June–July 1932: 22; *Workers Theatre* Mar. 1933: 15; *New Theatre* Sept. 1934: 28; all in Box 1 HF.

32. Jeliffe, Box 1 HF.

33. The most concentrated expression of this campaign is represented by the July 1935 issue of *New Theatre*. The entire issue is devoted to blacks in the arts. The editorial for that issue, by George Sklar, calls for a "Negro Theatre in America" and cites the leadership given by the workers theater movement to this effort, Sklar, Box 1 HF.

34. *New Theatre* Sept. 1934: 28 (that *James Victory* was a locally written and produced play contradicts the criticism of the Detroit John Reed Group cited earlier in this section); *New Theatre* Dec. 1934: 10–11; both in Box 1 HF. The decision to close the John Reed clubs followed the change in the party's political agenda from a class and revolutionary struggle against capitalism wherever it existed to a united front against war and fascism. See Aaron 281–3; Cowley 269–72. Paul Peters and George Sklar are the authors of *Stevedore*. Its first production was by the New York Theatre Union, a group primarily managed by Albert Maltz and George Sklar.

35. Carney interview; Hayden interview; Contemporary playbill for *Stevedore* 15–17 Oct. 1936, JB.

36. *Workers Theatre* Apr. 1933: *New Theatre* Dec. 1934: 29; both in Box 1 HF.

37. The quotation and other information about these events is from Alice Evans, "The Living Theatre"; see also Evans, "Below Chicago's Mason-Dixon Line," for a 1934 account of the Chicago campaign to integrate company and audience; both in Box 1 HF.

38. *Workers Theatre* July–Aug. 1933: 17; the fullest account of this theatre experience is in Hilberman and Mitchell.

39. Of course, Hallie Flanagan knew of the Russian innovations before the American workers theater implemented them here, but their implementation here, which she greeted enthusiastically, set up an American, albeit left-wing pre-

cedent that made the living newspaper for the FTP more acceptable and more likely to be successful with new mass audiences.

40. *Workers Theatre* Mar. 1933: 11, Box 1 HF.
41. *New Theatre* Apr. 1934: 8, Box 1 HF.
42. McDermott 69–72; Friedman, "Workers' Theatre Movement" 114; Stuart Cosgrove, "From Shock Troupe to Group Theatre" in Samuel, MacColl, and Cosgrove 268.
43. *New Theatre* Oct. 1935: 30, Box 1 HF.
44. Shapiro, Part II: 10–13.
45. *Workers Theatre* Mar. 1933: 11, Box 1 HF.
46. *Workers Theatre* July–Aug. 1933: 17, Box 1 HF.
47. *New Theatre* Sept.–Oct. 1933: 3, Box 1 HF.
48. Friedman, "Workers' Theatre Movement" 116; Ira Levine 96–9.
49. The League of Workers' Theatres also changed its name to the New Theatre League.
50. Janet Shapiro, "The History of the Detroit Contemporary Theater in the 1930s," a ms generously given to me by Charlotte Shapiro and hereafter referred to as J. Shapiro, Shapiro Part II: 11. Charlotte Shapiro interview; Leo Mogill (of the Contemporary Theatre) interview.
51. See the program for *Awake and Sing*, Eleventh Production, 19–20–21 Nov. 1936 and the one called Theatre Night, Fifteenth Production, 26 May 1938 for these and other plays in their repertoire. All in JB, ALU, WSU.
52. The quotation is from the playbill for *Stevedore*, Tenth Production, 15–16–17 October 1936, p. 4 JB ALU, WSU; J. Shapiro, Part II: 13–15. A heated dispute punctuated the first American Writers' Congress (1935) over Kenneth Burke's suggestion that the term "people" be substituted for "proletariat" to attract a larger cross section of the American population; "Revolutionary Symbolism in America," 89–91.
53. The 1936–37 sit-down strike at the Chevrolet installations in Flint and the flurry of strikes that followed at other shops and workplaces in the Detroit area motivated the group to produce plays in union halls and at struck facilities. In Flint, it performed on several occasions immediately outside the plant where the auto strikers were sitting down and once inside as well. Reports have it that the performers were lifted through the windows into the plant, a stage entrance that surely must be rare in theater annals. J. Shapiro, Part II: 13–15.
54. In the Soviet Union, the political and literary establishment thought it had made something new of realism and theatrical naturalism by coming up with the name socialist realism. But it forgot an important precept of dialectics: that form and content, as any dialectical contradiction (not to be confused with logical contradiction), are inseparable. A truly revolutionary process, in politics and art, must of necessity dismantle the old social and artistic relationships in form and content. To retain an old form and to attempt to insert a new content into it or the reverse (as we discover in essentialist modernism) is to doom the new to a transformation into the old. Socialist realism was adopted as the official direction of Soviet literature at the All-Union Congress of So-

viet Writers, August 1934. See particularly the reports of Maxim Gorky, "Soviet Literature," and Karl Radek, "Contemporary World Literature and the Tasks of Proletarian Literature."

9. Starting Out from Nowhere: Artists, Art-Officials, and Super-ficials

1. I am not proposing that money always or even preponderantly carries the day even in a materialistic and market-oriented culture such as ours. The belief in its absolute magical powers blinds one to the limits of its quite enormous power and often betrays its believers. At the same time the belief, since it is common, has a psychological effect that indeed extends its limits beyond the power it is enabled to exercise as the central medium and measure of value in the United States.

2. The Federal Theater was the first to go. A series of hearings by the Dies Committee in the spring of 1939 treated all the projects with contempt and suspicion, but especially impugned the Theater Project as evil and subversive. When the allocation for the WPA came up in May, Congress refused to approve funds for the Theater Project, forcing it to close down in June, while many units were still engaged in production runs. Although the other arts projects were allocated funds and remained nominally under federal jurisdiction, the essential power over them was dispersed to the states. They lasted for a little over three more years, no longer with any grand populist aim. Until the United States became embroiled in the Second World War, they wound down the various programs they had been engaged in. After December 1941, their programs became part of the war effort. For example, the Writers' Projects in the various states wrote pamphlets and booklets on how to operate and maintain war equipment and arms, and what to do in air raids.

3. There were, of course, other super-ficials outside the arts projects themselves, that is super-ficials in the WPA at the federal level. They determined the overall allocations of funds state by state, the general plan of organizational structure and authority, and the general, but not the specific policy governing the arts projects.

4. The public institutions funded are state and local ones. It will be recalled from Chapter 1 that these are almost always under the control of boards composed of persons of upper-class rank who wield enormous political and economic power and, of course, cultural power.

5. Of course, evaluators carry with them an unannounced and in many cases an unconscious aesthetic and thematic set of standards. But the judgments they render are presumed to be free of these. The assumption is that the aesthetic and thematic standards used are objective and universal in acceptance and are restrictors of specific aesthetic models or subjects.

6. Flanagan letter to Hopkins 1 May 1936, Box 88 HH.

7. See Chart No. 1 attached to letter cited in the previous footnote.

10. The Michigan FTP: Conflicted Authority and Censorship

1. Flanagan to Stevens, 14 Oct. 1935 and copy to Pierson; McClure to Pierson, 16 Oct. 1935; carbon memo Flanagan to Messrs. Baker and McClure, 12 Nov. 1935; all in WPA "State" Series, Box Michigan 651.3113 to 651.312 (1935–36) RG69.

2. Stevens to Flanagan, 20 Nov. 1935, WPA "State" Series, Box Michigan 651.3113 to 651.312 (1935–36) RG69.

3. Robison to Flanagan, 27 Dec. 1935, WPA "State" Series, Box 651.3113 to 651.312 (1935–36) RG69.

4. Stevens to Flanagan, 10 Jan. 1936, WPA "State" Series, Box Michigan 651.3113 to 651.312 RG69.

5. Ibid.

6. Ibid.

7. Henry A. Perry, program director for Michigan Centennial Celebration, letter to Flanagan, 13 Nov. 1935, Box Michigan 651.3113 to 651.312 (1935–36) RG69.

8. Marvin telegram to Flanagan, 14 Feb. 1936; letters and memos from Flanagan in February, WPA "States" Series, Box Michigan 651.3113 to 651.312 (1935–36) RG69.

9. On the advice of Schouman, Flanagan appointed Mountjoy as project director for Ohio and Michigan at $3800.00 a year, a salary she thought too high but went along with because his responsibilities covered two states and because Jacob Baker, after a call to Schouman, approved; Flanagan report and attached extract to McLure and Stein, 19 June 1936; see also Stein to Agnes S. Cronin, administrative assistant, Division of Women's and Professional Projects, 20 Aug. 1936; both in WPA "State" Series, Box: Michigan 651.3113 to 651.312 (1935–36) RG69.

10. The division of responsibilities did not last long. By July 1936, perhaps even by the last week in June, Beyer was producing director as well as state director and Mountjoy had become Midwest regional director of the FTP in place of George Kondolf, who had only a few months earlier replaced Stevens. By September or October McGee replaced Mountjoy as Midwest regional director. Fairclough activities report for May 1936; letterhead of director's bi-monthly production report for August 1st to 15th, 19 Aug. 1936: Beyer letter to Flanagan, 24 June 1936; Mountjoy letter to Kondolf, 15 May 1936; all in WPA "State" Series, Box Michigan 651.3112 to 651.312 (1935–36) RG69.

11. Beyer letter to Flanagan 24 June 1936, Beyer letter to William Farnsworth 24 July 1936, bi-monthly director's production report for August 1 to 15, 19 Aug. 1936, all in WPA "State" Series Box Michigan 651.3113 to 651.312 (1935–36) RG69. Frederic S. Schouman was the administrative assistant of the state WPA at time, or the super-ficial third in the line of authority, behind Harry Lynn Pierson, the head administrator, and William Haber, the deputy administrator.

12. Stannard to Farnsworth 2 Oct. 1936 and Stannard telegram to McGee 29 Sept. 1936, WPA "State" Series, Box Michigan 651.3113 to 651.312 (1935–36) RG69.

13. Beyer to Farnsworth 30 Sept. 1936 and Farnsworth to Stannard, 30 Sept. 1936, WPA "State" Series Box Michigan 651.3113 to 651.312 (1935–36) RG69. Stein's August investigation, in addition to concluding that Stannard's charges were unwarranted, except for the excessive labor costs, blamed Mountjoy for this, because he hired and fired people arbitrarily and because he approved misguided advertising. Stein recommended his dismissal. The bad relationships with the state administrators he attributed to Schouman and the feud between Schouman and Stannard. Schouman's intervention in the affairs of the Theater Project was interpreted by Beyer and project personnel as friendliness and was sought after, but Schouman was impinging on Stannard's jurisdiction. See Stein telegram to Cronin 19 Aug. 1936, his letter to Flanagan, and his salary and revenue accounting to her 20 Aug. 1936, WPA "State" Series Box Michigan 651.3113 to 651.312 (1935–36) RG69.

14. Stannard to Flanagan 2 Oct.1936, WPA "State" Series, Box Michigan 651.3113 to 651.312 (1935–36) RG69.

15. Flanagan, *Arena* 160.

16. Elizabeth R. Donnelly, Women's Division, Michigan WPA, to Flanagan 16 Jan. 1937, File 651.312 Michigan Jan. 1937, WPA "State" Series, RG69.

17. Mountjoy to Kondolf, 15 May 1936, Michigan, WPA "State" Series. Box Michigan 651.3113 to 651.312 (1935–36) RG69. A month later, Hallie Flanagan sent a memorandum to McLure and Stein that included an extract from a report by Russell F. Bender. The extract shows that Mountjoy, still trying to solve the problem, had also been negotiating to secure a theater connected to the Civic Arts Building, a site under the control of "a committee of wealthy and influential citizens headed by Edsel Ford." Bender thought this was not very desirable, nor did he think the theater would be attractive to ordinary citizens. "It is," he wrote," far too austere and cold appearing for theatrical purposes." Flanagan obviously agreed with this assessment. Bender was on the Midwest regional staff in Chicago. Flanagan memorandum to Bruce McClure, deputy director and Stein, director of procedures, Division of Women's and Professional Projects, 19 June 1936, WPA "States" Series, Box 651.3113 to 651.312 (1935–36) RG69.

18. Mountjoy to Flanagan, 19 May 1936; report to FTP in Washington, 12 Nov. 1936; both in WPA "State" Series, Box Michigan 651.3113 to 651.312 (1935–36) RG69. The information on the progressive and radical approach to solving the theater problem comes from Fireman interviews 12 Dec. 1978 and 11 July 1979.

19. Report 16 Jan. 1937, WPA "State" Series, Box Michigan 651.312 to 651.3122 (1937–39) RG69. The fact that the People's Theatre became the home of the FTP for a while is not to be attributed completely to a turn toward an unadulterated populism. That it was one of the few affordable theaters available also had something to do with the choice. Still populism also had its influence.

20. Mountjoy to Flanagan 19 May 1936, WPA "State" Series, Box 651.312 to 651.3122 (1935–36) RG69.
21. Flanagan, *Arena* 160.
22. Flanagan report on her Fall 1937 visit to Detroit to Laurence Morris; Robert C. Schnitzer, deputy national director, FTP; and Ellen S. Woodward, national administrator of the Women's and Professional Projects Division, WPA; 26 Oct. 1937, WPA "State" Series Box: 651.312 to 651.3122 (1937–39) RG69.
23. Fairclough statement in *Detroit News* 26 June 1938, File Michigan 1936 RG69. Ashton comments on his poor acting skills in a letter to Flanagan 29 June 1938, WPA "General Subject" Series, Box 211.2 1935–1939 (A) RG69 and in activity report to Flanagan, attention J. Howard Miller, national deputy director, Federal Theater Project 3 July, WPA "States" Series, Box Michigan 651.312 to 651.3122 (1937–39), RG69. Ashton also points out in the activity report that Matthews never mentions in his charges his own year-and-a-half membership in the Workers Alliance. Neither does he reveal in his complaint about Segal selling the *Daily Worker* to company members that "he himself sold the *Daily Worker* long before Miss Segal got the idea."
24. Ashton letter to Flanagan 29 June 1938, cited in en. 23.
25. Slutz, "Council to Hear Charges Against WPA Theatre, Wednesday" *Detroit News* 26 June 1938, WPA "States" Series, File Michigan 1938 RG69. Edith Segal interviews in Spring 1979 and 13 Nov. 1979. Ashton report to Flanagan 3 July 1938, Box 651.312 to 651.3122 (1937–39) RG69.
26. Ibid.
27. Ashton letter to Flanagan 29 June 1938, cited in en. 24 and report 3 July 1938, cited in en. 25.
28. Sims to Hopkins 2 Jan. 1936, Box Michigan 610: Special Litigations 1935–36 RG69.
29. Flanagan, *Arena* 115–7 gives an account of the chaos surrounding the writing of the play. "Written?," she exclaims at one point: "Too mild a word. The play was produced by polygenesis." Sinclair Lewis and Jack Moffitt, aided by their agents and the staff of New York City's Essex House, put the script together. Lewis kept putting in and taking out scenes at whim. Units all over the country were screaming for an unchanging, finished script. For local changes to suit local settings, issues, and audiences and for the national office's warnings not to be politically one-sided in presenting the play, see *Arena* 121–2.
30. Stannard to Farnsworth 2 Oct. 1936 WPA "State" Series, Box Michigan 651.3113 to 651.312 (1935–36) RG69.
31. Beyer to Farnsworth 30 Sept. 1936, WPA "State" Series, Box Michigan 651.3113 to 651.312 (1935–36) RG69.
32. Morrow interview 20 July 1978, SC. In this interview, Morrow says that the state WPA administration, apparently in the person of Mrs. Connolly, nixed the proposal.
33. McGee to Fred Morrow, the replacement for Mountjoy as state FTP director, 10 Apr. 1937, WPA "State" Series, Box Michigan 651.312 to 651.3122 (1937–39) RG69; Flanagan to Schnitzer, Morris, Woodward, Detroit, Michigan, 26

Oct. 1937, cited in en. 22. Morrow, claiming that Detroit was the only project that produced *Let Freedom Ring*, that it turned out to be far more radical than *Power*, and that his recommendation not to put the play on was rejected, Morrow interview cited in en. 32.

34. Flanagan memorandum to Florence Kerr, national administrator of the Division of Women's and Professional Projects (Kerr succeeded Ellen Woodward, who had gone off to the Social Security Board, in January 1939), 9 Feb. 1939, Box Mc-Mu RG69.

35. One example of congressional zealousness, and ignorance one needs to add, over subversion is the suspicion one member had about Christopher Marlowe. When Hallie Flanagan appeared before the House Committee for the Investigation of Un-American Activities, then more popularly know as the Dies Committee and after World War II as the House Un-American Activities Committee (HUAC), in December 1938, to defend the FTP against charges of being communistic, she quoted the phrase "Marlowesque madness" from an article she had written some years back. Congressman Joseph Starnes, a Committee member caught her up immediately: "You are quoting from this Marlowe. Is he a communist?" *Arena* 342.

36. For accounts of the *Ethiopia* contretemps, see Flanagan, *Arena* 65–7 and Connor and Brown 26–7. This particular act of censorship became one of the more famous cases because it led to the resignation of Elmer Rice from the directorship of the New York company. Perhaps even more famous was the masked censorship of Mark Blitzstein's *The Cradle Will Rock* being directed by John Houseman and Orson Welles. When it was canceled by Washington super-ficials on the night scheduled for its FTP opening, Houseman, Welles and the rest of the cast traveled through Manhattan streets in costume, carting stage sets and musical instruments to another theater, where it was performed with Marc Blitzstein all alone on stage at a piano and by the actors sitting among the audience in order to comply with Equity's ruling. See Flanagan, *Arena* 202–3; Houseman gives the most detailed account 245–79; Brown and O'Connor 27–8. One other case, *Sing for Your Supper*, a play produced by the New York unit, drew the ire of Flanagan herself because it mentioned America's sixty richest families unfavorably, a notable case of the self-censorship discussed in Chapter 2.

37. Flanagan, *Arena* 135–6; Flanagan notes, File MWEZ HFD.

11. The Michigan FWP: Self-Restraint and the Battle Within

1. Penkower 11.

2. The report is untitled, undated, and unsigned. But since it points out that the first undertaking of the project, the state guides, had nearly been completed and proposes a new undertaking, a systematic compilation of the Americana and folk materials collected while doing the guides, the date is clearly early or mid-1939. The writer of the report is clearly someone fairly high in the Washington staff of the project. On the first page, in pencil in the upper right-hand

corner is the word "June," possibly a reference to the month of the report, and the name "Niles," preceded by undecipherable initials, possibly those of David K. Niles, who was an assistant to Harry Hopkins. The bracketed words and phrases are my insertions for the sake of greater clarity. The item is in WPA:FWP, Box Miscellaneous Files of Alsberg and Harris 1935–39 RG69.

3. The idea for a guide-book series came from several sources around the country, going back to 1933 and the first relief programs for white-collar and professional workers adopted not only by the Roosevelt administration, but a few states, most notably Connecticut. See Penkower 21–6. Suggestions for a guide book also came from Michigan. More will be said about this in the next chapter.

4. There were three major instances of discomfort, the most intense being Massachusetts, the only truly external case of jitters. Governor Charles F. Hurley of that state, other Massachusetts politicians and businessmen, and Boston newspapers attacked the Massachusetts guide as too left-wing in the space it devoted to the Sacco-Vanzetti case, to the Lawrence strikes and over the inclusion of Labor Day among official holidays. The Massachusetts guide was sharply criticized by politicians and newspapers elsewhere in the nation. The first FWP publication out of New York City, *Your New York*, upset project administrators, but more for reasons of deficiency in good taste and moral sensibility. The project's associate director, George Cronyn, took Orrick Johns, the head of the New York City unit, to task for publishing a view of New York that was too lurid (Chinatown dens, checkered Greenwich Village hangouts). Curiously enough Johns was the one administrator with a large degree of authority on any level of administration closely associated with the Communist Party, and yet the one publication issued during his tenure contained nothing that aroused political misgivings. His free living and loving on and off the project aroused far more consternation, although he also participated in Writers Union protests against project cutbacks and drew some newspaper attention because of his associations with the *New Masses*. At any rate, the discomfort was more of an internal affair than a widely expressed external one, except for an attack on the pamphlet in the *Village Voice*. The same is true for the Idaho guide. Cronyn and Alsberg were displeased with Vardis Fisher, the director of the Idaho Writers Project. The charge was that Fisher had failed to be sufficiently detached (Fisher called Pocatello ugly, derogated Zane Grey, and was candid about trucker-railroad violence). See Penkower 97–9 (Idaho), 100–1 (New York City), 101–7 (Massachusetts); also Mangione 201–3 (Idaho), 217–20 (Massachusetts), and 83–4, 164 (New York).

5. Of course, the Writers' Project was frequently under attack, either separately or in conjunction with the other arts projects, from conservative and right-wing newspapers and politicians all over the country. In Washington, conservative and right-wing legislators on Capitol Hill kept up a steady barrage about New Deal and left-wing propaganda and personnel in the work particularly of the Arts, Theater, and Writers' projects. The story of these external campaigns

against federal patronage in the 1930s has been told at length in many of the works cited in this study and will be noted specifically later on in my account of how these attacks affected Detroit and other places in the Midwest.

6. For Barrett's responsibilities and the quotation about the American guide, see Chittenden to Alsberg 3 Nov. 1935; for Washington's inspiration, see Chittenden to Alsberg 20 Nov. 1935; both in WPA-FWP, Box Administrative Correspondence, Michigan-Minnesota (1935–1939) RG69.

7. Gaer to Chittenden 6 Nov. 1935, WPA-FWP, Box Adminstrative Correspondence, Michigan-Minnesota (1935–39) RG69.

8. Chittenden to Alsberg 3 Nov. and 11 Nov. 1935, WPA-FWP Box Administrative Correspondence Michigan-Minnesota (1935–39) RG69.

9. Ibid.

10. Chittenden to Alsberg 20 Nov. 1935, WPA-FWP, Box Adminstrative Correspondence Michigan-Minnesota (1935–39) RG69.

11. Mangione 228.

12. Chittenden to Alsberg, 20 Nov. 1935, cited in en. 10.

13. Chittenden to Alsberg 3 Nov. 1935, WPA-FWP, Box Adminstrative Correspondence Michigan-Minnesota (1935–39) RG69.

14. Kimon Friar proved Miss Barrett's evaluation of his writing ability before long, when he rescripted Christopher Marlowe's *Dr. Faustus* for production by the Detroit FTP. See Chapter 16 for a fuller account of this production. Friar became fairly well-known after the 1940s for his translations of Nikos Kazantzakis and other Greek writers, demonstrating even more persuasively the soundness of Barrett's judgement.

15. Gaer memorandum to Alsberg, Subject: *Confidential Michigan* 6 June 1936, Michigan Field Reports RG69.

16. Chittenden to Alsberg, 20 May 1936, Administrative Correspon- dence Michigan-Minnesota (1935–39) RG69.

17. Gaer memorandum to Alsberg 6 June 1936, cited in en. 15.

18. Mangione 101.

19. See editorial, ts. attached to letter from Schouman to Alsberg, 27 July 1936, WPA-FWP, Box Administrative Correspondence Michigan-Minnesota (1935–39) RG69.

20. Gaer field report to Alsberg 6 July 1936, Box Field Reports Michigan RG69.

21. Gaer to Alsberg 6 June 1936, cited in en. 15.

22. Isbell letter to Alsberg 9 Mar. 1937, WPA-FWP, Box Administrative Correspondence Michigan-Minnesota (1935–39) RG69.

23. Isbell letter to Alsberg 23 Feb. 1937. In this resignation letter, Isbell recommended Young, who had worked for two weekly newspapers and had been a Detroit editor and rewrite man for the Associated Press. He also proposed that Clifford's managing editor responsibilities be increased together with his salary, to bring it into line with his enlarged editorial jurisdiction. The increase in salary was approved by Alsberg and Nims, the head of the Michigan WPA, and finally authorized by Ellen Woodward, the national assistant director of the WPA, on March 15 in a letter to Nims; see also Alsberg letter to Wood-

ward 15 Mar. 1937; all citations from WPA-FWP, Box Administrative Correspondence, Michigan-Minnesota (1935–39) RG69.

24. Young letter to Alsberg 18 June 1937, WPA-FWP, Box Administrative Correspondence, Michigan-Minnesota (1935–39) RG69.
25. Laning field report to Alsberg 25 June 1937, Michigan Field Reports RG69.
26. Alsberg letter to Frederick 3 Feb. 1938, WPA-FWP, Box Administrative Correspondence, Michigan-Minnesota (1935–39) RG69.
27. Alsberg letter to Frederick 13 Apr. 1938, WPA-FWP, Box Administrative Correspondence, Michigan-Minnesota (1935–39) RG69.
28. Undated article on what the WPA achieved in the field of books, apparently from *Time Magazine*, WPA-FWP Articles 1938–67 KK. The layout, the style, and the sheet size of the article suggest *Time Magazine*. The nature of the material summarized suggests a date after 1939, when Newsom was the national director. In the summer of 1939, the new law dealing with work-relief turned all the projects that remained, from then on called programs, over to state control. The national office became an advisory unit, keeping tabs on what the states were doing but with no strong control of their activities, their personnel policies, or budget allocations. Congress refused to include a theater program in the new act. All the other projects remained but were now called by their states' names, such as the Michigan Writers' Program, the Michigan Arts Program, etc. Control from the Washington center revived after 7 December 1941 and continued until 1943, when work-relief ceased to be a government program. In that period, the Arts and Writers' programs had become auxiliaries of the war effort, producing maps, drawings for constructing military bases, and how-to pamphlets about a variety of military subjects.
29. Newsom to Alsberg 9 Jan. 1939; see also Alsberg's response in favor of publishing the Hayden manuscript as a monograph 27 Jan. 1939; both in WPA-FWP, Box Project Proposal, Underground Railroad RG69.
30. For full accounts of the attacks by the Dies Committee and the Woodrum Committee, of the Emergency Relief Act of 1939, the termination of Federal One, and of the reorganization of the arts projects into locally sponsored, state agencies, see Flanagan, *Arena* 334–65; McDonald 309–38; Mangione ch. 8; Mathews, *Federal Theatre*, ch. 6; and Penkower 194–210.
31. Falstein interview.
32. Tarini interview; Hayden interview. At the time of his interview, Tarini was the chief supervisor of the Detroit office of the United States Employment Service, an agency he had been with almost from the close of World War II.
33. We see the double-digiting of layoffs and the roller-coaster character of allocations from the employment quota documents for the Michigan FWP in the National Archives. The fall 1935 quota called for a staff of 200, but 188 were actually placed on the payroll and continued to be on it as of 27 July 1936, by which time Isbell was the director. In December 1936, Isbell reports the staff reduced to 120 and complains about it as unfair and an obstacle to carrying out the project's mission effectively. This is another indication of Isbell as a sympathetic art-official helpless to prevent the execution of an order from

above that he did not care for at all. By August of 1937, the FWP staff was down to 86. All this represents the steep downside of the roller coaster and betokens a period of slight, but detectable recovery. An upside begins in early 1938 with an increase to 96, goes up in August 1938 to 111, and in January 1939 to 121, all of which is a refiguring based on the downturn of that period, called by the New Deal government a recession—the first time in U.S. economic history that term was used to name an economic decline. The term is now the favored euphemism for depression. In July 1939, the figure drops to 90, beginning a new free fall that proved to be its final one, lasting until the end of the ride in 1943. The defense industry was growing in response to the oncoming war and Federal One was under sharp attack politically by the Dies Committee and fiscally by the Woodruff Committee. The ups and downs I have cited here are matched in ratio in all Federal One units nationwide. See the various employment quota documents in WPA-FWP, Michigan A Employment 1935–36 and 1937–38; also WPA-FWP Box Administrative Correspondence, Michigan-Minnesota (1935–39); both in RG69. See also Employment Quotas by Unit Office FWP from 1937 to July 1939 in "Portrait of a Democracy," ts., FWP History Mss. Portrait of Democracy, Manuscript Division LC.

34. AFGE-Lodge 322 leaflet, "Flash," on 25 Mar. 1937 report in the *Detroit News* misrepresenting the facts of the lodge's suspension, File Folder: Papers, undated, concerning the Federal Writers' Project; also Composition Book for fall 1937 concerning the Federal Writers' Project and the American Federation of Government Employees; all in Box 10 newspaper clippings and papers, RS. See also Bernice B. Heffner, AFGE National Secretary, to Frank Martel 2 Apr. 1937 for the national office's point of view that the local FWP people violated the AFGE constitution, in File Government Employees International Union, 1937–48, MDC.

35. The Workers Alliance and its close ally, The Writers' Union, were first organized in New York City in 1934. The Workers' Alliance was composed of unemployed workers, relief clients, and WPA and PWA employees. Later it formed a City Projects Council for white-collar workers who were not represented by professional unions. In both forms, Alliance and Council, it undertook to organize Federal One personnel. The Writers' Union and the Unemployed Writers' Association, also first formed in 1934, became an organization by 1935 and drew many but not most of its members from the John Reed Clubs. See Flanagan, *Arena* 55–6, Penkower 15–6, Mangione 34–8.

36. Minutes for June 1938 and other items in the union file of this collection indicate that by June 13, the UPOWA, Local 26 had begun to represent Detroit's Federal One personnel, Box 10 RS.

37. The *New York Sun*, the *New York American* (a Hearst newspaper), the *Chicago Tribune*, the *Baltimore Sun*, and other conservative journals led in such media publicity, but liberal organs, such as the *New York Times*, the *Los Angeles Times*, and the *Detroit Free Press*, also on occasion described the projects in the same way and treated witness charges of subversion at congressional in-

vestigations as credible. See Penkower footnotes to 182, 185, 186, 188, 189, 195.

38. Penkower, 181–6, 194–200; Mangione, 164–9, 289–326. Also Flanagan, whose view of Communists and union activity and of the congressional investigation of un-American activities in the FTP, is not given to hidden red motives where project personnel were roused to opposition; see *Arena* 57–9, 201–2, 333–73.

39. *Poetry* July 1938: 226.

40. Negotiations Committee leaflet Lodge 322, AFGE, Arthur Clifford, chairman, Box 10 Newspaper clippings and papers, RS.

41. It should be remembered that by 1937, Communist ideology and party line had adopted the popular front policy, which meant that revolution had been removed from the agenda in favor of a multi-class unity to confront the threat of fascism. With regard to the arts, Communists and their sympathizers opened the door to what they called progressive and democratic bourgeois work.

42. On the boycott plan, see minutes 20 July 1937; on the Cadillac Square Demonstration, minutes 1 Feb. 1938; on Tarini's eloquence, composition book with minutes 12 Oct. 1937; all in Box 10, newspaper clippings and papers, RS.

43. Shelley Rathmer interview.

44. Edmund Wilson testifies to this in "Communists and Cops," which appeared in the 11 Feb. 1931 issue of the *New Republic*, and Malcolm Cowley does so on several occasions, when reporting on events for the same journal that he had witnessed first-hand, such as coal miners' strikes and bonus marchers.

45. Flanagan, *Arena* 326.

46. Cowley, "Poetry Project" 224, 225, 227.

47. Minutes, PDWA meeting, 15 Feb. 1938 and minutes, stewards and officers meeting, 22 Feb. 1938, Box 10 Newspaper clippings and papers, RS.

12. Odd Couplings: Popular Arts, the Classics, and Populist Esthetics

1. There have been several extended studies of these works. For a general account see McDonald 720–32, Penkower 140–58, Mangione 255–85. FWP units in Florida, Georgia, South Carolina, and elsewhere began research on slave narratives as early as 1936, Penkower 144. The Massachusetts FWP began work on its Armenian population simultaneously with its work on the guide and published its study of them in 1937, quick results indeed; bibliography of FWP publications in Mangione 384. Once William T. Couch, of the University of North Carolina Press, became the assistant director of the South Carolina unit, he guided its personnel in the collection of life histories, which produced the well-known *These Are Our Lives*. A version of it, *Such as Us: Southern Voices of the Thirties*, edited by Tom E. Terrill and Jerrold Hirsch, was published in 1978. It led to a running controversy between the editors of *Such as Us* and Leonard Rapport, a Carolina FWP collector during the thirties, over the authenticity of the stories collected by the FWP; see Rappaport

and Terrill and Hirsch articles in *Oral History Review*. For examples of stage plays based on unprivileged publics that were quickly on hand and quite successful, we have Paul Green's *Roll Sweet Chariot*, performed by the New Orleans FTP, Flanagan, *Arena* 84; a play by Alabamian Thomas Hall-Rogers, *Altars of Steel*, performed by the Alabama FTP, *Arena* 88–9.

2. Editorial comment on Michigan Art and Architecture by F. A. Gutheim, 14 Jan. 1937, WPA-FWP, Box Michigan Editorial Notes RG69.

3. Michigan, Grand Rapids (Architecture) 28 Apr. 1937, WPA-FWP, Box Michigan Editorial Notes RG69.

4. Brown to Isbell 24 Aug. 1937, WPA-FWP, Box Project Negro Studies General 1935–39 RG69.

5. Alsberg to Newsom 10 May 1939, File Michigan Correspondence FWP.

6. Even the work created by the Writers' Project could not be produced by itself, in most cases, but had to funneled into the publishing industry. The Writers' Project had to make contractual arrangements with publishing companies to get its work into print.

7. Coggan letter to Murray 28 Jan. 1935, attached to Murray letter to Collier 30 Jan. 1935, Box FERA State Files 1933–36 Michigan RG69.

8. Crump to Goldschmidt 27 Dec. 1934, Box FERA State Files 1933–36 Michigan RG69.

9. Collier letter to Murray 5 Feb. 1935, Box FERA State Files 1933–36 Michigan RG69.

10. Mangione 206, 267. Alsberg and the other Washington administrators were chagrined and embarrassed that the Idaho guide appeared in print before the Washington, D. C., guide. *Idaho: A Guide in Word and Picture*, the very first guide to be published, came off the press in January 1937. *Washington: City and Capital* followed in April 1937. For a full account see Mangione 201–9; also Penkower 125–6.

11. Mangione 92, 267.

12. Mangione 209–10; Penkower 118–9.

13. Mangione 216–20, 354; Penkower 101–4.

14. McDonald 722; Mangione 259; Penkower 145. The Brown comment on idiom and pronunciation is from McDonald, the *American Mercury* citation from Mangione. The evidence is not absolutely clear about the composition of the team who produced *The Negro in Virginia*. Penkower is the source for the number of black writers and researchers, but his footnote documents other information in his account. Mangione, in speaking of Lewis's virtues as an editor, includes among them the fact that he got along well with both the blacks and whites who were involved in the study, but he doesn't provide documentary evidence that both blacks and whites were involved. Since Mangione played so important a role in the FWP, he himself constitutes a primary source of information, and hence, his comment should not be taken lightly. We know, however, what a tricky devil memory is. Although I have no hard evidence to add, my sense is that an all black team was responsible for the undertaking and the book published therefrom. Still the spirit of black and

white cooperation in some of the units is suggested by Mangione's comment. There were places, and not only in the deep South, where racist attitudes still dictated white-black relationships in the project units. The white project workers in Oklahoma, for example, did not allow blacks to drink from the office drinking fountain, Mangione 258.

13. Federal Writers' Project: Midwest Ups and Downs

1. The Massachusetts FWP is a reverse example to that of North Carolina and Virginia. It had a staff led by a highly trained academic, Frank Manuel, himself a product of the working class, but it followed more traditional and detached methods and never produced anything in folklore, life histories, or ethnic studies that compares with that put out by the two southern states. On Manuel, see Mangione 279; Penkower 153–4.

2. Falstein 45 LF. My reason for considering *Journey* a memoir very thinly disguised as a novel is that it follows actual life experiences very closely. As a novel it is clothed, with unblushing innocence, in see-through fabric. For example, the chief character, whose name is Alex Greenstein, shortens it to Alex Greene. He does this to avoid any anti-Semitic obstacles that might get in his way when applying for an auto-factory job; he continues using the alias, once he is laid off from his auto job, in order to maintain a consistent record to qualify for relief as an unemployed worker and thereby for a job on what the author re-labels the Writers Program. In his own experience, Falstein dropped the final syllable of his second name when he first came to Detroit in order to get a job in the automobile industry and continued to use the shortened form, Falls, when applying for and after getting an appointment to the Michigan FWP. Falstein's description in *Journey* of the associate director of the Writers Program matches almost exactly, in personality and physical traits, the Mangione description of Mary Barrett that I cited in the previous chapter. In *Journey*, Falstein names his interviewer, the art-official second-in-command, Myra Kelly—an obvious rescrambling of Mary into Myra. Equally obvious is the two-syllable, Anglo-sounding Kelly substitution for Barrett. Other personality and physical descriptions in the manuscript resemble those of other staff members, particularly Arthur Clifford and Kimon Friar; the first is represented, under another name, as a prize-winning university writer, wheel-chair bound, and often demandingly gruff, as documents and oral accounts indicate Clifford was; the latter is represented, also under another name, as an esthete interested mainly in writing poetry, as documents confirm Friar was. Finally, the name of the last director of the Writers Program in *Journey* is named John Folsom and is from the East. The last director of the Michigan FWP, last that is under centralized authority, was Jack Newsom, a transplant from New York.

3. Each of the Midwest guides, except the Illinois one, has an appendix as a fourth part. Since these appendices consist of chronologies of state events and bibliographies, I leave them out of my analysis. For a quick view of the overall

organization of the guides, see the table of contents for each. Page references to these guides hereafter will appear in parentheses in the text.

4. Mangione provides the fullest account of this cantankerous relationship 201–8. The Alsberg characterization is recorded in a memorandum to Hopkins and is cited in Mangione 207. Katherine Kellock considered Fisher "a pain in the neck" and the Idaho guide idiosyncratic—so much so that, if it were allowed to go unrevised, she believed, it would sink the Project 208. Kellock, the reader will remember, wanted a pure and simple tour-book series. She felt strongly that uniform structure and style were absolutely essential.

5. *New York Panorama* (New York: Random House, 1938); but see bibliography for latest edition.

6. A number of manuals and supplements represented official attempts to codify standards and literary quality and uniformity: *American Guide Manual*, Supplementary Instructions 9–A (27 July 1936), 9–C (4 Aug. 1936), 9–D (31 Aug. 1936), 16 (21 Oct. 1936), 14–A (28 Oct. 1937) all to the *American Guide Manual* and in RG69.

7. McDonald 653, 667, 740, 744; Penkower, 31–2, 34–5, 75–95, 97. Mangione 144–5, 204–5.

8. The fact that it had gone through eight printings by 1964 gives us some idea of its favorable reception by the public at large.

9. The first of the two in the sequence of essays in Part I is "Marine Lore" by Ivan H. Walton, a folklorist on the faculty of the University of Michigan. The second is "The Development of Architecture" by Emil Lorch, also a faculty member of the University of Michigan. These experts were requested to deal with these subjects by the FWP art-officials in consultation with the FWP field representatives and the Washington officials because they felt the research required to do justice to both was beyond the ability of the regular staff. To be fair, it must be said that Walton's essay is livelier than Lorch's and all the others, except one. But Walton's essay, like Lorch's, is consistent with the formula for style and tone required by Washington. The reason is probably not that Walton and Lorch were following Washington or knew about its formula but that they were conforming to academic decorum. A good part of the Washington formula was based upon that approach to writing, although it took care to guard against pedantry and over formal stuffiness.

10. Regretfully, I point out that the Stott Building is now abandoned and the David Whitney Building is on the verge of being abandoned. It is a shameful waste of space and esthetic achievement that these two handsome buildings, which soar over the northern end of Detroit's downtown, are victims of the social, economic, and political prejudices that are at the heart of Detroit's present neglect.

11. The phrase, in Spanish "mareveilloso realismo," comes from Alejo Carpentier and is the precursor of "magical realism." It actually comes closer to what Latin-American writers, like Gabriel Garcia-Marquez, really do in most, if not all, of their work.

12. Orwell 353–67, but especially 363–4.
13. The Battle of Bad⸱Axe took place on August 2, 1832. it was the last of the Indian-U. S. wars in Illinois, for it led to the forced removal of the last Native Americans from Illinois. The capture of Detroit and the Fort Dearborn massacre occurred on August 15, 1812.
14. My analysis is based largely on the absence of written documentation dealing with the issue and my oral interviews with FWP people—Falstein, Tarini, and Maxine Wood in particular—and with WPA artists Charles Pollack and Barbara Wilson Benetti. As we shall see in the FTP chapter, my interviews with theater people, including Hy Fireman and Edith Segal, support it as well. Mangione writes that "most of the parties they [the Chicago staff] attended were usually for the purpose of raising money for some left-wing cause; for several years the main cause was that of the Spanish loyalists and their war against the forces of Franco" 131. This is fairly typical of the strategy followed by the left wing: politics yes, but not the politics of esthetic work.

14. Shreds and Patches: The Unfinished Business of Folklore

1. We have mentioned Idaho (*Idaho Lore*), North Carolina (*These Are Our Lives*), and Virginia (*The Negro in Virginia*). Other notable cases are Massachusetts (*The Albanian Struggle in the Old World and New* [1939], *The Armenians in Massachusetts* [1937]); and New York City (*The Italians of New York* [1938], also published in Italian in 1939; *Jewish Families and Family Circles of New York*, in Yiddish [1938], *The Jewish Landsmanschaften of New York*, in Yiddish [1939]).
2. They are *God Sends Sunday* (1931), *Black Thunder* (1935), and *Drums at Dusk* (1939).
3. *Pioneer Days in Illinois* (1940); *Stories from Illinois History* (1941).
4. For a complete list of the FWP editors who engaged in the study see the preface to the edition by Jean Blackwell Hutson. Also see Mangione 261–2.
5. The warehouse is in Loveland, Maryland, which has since become famous also for tennis tournaments starring the most important women professionals. Although I have acknowledged their help in the preface, it seems only right to mention the names of the people who were party to my adventure: Paul T. Heffron, acting chief; Dr. Ronald S. Wilkinson, assistant chief; Richard Bickell and Joseph Sullivan, the two archivists. Without their professional guidance as well as their crowbar skills, this book would have of necessity had a greater hole in it than it now has.
6. From 1935 on, that is during the united-front period, the left wing based its policy less on struggle between classes and more on an alliance of classes opposed to fascism. Hence, it moved closer to liberal ideology. This movement by the left toward the center may explain why the left in the FWP gave little theoretical impulse to populist esthetics. While it continued throughout the united-front period to include in its view the importance of the inspirational energy to be drawn from disenfranchised publics, it tended to see the FWP

334

more as a professional work-relief agency and as a benign provider of cultural products to those publics rather than a recipient of inspiration from them.

7. See letter from Alsberg to Isbell on the need for field workers to follow folklore collecting instructions carefully, also on John Lomax as special consultant for folklore, and on professional folklorists in Michigan for help 12 Aug. 1936, Box WPA-FWP Folklore, Alabama-Mississippi 1935–39, RG69. Soon after the project got underway in 1935, Katherine Kellock formulated a set of instructions for local unit folklore collecting, Mangione 265. Botkin became folklore consultant in May 1938, and folklore editor in August 1938 and he issued a more complete set of instructions than the ones formulated by Lomax in September 1938, the *Manual for Folklore Studies* RG69. McDonald 704, 709.

8. On usefulness and affectiveness in storytelling, see Benjamin 86.

9. Ibid. 84–5.

10. Inventory of folklore manuscripts and ex-slave narratives, LC Project 18 Sept. 1940, Box WPA-LC Writers' Unit RG69. The number of manuscripts for one of the 33 thematic categories "New Year Lore" is entered as a question mark. The other 32 number 348.

11. This turnover information comes from Rebecca Shelley in a letter to her husband Felix Rathmer 24 Feb. 1937, Box 2 RS.

12. Shelley to Adams undated January 1937; Shelley letter to Isbell 20 Jan. 1937; both in Box 2 RS. The letter to Adams, although in a 1936 file, belongs to January 1937 for it deals with Isbell's January phone call informing her of her placement in the project.

13. Shelley to Rathmer 3 Feb. 1937, Box 2 RS.

14. Shelley to Rathmer 13 Jan. 1938, Box 2 RS.

15. Shelley to Rathmer 3 Feb. 1937, cited in en. 13.

16. Shelley to Rathmer 2 Apr. 1937, Box 2 RS.

17. Shelley to Benjamin Botkin 16 Oct. 1938, Box WPA-FWP Folklore Alabama-Mississippi 1935–39, RG69. In this letter, Shelley cites the uncertainties over method and concept that she and her fieldworkers were having and informs Botkin that Professor Emelyn Gardner, a trained folklorist, has finally consented to work with her on a more sustained basis to provide the Michigan FWP with professional know-how.

18. Shelley letter to Emily Balch 4 May 1937, Box 2 RS. In the letter she explains her separation from Felix as a way to get on the state's relief roles. The separation was more complex than that. Her letters to Felix indicate that the economic reason was reinforced by a faltering personal relationship. She was particularly pleased at being appreciated by FWP members for her writing because she felt that the regard of others would make Felix esteem her more. See Feb. 3 letter cited above. Elsewhere she writes of not being willing to return to abuse and insult. See letter to Felix, undated, among a series of undated letters in Box 14 RS.

19. Shelley to Balch 10 Aug. 1937; John Safran informs the Washington office that Shelley was dismissed for being an alien; Balch to Shelley, 16 Aug. 1937; all in Box 2 RS.
20. Newsom to Botkin 27 Sept. 1938; Newsom to Alsberg, att: Dr. Botkin 1 Mar. 1939; both in Box WPA-FWP Folklore Alabama-Mississippi 1935–39 RG69.
21. Newsom to Alsberg, att: Botkin 31 Oct. 1938 announces the Wayne assignment. See Shelley to Alsberg 29 July 1938 about political favoritism; Shelley to Balch, posted from Houston, 28 Dec. 1938; all in Box 2 RS.
22. Newsom to Botkin 1 Mar. 1939, File Michigan Folklore RG69.
23. Newsom to Alsberg, att: Botkin 1 Nov. 1938 mentions that Alan Lomax has the Polish ballads collected in Michigan in his possession; Newsom to Alsberg, att: Botkin 1 Mar. 1939 discusses inadequacy of the Paul Bunyan work and the plans for the ballads; both in Box Folklore Alabama-Mississippi 1935–39, RG69.
24. For folklore classifications from national office, see Folklore Classifications (Ralph S. Boggs), Box WPA-LC Writers' Unit; for classifications used in Michigan, see Shelley to Botkin 16 Oct. 1938 Box WPA-FWP Folklore Alabama-Mississippi; for inventory of Michigan folklore, see Inventory of Folklore Manuscripts 18 Sept. 1940, Box WPA-LC Writers' Unit; all in RG69.
25. Shelley to Rathmer 11 Apr. 1937, Box 2, RS.
26. Folklore of Flint, File Beliefs and Customs—Michigan, FWP.
27. "De Old Shaintee," File Songs and Rhymes, Shanty Songs, Work Songs, Dance Calls, Box 45–2 FWP.
28. "The Jam on Gerry's Rock" and "Young Monroe," File Songs and Rhymes, Box 45–2, FWP.
29. "The Death of Harry Vail," about a mill worker accidentally sliced to death in 1879 by a power saw, is an example of poor re-writing, File Songs and Rhymes, Great Lakes Folk Speech and Worker's Jargon—Michigan; "The Cornish Miner," while good in capturing the dialect of the English immigrant miner, seems like an outside view of a passing way of life, File Songs and Rhymes; both in Box 45–2, FWP.
30. The crop-lore saying is from a series, Folklore—Farmers, collected by Elizabeth Wood in the Charlevoix region, File Beliefs and Customs, Taboos—Weather and Crop Lore, Michigan; the second saying is from a series of items, "Metaphors," collected by Walter C. Meyland around Munising, File Phrases and Sayings, Proverbial Similes—Michigan; the third on superstitions related to Friday was collected by Helen Arnold and is in the same file as the first; all are in Box 45–2, FWP.
31. The author is cited in some sources as Clifford Allen. But officially it is described as compiled by workers of the Writers' Program of the Works Project Administration of Michigan. By 1940 the FWP had become a "Program," the WPA had dropped "Progress" from its name for "Project," and both had become state agencies. The work is not available nationally, except perhaps in the most leading libraries, such as the New York Public Library. It is available at LC and in many Michigan public and university libraries.

32. Holbrook to Newsom 26 Mar. 1942, WPA-FWP, Box 211.17 to 211.19, RG69.

33. "A Note to Consultants on the Method Used in Compiling a Lexicon of Trade Jargon," 12 page carbon ts, File Correspondence—Trade Jargons, Box 42–1, FWP. This note is interesting for it eliminates from consideration light industry; trades where workers have little contact with one another; the slang of Hollywood, Broadway, the campus, sports, prisons, hoboes, criminals, the underworld, and Harlem. It was clearly after heavy industry and industry where the work process was such that workers had close, hour-after-hour contact with each other. The state assignments are included in a two-page attachment following page 4 of the note. In addition to the logging language recorded in ballad, story, and historical essay, the Michigan FWP also compiled a lexicon of lumber jargon for the trade project.

34. Botkin memorandum to Newsom on the subject, Lexicon of Trade Jargon 10 May 1940, the first two pages unnumbered, the last eight numbered starting with 2. The comments I have cited are drawn from the unnumbered pages.

35. Automobile Workers' Slang, Michigan 1938–9, six page ts; Lexicon of Trade Jargon, Furniture Industry, two page ts; both from File Michigan—Trade Jargons, Box 42–1, FWP.

36. Newsom to Harry Shaw (a New York University instructor who, in 1938, became the fourth of seven New York FWP directors) 12 Aug. 1938; Goodwin (not more fully identified) memorandum to Alsberg, Subject: Argot of the Automotive Industry, attached to a two-page list of terms called "Dictionary of Slang"; both in File Michigan—Trade Jargons, Box 42–1, FWP. The memorandum is undated, but the top of the first page of the list to which it is attached has the pencilled-in information Michigan/ 1938–9.

37. Alsberg to Newsom 8 July 1938, File Correspondence—Trade Jargon, Box 42–1, FWP. For Brown and Haessler, see the biographical notes in the catalogues of the Joe Brown and Carl Haessler Collections, ALU.

38. File Labor Vocabulary, Box 15, JB.

39. Folklore and Folk Customs by George Henry Meyers, Croswell, Michigan, 1 Apr. 1937, Box: 45–2, FWP.

40. "The Ghost on the Hill," 26 Apr. 1938, File Ghosts—Michigan Box, 45–2; "Pat and the Ghost," 19–23 in "Folklore and Folk Customs"; both in FWP.

41. Mitcoff letter to Young 15 Feb. 1938 and the attached tale about the significance of Russian beggars, entitled "Bread" in Box 2, RS. See also "Baba-Yaga" and other Russian folk tales by Mitcoff in File Tales Michigan, Box 45–2, FWP.

42. Both stories are in File Ghosts—Michigan, Box 45–2, FWP.

43. For the Meyers' version see "The Haunted House that Was," 17–9, in "Folklore and Folk Customs," FWP. For the particular phrases cited see pp. 18 and 19.

44. "Hi Robinson," File Tales, Anecdotes, Local Legends—Michigan, Box 45–2, FWP.

45. "Paul Bunyan Legends" 12 Apr. 1937; File Devil Lore—Michigan and Paul Bunyan Tales, Box 45–2, FWP. That there is any merit to the explanation of how Bunyan legends got started is uncertain.

46. The last two stories, "Paul Bunyan Up-To-Date" 8 Mar. 1937 and "Paul Bunyan Story" by L. E. Sherman 12 Feb. 1937 are in File Devil Lore—Michigan and Paul Bunyan Tales, Box 42, FWP. It is not at all certain that the stapling story is a new find. The staple as the centerpiece of the third story suggests a twentieth century, perhaps a 1930s, addition to Bunyan lore.

15. Neglected Publics: Ethnic, Black, and Social-Class Studies

1. See for example *The Albanian Struggle in the New and Old World, The Armenians in Massachusetts, The Italians of New York, The Jewish Landmanschaften of New York.*

2. Royse to MacLeish 7 June 1940, Records of the WPA, RG69.

3. *These Are Our Lives* xii.

4. American Council letter to Colby 24 July 1942, File Men at Work, Box 211.17 to 211.19, RG69.

5. Mangione 285.

6. Pennsylvania-Dutch was here used, mistakenly, as a generic term.

7. W. M. Kiplinger, director of Public Activities Program, letter to James H. Cruther, Louisiana Works Program Administrator, att: Alma S. Hammond, Division of Community Service Programs 12 Aug. 1941, File 1941 America Eats, FWP. Evelyn S. Byron, State Director of Illinois Services Division to Florence Kerr, last director of Professional and Women's Projects, 22 Apr. 1942, File America Eats, Box 211.17–211.19, RG69.

8. See Henry Becker "Forty-Eighters Who Came to Detroit," ts., and "My Immigration and Its Reaction," ts., Box 2, RS.

9. File "Men at Work," FWP.

10. Genette 94–5, 109–12.

11. The seventeen-volume LC collection was reassembled for publication as *The American Slave: A Composite Autobiography*, general editor George P. Rawick, 19 vols. (1972); Supplement, Series 1, 12 vols. (1977); Supplement, Series 2, 10 vols. (1979). The additional volumes were needed to accommodate the find of more FWP narratives. The Ohio and Indiana narratives are in volume 5 of Supplement Series 1. More Indiana material shares volume 6 of the 1972 publication Supplement, with Alabama and more Indiana material is in volume 1 of Series 2.

12. Tarini announcement, Box 10 RS.

13. *American Stuff* viii. The sponsor of *American Stuff* was the Guilds' Committee, which consisted of Franklin P. Adams, Bruce Bliven, Morris L. Ernst, Lewis Gannett, and Margaret Marshall.

14. The Clifford play, other Hopwood award manuscripts that Clifford wrote, and the Mitcoff novel are available at the Avery Hopwood Room, University of Michigan.

16. Smoky Cyclorama: Putting on Shows in the Midwest

1. Flanagan to Hopkins, Box 88 HH.
2. *Arena* 153.
3. *Arena* 157.
4. *Arena* 159.
5. On *Swing Mikado*, see *Arena* 145–8, for Cincinnati 172. A ts. manuscript, "The Negro in the Federal Theatre" by Harold Rogers says that a play based on Shakespeare's *Romeo and Juliet* and called *Romy and July*, with music by Margaret Bonds and lyrics by Robert Dunsmore, was the forerunner of *Swing Mikado*, File Negro in the Federal Theatre, ISH.
6. Lindemulder to Flanagan 23 Sept. 1935, Box 651.3113–651.312 Michigan 1935–36 RG69.
7. Mountjoy to Flanagan 19 May 1936; Flanagan to Mountjoy 14 May 1936; both in Box 651.3113 to 651.312 Michigan 1935–36 RG69.
8. Beyer to Flanagan 10 Sept. 1936; McGee to Morrow 10 Apr. 1937; Woodward to Nims 24 Feb. 1938; Haldene to Miller 28 Feb. 1939; all in Box 651.312 to 651.3122 Michigan 1937–39 RG69.
9. See last page of *Let Freedom Ring* playbill, Detroit Federal Theatre 21–30 May 1937, playbill collection FTG.
10. The production information is from Wood 3.
11. *Dr. Faustus* playbill 1–11 July 1937, Detroit Federal Theater, playbill collection; production records and reports, along with critics' and audience responses 1 July 1937–19 Jan. 1938 Box 130 (plays actually performed); all in FTG. See also "Federal Actors Open Isle Plays," the *Detroit Free Press* 17 Aug. 1937; "Federal Theatre Presents Belle Isle Performance," the *Detroit News* 17 Aug. 1937.
12. "Strike Marches On" script, File Flint Notes; Vorse account of getting the play together and background events, File Flint News Articles; all in Box 109 MHV. None of the union people who were at Pengelly Hall that night, nor Henry And Dorothy Kraus, who were closely involved in the daily events of the sit-down, remember the play being performed. Dycke writes that Watson, who was in Flint to give a lecture, was requested by union men to do a living newspaper on their strike, see Dycke 140, 160; also see Watson's own account in *New Theatre and Film*.
13. Morrow interview; see last page of *200 Were Chosen* playbill collection; production records and reports for *200 Were Chosen* Box 457; all in FTG.
14. See last page of *Paths of Glory* playbill 16–25 Apr. 1937, play-bill collection, FTG; production bulletin of *Let Freedom Ring*, RG69; production figures and report of *They Too Arise*, Box 430 FTG.
15. Doll, Play Production Report, Art Directors Report 1–3; FTG audience comments also from Play Production Report, Audience Reaction 1–2; FTG.

Selected Bibliography

Manuscript Collections

(AH)   Amas K. E. Holmio, "History of the Michigan Finns." 3 vols. ts. 1967. BHL, UM. [Published in Finnish. *Michigan in Suomi-laisten Historia.* Hancock, MI: Society for the Publication of the History of Michigan Finns, 1967].

(AME)   AME, St. Matthews, and Second Baptist Churches (Records), Historical Records Survey, BHC, DPL.

(AWH)   A. William Hoglund, "Finnish Immigrant Fiction and Its Evolution from Romanticism to Realism in the United States, 1885–1925." 15–30. In *Studies: No. 9.* ed. Vilho Nutemaa and Keijo Virtanen. Vaasa: Institute for Migration. BHC, DPL.

(BE)   Congregation Beth El Papers, BHC, DPL.

(BTC)   Second Baptist Church Tape Collection, The Second Baptist Church, Detroit.

(BTW)   Booker T. Washington Play Program, ts. Photographs of Robert Hayden and other performers. In author's possession. Generously provided by Josephine Love, Director Your Heritage House, Detroit.

(CH)   Carl Haessler Collection, ALU, WSU.

(CT)   Contemporary Theater Playbill Collection, Department of Music and Performing Arts, DPL.

(DBA)   Detroit Bethel African Methodist Episcopal Church, "Historical Sketch, 1841–1927." BHC, DPL.

(DLT)   Detroit-Little Theatre Vertical Files, Department of Music and Performing Arts, DPL.

(DN)   *Detroit News*, BHC, DPL.

(DP)   *Detroit Plaindealer*, BHL, UM. Copies of the newspaper are difficult to obtain. Microfilm of its few years span (28 Sept. 1889–19 May 1893) is available at BHL.

(DPB)   Detroit Playhouse Bound Programs and Announcements. Department of Music and Performing Arts, DPL.

(DT)   *Detroit Tribune*, BHC, DPL.

(DUL)   Detroit Urban League Collection, BHL, UM.

(EAH)   E. Azalia Hackley Collection, DPL.

341

Bibliography

(EG) Metropolitan Theatre Presents Eulalia Gaines. Detroit Drama Vertical Files, E. Azalia Hackley Collection, DPL.

(EK) Edith Koivisto Papers. IHR, UMI.

(FA) Folk Music and Folklore Files, Folklore Archives. Purdy Library, WSU.

(FB) First Baptist Church. Misc. Materials, BHC, DPL.

(FS) Fern Stevenson, Department of Recreation, Temple Beth-El Archives, Bloomfield Hills, MI.

(FTG) Federal Theater Project Collection (LC), GMU.

(FWP) US WPA Collection (Federal Writers' Project), Manuscript Division, LC.

(HC) Harold Courlander File, E. Azalia Hackley Collection, DPL.

(HCT) "The History of the Detroit Contemporary Theatre." Unpub. essay. n.d. In author's possession. Courtesy of Charlotte Shapiro, a founder of the Contemporary Theatre. Part II, 11.

(HCW) History of Michigan State Association of Colored Women. Ms. 1935 BHC, DPL.

(HF) Hyman Fireman Collection, ALU, WSU.

(HFD) Hallie Flanagan Davis Collection, Performing Arts Research Center, Lincoln Center Library and Museum of Performing Arts, New York Public Library.

(HH) Harry L. Hopkins Papers, FDR.

(HM) Helmi Dagmar Mattson Papers. IHR, UMI.

(HRS) Historical Records Survey, BHC, WSU.

(ISH) Federal Writers' Project Collection, Manuscript Section, ISH.

(J) Jabberwock. E. Azalia Hackley Collection, DPL.

(JB) Joe Brown Collection, ALU, WSU.

(JEB) Jessie Bonstelle Theatre Scrapbook, Department of Music and Performing Arts, DPL.

(KK) Katherine Kellock Papers, Manuscript Division, LC.

(LF) Louis Falstein Collection, "Journey to a Violent Land." New York: n.p., n.d. ALU, WSU.

(MDC) Metropolitan Detroit AFL-CIO Collection, ALU, WSU.

(MHV) Mary Heaton Vorse Papers. ALU, WSU.

(RG69) Record Group 69, U.S. WPA Federal Writers' Project Collection, NA.

(RH) Robert Hayden. "The History of the Negro in Michigan." BHC, DPL.

(RO) "The Romance of a People" Playbill, A Musical and Dramatic Spectacle. Sponsored by the Jewish Welfare Federation in cooperation with the Detroit Free Press, the Detroit News, the Detroit Times. Detroit: Olympia Auditorium, 16 Apr. 1934. Department of Music and Performing Arts, DPL.

(RS) Rebecca Shelley Papers, BHL, UM.

(SBC) Second Baptist Church, Church Vertical Files, E. Azalia Hackley Collection, DPL.

(SC) Scrapbooks of the Detroit Institute of Arts, DIA Library. Detroit.

(SL) Stanislawa Leskiewicz Papers. BHC, DPL.

(SW) Stanislaw Wachtel Papers, BHC, DPL.

(TI) *Tribune Independent* (Detroit), BHC, DPL.

342

(VJ)   Virtanen Keijo, *Letters to Finland.* Bulletin 26. Michigan Historical Collections, June 1976. BHC, DPL.

(WC)   Workmen's Circle (U. S.) Michigan District Committee Papers, BHS, UM.

FWP Publications

The Albanian Struggle in the Old World and New. Boston: Writer, Inc., 1939.

Allen, Clifford. *Michigan Log Marks.* Detroit: 1940.

American Stuff: An Anthology of Prose and Verse by Members of the Federal Writers Project. Foreword by Henry G. Alsberg. New York: Viking Press, 1937.

"Annals of Labor and Industry." 2 Vols. Mimeo. Chicago: 1939–40.

The Armenians in Massachusetts. Boston: Armenian Historical Society, 1937.

Cavalcade of the American Negro. Chicago: Diamond Jubilee Exposition Authority, 1940.

Gumbo Ya-ya: A Collection of Louisiana Folk Tales. Comp. Lyle Saxon, Edward Dreyer, and Robert Tallant. Boston: Houghton Mifflin, 1945.

Idaho: A Guide in Word and Pictures. Caldwell, Idaho: Caxton, 1937.

Illinois: A Descriptive and Historical Guide. Chicago: A. C. McLurg, 1939.

Indiana: A Guide to the Hoosier State. New York: Oxford UP, 1941.

The Italians of New York. New York: Random House, 1938. Also in Italian. *Gli Italiani di New York.* New York: Labor P, 1939.

Jewish Families and Family Circles. In Yiddish. New York: 1939.

Jewish Landsmanschaften of New York. In Yiddish. New York: I. L. Peretz Yiddish Writers' Union, 1938.

Lay My Burden Down: A Folk History of Slavery. ed. Benjamin Botkin. Chicago: U Chicago P, 1945.

Michigan: A Guide to the Wolverine State. 1941. New York: Oxford UP, 1964.

Michigan Log Marks. (attr. Clifford Allen.) East Lansing: Michigan State College, 1940.

The Negro in New York: An Informal Social History. Roi Ottley and W. J. Weatherby, ed. New York: New York Public Library and Oceana, 1967.

The New Orleans City Guide. 1938. Boston: Houghton Mifflin, 1972.

New York Panorama. 1938. St. Clair Shores, Mich.: Scholarly P, 1976.

The Ohio Guide. New York: Oxford UP, 1940.

"Pioneer Days in Illinois." Mimeo. Chicago: 1940.

"Stories from Illinois History." Mimeo. Chicago: 1941.

These Are Our Lives. Ed. and preface by W. T. Couch. (FWP) Chapel Hill: U North Carolina P, 1939.

Wisconsin: A Guide to the Badger State. New York: Duell, Sloan and Pearce, 1941.

Government Documents

Thirteenth Census of the United States: Abstract of the Census with Supplement for Michigan. Washington: GPO for Department of Commerce, Bureau of Census, 1913.

Bibliography

Fourteenth Census of the United States: State Compendium, Michigan. Washington: GPO for Department of Commerce, Bureau of Census, 1923.

Fourteenth Census of the United States: 1920 Population: Occupations. Vol. 4. Washington: GPO for Department of Commerce, Bureau of Census, 1923.

Fifteenth Census of the United States: 1930 Population, Alabama-Missouri. Vol. 3, Part 1. Washington: GPO for Department of Commerce, Bureau of Census, 1933.

Fifteenth Census of the United States: 1930 Population: Occupations. Vol. 13. Washington: GPO for Department of Commerce, Bureau of Census, 1933.

Detroit Bureau of Governmental Research. *The Negro in Detroit*. Detroit: Pre. for the Mayor's Interracial Comm. by a special survey staff, 1926.

Monthly Labor Review. U. S. Department of Labor, The Bureau of Labor Statistics. Washington: GPO Vols. 31–50, 1930–1940.

Unemployment and Relief in Michigan. 1st Report of the State Emergency Relief Commission. July 1933–Oct. 1934. 1935.

Haber, William. *Unemployed Persons on the Emergency Relief Rolls in Michigan*. Lansing: Michigan, State Emergency Welfare Relief Commission, 1935.

Presentations

Carney, Nimrod. Untitled paper presented at the conference "Black Family Life as Portrayed in the Black Theatre." Detroit: The Fred Hart Williams Geneological Society, 5 Jan. 1985.

Du Plessis, Lillian. Untitled paper presented at the conference "Black Family Life as Portrayed in the Black Theatre." Detroit: The Fred Hart Williams Geneological Society, 5 Jan. 1985.

Tuomi-Lee, Sirkka. "Stage Recollections Among Finns." Paper presented at the Finn Forum.Toronto: Nov. 1–3, 1979. The Multicultural History Society of Ontario.

Interviews

Unless otherwise noted the interviews were taped and transcribed

Barbara Wilson Benetti. 3 Nov. 1930.
Shirley Benyas. Telephone conversation 14 June 1986.
Irja Connolly. 14 Jan. 1986.
Velma Lehtela Duletsky. 18 Feb. 1986.
Louis Falstein. 27 Mar. 1980.
Hy Fireman. 12 Dec. 1978 and 11 July 1979.
Lillian Genser. Telephone conversation 14 June 1986.
Lillian Gold. Telephone conversation 14 June 1986.
Molly Haar. Telephone conversation 14 June 1986
Robert Hayden. 30 Aug. 1978.
Irving Kroll. Telephone conversation 14 June 1986.

Leo Mogill. 2 Aug. 1978 and telephone conversation 14 June 1986.
Stanley Nowak. 4 April 1984.
Charles Pollack. 9 Sept. 1979. Paris, France.
Rebecca Shelley Rathmer. 6 Aug. 1979.
Kenneth Rowe. 14 Aug. 1979.
Edith Segal. Spring 1979 and 13 Nov. 1979.
Charlotte Shapiro. July 1978.
Louis Sirotkin. 22 Aug. 1978.
Anteo J. Tarini. 14 Aug. 1978
Ruth Whitworth. 19 Nov. 1979.
Maxine Wood. Spring 1979.

Books

Aaron, Daniel. *Writers on the Left*. 1961. New York: Oxford UP, 1977.

Ahokas, Jaako. *A History of Finnish Literature*. Bloomington: Indiana UP, 1973.

Algren, Nelson. *America Eats*. Preface by Louis I. Szathmàry II, ed. by David E. Schoonover. Iowa City: U Iowa P, 1992.

The American Economy During the Great Depression. New York: Garland, 1990.

The American Slave: A Composite Autobiography. Genl. ed. George P. Rawick. 17 vols. Westport, Conn.: Greenwood P, 1972; Supplement, Series, 1, 12 vols. Westport, Conn.: Greenwood P, 1977; Supplement, Series 2, 10 vols. Westport, Conn.: Greenwood P, 1979.

Aptheker, Herbert. *American Negro Slave Revolts*. Studies in History, Economics and Public Law 501. New York: Columbia UP, 1943.

Arian, Edward. *The Unfulfilled Promise: Public Subsidy of the Arts in America*. Philadelphia: Temple UP, 1989.

Baker, Houston. *Afro-American Poetics: Revisions of Harlem*. Madison: U Wisconsin P, 1988.

———. *Blues, Ideology, and Afro-American Literature Vernacular Theory*. Chicago: U Chicago P, 1984.

Bakhtin, Mikhail. *The Dialogic Imagination*. Ed. Michael Holquist, trans. Caryl Emerson and Michael Holquist. 1981. Austin: U Texas P, 1988.

Balch, Jack. *Lamps at High Noon*. New York: Modern Age, 1941 [novel about FWP].

Bell, Bernard W. *The Afro-American Novel and Its Tradition*. Amherst: U Massachusetts P, 1987.

Benjamin, Walter. *Illuminations*. Hannah Arendt, ed. and intro. Harry Zohn, trans. [German ed. 1955]. 1968. New York: Schocken, 1969.

Bianco, Carla. *Italian and Italian-American Folklore: A Working Bibliography*. Folklore Forum, Bibliographic and Special Series 5. Bloomington: Folklore Institute, 1970.

Blake, Ben. *The Awakening of the American Theatre*. New York: Tomorrow Publishers, 1935.

345

Bibliography

Bolkosky, Sidney. *Harmony and Dissonance: Voices of Jewish Identity in Detroit, 1914–1967*. Detroit: Wayne State UP, 1991.

Bontemps, Arna. *Black Thunder*. 1935. Boston: Beacon P, 1968.

———. *Drums at Dusk*. London: Harrap, 1940.

———. *God Sends Sunday*. New York: Harcourt, Brace, 1931.

——— and Jack Conroy. *They Seek a City*. Garden City: Doubleday, Doran, 1945.

Botkin, Benjamin. *A Treasury of American Folklore*. New York: Crown, 1944.

Bradley, David Henry, Sr. *A History of the A. M. E. Zion Church*. Nashville: Parthenon P, 1956.

Braudel, Fernand. *Civilization and Capitalism: 15th–18th Century*. 3 vols. Siân Reynolds, trans. New York: Harper and Row, 1981–84. Vol. 1. *The Structures of Everday Life*. 1981. Vol. 2. *The Wheels of Commerce*. 1982. Vol 3. *The Perspective of the World*. 1984.

Brink, Alice Martin. "The Drama of Detroit from Its Inception to 1870." Unpublished M. A. thesis. History Dept. Wayne State U, 1937.

Broadus, Mitchell. *Depression Decade: From New Era through New Deal, 1929–1941*. New York: Rinehart, 1947.

Brown, Frederick. *Theatre and Revolution: The Culture of the French Stage*. New York: Viking, 1980.

Brown, Lawrence Guy. *Immigration: Cultural Conflicts and Social Adjustments*. New York: Arno P, 1969.

Brown, Lorraine and John O'Connor, ed. *Free, Adult, Uncensored: The Living History of the Federal Theatre Project*. Washington, D.C.: New Republic Books, 1978.

Brożek, Andrzej. *Polish Americans, 1854–1939*. Warsaw: Interpress, 1985.

Burke, Kenneth. "Revolutionary Symbolism in America." 87–94. *American Writers' Congress*. Henry Hart, ed. New York: International P, 1935.

Cahill, Holger. *American Folk Art: The Art of the Common Man in America, 1750–1900*. New York: The Museum of Modern Art, 1932.

———. *Art in America in Modern Times*. New York: Reynal & Hitchcock, 1934.

———. Foreword. *Art for the Millions: Essays From the 1930s by Artists and Administrators of the WPA Federal Art Project*. Ed. and intro. Francis V. O'-Connor. 1973. Boston: New York Graphic Society, 1975.

———. *New Horizons in American Art*. New York: The Museum of Modern Art, 1936.

Chandler, Lester Vernon. *America's Greatest Depression*. New York: Harper & Row, 1970.

Conroy, Jack and Curt Johnson. *Writers in Revolt: The Anvil Anthology, 1933–40*. New York: Laurence Hill, 1973.

Cowley, Malcolm. *The Dream of the Golden Mountains: Remembering the 1930s*. New York: Viking, 1980.

Dancy, John. *Sand Against the Wind*. Detroit: Wayne State UP, 1966.

D'Angelo, Pascal. *Pascal D'Angelo: A Son of Italy*. New York: MacMillan, 1924.

Davenport, Marguerite. *Azalia, the Life of Madame E. Azalia Hackley*. Boston: Chapman and Grimes, 1949.

Davidson, Donald. *The Attack on Leviathan: Regionalism and Nationalism in the United States*. Chapel Hill: U North Carolina P, 1938.

Davis, John H. *The Guggenheims: An American Epic*. New York: William Morrow, 1978.

Davis, Philip, ed. and comp. *Immigration and Americanization*. Boston: Ginn, 1920.

Dean, William Luther. "A Biographical Study of Miss Laura Justine Bonstelle-Stuart Together with an Evaluation of Her Contribution to the Modern Theatre World." Unpublished dissertation. U Michigan, 1934.

Deitch, Mattes. *Inm Land fon Die Yanjis*. Chicago: Fireside, 1935.

——, Ben Sholem and Shloime Schwartz, comp. *From Midwest to North Pacific: An Anthology of Yiddish Verse*. Chicago: M. Cheshinsky, 1933.

etweiler, F. G. *The Negro Press in the United States*. 1972. New York: Vintage, 1973.

Dillard, J. L. *Black English: Its History and Usage in the United States*, 1972. New York: Vintage, 1973.

Dorson, Richard M. *Bloodstoppers and Bearwalkers: Folk Traditions of the Upper Peninsula*. Cambridge, Mass.: Harvard UP, 1952.

——. *Land of the Millrats* [Indiana folklore]. Cambridge, Mass.: Harvard UP, 1981.

——, ed. *Folklore and Folklife: An Introduction*. Chicago: U Chicago P, 1972.

——. *Negro Folktales in Michigan*. 1956. Westport, Conn.: Greenwood P, 1974.

Dycke, Marjorie Louise. "The Living Newspaper: A Study of the Nature of the Form and Its Place in Modern Social Drama." Ph.D. dissertation. New York University, 1948.

Eagleton, Terry. *Criticism and Ideology: A Study in Marxist Literary Theory*. London: New Left Books, 1976.

——. *The Function of Criticism: From "The Spectator" to Post-Structuralism*. London: Verso, 1984.

——. *Ideology: An Introduction*. London: Verso, 1991.

——. *The Ideology of the Aesthetic*. Oxford: Basil Blackwell, 1990.

——. *Literary Theory: An Introduction*. Minneapolis: U Minnesota P, 1983.

——. *Marxism and Literary Criticism*. Berkeley: U California P, 1976.

Ekirch, Arthur A. *Ideologies and Utopia: The Impact of the New Deal on American Thought*. Chicago: Quadrangle Books, 1969.

Epstein, Dena J. *Sinful Tunes and Spirituals: Black Folk Music to the Civil War*. Urbana: U Illinois P, 1977.

Evans, Walker. *Walker Evans, America*. New York: Rizzoli, 1991.

Falstein, Louis. *Face of a Hero*. New York: Harcourt, Brace, 1950.

——. *Laughter on a Weekday*. New York: I. Oblensky, 1965.

——. *The Man Who Loved Laughter*. Philadelphia: Jewish Publication Society of America, 1968.

——. *The Martyrdom of Jewish Physicians in Poland*. New York: Exposition P, 1963.

Bibliography

Fauman, S. Joseph. "Occupational Selection Among Detroit Jews." *The Jews: Social Patterns of an American Ethnic Group*. ed. Marshall Sklare. Glencoe: Free P, 1958. 119–37.

Febvre, Lucien. *Life in Renaissance France*. A series of essays first published in French in *Revue des cours et conferences*, 1921, 1925. Marian Rothstein, ed. and trans. Cambridge, Mass.: Harvard UP, 1977.

Flanagan, Hallie. *Arena*. New York: Duell, Sloan, and Pearce, 1940.

———. *Dynamo*. New York: Duell, Sloane and Pearce, 1943.

Foner, Eric. *Reconstruction: 1863–1877*. New York: Harper and Row, 1988.

Foss, Michael. *The Age of Patronage: The Arts in Society, 1660–1750*. London: Hamish Hamilton, 1971.

Foucault, Michel. *The Birth of the Clinic: An Archaeology of Medical Perception*. New York: Pantheon, 1973.

———. *Discipline and Punish*. New York: Pantheon, 1977.

———. *Madness and Civilization: A History of Insanity in the Age of Reason*. New York: Pantheon, 1965.

Fraser, Steve and Gary Gersfee. ed. *The Rise and Fall of the New Deal Order, 1930–1980*. Princeton: Princeton U P, 1989.

Friedman, Daniel. "A Brief Description of the Workers' Theatre Movement of the Thirties." *Theatre for Working-Class Audiences in the United States, 1830–1980*. Bruce A. McConachie and Daniel Friedman, ed. Westport, Conn.: Greenwood, 1985. 111–20.

———. "The Prolet-Beuhne: America's First Agit-Prop Theatre." Unpublished Ph.D. dissertation. Madison: U Wisconsin, 1979.

Galbraith, John Kenneth. *The Great Crash, 1929*. 2nd ed. Cambridge: Houghton Mifflin, 1961.

Gard, Robert Edward. *Community Theatre: Idea and Achievement*. New York: Duell, Sloan and Pearce, 1959.

———. *Grassroots Theater: A Search for Regional Arts in America*. Madison: U Wisconsin P, 1955.

Gates, Henry Louis, Jr. *The Signifying Monkey: A Theory of Afro-American Literary Criticism*. New York: Oxford U P, 1988.

Gayle, Addison, ed. *The Black Aesthetic*. Garden City: Doubleday, 1971.

Geertz, Clifford. *The Interpretation of Cultures*. New York: Basic Books, 1973.

Goldstein, Kenneth S. *A Guide for Field Workers in Folklore*. Hatboro, Pa.: Folklore Associates, 1964.

Goldstein, Malcolm. *The Political Stage: American Drama and Theater of the Great Depression*. New York: Oxford UP, 1974.

Gordon, Mel. "The Yiddish Theatre in New York: 1900." *Theatre for Working-Class Audiences in the United States, 1830–1980*. Bruce A. McConachie and Daniel Friedman, ed. Westport, Conn.: Greenwood, 1985. 69–73.

Gould, Stephen Jay. *Time's Arrow, Time's Cycle*. Cambridge: Harvard UP, 1987.

Gross, Nahum. ed. *Economic History of the Jews*. New York: Schocken, 1975.

348

Halkola, David T. "Finnish Language Newspapers in the United States." *Finns in North America: A Social Symposium.* Ralph J. Jalkanen, ed. Hancock, Mich.: Michigan State UP for Suomi College, 1969.

Hannula, Reino Nikolai. *Blueberry God: The Education of a Finnish-American.* San Luis Obispo, Calif.: Quality Hill Books, 1981.

Harshav, Benjamin and Barbara Harshav, intro., trans., ed. *American Yiddish Poetry: A Bilingual Anthology.* Berkeley: U California P, 1986. See especially the introduction, "American Yiddish Poetry and Its Background," 3–61.

Haviland, Laura S. *A Woman's Life Work.* 1881.

Hayden, Robert. *Heart-Shape in the Dust.* Detroit: Falcon P, 1940.

Hill, Christopher. *Reformation to the Industrial Revolution, 1530–1780.* The Pelican Economic History of Britain 2. 1967. Hammondsworth: Penguin, 1974.

———. *The World Turned Upside Down: Radical Ideas During the English Revolution.* 1972. Hammondsworth: Penguin, 1980.

Himelstein, Morgan Y. *Drama Was a Weapon: The Left-Wing Theatre in New York, 1929–1941.* New Brunswick: Rutgers UP, 1963.

History and Directory of the Churches of Detroit. Detroit, 1877.

History of Michigan State Association of Colored Women. Detroit, 1953.

Hobsbawm, Eric. *The Age of Revolution, 1789–1848.* Cleveland: World, 1962.

———. *Industry and Empire: From 1750 to the Present.* The Pelican Economic History of Britain 3. 1968. Hammondsworth: Penguin, 1969.

Hoglund, A. William. *Finnish Immigrants in America, 1880–1920.* Madison: U Wisconsin P, 1960.

Holcombe, A. N. *The New Party Politics.* New York: W. W. Norton, 1933.

Holmio, Amas K. E. *Michiganin Suomilaisten Historia.* Hancock, Mich.: Society for the Publication of the History of Michigan Finns, 1967. English version "History of Michigan Finns." 3 vol. ts. BHL.

Hopkins, Harry Lloyd. *Spending to Save: The Complete Story of Relief.* New York: W. W. Norton, 1936.

Houseman, John. *Run-Through: A Memoir.* New York: Simon and Schuster, 1972.

Howe, Irving, and Eliezer Greenberg, ed. *A Treasury of Yiddish Poetry.* New York: Holt, Rinehart and Winston, 1969.

———, ed. *A Treasury of Yiddish Stories.* New York: Viking, 1954.

———, ed. *Voices From the Yiddish: Essays, Memoirs, Diaries.* Ann Arbor: U Michigan P, 1972.

Hughes, Catharine. *Plays, Politics, and Polemics.* New York: Drama Book Specialists, 1973.

Hummasti, Paul George. *Finnish Radicals in Astoria, Oregon, 1904–1940: A Study in Immigrant Socialism.* New York: Arno P, 1979.

Hutchinson, Edward Prince. *Immigrants and their Children, 1850–1950.* New York: Wiley, 1956.

Inglehart, Babette F. and Anthony R. Mangione. *The Image of Pluralism in American Literature: Annotated Bibliography on the American Experience of European Ethnic Groups.* New York: Institute on Pluralism and Group Identity of the American Jewish Committee, 1974.

349

Bibliography

Innes, C. D. *Erwin Piscator's Political Theatre: The Development of Modern German Drama.* Cambridge: Cambridge U P, 1972.

Jewish Population Studies. ed. Sophia Robison. Jewish Social Studies, 3. New York: Conference on Jewish Relations, 1943. Henry J. Meyer, "A Study of Detroit Jewry." 109–127.

Johns, Orrick. *Time of Our Lives: The Story of My Father and Myself.* New York: Stackpole, 1937.

Karni, Michael. ed. *Finnish Diaspora II: United States.* Toronto: Toronto Multicultural Historical Society, 1981.

———, Matti E. Kaups, Douglas J. Ollila, ed. *The Finnish Experience in the Western Great Lakes Region: New Perpsectives.* Duluth: Immigration History Research Center, U Minnesota, 1975.

Katzman, David M. *Before the Ghetto: Black Detroit in the Nineteenth Century.* Urbana: U Illinois P, 1973.

Kazin, Alfred. *On Native Ground.* 1942. Garden City: Doubleday, 1956.

Kennedy, Louise Venable. *The Negro Peasant Turns Cityward: Effects of Recent Migrations to Northern Centers.* New York: Columbia UP, 1930.

Koch, Frederick Henry. *Carolina Folk-Plays: First, Second, and Third Series.* New York: H. Holt, 1941.

Kolehmainen, John I. *The Finns in America: A Bibliographical Guide to Their History.* Hancock, Mich.: Finnish Lutheran Book Concern, 1947.

———. *From Lake Erie's Shores to the Mahoning and Monongahela Valleys: A History of the Finns in Ohio, Western Pennsylvania, and West Virginia.* Painsville: Ohio Finnish-American Historical Society, 1977.

Korman, E. *Yiddishe Dicterinim.* Chicago: L. M. Stein, 1928.

Kridl, Manfred. *A Survey of Polish Literature and Culture.* Olga Scherer-Virski, trans. New York: Columbia UP, 1967.

Kunka, Natalia. "The Amateur Theatre Among Poles." 67–90; Majewska, Halina J. "The Polish Stage in Chicago." 90–4; *Poles of Chicago, 1837–1937: A History of One Century of Polish Contribution to the City of Chicago.* Chicago: Polish Pageant. 1937.

Labor. New York: Garland, 1990.

Larson, Gary O. *The Reluctant Patron: The United States Government and the Arts, 1943–1965.* Philadelphia: U Pennsylvania P, 1983.

Lefkowitz, Helen. *Culture and the City: Culture, Philanthropy in Chicago from the 1880s to 1917.* Lexington: Kentucky UP, 1976.

Levine, Ira A. *Left-Wing Dramatic Theory.* Ann Arbor: UMI, 1985.

Levine, Lawrence. *Black Culture and Black Consciousness.* New York: Oxford UP, 1977.

Levine, Philip. *One for the Rose.* New York: Atheneum, 1981.

———. *They Feed The Lion.* (1972). New York: Atheneum, 1980.

Lifson, David, trans. and ed. *Epic and Folk Plays of the Yiddish Theatre.* Rutherford, N.J.: Fairleigh Dickinson UP, 1975.

———. *The Yiddish Theatre in America.* New York: Thomas Yoseloff, 1965.

Lipsky, Louis. *Tales of the Rialto: Reminiscences of Playwrights and Players in New York's Jewish Theatre in the Early 1900s*. New York: Thomas Yoseloff, 1962.

Liptzin, Sol. *The Flowering at Yiddish Literature*. New York: Thomas Yoseloff, 1964.

———. *A History of Yiddish Literature*. Middle Village, N.Y.: Jonathan David, 1975.

Locke, Alain Le Roy. *The Negro and His Music*. 1936. New York: Arno P, 1969.

Loften, Mitchell. *Black Drama: The Story of the American Negro in the Theatre*. New York: Hawthorne Books, 1967.

Lomax, Alan. *American Folk Song and Folklore: A Regional Bibliography*. New York: Progressive Education Assoc., 1942.

Lönnrot, Elias, comp. *The Kalevala or Poems of the Kalevala District*. Cambridge: Harvard UP, 1963.

Lynes, Russel. *Good Old Modern: An Intimate Portrait of the Museum of Modern Art*. New York: Atheneum, 1973.

Machiavelli, Niccolò. *The Prince*. 1648. Chicago: U Chicago P, 1985.

Madden, David, ed. *Proletarian Writers of the Thirties*. Carbondale: Southern Illinois UP, 1968.

Madison, Charles A. *Jewish Publishing in America: The Impact of Jewish Writing on American Culture*. New York: Sanhedrin P, 1976.

Mangione, Jerre. *The Dream and the Deal: The Federal Writers' Project, 1935–1943*. Boston: Little Brown, 1972. New York: Avon, 1972.

Marcus, Steven. *Engels, Manchester, and the Working Class*. 1974. New York: Vintage, 1975.

Marling, Karal Ann. *Wall-to-Wall America: A Cultural History of Post-Office Murals in the Great Depression*. Minneapolis: U Minnesota P, 1982.

Marx, Karl. *Capital: A Critique of Political Economy*. New York: International P, 1987.

———. [Economic and Philosophic Manuscripts of 1844]. *Karl Marx/Frederick Engels: Collected Works*. Vol. 3. New York: International Publishers, 1975. 229–346.

Mathews, Jane De Hart. *The Federal Theatre, 1935–39: Plays, Relief, and Politics*. Princeton: Princeton UP, 1962.

Mattila, Walter. *The Theater Finns*. Portland: Finnish American Historical Society of the Midwest, 1972.

McConachie, Brucca, and Daniel Freidman, ed. *Theatre for Working-Class Audiences in the United States, 1830–1980*. Westport, Conn.: Greenwood P, 1985.

McCreery, Kathleen and Richard Stourac. *Theatre as a Weapon: Workers' Theatre in the Soviet Union, Germany, and Britain, 1917–1934*. London: Routledge & Keegan Paul, 1986.

McDonald, William F. *Federal Relief Administration and the Arts: The Origins and Administrative History of the Arts Projects of the Works Progress Administration*. Columbus: Ohio State UP, 1969.

McKinzie, Richard D. *The New Deal for Artists*. Princeton: Princeton UP, 1973.

351

Bibliography

McKinzie, Kathleen O'Connor. "Writers on Relief: 1935–1942." Unpublished Diss. U of Indiana, 1970.

McLoed, Norman. *You Get What You Ask For* [Novel about FWP]. New York: Harrison-Hilton Books, 1939.

McWilliams, Carey. *The New Regionalism in American Literature*. Seattle: U Washington Bookstore, 1930.

Meltzer, Milton. *World of Our Fathers: The Jews of Eastern Europe*. New York: Farrar, Straus and Giroux, 1974.

Meneghel, David L. *A History of the Schubert Theatre in Detroit*. Unpublished dissertation. Wayne State University, 1966.

Meyer, Henry J. "A Study of Detroit Jewry, 1935." In *Jewish Population Studies*. 1943. 109–30.

Miller, James. *The Detroit Yiddish Theatre, 1920–1937*. Detroit: Wayne State UP, 1967.

Miller, Lillian. *Patrons and Patriotism: The Encouragement of the Fine Arts in the United States, 1790–1860*. Chicago: U Chicago P, 1966.

Milosz, Czeslaw. *The History of Polish Literature*. Berkeley: U California P, 1983.

Minihan, Janet. *The Nationalization of Culture: The Development of State Subsidies to the Arts in Great Britain*. New York: New York UP, 1977.

Mocha, Frank, ed. *Poles in America: Bicentennial Essays*. Stevens Point: Worzala Publishing, 1978.

Montgomery, David. *The Fall of the House of Labor: The workplace, the state, and American labor activism, 1865–1925*. Cambridge: Cambridge UP, 1987.

National Bureau of Economic Research. *International Migrations*. 2 vols. New York: National Bureau of Economic Research, 1929–1931. Vol. 1 ed. and intro. Imre Ferenczi. Vol. 2 ed. Walton F. Wilcox.

Netzer, Dick. *The Subsidized Muse: Public Support for the Arts in the United States*. New York: Cambridge UP, 1978.

Nye, Russel. *Midwestern Progressive Politics: A Historical Study of Its Origins and Development, 1870–1958*. East Lansing: Michigan State CP, 1951.

Niitemaa, Vilho, et al., ed. *Old Friends–Strong Ties*. Turku, Finland: Institute for Migration, 1976.

O'Connor, Francis, ed. *Art for the Millions: Essays from the 1930s by Artists and Administrators of the WPA Federal Art Project*. Boston: New York Graphic Society, 1975.

———. *Federal Support for the Visual Arts: The New Deal and Now*. Boston: New York Graphic Society, 1969.

Odum, Howard W. *American Regionalism*. New York: Henry Holt, 1938.

———. *The Negro and His Songs: A Study of Typical Negro Songs in the South*. 1925. Hatboro, Pa.: Folklore Associates, 1964.

———. *The Regional Approach to National Social Planning*. Chapel Hill: U North Carolina P, 1935.

——— and Guy Johnson. *Negro Workaday Songs*. Chapel Hill: U North Carolina P, 1926.

Odum, Howard W. and Harry E. Moore. *American Regionalism: A Cultural-Historical Approach to National Integration.* New York: Henry Holt, 1938.

Olszuk, Edmund G. *The Polish Press in America.* Milwaukee: Marquette UP, 1940.

Ortega y Gasset, José. *The Revolt of the Masses.* 1930. New York: W. W. Norton, 1957.

Orwell, George. *Collected Essays.* London: Secker and Warburg, 1961.

Osada, Stanislaw. *Literatura Polska i Polsko-Amerykanska dla ludu Polskiego w Ameryco.* Chicago: W. Dyniewicz, 1910.

Overmeyer, Grace. *Government and the Arts.* New York: W. W. Norton, 1939.

Pawlowska, Harriet M., collector and ed. *Merrily We Sing.* Detroit: Wayne State UP, 1961.

Payne, Bishop Daniel A. *Sermons and Addresses, 1853–91.* ed. Charles Killian. New York: Arno P, 1972.

Peeler, David P. *Hope Among Us: Social Criticism and Social Solace in Depression America.* Athens, Ga.: U Georgia P, 1987.

Pells, Richard. *Radical Visions and American Dreams: Culture and Social Thought in the Depression Years.* Middleton, Conn.: Wesleyan UP, 1973.

Penkower, Noam. *The Federal Writers' Project: A Study in Government Patronage of the Arts.* Urbana: U Illinois P, 1977.

Perry, Joseph McGarity. *The Impact of Immigration on Three American Industries, 1865–1914.* New York: Arno P, 1978.

Peterson, W. A. A *History of the Professional Theatre of Detroit, Michigan from September 13, 1875 to July 3, 1886.* Gainseville: U Florida P, 1959.

Pinski, David. *Three Plays* [*Isaac Sheftel, The Last Jew, The Dumb Messiah*]. New York: Arno P, 1975.

Piscator, Erwin. *The Political Theatre: A History, 1914–1929.* New York: Avon Books, 1978.

Poggi, Jack. *Theater in America: The Impact of Economic Forces, 1870–1967.* Ithaca, New York: Cornell UP, 1968.

Puotinen, Arthur Edwin. *Finnish Radicals and Religion in Midwestern Mining Towns, 1865–1914.* New York: Arno P, 1979.

Rabkin, Gerald. *Drama and Commitment: Politics in the American Theatre of the Thirties.* Bloomington: Indiana UP, 1964.

Re, Vitorio. *Michigan's Italian Community: An Historical Perspective.* Detroit: Office of International Exchange and Ethnic Studies, WSU, 1981.

Riegel, Milton M. *The Midland: A Venture in Literary Regionalism.* Iowa City: U Iowa P, c.1975.

Reynolds, Clay. *Stage Left: The Development of the American Social Drama in the Thirties.* Troy, N.Y.: Whitston P, 1986.

Rodgers, James Williams. "The History of the Garrick Theatre, Detroit: 1909–1928." Unpublished thesis. Wayne State U, 1967.

Rosenfeld, Lulla Adler. *The Yiddish Theatre and Jacob P. Adler.* 1977. New York: Shapolsky Publishers, 1988.

Rosenfeld, Morris, *Songs From the Ghetto.* Trans. Leo Weiner. Boston: Copeland and Day, 1898.

353

Bibliography

Ross, Carl. *The Finn Factor in American Labor, Culture, and Society.* New York: Parta Printers, 1977.

Rothbard, Murray Newton. *America's Great Depression.* Los Angeles: Nash Pub., 1972.

Rothschild, Steven B. "A General History of the Detroit Jewish Community: 1933–49." Unpublished honors thesis. Department of History, U Michigan, 1974.

Rubin, Ruth. *Voices of a People: Yiddish Folk Songs.* New York: Thomas Yoseloff, 1963.

Rudick, Lawrence W. *A History of the Theatre of Detroit, 1862–1875.* Ann Arbor: n.p., 1971.

Russell, John Andrew. *The Germanic Influence in the Making of Michigan.* Detroit: U Detroit, 1927.

Sachar, Howard M. *The Course of Modern Jewish History: The Classic History of the Jewish People, from the Eighteenth Century to the Present Day.* New rev. ed. New York: Vintage Books, 1990.

Samuel, Joseph. *Jewish Immigration to the United States.* New York: Columbia U P, 1914.

Samuel, Ralph, Ewan MacColl and Stuart Cosgrove., ed. *Theatres of the Left, 1880–1935: Workers' Theatre Movements in Britain and America.* London: Routledge & Kegan Paul, 1885.

Schwartz, Lawrence H. *Marxism and Culture: The CPUSA and Aesthetics in the 1930s.* Port Washington, N.Y.: Kennikat P, 1980.

Selden, Samuel. *Frederick Koch, Pioneer Playmaker: A Brief Biography.* Chapel Hill: U North Carolina Library, 1954.

Sernett, Milton C. *Black Religion and American Evangelicalism: White Protestants, Plantation Missions, and the Flowering of Negro Christianity, 1787–1865.* Metuchen, N.J.: Scarecrow P, 1975.

———. *Afro-American Religious History: A Documentary History.* Durham: Duke University Press, 1985.

Shoeman, Charles Henry. *A Dream and Other Poems.* Ann Arbor: 1899.

Sjöblom, George. "Finnish-American Literature." *The History of Scandanavian Literatures.* Frederika Blankner, comp., trans., ed. New York: Dial, 1938.

Slonim, Marc. *Russian Theater: From the Empire to the Soviets.* Cleveland: World Publishing Company, 1961.

Smitherman, Geneva. ed. *Black English and the Education of Black Children and Youth.* Detroit: Center for Black Studies, WSU, 1981.

———. *Talkin and Testifyin: The Language of Black America.* Boston: Houghton Mifflin, 1977.

Sobel, Mechal. *Trabelin' On: The Slave Journey to an Afro-Baptist Faith.* Princeton: Princeton U P, 1988.

Sohn-Rethel, Alfred. *Intellectual and Manual Labour.* Martin Sohn-Rethel, trans. Atlantic Highlands, N. J.: Humanities P, 1978.

Spearman, Walter. *The Carolina Playmakers: The First Fifty Years.* Samuel Selden, asst. Chapel Hill: U North Carolina P, 1970.

354

Spencer, Jon Michael. *Sacred Symphony: The Chanted Sermon of the Black Preacher*. Westport, Conn.: Greenwood P, 1987.

Sporn, Paul. "Working-Class Theatre on the Auto Picket Line." *Theatre for Working-Class Audiences in the United States, 1830–1980*. Bruce A. McConachie and Daniel Friedman, ed. Westport, Conn.: Greenwood, 1985. 155–70.

Stearns, Marshall W. *The Story of Jazz*. New York: Oxford UP, 1956.

Stoneman, William E. *A History of the Economic Analysis of the Great Depression in America*. New York: Garland, 1979.

Storey, Margaret Hamilton and Hugh Gillis. *Players' Nursery*. Palo Alto: Dramatists' Alliance of Stanford U, 1940.

Stott, William. *Documentary Expression and Thirties America*. 1973. Chicago: U Chicago P, 1986.

Stourac, Richard and Kathleen McCreery. *Theatre as a Weapon: Workers' Theatre in the Soviet Union, Germany and Britain, 1917–1934*. London: Routledge & Kegan Paul, 1986.

Straker, D. Augustus. *Negro Suffrage in the South*. Detroit, 1888.

———. *The New South Investigated*. Detroit: 1906.

———. *Reflections on the Life and Times of Toussaint L' Ouverture, the Negro Haytien*. Detroit, 1886.

———. *A Trip to the Windward Islands or Then and Now*. Detroit, 1896.

Swados, Harvey. *The American Writer and the Great Depression*. Indianopolis: Bobbs-Merrill. 1966.

Symanski, Edward Alan. *Fallen Stars*. London: Poets and Painters P, 1961.

———. *From the Fourth Province*. Florence: Tyskiewicz Private P, 1952.

Syrjala, Frans J. *Historical Essays about the Finnish-American Labor Movement*. Fitchburg, Mass: Finnish Socialist Association, 1929.

Taras, Piotr. *Polonia w Detroit*. Warsaw: Pallotinum, 1989.

Taylor, Abner. *Bad Poems and Happy Verses*. New York: Scribner's, 1973.

Terrill, Tom E. and Jerrold Hirsch, ed. *Such As Us: Southern Voices of the Thirties*. Chapel Hill: U North Carolina P, 1978.

The Theater Finns. ed Walter Mattila. Portland: Finnish American Society of the West, 1972.

Thomas, William Isaac. *Old World Traits Transplanted*. New York: Harper, 1921.

Thomas, William Isaac and Florian Znaniecki. *The Polish Peasant in Europe and America*. 1927. 2 vols. New York: Dover, 1958.

Tocqueville, Alexis de. *Democracy in America*. 1833. 1848. 1966 J. P. Mayer, ed. George Lawrence, trans. New York: Anchor, 1969.

———. *Journey to America*. ed. J. P Mayer. New Haven: Yale Paperback Series, 1962.

Trachtenberg, Alan. *Reading American Photographs*. New York: Hill and Wang, 1989.

Vance, Robert Bayliss. *Regional Reconstruction: A Way Out for the South*. Chapel Hill: U North Carolina P, 1935.

Velikonja, Joseph. *Italians in the United States: Bibliography*. Carbondale, Ill.: Dept. of Geography, So. Illinois U, 1963.

355

Bibliography

Wargelin, John. *The Americanization of the Finns*. Hancock, Mich.: Lutheran Book Concern, 1924.

Warren, Francis H., comp. *Michigan Manual of Freedman's Progress*. 1915. 3rd ptg. Detroit: John M. Green, 1985.

Wasastjerna, Hans R. *History of Finns in Minnesota*. Duluth: Finnish-American Historical Soceity, 1957.

Weinreich, Max. *History of the Yiddish Language*. Shlomo Noble, trans. Chicago: U Chicago P, 1980.

Wichorek, Martha and Michael Wichorek. *Ukrainians in Detroit*. Detroit: Wichorek, 1955.

Wiernik, Peter. *History of the Jews in America from the Period of the Discovery of the New World to the Present*. 3rd ed. With a Survey of Forty Years of Jewish Life, 1932–72 by Irving J. Sloan. New York: Hermon P, 1972.

Williams, Jay. *Stage Left*. N.Y.: Charles Scribner's Sons, 1974.

Williams, Raymond. *Problems in Materialism and Culture*. London: Verso Editions, 1980.

Wilmore, Gayraud S. *Black Religion and Black Radicalism: An Interpretation of the Religious History of Afro-American People*. 2d ed. Maryknoll, N.Y.: Orbis Books, 1983.

Wisse, Ruth R., intro., ed. *A Stetl and other Yiddish Novellas*. Detroit: Wayne State UP, 1986.

Wood, Arthur Evans. *Hamtramck: A Sociological Study of a Polish-American Community*. New Haven: College and University P, 1955.

Wood, Maxine. *On Whitman Avenue*. New York: Dramatists Play Service, 1946.

Woodson, June Barber. *A Century with the Negroes of Detroit, 1830–1930*. Detroit: 1949.

Wright, Richard. *Black Boy*. New York: Harper and Brothers, 1945.

———. *Uncle Tom's Children*. New York: Harper and Brothers, 1940.

Journal and Periodical Essays

Anderson, David D. "Michigan Proletarian Writers." *Mid America* 9 (1982): 76–97.

Beynon, Erdmann Doanne. "The Hungarians of Michigan." *Michigan History Magazine* 24 (1937): 90–102.

Botkin, B. A. "Regionalism: Cult or Culture?" *English Journal* 25 (1936): 181–5

———. "Regionalism: The Next Step." *Space* 1 (1934): 86–8.

———. "We Talk of Regionalism: North, East, South, and West." *Frontier* May 1933: 1–11.

———. "WPA and Folklore Research." *Southern Folklore Quarterly* 3 (1939): 7–14.

Cantwell, Robert. "America and the Writers' Project." *New Republic* Apr. 26, 1939: 323–5.

Cowley, Malcolm. "Poetry Project." *Poetry* (1938): 224–7.

Cuba, Stanley. "Polish Amateur Theatricals in America: Colorado as a Case Study." *Polish American Studies* 38 (1981): 23–49.

————. "A Polish Community in the Urban West: St. Joseph's Parish in Denver, Colorado." *Polish American Studies* 36 (1979): 33–74.

Current-Garcia, E. "Writers in the Sticks." *Prairie Schooner* 12 (1938): 294–309.

Elion, Harry. "A Playwriting Group." *Workers' Theatre* Sept.–Oct. 1932, 7–8.

Estreicher, Karol. "Teatr Polski Za Oceanem" [The Polish Theater Beyond the Ocean]. Trans. Matthew J. Strumski as "The Beginnings of Polish American Theatre." *Polish American Studies* 4 (1947): 31–6.

Evans, Alice. "Below Chicago's Mason-Dixon Line." *New Theatre* 1934, 10. HF, Box 1, File 9.

————. "The Living Theatre." *Workers' Theatre* Mar. 1935, 15. HF, Box 1, File 10.

Farran, Dan. "The Federals in Iowa: A Hawkeye Guidebook in the Making." *Annals of Iowa*. 3rd Series. 41 (1973): 1190–6.

"Federal Poets." *New Republic* 11 May 1938: 10–12.

"Federal Poets' Number." *Poetry* July 1938.

"Federal Writers' Issue." *Directions* Apr. 1939.

"Federal Writers' Number." *New Masses* May 10, 1938: 97–127.

Fine, David M. "Immigrant Ghetto Fiction, 1885–1918: An Annotated Bibliography." *American Literary Realism, 1870–1910* 1 (1973): 169–95, 1190–6.

"Finnish Labor Songs from Northern Michigan." *Michigan History Magazine* 31 (1947), 331–43.

Flanagan, Hallie. "A Theatre is Born." *Theatre Arts Monthly* Nov. 1931: 908–15.

Fletcher, J. G. "Regionalism and Folk Art." *Southwest Review* 19 (1934): 429–34.

Fox, Daniel. "The Achievement of the Federal Writers' Project." *American Quarterly* 13 (1961): 3–19.

Franklin, Leo M. "Jews in Michigan." *Michigan History Magazine* 23:1 (1939), 77–92.

Friend, Irja Koski. "Recollection Restaged." *Finnish Americana* 6 (1983–84), 16–22.

Garvett, Morris. "The Development of Jewish Education in Detroit." *Michigan Jewish History* 5:2 (1965), 4–10.

"The Ghetto." *Michigan Journal of History* (June 1966): 9–13.

Glicksberg, Charles. "The Federal Writers' Project." *South Atlantic Quarterly* 37 (1938): 157–69.

Greber, J. "Aesthetic and Sociologic Aspects of City and Regional Planning." *American Philosophical Proceedings* 74 (1934), 15–9.

Hacker, Louis R. "Sections or Classes?" *Nation* 26 July 1933: 108–10.

Hilberman, Dave and Henry Mitchell. "Creative Drama on the Ohio Relief March." *New Theatre* Sept.–Oct. 1933, 10–1, HF, Box 1, File 5.

Hoglund, A. William. "Finnish Immigrant Letter Writers: Reporting to Finland, 1870s to World War I." 13–31. *Finish Diaspora II*. Michael Karni, ed. Toronto: Multi-Cultural Historical Society of Ontario, 1981.

Jeliffe, Rowena Woodham. "A Negro Community Theatre." *New Theatre* July 1935, 13, 32.

Johnson, Aili Kolehmainen. "Finnish Labor Songs from Northern Michigan." *Michigan History* 31:3 (1947), 331–43.

Bibliography

Kellock, Katherine. "The WPA Writers: Portraitists of the United States." *American Scholar* 9 (1940): 473–82.

Kistler, Mark O. "The German Language Press in Michigan: A Survey and Bibliography." *Michigan History Magazine* (1960): 303–25.

———. "The German Theater in Detroit." *Michigan History Magazine* (1963): 289–300.

Knuuti, Rosa Alexander. "The Workers' Play." *Industrial Pioneer* 3: 7 (1925), 26–8.

Kolehmainen, John Ilmari. "The Finnish Immigrant *Nyrkkilehti*." *Common Ground* 6 (1943), 105–6.

———. "Finnish Newspapers and Periodicals in Michigan." *Michigan History Magazine* 24:1 (1940), 119–27.

———. "The Inimitable Marxists: The Finnish Immigrants." *Michigan History Magazine* 36: 4 (1952) 395–405.

Larkin, Margaret. "Ella Mae's Songs." *Nation* 129 (9 Oct. 1929): 382–3.

Loukinen, Michael M. "Second Generation Finnish-American Migration from the North Woods to Detroit, 1920–50." 107–25. *Detroit*. ed. Melvin Holli. New York: New Viewpoints, 1976.

Mathews, Jane De Hart. "Arts and the People: The New Deal Quest for a Cultural Democracy." *Journal of American History* 62 (1975): 316–39.

McDermott, Douglas. "The Theatre Nobody Knows: Workers' Theatres in America, 1926–1942." *Theatre Survey* 6: 1 (May 1965): 65–82.

McWilliams, Carey. "Localism in American Criticism." *Southwest Review* 19 (1934): 410–28.

"Michigan's Italian-American Heritage." *Family Traits*. Lansing: Michigan Dept. of Education, 1977–78, 1–29.

Michlin, Michael. "Memories of an Earlier Detroit." *Michigan Jewish History* 9:1 (1969), 3–9.

Milewicz, Stanislaw. "Mody Teatr-Polska Szko a Dramatyczna Tanecz-no-Wokalna." *Wiedza o Poloni Amerykanskiej* 1 (1947): 85–7.

Morrison, Toni. "Unspeakable Things Unspoken: The Afro-American Presence in American Literature." *Michigan Quarterly Review* 28 (1989): 1–34.

Moss, Leonard W. "Folklore among Detroit Jews." *Michigan Jewish History* 3 (1963), 2–10.

Mumford, Lewis. "Regionalismm and Irregionalism." *Sociological Review* Oct. 1927: 277–88 and Apr. 1928: 131–41.

Napolska, Sr. M. Remigia. "The Polish Immigrant in Detroit to 1914." Polish American Studies 2: 4–11.

New Theatre Feb. 1934, 23; Sept. 1934, 28; Nov. 1934, 24. HF.

New Theatre. July 1935 [entire issue on African-Americans in the Arts]; Apr. 1934, "From Atlantic to Pacific: The Revolutionary Theatre Holds Its Second National Festival." pp. 5–8. HF, Box 1, File 7; Sept. 1934, 28; Dec. 1934, Box 1, File 9 p. 29; FH, Box 1, File 11. Oct. 1935, p. 30 [Cleveland]; Sept.–Oct. 1933, p. 3 HF, Box 1, File 6.]

Rankin, Lois. "Detroit Nationality Groups." *Michigan History Magazine* 23:2 (1939): 129–211.

Ransom, John Crowe. "The Aesthetic of Regionalism." *American Review* 2 (1934): 290–310.

Rapport, Leonard. "How Valid Are the Federal Writers' Project Life Stories: An Iconoclast among True Believers." *Oral History Review* 1979: 6–17.

Riipa, Antero. "Books for the Finnish Immigrant." *The Interpreter* 2 (1923), 3–8.

Riipa, Timo. "The Finnish Immigrant Theatre in the United States." In *Finnish Diaspora II: The United States*, ed. Michael G. Karni. 277–89. Toronto: Multicultural Historical Society of Ontario, 1981.

Rockaway, Robert A. "The Detroit Jewish Ghetto Before World War I." *Michigan History Magazine* 52:1 (1968), 28–36.

Rosenberg, Harold. "Anyone Who Could Write English." *New Yorker* 20 Jan. 1973: 99–102.

Rosenshine, Jay. "History of the Sholom Aleichem Institute of Detroit." *Michigan Jewish History* (June 1974) 12–7.

Shrode, George. "Mary Zuk and the Detroit Meat Strike in 1935." *Polish American Studies* 43 (1986): 5–39.

Sjoman, Sophie. "The Mighty Gods." *Industrial Pioneer* 3:9 (1926), 18.

Sklar, George. "Negro Theatre in America." *New Theatre* July 1935. 3. HF, Box 1, File 10.

Stocker, Deveva Steinberg. "When 'Bubie Gitel' Came to Detroit." *Michigan Jewish History* 3:2 (1962), 20–2. [Frederic Warde Dramatic society 22].

Strumski, Matthew J. "The Beginnings of Polish American Theater." *Polish American Studies* 4:31–6.

Tanne, Laura. "Evening" and "Restaurant" Industrial Pioneer 3:7 (1925), 8.

Terril, Tom E. and Hirsch, Jerreld. "Replies to Leonard Rapport's How Valid Are the Federal Writers' Project Life Stories." *Oral History Review* 1980: 81–9.

Thomas, Richard. "The Detroit Urban League: 1916–1923." *Michigan History Magazine* 60 (1976): 315–38.

Thorson, Gerald. "Norwegian Immigrant Novels Set in Chicago." *Mid America* 4 (1977): 74–88.

Tuomi-Lee, Sirkka. "Reminiscences of the Finnish-American Cultural Movement." 201–5. *Finnish-American Horizons*. Comp. John Kelonen. New York and Mills, Minn.: Russell Parta Pub., 1976.

———. "Stage Recollections among the Finns." ts. provided me by author. 1–16. A printed version is also in *Finnish Diaspora II: United States*. ed. Michael Karni. Toronto: Multi-Cultural Historical Society of Ontario, 1981.

Vismara, John C. "The Coming of Italians to Detroit." *Michigan History Magazine* 2 (1918): 110–24.

Wargelin, John. "The Finns in Michigan." *Michigan History Magazine* 24 (1937): 179–203.

Warren, Robert Penn. "Some Don'ts for Literary Regionalists." *American Review* 3 (1936): 142–50.

Watson, Morris. "Sitdown Theater." *New Theater and Film* 4: 2 (1937), 5–6.

Bibliography

Workers' Theatre Mar. 1933, 11; Apr. 1933, 9; July–Aug. 1933, 17, all in HF, Box 1, File 5.

Workers Theatre Nov. 1931, 38; Dec. 1931, 27, both in HF, Box 1, File 4. June–July 1932, 22; Sept–Oct. 1932, 7–8, both in HF, Box 1, File 3. Mar. 1933, 15; Apr. 1933, 9, both in HF, Box 1, File 5.

Wright, Richard. "I Have Seen Black Hands." *New Masses* 26 June 1934: 16.

Zand, Helen Stankiewicz. "Polish-American Folk-ways." *Polish American Studies* 6 (1949): 33–41;

———. "Polish-American Folkways." *Polish American Studies* 17 (1960): 100–4.

———. "Polish-American Leisureways." *Polish American Studies* 18 (1961): 34–6.

———."Polish Folkways in the United States." *Polish American Studies* 12 (1955): 65–72.

———. "Polish Family Folkways in the United States." *Polish American Studies* 13 (1956): 77–88.

Newspaper Articles

Detroit Free Press. 17 Jan. 1879. 1:2.

Detroit Jewish Chronicle. Poem by Rabbi Louis I. Newman about why synogagues have no bells. Philip Raskin, "The Feast of Freedom." A poem about Passover. 8 Apr. 1932; Edith Hartman, "Realization." A poem about words transforming grief into bliss. 4 Dec. 1931.

Detroit News 22 Dec. 1924: 9.

Detroit News-Tribune. 1 Apr. 1900: 18–4.

Detroit Tribune 14 Apr. 1933, 6 May–30 Dec. 1933; as *Detroit Tribune* 31 Dec. 1933–7 Sept. 1935; and again as *Detroit Tribune* 14 Sept. 1935–5 July 1941, all on Microfilm 685 BHC.

Dziennik Polski. Detroit: Microfilm 1166. 1904–1985. BHC.

Jewish American. Wolf, Emma, "Other Things Being Equal." An installment of a serialized novel published by A. C. McClurg. "Watchman." A poem based on Isaiah, XXI: 11–12. 2 Jan. 1903; Emile Poulsson, "Giving." A poem translated from Norwegian. 9 Jan. 1903. Nathan Bernstein, "Israel's Talisman." A poem in praise of God. 23 Jan. 1903. S. Montreve, "In the Wilds of Africa." An installment of a serialized novel subtitled "A Romance of a Lost Jewish Tribe. 18 Oct. 1907.

Lawrence, Richard. "The Bonstelle Playhouse Will Be New Civic Center for Detroit Public." *Detroit News* 22 Dec. 1924, 9.

McLauchlin, Russell. Rev. of "Underground Savage." *Detroit News* 3 Oct. 1931.

"Michigan's Rugged Little Finland." *Detroit News.* 17 Mar. 1940, 12–13.

Rekord Godzienny. Detroit: Microfilm 1136, 1927–35. BHC.

Shaw, Lew G. Rev. of "Hamlet." *Detroit Free Press* 17 May 1927, 6.

Stark, George W. "Juliet in Flappermood." Rev. of "Romeo and Juliet." *Detroit News* 18 Mar. 1926, 25.

———. "Shakespeare, Mendelssohn." Rev. of "A Midsummer Night's Dream." *Detroit News* 24 July 1928.

"Summer Plans at the Bonstelle." *Detroit News* 4 Apr. 1927.

Trybuna Robotnicza. Detroit: 1924–41, ALU.

Der Weg. S. Nefam, "Dr. Herzel." A poem in memory of this leading Zionist. L. Malamud, "My Literary." A short story. 24 July 1919.

INDEX

Index

Index

Index